"This innovative work—part intellectual history and part memory study—reveals the shifting cultural landscape of late nineteenth-century and early twentieth-century America and the crucial of role of military cemeteries within this national, transatlantic, and transpacific narrative."

—Tracy L. Barnett, *North Carolina Historical Review*

"Shannon Bontrager's *Death at the Edges of Empire* joins a list of other seminal works on war and memory, such as Kristin Ann Hass's *Carried to the Wall*. He shows the importance of culture on shaping American narratives regarding war. It is a very important addition to the literature. Highly recommended!"

—Kyle Longley, author of *Grunts: The American Combat Soldier in Vietnam*

"Dense and absorbing. I'm particularly impressed by Bontrager's deft rhetorical analysis of various speeches—many of them by presidents—delivered at remembrance functions between 1863 and 1921.... This is an effective way of tracking the ideological twists and turns in American war commemoration. In addition, the author knows how to tell a story. Some of my favorite sections of this book are simply compelling narratives."

—Steven Trout, author of *On the Battlefield of Memory: The First World War and American Remembrance, 1919–1941*

DEATH AT THE EDGES OF EMPIRE

Studies in War, Society, and the Military

GENERAL EDITORS
Kara Dixon Vuic
Texas Christian University
Richard S. Fogarty
University at Albany, State University of New York

EDITORIAL BOARD
Peter Maslowski
University of Nebraska–Lincoln
David Graff
Kansas State University
Reina Pennington
Norwich University

DEATH at the EDGES of EMPIRE

Fallen Soldiers, Cultural Memory, and the Making of an American Nation, 1863–1921

SHANNON BONTRAGER

UNIVERSITY OF NEBRASKA PRESS · LINCOLN

© 2020 by the Board of Regents of the University of Nebraska

All rights reserved

The University of Nebraska Press is part of a land-grant institution with campuses and programs on the past, present, and future homelands of the Pawnee, Ponca, Otoe-Missouria, Omaha, Dakota, Lakota, Kaw, Cheyenne, and Arapaho Peoples, as well as those of the relocated Ho-Chunk, Sac and Fox, and Iowa Peoples.

Library of Congress Cataloging-in-Publication Data
Names: Bontrager, Shannon, author.
Title: Death at the edges of empire: fallen soldiers, cultural memory, and the making of an American nation, 1863–1921 / Shannon Bontrager.
Description: [Lincoln, Nebraska] [University of Nebraska Press], [2020] | Series: Studies in war, society, and the military | Extensive and substantial revision of the author's thesis (doctoral)—Georgia State University, 2011, titled Nationalizing the dead: the contested making of an American commemorative tradition from the Civil War to the Great War. | Includes bibliographical references and index.
Identifiers: LCCN 2019015608
ISBN 9781496201843 (cloth)
ISBN 9781496229045 (paperback)
ISBN 9781496219091 (pdf)
ISBN 9781496219084 (mobi)
ISBN 9781496219077 (epub)
Subjects: LCSH: Collective memory—United States. | War and society—United States—History. | War casualties—Social aspects—United States—History. | War memorials—Social aspects—United States—History. | Memorialization—United States—History. | Death—Social aspects—United States—History.
Classification: LCC HM1027.U6 B65 2020 | DDC 303.6/6—dc23
LC record available at https://lccn.loc.gov/2019015608

Set in Arno Pro by Mikala R. Kolander. Designed by N. Putens.

For Julie S. Bontrager (1949–2019) and Andrew R. Cumming (1944–2019), both of whom we lost too soon.

CONTENTS

List of Illustrations   ix

Acknowledgments   xi

Introduction: Lincoln's Promise   1

PART 1. STORAGE

1. Where the Grapes of Wrath Are Stored   37

2. The Nation, a Monument of Empire   61

3. Remembering Domestic Foreign Spaces   85

PART 2. RETRIEVAL

4. Retrieve the *Maine*!   119

5. Memories of a Foreign Land   149

PART 3. COMMUNICATION

6. Exiles of American Cultural Memory   187

7. Cultural Memory in the Information Age   213

8. That Cause Shall Not Be Betrayed   245

9. Listening to Empire   275

   Epilogue: Reclaiming Lincoln's Promise?   301

   Appendix A: Stops in D. H. Rhodes's Tour of the Philippines   319

   Appendix B: Stops in F. S. Croggon's Tour of the Philippines   327

   Notes   333

   Bibliography   357

   Index   371

ILLUSTRATIONS

Following page 164

1. The boneyard of Paco Cemetery
2. War is hell
3. On the road to Caloocan
4. Wreckage of the USS *Maine*
5. A view of the wreckage
6. Inside the cofferdam
7. The completed cofferdam
8. Building the cofferdam
9. Arthur Bluethenthal, Princeton All-American
10. Bluethenthal at his writing desk on the eastern front
11. Bluethenthal at Wrightsville Beach

12. Documenting a tragedy

13. Robert Burton House

14. Kiffin Yates Rockwell

15. North Carolina nurses of Hospital No. 65

16. Hospital nurses in France

17. Base Camp Hospital No. 65

18. Thomas J. Bullock

19. Chaplains working for the Graves Registration Service

20. Early temporary cemetery of the American dead in France

21. North Carolina officers viewing a temporary cemetery of American war dead in France

22. Landscape of retrieval

23. American bodies in a local cemetery in France

24. Constructing a temporary cemetery in France

25. Twilight Mass on November 12, 1918

26. Warren Harding dedicating the Tomb of the Unknown Soldier

27. The crowd witnessing the burial of the Unknown Soldier

28. The Santiago Surrender Tree

ACKNOWLEDGMENTS

My grandfather, Benedict Bontrager, was born and baptized Amish, but he left the agrarian, anti-intellectual, moral life that his family lived, taking his wife and his children with him. Ben's family shunned him when he left. The rejection of a first-born son and oldest sibling constituted a shocking rift within the family, but it also created a profound fissure between the past and the present, as they rarely spoke to Ben for the rest of his life. Their family life forevermore remained in the past while my grandfather's non-Amish life existed in the present. On occasion, memories of the past drifted into the present, but only momentarily. For example, when my grandmother, Mary Bontrager, died of cancer in the 1980s, many Amish Bontragers defied their bishop's decree and attended her funeral alongside their ostracized brother in an illicit yet profound statement of sympathy. They didn't speak to him, however, beyond the customary condolences one utters over the dead. In essence the presence of my grandfather's Amish kin at my grandmother's funeral represented the flickering memory of a family long ago ripped asunder by a shunning.

I was born just days before the last U.S. combat troops left Vietnam in March 1973. This war separated the American past from the present in powerful ways. The dishonesty of politicians and the failures of military leadership produced a culture not only of concealing the truth from the American people but also of concealing the history of American empire. The consequences of these kinds of fissures were profound. I could feel this legacy of Vietnam growing up in St. Joseph County, Michigan, which had its fair share of Vietnam veterans who almost never talked about their experiences. Our neighbor served as a medic during the war, but that was about all he could bring himself to mention. Those who occasionally spoke sometimes broke down in fits of sadness. Some men I knew suffered from flashbacks and post-traumatic stress disorder (PTSD). Some never recovered from their trauma. While growing up, I saw the illness shockingly manifest itself on a few occasions as ghosts of memory returned to wounded men to haunt even the strongest of them. But despite living through debates about Agent Orange and the recovery of POW/MIAs, the anguish felt by these members of our community never directly touched my family. Most Amish people religiously opposed wars on the grounds that Jesus of Nazareth required his followers to turn the other cheek. Ben's own grandfather and my great-great-grandfather, Manassas, was punished for this religious belief during the First World War. Manassas Bontrager, a bishop, wrote a letter that an Amish periodical published advocating that young Amish men should attempt to live the pacifist life of Christ and avoid military duty. He wrote this letter after Congress had passed the Sedition Act in 1918, and federal authorities quickly arrested him. He pled guilty and served jail time. The U.S. military developed Conscientious Objector (CO) protocols in earnest, in part, as a consequence of the many thousands of American Mennonite, Amish, and other religious followers who believed in their Christian duty to refuse to fight in the First World War. As evidence suggesting that shunning cannot completely separate the past from the present, I like to think that Manassas's trial helped our family, as my own father claimed CO status in the 1960s when his draft number came up. My father passed his CO examination and served time working in a local hospital in lieu of military service. I grew up sad that some in our community suffered from their war experiences, yet I was thankful that my father never had to endure this trauma.

This gratitude did not shield me, however, from the chasm that separated me from my family and insulated me from the American past. I carved my own identity in the shadows of this post-shunning/post-Vietnam world. The shunning of my grandfather separated him from his brothers and sisters (and me from hundreds of kinfolk) while the conflict in Vietnam invigorated a culture of forgetting even when symptoms of PTSD or cancer from the use of Agent Orange signified to everyone just how traumatic the experiences of war continued to be. The lack of government transparency coupled with the public's unwillingness to critique the American empire robbed veterans of their ability to talk about the war. This separated people of my generation from the conflict and quarantined us from the past. While completing this project, I realized how my grandfather's shunning and the Vietnam War intersected within my own memory. My ability to make my individual identity depended on my association to a kinship network of which I was not a member while my social identity required access to a cultural memory that concealed the past from me. I had to work around these limitations by seeking out alternative networks that could help me recover the past more effectively. I am not alone in this labor. Millions of people have had to perform similar work, and although our individual memories and our own interpretations may be different, all of us have carved our identities from sharing our memories with others. To those in my family and those who endured the Vietnam conflict at home and on the battlefield, I owe a profound debt of gratitude.

There are many other debts that this project has accumulated. Ian Christopher Fletcher, Joe Perry, Michele Reid-Vazquez, and Larry Youngs provided important early criticism that has helped make this project infinitely better. Their willingness to read, to encourage, and to offer feedback was equaled only by my friend and colleague Steven Blankenship, who not only volunteered to read multiple drafts of all of my chapters but also provided valuable professional and personal mentorship over the years. He is a senior colleague that anyone would be grateful to have, as I am. I have benefited immensely from participating in the National Endowment for Humanities Bridging Cultures: The U.S. in the Atlantic and Pacific Worlds initiative jointly operated with the American Historical Association, which provided valuable opportunities to perform research at the Huntington Library in San Marino, California, and the Library of Congress in Washington DC. Philip Morgan, John R. McNeil, Denver Brunsman, Marcy Norton, William Deverell, David Igler, Kariann Yokota, and several others all produced conversations that helped transform this project in important ways by helping me think about how the United States operated in the Atlantic and the Pacific worlds. The postdoctoral fellowship I received from the Memory and Memorialization: Representing Trauma and War project jointly sponsored by Edward Berenson at New York University and Denis Peschanski at the Centre National de la Recherche Scientifique allowed me to research in Paris and continue to think about the transatlantic nature of American memory. Too many librarians and archivists to name helped me access documents and suggested insightful lines of query. I would like to extend a special thanks to Senior Military Archivist (retired) Richard L. Boylan, who spent several hours with me at the National Archives in College Park, Maryland, helping me fill out request forms, escorting me to the stacks, and alerting me to sources that only someone with his vast experience could locate. It was heartwarming and encouraging to work with such a seasoned scholar who went out of his way to help me. The blind reviewers working with the University of Nebraska Press, as well as the entire editorial staff including Bridget Barry's continually good advice and encouragement, added immense insight to my project and made it better. I thank all of these people for their valuable help while acknowledging that any errors are my responsibility alone.

Perhaps the greatest debt I owe to my wife, Eleanor, and our three children, Mairi, Adam, and Ronan. Eleanor continually reminds me about what is important in life. Mairi patiently indulges me in my "boring" history work, offsetting it with clever historic tales of her own making. Adam is an exuberant son full of ideas about how to make the world a better place. His earnest no-nonsense pursuit of his own goals is inspiring if not humbling. Ronan has made me remember the importance of being a father and has made me laugh while doing so. I am very thankful to have my family. To all of these people and the many others who I was not able to name, thank you.

DEATH AT THE EDGES OF EMPIRE

Introduction

Lincoln's Promise

> Man is an animal suspended in webs of significance that he himself has spun.
> —Clifford Geertz

On the evening of July 3, 1863, Corp. Alfred P. Carpenter of the First Minnesota fell asleep near Cemetery Hill after the Battle of Gettysburg. Wounded twice, Carpenter had been one of the 252 men who had charged advancing Confederate soldiers who were trying to take the Union artillery pieces stationed on Little Round Top. It was a costly battle for the threadbare regiment, which lost more than 80 percent of its men, but this stopped the rebel advance and set the stage for the Union Army's victory by thwarting General Pickett's infamous charge. On this night, Carpenter's fallen comrades remained on the field as the Union troops prepared for another attack that never came. "Hospital attendant[s]," wrote Carpenter, "must take care of the wounded till darkness closes down about us. Then we go supperless to sleep, our bed, Mother Earth; our covering, the broad canopy of the starry decked Heavens; the unburied dead sleeping around us." Carpenter rose on Independence Day to help the living bury their dead. He took stock of the decimated regiment: "Where are the other fourteen hundred whose names are borne upon our rolls? Some are sleeping on nearly all the Eastern battlefields from 1st Bull Run to Gettysburg. They have gone to rest; they are sleeping in soldiers' graves, among the unknown and unnumbered dead."[1] Carpenter's journal entries represented an attempt to explain the high cost his regiment paid not only at Gettysburg but throughout the war. Sleeping with the dead produced, for Carpenter, a community of soldiers whose sacrifices in every major battle deserved recognition and remembrance. The corporal seemed to have found comfort in Minnesota soldiers sharing one last night together as comrades.

In contrast, Laurence Kent died alone in his Paris apartment. Kent served as a sergeant in Company B with the Second Engineers Company during the First World War. He had suffered gas attacks six times. Although he survived the war, the exposure to chemical weapons would plague him for the rest of his life. Kent soon became a historian of the Graves Registration Service. The War Department charged this new service with registering the graves of the American dead. While Carpenter could only imagine his comrades spread out across the entire landscape of war, Kent could see the names of his brethren cross his desk, and he played an active role in consolidating their remains into centralized cemeteries. But he continued to have difficulty breathing. In July 1921 Kent again went to the American hospital in Paris for the painful treatment of his ailments. A few days later, no longer willing to deal with his chronic condition, he shot himself in the heart while in his bed at home. He died as an individual, alone, as did hundreds of thousands of others, unable to overcome the horror of trench warfare—gas, machine guns, barbed wire, artillery, and mud. Such misuse of soldiers seemed to violate the basic core doctrines of humanity reaching beyond the battlefield and into the postwar years. Existing on the other side of a great technological and bureaucratic divide from Carpenter, Kent's suicide was suggestive of a culture of forgetting. He ended his suffering in solitude.[2]

Carpenter's and Kent's experiences came at a time when the relationship between the individual and the state underwent a radical transformation of citizenship. This transformation revolved around the Janus-faced dilemma of remembering and forgetting, which was fixated on the very nature of republicanism within the United States, according to Alexis de Tocqueville. Unlike European society, Tocqueville claimed, where subjects perpetually remembered their location within society (and their individual obligation to the community) through the ever-present relationship between the peasant, the landlord, and the church, republicanism helped citizens forget their social obligations. Tocqueville observed that "not only does democracy make every man forget his ancestors, but it hides his descendants and separates his contemporaries from him; it throws him back forever upon himself alone and threatens in the end to confine him entirely within the solitude of his own heart."[3] Forgetting was a democratic process for the Frenchman, and republicanism helped produce amnesiacs who forgot their individual commitments and obligations to society.

Republican collective memory was unraveling indeed in the wake of a devastating civil war, the ensuing pursuit of empire across the Great American Desert and into the vast oceanic spaces of the Pacific, and the unfolding Industrial Revolution, which served to disrupt local social networks. Whether through death, caused by war, or as individuals moved away to western landscapes and urban centers, social networks were loosening at an unprecedented rate. The Spanish-Cuban-American War and the First World War further transformed society. America became a burgeoning empire with colonies in the Philippines, a growing monopoly of influence in the Western Hemisphere, and an industrial capacity that saw the nation as the leading producer economy in the world.[4] People now had to navigate the wide-open spaces of a "distended society" that had limited communication and transportation capacity. The mechanized strategies of war accelerated this process. The violence of war literally killed kinship when a family member died, while the experiences of traumatic violence often made talking about it too painful to remember for those who survived. All of these helped further sever the individual from society. Modernity and materialism had taken its toll on memory, making it easier for Americans to forget the obligations that an individual owed to society. Laborers out of work, soldiers returning home, women returning to the domestic sphere, or African Americans retreating from the color line—all were vulnerable to experiencing isolation from society during the nineteenth century. Grief and trauma brought on by progress and warfare had penetrated the intimate alcoves of relationships that made disconnected local social networks possible and functional. Tocqueville feared voluntary isolation of the individual, but industry, empire, and war induced and accelerated it, often tearing the individual from their memories and their obligations.

Examining the way that Americans remembered the military dead provides an opportunity to explore how politics of race, class, and gender shaped the rituals of commemoration and cultural memory as the American republic overlapped with the American empire. While early nineteenth-century attempts to build cultural memory successfully connected many people, invigorating social bonds and reducing trauma through new mourning traditions, those whose citizenship status prevented them from accessing the network experienced severed social bonds and exclusion from the national identity. This project sought to exclude those who could not fit the depictions of whiteness, capitalism, or Protestantism. American expansion in the West, the Caribbean, and the Pacific often produced cultural trauma for indigenous people who could not align their interests with those of the Americans, even if members of those communities fought and died for the security of the U.S. economic and political system. Thus the language and practice of death and burial in the military exposed a key landscape where agents of nation and empire collaborated to define who belonged within the criteria of citizenship. Rising bureaucratic and technological reform in the care of military dead took individual and collective mourning and grief from the small-scale individual context of early nineteenth-century republicanism and placed it in the context of the War Department's new bureaucratic traditions of large-scale organization. If Americans officially understood their experiences as part of a democratic-republican nation, but military agents of the nation engaged in imperialistic and (neo)colonial expansion based on racial subordination and exclusion, then this discrepancy would repeatedly manifest itself in ways shaped by specific situations in the storage of *cultural* memory, its retrieval through the performance of *public* commemoration, and its communication through collective participation in *national* identity.

Historian of memory Jan Assmann underscores Tocqueville's belief in "the fact that man's basic and natural disposition would seem to favor forgetting rather than remembering." Societies could forget the past, based on what Assmann describes as a system of cooling memory. He contends that "cold" societies insulate themselves from the past and "put up desperate resistance to the penetration of history" by "freezing history" and by stressing the "recurrence and regularity, as opposed to the unique and the extraordinary" of society "whereby change is frozen."⁵ There was no shortage of deadening the past in the United States, as the early republican society cooled off the hot transformative revolutionary era. The political ineffectiveness of the Articles of Confederation and the related economic decline, the continual impressment of Americans by British officials and British presence in the Northwest Territory and Canada, the Northwest Indian War, the republican overtures of Federalists (outlined, for example, in Federalist no. 10) to safeguard the union against internal factions and democratic change, the codification of slavery within the U.S. Constitution and the preservation of chattel slavery in American society, the War of 1812, and the numerous economic recessions and depressions from the 1780s to the 1830s serve as a few reminders of how untethered Americans had become from a revolutionary past. Americans built "cold" early republican traditions within a "structural amnesia," especially around the institution of slavery, which accentuated the present and minimized the past. This had devastating effects for black Americans who remained enslaved and excluded from cultural memory.

Slavery itself amounted to a peculiar institution that the past could not penetrate. The present seemed frozen in time on the plantation as planting and harvest seasons folded into each other. Slave masters stymied literacy efforts, prevented marriage, sold children from underneath their mothers, and inflicted severe physical and psychological punishment—all with the design to keep slaves disconnected from the(ir) past. In her slave memoir, Harriet Jacobs described her imprisonment when her owner, Dr. Flint, began grooming her for his extramarital sexual gratification when she turned fifteen. He would approach her continuously with descriptions of sex acts, psychological manipulation, and intimidation. She remembered:

> My master met me at every turn, reminding me that I belonged to him, and swearing by heaven and earth that he would compel me to submit to him. If I went out for a breath of fresh air, after a day of unwearied toil, his footsteps dogged me. If I knelt by my mother's grave, his dark shadow fell on me even there.

Almost every waking moment Jacobs's "light heart which nature had given" had "turned heavy with sad forebodings." He was there to remind her of her present even when she confronted the past at her mother's grave. Everyone around her knew why her personality had changed. "Many of them [fellow slaves] pitied me," she noted, "but none dared to ask the cause. They had no need to inquire. They knew too well the guilty practices under that roof; and they were aware that to speak of them was an offence that never went unpunished. I longed for someone to confide in."[6] Flint took all kinds of measures to make sure that Jacobs would forget her personality if not her genealogy.

Jacobs had no one to talk to. She was completely isolated in the present. Her friends and family—fellow slaves—knew about their owner's sexual past, but they could not help her connect the past to the present without suffering severe punishment themselves. Maurice Halbwachs argued in the early twentieth century that memories are socially constructed and that humans make individual memories by sharing their experiences with others.[7] Twenty-first-century neuroscientists have investigated the biological capacity for human memory and have begun mapping the seemingly immeasurable neural pathways networked together by synapses that allow individuals to build memories from their experiences. This research has confirmed many of Halbwachs's theories. Synaptic connections form an incredibly complex network that functions powerfully in social relationships. When neurons are stimulated by a social interaction, they send an abundance of data to the brain. The brain receives these messages from the neural pathways, sifts the data into usable and unusable information, and then filters this information through previous social experiences and memories before interpreting it and storing the selected data internally. Social experience thus shapes an individual's memory: generally the more intense the experience, the stronger the association exists in the mind.[8] This biological process is an internal one and lasts for about as long as the individual stays alive and plays a crucial role in the way that individuals form memories. Halbwachs suggested that individuals could only validate their memories after sharing them with others. The interaction between individuals and groups produces what Halbwachs calls "collective memory." Remembering thus socializes people and provides individuals with the building blocks for their own identity and the access of belonging to a group. Those who do not share the group's memory cannot access its shared identity. Dr. Flint's illicit sexual exploitation of Jacobs thus isolated her from the boundaries, the refuge, and the respite of the group identity that her fellow slaves made. It was taboo for them to share their memories and experiences of the past with her. White plantation owners could wield a profound power of memory over their slaves.

The structural amnesia of the early republic, however, was counterbalanced by the memories formed at the local level. Unlike Jacobs, free Americans in small towns, college campuses, workshops, and churches across the nation socially reproduced collective memories countless times precisely because they offered refuge and respite for group members. Assmann describes this as "communicative memory" in which individuals within a group share, or communicate, their memories spontaneously with each other in the everyday spaces of life. Bostonians who experienced the Battle at Bunker Hill, evangelicals who experienced the Second Great Awakening, the jobless who experienced economic calamity in the Panic of 1837, Catholics, or slaves all formed their own disparate groups based on shared experiences. Although some individuals may have crossed the borders of these groups, they did so individually; for the most part, groups did not blend into other groups. Communicative memories are experience-based and can only be regulated from within by group members. They need no external interpreters such as poets, clerics, historians, or government officials to remember on their behalf because they experienced a vibrant past together. Within the group, members are equal and could share memories because they had similar experiences. This was why the era of the early republic had few national monuments, in part, because they had no need for them. Local monuments proliferated in this era because they spoke to the experiences of people who shared their memories with each other in the local community. More than that, Assmann suggests that group members often tie their memories of the past to specific locations. One can describe slaves' memories that revolve around the middle passage, the plantation, or the fields; soldiers' memories of the battlefield; shopkeepers' memories of the shop floor; or grievers' memories of the cemetery or the dead body. Communicative memories are constantly tied to locations and are continually under construction and reconstruction each time they are passed on from individual to individual, and thus they are prone to distortion, interpretation, and mythology each time they are recalled and shared. Communicative memory is thus made out of the shared experiences of individuals and perishes with each individual and each generation. They are nevertheless sacred to the group and its members.[9]

Societies of the early republic were built largely on communicative memories. Individuals living in the disconnected rural agrarian communities of the early nineteenth century shaped their collective memories through local, instinctive, and mostly oral processes. Few institutions, outside of Protestant Christianity, could influence these memories, and federal government officials certainly had limited capacity to shape the memories of largely local communities dispersed across a vast landscape. Group members could cool collective memories based on local politics and economics, but they could heat them up, too, when their security and sense of collective identity called them to connect the present to the past. Early republicans such as Thomas Jefferson, Andrew Jackson, and Ralph Waldo Emerson embodied what Assmann describes as a "foundational function" of heating memory. They were men who believed that Jeffersonian agrarianism, the pursuit of letters, or universal white male suffrage knitted the past together to the disconnected "archipelagos of democracy" within the rural landscape. They stressed a mythologized past that produced a meaningful present as the foundation of society. Americans thus tapped into the mythology of the revolutionary era in order to connect it to the "divinely inspired" foundations of the republican present. Individuals caught up in abolitionism provide excellent examples of what Assmann describes as a second incubator or "contrapresent" function of heating memory. Abolitionists who saw defects in the present emphasized the marginalized, the lost, and the sinful aspects of republican culture. They stressed how the present had broken from the past as they often looked to the past for antidotes to the present.[10] Abolitionists and their evangelical allies often used moralistic and religious memories to critique and condemn the immoral present. Foundational and contrapresent functions coexisted and helped Americans from different places and perspectives understand their early nineteenth-century national identity in relation to the past.

Whether warming or cooling, nineteenth-century Americans' ability to remember was limited. They carved out a contingent national mythology with very few memories to draw upon. Whereas Europeans had accumulated centuries of people who had fallen in war and could rise again as national heroes, Americans had very few such figures. The unfolding of the republic, however, provided opportunities to commemorate both the dead and the nation. America's heroic dead—from George Washington to the soldiers at Bunker Hill, from Gen. Anthony Wayne to Andrew Jackson, and from Winfield Scott to Zachary Taylor—dotted the landscape of the nation (and Mexico City) but in isolation from each other. While antebellum Americans, as historian William A. Blair contends, "had ample spirit for holidays and public commemoration," they did not have "a unified interpretation of commemorations that honored the republic."[11] What the new nation needed was a collective memory that could incorporate local communicative memories into a national idea. This task also had to navigate the diverse groups of Native Americans who had long ago claimed commemorative spaces for their own social, cultural, and political means in the very locations that citizens of the new nation now coveted. Death rituals delineated these sacred indigenous locations. American Methodist missionary James B. Finley described in the 1810s one example of a Wyandot "feast of the dead" performed in Ohio along the Sandusky River. "They kindle a fire, and each person, before he begins to eat, bites off a small piece of meat, which he casts into the fire. The smoke and smell of this attracts the *Jebi* (or spirit) to come and eat with them."[12] Finley believed the ritual was superstitious nonsense and called for its eradication, but this feast of the dead represented an indigenous sacred space and memory.

Diverse Native American commemorative spaces, spread out across the North American continent, stood in the way of Americans making sites of memory that could help produce an American mythology. American removal policies made "empty" the land that covered indigenous ancestors just as the U.S. government emptied the land of Indian presence. This effectively desacralized Native American space and produced "blank" space that could now be transferred to settlers. Americans rushed in and resacralized "uncontextualized" spaces of North America with their own cemeteries and their own mourning traditions. American settlers thus used death as a tool of colonialism. As frontier and borderland communities sprang up, settlers ignored Native American burial sites and built their own where the living and the dead were located in proximity to the church and individual plots accentuated the individual's relationship to Christianity. Cemeteries were important in eradicating Native American sacred space and expanding the American frontier.[13] The recontextualized "empty" spaces allowed Americans to reinterpret the natural surroundings of death and nature efficaciously. Henry David Thoreau noted this in his travels on the Merrimack River. As he passed by "some graves of the aborigines," he noted, "Time is slowly crumbling the bones of a race." He predicted, "These mouldering elements are slowly preparing for another metamorphosis, to serve new masters, and what was the Indian's will ere long be the white man's sinew."[14]

In the context of this imperialistic republicanism, Americans built cemeteries that would speak to the civil religion of states united by common values of capitalism, Protestantism, and nativism. Cemeteries sprang up everywhere Americans expanded the nation's borders.[15] Middle-class people spent their leisure time in garden cemeteries contemplating their Christian mortality while breathing fresh air; they picnicked, exercised, and experienced the "museum" of the local community that contained the remains of Americans, some heroic, who made its history.[16] Historian David Sloane points out that although the family plot was the cornerstone, the new garden "cemeteries were designed to heighten cultural consciousness about the past and about salvation." He notes, "The creation of a national past was inextricably linked to the establishment of local histories throughout America. Communities searching for a local history used the rural cemetery as a repository and a shrine." Sloane adds, "Cemetery associations took several steps to link the cemetery to the community's memory, the most obvious of which was to bury and honor the nation's war dead or the place that they died."[17] Garden cemeteries accentuated local history while also connecting the living to larger national and Christian memories.[18] No overarching government entity had the power to produce a competing comprehensive collective memory at the national level, and the relative weakness of official government attempts allowed local elites to use the social norm of burial to make memory and produce identity according to local tastes.

But the United States was undergoing a process that historian Robert Wiebe has described as "the search for order" in which the country moved from a society of disconnected archipelago communities to a "distended society" of a modern nation-state.[19] This changing relationship between the individual and society reflected the ways urban middle-class definitions were replacing sectional and rural identities. It also illustrated how growing government bureaucracy and corporate behemoths were eroding the power of small businessmen, local culture, and traditional values expressed through families and homegrown communities. Bureaucratic reform and capitalist expansion often dissolved the social bonds of community and family. As the nineteenth century unfolded, privatization of burial and mourning weakened the reified power of death to tie together the imagined community to the republic. Rural cemeteries became jumbled with unique and gaudy tombstones and monuments that reminded people—at a time when society privileged republicanism—of the inequality of death and thus the inequality of life. Within a few decades, the rural cemeteries of republicanism had become the very symbols of the inequality of capitalism. As rural garden cemeteries, filled with elaborate monuments, became places of overcrowded sepulchers and muddled memories, it became difficult for people to contemplate the national history and to experience the therapeutic benefits of the natural environment when walking among the dead. The rural cemetery had lost its romanticism; it had become cluttered and unseemly. Thus the locations where collective memory was supposed to connect locals with national identity became disrupted and strained.

One response to this secularization of death in the early nineteenth century was an attempt by middle-class Christian Victorians to control death—to bring it out of the profane and into the sacred realm of Protestantism. They created a ritual of the so-called Good Death characterized by perishing on a deathbed in the home, surrounded by loved ones. Ideally, the dying would utter reassuring words with the last few breaths of mortal life that signified his or her acceptance of salvation, then display calmness in their eyes. This process was important as it gave witnesses valuable clues as to whether the soul had accepted salvation, and it shaped the way the living would remember the dead.[20] The religious understanding of the Good Death carried with it overtones of secular nationalism too. The Civil War had given Americans unprecedented opportunities to make munificent meanings from their individual and collective losses, often using interchangeably religious and secular language to explain their grief. Historian Mark S. Shantz claims that "'The Soldier's Grave' begins to take us into an ideological terrain in which the national government has taken the place of the church."[21]

Despite the reliance on the Good Death, social and family disruptions were especially acute when corporate and government leaders, bent on expanding the nation's boundaries, committed the state to war, thus producing massive voids within individual families across the nation when soldiers died far from home where the Good Death could not be verified. These disruptions within family networks posed significant threats to disrupt the social stability born out of people sharing their memories locally. How could a family in Vermont explain the death of their son on a battlefield in Georgia? For what purpose did his life serve if he died so far away from home? To alleviate the potential blowback from this burgeoning social alienation, government and corporate agents, collaborating with middle-class Americans, created functional collective memories that were more receptive to the needs of citizens and also more supportive of the structures of state. Middle-class professionals gradually came to manage the symbiotic relationship between the living and the dead. A death industry emerged that increasingly took the experience of grief and the accompanying mourning rituals more and more out of its religious context and commoditized them. The rise of funeral directors, funeral homes, and life insurance companies invaded the communicative aspect of remembering by bringing death out of the private home and into public places while turning dead bodies and graves more and more into cultural artifacts.[22] The Civil War meanwhile killed so many people from nearly every nook and cranny of American society that grief and mourning rituals networked the agrarian republic together in ways that previously only Christianity had accomplished. Memories of those who died for their country now rivaled and cooperated with memories of the Christ as the lubricant of republican communicative memory. Yet in this secularizing age, the living and the dead maintained a symbiotic relationship now refracted through social obligations more so than religious salvation.

People still needed the dead to authenticate the meaning of life while the dead needed the living to remember them. As corporations increasingly came to manage death and grief, people found reliable new ways to verify life and the living's relationship to the dead. Focusing on memories of the dead illuminates how Americans utilized communicative memory to adapt older agrarian Protestant rituals to newly invented traditions of cultural memory.[23]

Perhaps this context helps explain Abraham Lincoln's interpretation of republican memory, which provided one of the most potent rebukes of Tocqueville. In his first inaugural address Lincoln proposed to warm the memories of his countrymen who seemingly had been disconnected from their shared revolutionary past. Lincoln reminded Northerners and Southerners of the "mystic chords of memory, stretching from every battlefield and patriot grave to every living heart and hearthstone all over this broad land." These mystic chords summoned a cultural memory of grief and memory that Lincoln believed defied the gravitational pull of republican amnesia. The patriot dead, Lincoln surmised, helped stimulate a social memory expressed through a harmonious chord progression connecting the war dead's sacrifice to the living's collective memory. Many Northerners and Southerners had family connections, experiential connections, or political connections to the patriot dead. Lincoln hoped most would remember their sacrifices and still hear the chords and the harmony that "will yet swell the chorus of this union, when again touched, as surely they will be, by the better angels of our nature." Human nature inclined people to remember the war dead, and Lincoln hoped this shared memory would provide the social connective tissue necessary to bind individuals together. Collective memory formed a usable way of remembering that Lincoln hoped would help keep Americans from atomizing into a nation of Tocquevillian individuals.

Assmann argues that people actually practice collective memory by two different methods. Lincoln's call for the "better angels of our nature" was intended to influence the cultural aspect (and not the communicative characteristic) of collective memory. Whereas communicative memory is experience-based and resides in the common everyday face-to-face interactions of people within groups, cultural memory is cultural-based and is communicated through scripted rituals, cultivated myths, and sacred nationalistic ceremonies such as the Fourth of July or Memorial Day, or the dedication of national monuments, or the reverent burial of the soldier dead. Unlike communicative memory, which is regulated by people from within the group, cultural memory is regulated externally by highly skilled cultural interpreters. Assmann describes this feature of collective memory as a vibrant interplay of material objects, communication abilities, and representations of the past wielded by skilled individuals who deploy monuments, print media, and icons to connect people from distant regions who may not even know that each other exists. Poets, historians, archivists, clerics, and politicians regulated this kind of memory, not shopkeepers, soldiers, laymen, or laborers. To participate in cultural memory, individual citizens and the groups they identify with had to acquire a range of memory techniques (mnemotechniques) utilizing dynamic memory technologies (mnemotechnologies) that skilled interpreters developed to make national identity out of the past. Republican memories were largely communicative before the Civil War because of the absence of mnemotechniques—outside of the religious memory of the Christ—to tie disconnected agrarian communities together. Cultural memory that existed in the republic was limited and thin before the Civil War. After the conflict, people developed new memory techniques to help them cope with the loss of loved ones and also to help them define and redefine citizenship in a new era of emancipation. They used these methods to transcend wide-open agrarian spaces and connect disparate communities. Just as the mind interprets biological memories through a selection process—adding useful information while eliminating unhelpful information—to help an individual explain the present, so too does cultural memory adapt to the changing societal perceptions of the past in relation to the present. Cultural memory is not fixed, and it can be passed on from generation to generation through a process Assmann calls "hypolepsis." In this process, younger people not only learn the memory techniques of the previous generation but also foster new technologies to remember through their own interpretations.[24] Cultural memory dynamically and perpetually forms and reforms as the tensions between individuals' internal biological memories and the social memories of society are worked out, reworked, and synchronized. Cultural memory thus has a history and a historiography. By looking at the history and historiography of cultural memory, historians can identify strong indicators of how U.S. citizens understood their memories of the past and how they used them to justify the contradictions evident between imperial violence and republican virtue.[25]

Cultural memory centered on the symbiotic relationship between the living and the dead "stretching from every battlefield and patriot grave to every living heart and hearthstone all over this broad land." According to Assmann, remembering the dead efficaciously bridges the space between communicative and cultural memory. Everybody dies—it is a truly democratic process—and thus death governs the profane unruly communicative memories of the living. People must share their memories of the dead with each other to heal their grief and also to explain their own personal loss. But death is also opposite to life, and thus it carries with it a sacredness that can be ritualized and institutionalized, such as through last rites. Death thus provides citizens an opportunity to transcend the banality of death with the sacred obligation to remember the dead using festivals that can take on a retrospective and/or prospective function. Assmann describes the retrospective as the natural idea that the living can keep the dead "alive" in the present by remembering them. Retrospective memories of the dead help people define themselves in relation to group identity. Prospective memories of the dead, suggests Assmann, focuses on the achievements of how "the dead have rendered themselves unforgettable."[26]

On the one hand, remembering the dead made it easier for Americans to express their communicative memories in the face of new corporate and government rituals of cultural memory. But on the other hand, it also helped them locate the boundaries of nation and empire. "Most Americans," claims one historian, "could unite over the appeals of an imagined empire, in economic, political, and cultural terms, but the process of empire making proved to be deeply divisive and contradictory."[27] This was especially true as plantation owners in the South and trans-Mississippi West clashed with manufacturing and corporate interests in the Northeast more and more over the direction that American expansion should take and the contradictions regarding extending citizenship to nonwhites slaving on plantations, to indigenous peoples in the West, and even to Hispanics and Latinos on the borderlands of this expansion. Death, especially valiant deaths in times of war, allowed Americans to remember the individual hero; forget malignancies based on race, class, and historic boundaries; and embrace the new realities of the imagined community. The heroic dead refracted the integrity of the nation onto citizenship. If the ability to forget, according to French historian Ernest Renan, paved the way for people to construct the nation, so did the ability to mourn.[28] Dead bodies became crucial justifications supporting the imagined ideals of national rebirth through what historian Jackson Lears has described as "militarist fantasies" where national regeneration emerges from the ashes of violent destruction. Not only did the martial dead form what George Mosse described as the "cult of the fallen" but commemorating the war dead helped people validate the "creative destruction" of the living.[29] The meaning of the soldier dead gave citizens memories through which to interpret their identities especially in relation to the bureaucracy of the state. The bodies of the martial dead thus befitted key material artifacts or relics central to cultural memory. Individuals could interpret their own memories through the cultural memory of the "cult of the fallen" and share them with other people in other locations around the nation who were likewise struggling with interpreting national identity out of the catastrophe of war.[30]

Making an imperial citizenry and making imperial politics required cultural memory that could quickly and efficiently incorporate the atomizing memories of millions of Americans. Collective memory usually took shape when citizens expressing a dominant form of communicative memory and officials advocating a powerful form of cultural memory collaborated. Collaboration usually occurred through *hypolepsis*. Assmann uses this Greek word to describe how societal gatekeepers use interpretation and variation simultaneously to code and decode the established textual canon. Through the hypoleptic process, Assmann suggests, memories of ancient times stand equidistant from memories of the recent past. Memory-makers use these equidistant memories not "to change their function but to give them new life" within the ever-changing context of making civilization.[31] This was especially true for Americans during times of war in the late nineteenth and early twentieth centuries when casualty rates became increasingly alarming and when the definitions of national identity were most vulnerable. Americans could seamlessly juxtapose memories of Lincoln with Napoleon or the biblical Jacob, Jefferson with Aristotle, or even soldiers of American democracy with the hoplites of the Athenian phalanx because these memories stood culturally equidistant from one another and bore the reinterpretations of nation and empire.

The beginnings of this modern cultural memory culminated after the Civil War when government officials, elites, and middle-class Americans collaborated to interpret variations of republican agrarian communicative memory around their own anxieties and interests. Citizens and government officials remade this collective memory during America's wars of empire with Spain, Cuba, and the Philippines in response to the real anxieties posed by expanding the boundaries of the nation, which brought new interpretations and variations on who should be included or excluded from the national identity. Americans cemented the infrastructure of cultural memory in the domestic politics of Jim Crow segregation, Protestant Christianity, and capitalist enterprise but also in the xenophobia and Orientalism of imperialist adventures. These memories were especially vivacious for those trying to make sense of the contradictions of overseas wars of empire. Americans deployed the hypoleptic process again to reinterpret collective memory during the First World War in an attempt to sustain the rigidity of national identity posed by the rapid global expansion of U.S. influence on the world system and the waning of Progressivism.

But it was the Civil War when Americans first developed sustainable memory techniques through which to interpret cultural memory. Hundreds of thousands died in the conflict. Many of the living sought to justify these deaths by expanding the definitions of citizenship beyond the traditional rituals of nativist, capitalist Protestants while yet retaining the integrity of the Union. Lincoln's Gettysburg Address, delivered a few months after Carpenter's sleep with the dead, perhaps best voiced the public yearning to remember the dead who fought for the noble causes of slave emancipation and unification of the nation.[32] It also provides a classic example of the hypoleptic process of memory. The speech drew inspiration from the canon, ancient and recent, of western civilization. Lincoln drew from the Declaration of Independence, and although he was not an evangelical Christian, historian Mark Shantz suggests that the language of the Gettysburg Address "culled the language of theology," especially Lincoln's utterance of a "new birth of freedom."[33]

Lincoln applied the ritual of the Good Death to the nation's dead, obliging Americans to commemorate those who sacrificed for the nation. Even if men died alone on the battlefield, their actions, not their words, brought the assurance of their sacrifice for republicanism. Historian Garry Wills claims that Lincoln crafted his speech out of a long democratic tradition of Greek funeral eulogies that included Pericles's tribute to the Athenian dead from the Peloponnesian War. Wills extends this argument to suggest that the speech not only interpreted the American canon but also became part of it. "The Gettysburg Address," he suggests, "had become an authoritative expression of the American spirit—as authoritative as the Declaration itself, and perhaps even more influential, since it determines how we read the Declaration."[34] Lincoln interpreted ancient and recent canonical traditions not to change them but to apply them to the context of the war and of emancipation.

As a wartime speech, the commander in chief harnessed battlefield sacrifices to public opinion to justify his administration's continuation of the war and to "offer a deep history of a 'nation' that in fact was being born almost as he spoke." He used the speech to shore up the eroding support of abolitionists and radical Republicans who had begun to criticize his handling of the conflict. But Lincoln's speech also signaled a reorganization of the relationship between government and the people. As historian Steven Hahn suggests, Lincoln articulated a nation without borders, "a distinctive form of political organization and a distinctive form of state, with specific sorts of territorial reach, political economies, sets of social relations, and cultural projects." This new nation included maintaining a large national army, supporting an emerging industrial base of manufacturing, setting rules for banking and financial services, transforming slave labor to contract labor in the South, and expanding the federal government's territorial reach well beyond the trans-Mississippi West. "A federal state," suggests Hahn, "with an immensely expanded reach and capacity would emerge, connected in significant ways to powerful private interests." As a cultural project of this new state, understanding memory as a fundamental human need and placing it in the context of national identity was one of the most enduring political legacies of Lincoln's Gettysburg Address. In a moment of national crisis, Lincoln reached for the revolutionary ideals of liberty and self-government and attached them to the sacrifice of the dead, not just restating the ideals but obliging the living to honor the dead by recommitting themselves to "a new birth of freedom." In this way the Gettysburg Address called for a retrospective memory of the dead and served as a gateway allowing the past to seep into the present. It warmed the collective memory of a long-cooled early republican age as it obliged the living to carry the memories of the dead with them into the present as an indication of citizenship. Lincoln's speech combined this retrospection while adding a prospective memory of the dead. It venerated the achievements of soldiers who fought and died at Gettysburg and elsewhere. Although Lincoln's earlier Emancipation Proclamation first attempted to glean from the war a noble cause, it could not fully accomplish what "these honored dead" at Gettysburg could. Their sacrifice made them utterly unforgettable and gave the war a tangible political meaning. The president charged the state with the obligation to remember those who made the final sacrifice and thus joined retrospective and prospective memories of the dead. Remembering the dead gave new meaning and a sense of urgency to the idea that self-government meant the abolition of slavery. This produced a cultural memory of emancipation and liberty because all who visited Gettysburg, all whose loved ones died in the war, and all who were never able to reclaim their loved ones' bodies could remember the war as an exercise—an experience—of emancipation and state building. Lincoln thus took the language of American radicalism constructed at the edges of American societies before the war and moved it to the center of the American political tradition.[35]

This signaled the beginning of a new cultural tradition and constituted what can be described as Lincoln's promise to the dead and an obligation for the living.[36] This undertaking contained three necessary techniques of remembering described by Assmann: storage, retrieval, and communication. First, Lincoln's speech transformed Gettysburg from a battlefield to a sacred place that venerated the ideals of the bureaucratic nation by officially reshaping the relationship between the state and the citizenry. In this way it was poetic foundational memory that tied the origins of the republic to the cause of the dead. This newly sanctified republican space, mass-produced through congressional authorization of the national cemetery system, provided a kind of initial storage system of cultural memory. Row upon row of graves archived memories of the symbiotic bonds between the living and the dead. By placing the burden of memory on citizens to remember the sacrifice of fallen soldiers, Lincoln obligated citizens to a retrieval system of cultural memory. He burdened the nation-state and the citizens to a collaborative project of ritual performance in the repetitious recovering, burying, and commemorating of the dead. Memorial Day ceremonies, decorating graves, or simple visits to the national cemetery stimulated Americans to perform the rituals that powered their retrieval of memory. The president compressed feelings of patriotism, glory, and liberty onto the actual sacrifice of soldiers and used their corpses to communicate the need for collective participation in ending slavery and defeating the Confederacy. Hundreds of thousands of fallen soldiers became symbols that consolidated feelings of democracy, nationalism, and liberty into the politics of national identity and modern warfare. In a single speech, Lincoln had articulated a powerful cultural memory of the United States that up until then had been mostly absent in American identity; the nation-state and the world would remember "the brave men, living and dead," who fought for the principles of liberty. The Gettysburg Address democratized the sanctification process by claiming that the thousands who died there—not founders and framers, generals and statesmen, sages and poets—produced sacred space; it represented the best that American democracy had to offer to modern civilization. Thus Lincoln used the deaths at Gettysburg to symbolically defeat the Confederacy, slavery, and the Jeffersonian agrarianism that privileged states' rights over federalism while also initiating cultural memory through which Americans could reshape the relationship between the past and the present.[37]

Individual soldiers and their families had demanded this sort of cultural recognition long before the president was willing to articulate it. Lincoln was not at the forefront of this cultural movement; rather, he was trailing it. But he successfully harnessed the Republican state-building agenda to it and used the resources of the federal government to guarantee his promise. In exchange, citizens, particularly the grieving, received something that they had been demanding since the early stages of the war: remembrance. But from the very utterance of the promise, Lincoln's remaking of republican collective memory into cultural memory was contested. Cultural memory is by no means a natural phenomenon; it is socially constructed. This book examines the many tensions that existed within this social contract and that would continually play out in the relationship between citizen and government. It is a study of cultural memory that examines the rituals invented to commemorate the war dead. This study focuses on how government officials invented institutions and traditions to serve the needs of the government but also made cultural memory to meet the demands of middle-class Americans. By comparing the making of the Marietta, Georgia, Arlington, Virginia, and Sitka, Alaska, National Cemeteries, chapters 1–3 focus on the prospective and retrospective work of the dead to remake foundational memories. Comparing these cemeteries as case studies allows the reader to think about the consequences of Lincoln's promise in the early years of Reconstruction. Who would be remembered? Lincoln tied cultural memory to soldiers' sacrifices for freedom. Would freedmen be included in the American cultural memory? Nearly 200,000 blacks served and thousands died in the Union Army, many of whom had run away from slavery. But what of slaves who did not run away or who did but did not serve in the federal military? Would their sacrifices for freedom be considered valuable enough to obligate citizens to remember them? Would women be included in cultural memory? Women who sacrificed for constitutional freedom well before the war as well as women, particularly nurses, who served the cause of emancipation near the front lines seemed to be left out of Lincoln's promise. Additionally, would cultural commemoration of the dead effectively heal the individual's grief?

Carrie Chamberlin of Westfield, Pennsylvania, for example, wrote to the War Department in 1866 asking for the location of her husband's body and whether it could be transported to her home once it was located. Isaac

Chamberlin had been captured September 30, 1864, and died December 27 as a prisoner at Salisbury, North Carolina, but his body had been lost. "Trusting you have a heart full of sympathy for the afflicted," she wrote military officials, "the expense will be nothing ... for nothing in the world can give me the peace and consolation which would be in having his grave where I could know it were taken care of. I visit it in my loneliness."[38] Her affliction of grief lingered in the absence of her husband's body. What good was cultural memory of the dead if it could not be responsive to people like Mrs. Chamberlin? People, not institutions, made memories, and any memories of the dead at the cultural level had to serve both the sacred purposes of the republic and the everyday needs of the grief-stricken.

Many questioned the relationship between memory and place in Lincoln's promise. Was it specific to Gettysburg, or was it boundless? Or, asked another way, was it an artifact of space and time, or could it be mythologized, varied, and interpreted along the contours of U.S. expansion? How did Americans remember empire? The second section seeks to answer these questions. Well before the Civil War, many Americans were interested in going past the Mississippi, beyond Colorado and California, and into the Pacific Ocean writ large, and the federal government often collaborated and supported these efforts. Northerners and Southerners jointly held (albeit contradictory) imperialistic visions of the West and often competed and cooperated in their shared pursuit of empire. Southern plantation owners desired to connect the cotton belt of the Caribbean South to the bird guano repositories of Peru via the fertile cotton fields of Texas and the potential marketplaces in the Pacific world. Filibusters launched assaults into Mexico, Cuba, and Nicaragua using unauthorized military adventures to expand cotton and slavery into Latin America. Many New England whalers made their livings scouring the vast hunting grounds of the Pacific while steel, railroad, mining, and oil tycoons sought to tie their far-flung operations to the financial center in New England. Some Americans had migrated into Texas, instigating a war of independence primarily over the issue of slavery and then helping initiate a war between the United States and Mexico. U.S. officials capitalized on the war with Mexico using federal soldiers to acquire valuable Pacific ports for whalers, fur traders, cotton producers, miners, and other merchants to use while also giving the U.S. Navy important ports from San Francisco to San Diego from which to patrol the eastern Pacific. The discovery of gold in California in 1848 and other parts west brought Easterners and Southerners to the West in abundance.[39]

These antebellum imperial adventures continued full throttle during and after the war. The U.S. government subsidized the construction of the transcontinental railroad through the Homestead Act (a wartime measure designed, in part, to thwart Confederate expansion into the West that could connect the Pacific to the Caribbean, creating a Confederate thoroughfare for their King Cotton–based economy) and encouraged Americans to migrate west, claiming that "rain will follow the plough." Many Americans hoped to escape the traumatic aftermath of the Civil War by migrating west. The U.S. government had difficulty controlling this impetus. They tried to regulate it on the cheap by building too few forts maintained by a severely downsized postwar military. This effort was simply too small to prevent Native Americans and migrating Americans from engaging in violence when their respective interests overlapped. The U.S. government also attempted to regulate westward expansion through treaties with Indians, the Homestead Act, and other legislative edicts that established the overall rules and procedures of annexing states and supporting private enterprise (such as railroad, mining, and cattle industries) to "settle" the West. Key to regulating westward expansion was the willingness of soldiers to sacrifice their lives for Americans who insisted on migrating beyond the Mississippi River. "Nowhere did capitalists rely more heavily on the use of force than in the West," claims Hahn. Federal officials with their local white allies and territorial governors relied on federal troops "to defeat the resistance of Native peoples to railroad building and the white settlement that accompanied it and then were left to protect the lines that were in private lands."[40] Would Lincoln's promise oblige citizens of the republic to commemorate those who died during imperial expansion in the West? Could soldiers' sacrifices, committed beyond the emancipatory cause of the Civil War, be justified by the living back east?

With the Confederate rebellion defeated, federal officials such as Secretary of State William Seward sought to materialize an "idea of empire [that] intricately linked domestic and foreign affairs" and "knew no clear borders or boundaries." This kind of empire "required strong and stable social order at home, built upon flourishing agricultural and industrial economies" in which a federal government would "support the aspirations of merchants, manufacturers, and farmers." Seward thus sought "American commercial supremacy in the Pacific and control over the waterborne highways that led to Asia," believing that "the empire of the seas alone is the real empire." Seward acquired new territory in Alaska, procuring the strategic fur trading port of Sitka as well as the Aleutian Islands that could provide a "vital coaling station to Japan and China." He supported California statehood, which supplied the key ports in San Francisco, Monterrey, and San Diego. This expansive domain included enough civilian communities to support the whaling industry, the fur trade market, and the transportation of commodities across the Great American Desert via the railroad and throughout the Pacific Northwest. It extended American presence into the Pacific, but also gave the United States jurisdiction over indigenous peoples in the Aleutian Islands. Continental indigenous people living on the Great Plains and in the Pacific Northwest not only occupied valuable real estate where livestock, minerals, and agricultural resources could be exploited. They also occupied places that stood in the way of a United States bridging the Atlantic and Pacific worlds. Seward and his supporters understood that nation-states "perpetually and necessarily coloniz[ed] their own domains even as they prepare[d] to find new ones."[41] Americans connected these oceanic worlds with steel, railroads, imaginings of manifest destiny, and memories of a civilizing mission supported by government policies of expansion that excluded people who could not fit into the white-dominated worlds of Protestantism and capitalism.

This effort was a project of hemispheric imagining, as Gretchen Murphy suggests, that had messianic and pragmatic supporters from government officials and citizens, as Perry Anderson contends in *American Foreign Policy and Its Thinkers*. The work of bridging the Atlantic and Pacific worlds would incorporate the lives of many indigenous peoples and also immigrants from Asia, Europe, and Latin America as well as native-born Americans who lived and died building the infrastructure of empire. Would all of these sacrifices be remembered? Chapters 4–5 examine the war dead from the

Spanish-Cuban-American War in Cuba and the Philippine-American War to explore the way Americans built a nation using their memories of the republic to (re)imagine their importance in bridging the Atlantic and Pacific. American soldiers patrolled, regulated, protected, and enforced this hemisphere, often seeking cooperation from the Native American tribes as well as Cuban and Filipino authorities but also enforcing U.S. government policy with lethal force. Sometimes U.S. soldiers made up the rear guard of westward expansion, and sometimes they were the first into the fray of an imagined "untamed" land. They were charged with executing the federal policy of expansion into the West and later into the Caribbean and the Pacific; many of them made the ultimate sacrifice in this pursuit. Their deaths became a convenient opportunity to mark the new boundaries of the ever-expanding empire. Where they died mattered. Their graves served as monuments of stone marking the expanding boundaries of the nation and confirming the obligations of Lincoln's promise. Those who grieved the dead could also serve to help other Americans remember where boundaries were located and what kind of sacrifice contributed to their expansion. Remembering the dead could offer people a very compelling map of nation and empire.

Americans had to adapt their understanding of citizenship to the expanding history of American empire that often contradicted the virtues of republicanism. The historical context of empire could be minimized by redefining cultural memory as people applied Lincoln's promise to the changing terrain of nation and empire. As historians Frederick Cooper and Jane Burbank illustrate, nation and empire often overlapped and had to negotiate these boundaries at the core and at the edge of empire. The politics of exclusion shaped the memories of citizenship. With some obfuscation, republicanism and Jim Crow could be made to lie side by side, and so could democracy and Orientalism.[42] The competing nature between empire and nation forced Americans to interpret cultural memory through the rapidly changing identity of the republic. U.S. officials and citizens obliged to fulfill Lincoln's promise again used hypolepsis to do so. Americans thus adapted the canonical obligations of memory that Lincoln uttered at Gettysburg and applied them to new locations on the frontier to soften the violent legacy of an imperial history that often invalidated memories of republicanism.

Lincoln's promise would again establish the precedent for how Americans would commemorate the First World War. Chapters 6–9 examine how Americans remade their memories of the frontier experience during the early twentieth century, this time within the context of an emerging military-industrial complex. Citizenship was remade during this period, as Christopher Capazolla suggests, but this citizenry used specific memories of America's past to craft new rules of inclusion and exclusion. Cultural memory of the dead again had to accomplish two very difficult and even oppositional tasks. On the one hand, they had to heal people's grief. This healing process was riddled with racial tension, class animosity, religious opprobrium, and resentment of a federal government that could send loved ones to their deaths so barbarically. On the other hand, just as living soldiers could fight to extend the boundaries of the nation and the definitions of citizenship, dead soldiers could mark those territorial and ideological sites and sanctify them with the blood of their bodies and dirt of their graves. Political elites and U.S. citizens together constructed nationalistic commemorative traditions that could reduce collective trauma of war and economic devastation by reconnecting "the basic tissues of social life" through cultural memory that could negotiate the shared, overlapping, and even contradictory spaces of republic, nation, and empire.[43]

This work is not a history of warfare or foreign policy. It is an analysis of how American identity was constructed in the memories of the dead as their graves were dug throughout the North American continent as well as in the Atlantic and Pacific worlds. By studying the military dead of American expansion in the West and the Caribbean, I will chart the ways in which people enacted Lincoln's promise and evaluate how well the U.S. government and its citizens collaborated to keep Lincoln's vow. But most of all, this examination of cultural memory produces an analysis and an evaluation of the evolution of citizenship as it unfolded within the process of expansion. By looking at the public memory, official commemorations, monuments, and other displays of cultural memory displayed over the bodies of those who carried out the official policies of U.S. expansion, the collaboration between Americans and government officials negotiating republican and imperial terrains will become evident. People and communities needed to convince themselves and each other that they belonged to the American republic while middle-class and elite Americans sought to wield imperial power by excluding communities of people through racial, ideological, gender, or racial definitions. If empire was a process of inclusion and exclusion in overlapping places, then the techniques people used to remember the American republic and its imperial ambitions is one method through which scholars can identify and even plot the imperial repertoire of American power. Lincoln's promise continually obliged Americans to (re)connect their biographical memories to cultural memories. Mourning traditions reflected the way Americans counted the cost of conflict and imagined the nation's role in the world. Constructing, maintaining, and refreshing an American cultural memory was a fundamental aspect of the imagined community that helped justify the construction of the bureaucratic nation-state in the late nineteenth century.

PART 1

Storage

The Kingdom of the Dead gathered in the Theater of the Universe led by the music of Ludwig von Beethoven. Allan, a mortal, trespassed through the Hall of the Dark Brotherhood to a hallway that opened to an amphitheater one hundred thousand times bigger than the Capitol Building in Washington DC. Allan took his unlikely seat and quickly identified a "who's who" of western civilization's immortals in attendance. He saw Hannibal of Carthage, Alexander the Great, Cleopatra, Julius Caesar, Mark Antony, Joan of Arc, Oliver Cromwell, and Napoleon. Christopher Columbus attended, too, surrounded by the signers of the Declaration of Independence while William Shakespeare reclined in his throne as reigning monarch of the Kingdom of the Dead. All had gathered in the enormous amphitheater, unaware of the forbidden mortal among them, to watch *The Play of Destiny*, which was about to begin. This was an interaction between the living and the dead.[1]

Stephen Wheeler Downey wrote *The Play of Destiny* in 1867, two years after Lincoln's assassination and in the same year that federal authorities released former Confederate president Jefferson Davis from prison. While in the Union Army, Downey attained the rank of colonel before his honorable discharge in 1863 due to wounds suffered at the Battle of Harpers Ferry. In 1869 he and his brother William would venture to Wyoming where Stephen served in the territorial legislature, practiced law, speculated in mining, and helped create the University of Wyoming, later serving as its president.[2]

He penned this play within a play in 1867 "to perpetuate and keep green the memory of Abraham Lincoln in the hearts of the American people." Downey intended his monument to Lincoln to serve also as a memory of vengeance against "the master spirits who directed the hand of the assassin."[3] Downey used the Theater of the Universe as a sort of mystical playback through which he could dramatically retell a behind-the-scenes fantasy of the entire war over five acts liberally mixing fact and fiction. The theater thus provided a medium through which to remember the past. But instead of actors interpreting the past while on stage, the Theater of the Universe itself played back scenes as if the dead spectators were watching events as they happened. In this way the theater acted as an archive of memory storage. Allan, as the narrator, occupied a prime seat among the dead heroes of western civilization, and together the living and the dead became witnesses to the canonization of Lincoln's death and Confederate malfeasance. The message became clear as the play unfolded; renowned men (and a few women) of western civilization gathered to canonize the experiences of the Civil War and Lincoln's assassination. By witnessing this spectral play on the actual audience's behalf, Allan interpreted this supernatural process to the paying customers in attendance.

This play was a small part of an emerging memory boom that transfixed Americans in the immediate aftermath of the Civil War. The militarist regeneration of memory was reflected in the late nineteenth-century explosion of institutions such as the Grand Army of the Republic, the United Confederate Veterans, the mass production of print media and later visual and audio networks, the prevalence of sermons, obelisk monuments, museums, and official commemorations all signaling a profound desire for Americans to participate in the emerging memory industry surrounding the Civil War and Reconstruction. Indeed while early twentieth-century European thinkers provided much of the intellectual and cultural language used to describe collective memory and societal responses to war and mass violence, nineteenth-century Americans had built an industry of memory to help them explain the magnitude of loss from the Civil War.[4] Nevertheless, the initial memory problem facing American society was that of facility. There simply were too many names spread across too many places for individuals to remember. So many people died in the war that it far outstripped the capacity for people in small agrarian communities to remember them effectively. The living risked forgetting the dead, and thus transgressing Lincoln's promise, because the capacity to remember could not keep pace with the amount of data needed to be stored. Thus the living had to develop new strategies for memory storage at scale in order to cope with mass grief and explain the slaughter of loved ones who died amid strangers. Storage capacity could be increased if people could leverage their individual memory capacities together into a network. This network would need to be external to individuals and would need a method to communicate large amounts of data across large expansive spaces inhabited by disconnected communities. People thus developed techniques to network themselves together through the medium of culture.

The Play of Destiny provides one small example of how a functioning external memory network allowed people to store memory within culture. Downey felt an intense fear that Americans were stripping the past from the present too much. He was dismayed at Jefferson Davis's release from prison, which seemed, at least to him, symptomatic of an emerging cultural amnesia surrounding Lincoln's assassination. He hoped his play would keep the past a relevant part of the present and Lincoln a relevant symbol of politics. Many Northerners shared Downey's fears, and they sought to organize and institutionalize cultural memory to prevent further amnesia. Together, government officials and anxious middle-class Americans stored socially constructed memories within innovative rituals to help Americans understand the sacrifice of citizenship, to disperse the trauma of war still present in survivors' minds, but also to socially and economically "regenerate" the Republic. Downey used the theater as a visual medium to mythologize the memory of the conflict and store it within the rituals of the theater and the performance of the play. Audience members could retrieve it individually and use it to shape their respective memories, but the play also had the potential to link audience members—who would not have known or even known about each other beforehand—into a network that was based on sharing the themes of the play. Even if the individuals in the audience remained complete strangers and never spoke to one another, the play allowed them to sync their internal memories through the shared experience of the performance.

Neuroscientist Merlin Donald describes an external memory storage system that mimics the neurological connections of the mind. Just as biological neuro networks are seemingly too numerous to count, so too are the networked social memory pathways traversing and overlapping as humans interact with each other. This external system allowed people to leverage each other to store collective memories within culture. By relying on network users to store information, people could manipulate the network to transcend geographic boundaries and reach other people through outlets such as the theater but also through media channels such as music or public speaking. This network could store an incalculable amount of memory in the minds of potentially millions of other network users. It was limited only by the speed, convenience, and capacity of the technology that serviced the network. The friction initiated by this process, contends Donald, allows individuals to reinterpret their internal memories on a much larger scale then previously possible, adding and subtracting key facts from their recollections, then syncing these reformulated remembrances to social memory. In this way people were continually uploading, downloading, and syncing memories, which significantly enlarged the number of people within their group(s) and required them to develop better memory techniques to access and interact with the evolving technology of the network.[5]

Individuals during Reconstruction were thus continually rebalancing their sense of self and their sense of citizenship every time they accessed the cultural network when they listened to a church sermon, took in a show at the theater, read a newspaper, or visited a cemetary; all of these and more had profound effects on how individuals (re)interpreted their memories. Downey's play provides a window into how culture animated this external memory network while also highlighting the main problem with external storage systems during Reconstruction. Northern network users relied heavily on mythologizing Lincoln or the Union dead and too often neglected the work of incorporating culture into freedmen's calls for equality that came from their memories of slavery. It also failed to adequately create firewalls against competing memories eventually gaining access to the network born of the Lost Cause movement and white supremacy.

Downey, nevertheless, seems to suggest that through his unnatural access to the Theater of the Dead, Allan exposed to the paying audience a functioning external memory system of the war. The protagonist saw that the great heroes of the past, now dead, instantly canonized Lincoln's assassination as one of the great events of western civilization and remembered Confederate leadership as a group of men, led by Jefferson Davis, bent on undermining civilization. But Allan's transgression against nature threatened to keep the secrets of the dead from reaching the living. As the play concluded Allan sensed that he had been discovered as a "traitor" by the Kingdom of the Dead. Exposed, he ran out of the Theater of the Universe as the dead tried to entrap him forever in the Hall of the Dark Brotherhood. As the play concluded, Allan narrowly escaped and secured a carriage that whisked him away to safety and procured the memories of the dead so that they could be shared with the living.

CHAPTER 1

Where the Grapes of Wrath Are Stored

> Let me hasten to commend to the grateful consideration of this noble, generous people, alike the soldier who has given his strength, the prisoner who has sacrificed his health, the widow who has offered up her husband, the orphan that knows only that its father went out to battle and comes no more forever, and the lonely, distant grave of the martyr, who sleeps alone in a stranger soil, that freedom and peace might come to ours.
> —Clara Barton

The postwar memory boom that followed Lincoln's speech at Gettysburg transformed republican identity into a much broader middle-class national identity. New traditions emerged and melded hot memory with older ones. Lincoln's words transformed the Good Death beyond bourgeois private families to include soldiers and martyrs who suffered a Good Death for the nation even if nobody heard their last cries of assured belief in the national cause for which they suffered. Evidence of these new traditions emerged within a memory industry that included the creation of national cemeteries and the commemoration of soldiers not as local heroes but as national icons. Federal authorities and middle-class citizens built a network of sacred spaces. Sometimes the bureaucratic version of Lincoln's promise was resisted, sometimes it could be implemented with the help of local elites, and sometimes it was hegemonic. These collaborations produced a cold cultural memory that significantly left out African American communicative memories while excluding Confederate memories altogether. In all cases, these national spaces expressed a Northern interpretation that failed to adequately incorporate the symbolism of African American liberation.

Storing memory within the cult of Lincoln to sound the warnings of Confederate wickedness was innovative, but Downey's play failed to recognize, in the cult of the dead, an even more powerful storage system based less on uncommon men of reputation and more on common men of obligation in the wake of the Civil War. Lincoln himself helped initiate this cult as postwar commemorative rituals coalesced around the traditions emerging from Lincoln's promise and what historian George Mosse describes as the cult of the fallen soldier.[1] In July 1862 Congress authorized Lincoln to purchase land and build new national cemeteries at a moment when he was about to articulate a new official meaning of the war. His Gettysburg Address, delivered in the autumn of 1863, promised to dedicate the Gettysburg battlefield as a place that, along with many other locations, stored the memories of a new birth of freedom. The president promised the soldiers that the living would remember them as a noble community who furthered the cause of slave emancipation and democratic government. Many citizens took this promise seriously and found themselves supporting the federal government as officials assumed control over Union—but not Confederate—corpses after the war and supplied the grave markers, superintendents, and finances needed to keep cemeteries in pristine condition. "The War of the Rebellion was enabling the ruling Republicans to define the boundaries of the nation-state," and to aid their agenda, federal officials built a storage system of cultural memory out of this military cemetery system.[2] This network served Republican congressmen well as they consistently sought out the politics of "waving the bloody shirt"—a way to remind voters of the failures of the Democratic Party and their Confederate supporters in the South. But the federal support of a national military system also fit within the larger context that Republicans, particularly Radical Republicans in the Northeast, supported that used federal power to dramatically reshape the nation. They supported financial reform bills that brought banking and currency under federal regulation, supported the development of railroad, mining, and oil industries, and required states to create land-grant colleges through the Morrill Act.

Winning the war meant that Northern officials could influence Southerners through hot cultural memory at a time when radical Republicans in Congress were trying to reshape the socioeconomic structure of the South. They entirely transformed the labor system that planters had relied on to grow, harvest, and process cotton. They passed the Military Reconstruction Act in 1867, which oversaw state constitutional conventions in the former Confederacy and the enfranchisement of African Americans, who served on these constitutional conventions that helped ratify the Fourteenth Amendment, establishing national citizenship requirements and equal protection under the law. Republicans funded the Freedmen's Bureau in which government agents, often men who formerly served in the military, operated in the South delivering health care to former slaves, working with freedmen to negotiate labor contracts, redistributing land, establishing free education, and conducting freedmen's courts. Republicans often gained political influence in districts where black freedmen benefited from Freedmen's Bureau activities and the military protected their enfranchisement. In response, terrorist and paramilitary groups attempted to undermine Republican-friendly districts using violence and intimidation. Groups such as the Ku Klux Klan had limited success, but "far more effective in this work were rifle clubs—known variously as the White Leagues or the Red Shirts," who attacked Republican meetings, killed black voters, and used the force of arms to drive duly elected Republicans from office. "More and more counties were 'redeemed' in this way," argues Steven Hahn, "effectively undermining Republican state and local regimes or isolating them in a rising sea of paramilitarism." In the face of such violence, Freedmen continued to turn out to the polls, incorporating themselves politically into the Union League and using the African Methodist Episcopal Church to reach new voters. Some took up weapons and used their "arms-bearing militancy effectively [to] stare down the rifle clubs." Hahn asserts, "Former slaves were therefore the most numerous and reliable allies the Republicans had for the task of incorporating the rebellious states into their new nation-state."[3]

The presence of federal troops throughout much of the former

Confederacy coupled with the emergence of a vulnerable but sustainable Republican political movement in the South weakened and restricted the violence of paramilitary operations. Confederates thus cultivated new places, especially in cemeteries, to organize politically, writes historian William A. Blair. The ceremonial rituals performed within the cemeteries were "not simply reflections of social behavior but an active means of practicing politics." Confederates often went to cemeteries using their opportunity to commemorate the dead as an effective tool to resist Reconstruction all the while plotting their political reinvention.[4] As Hahn argues, "Democrats, without massive electoral fraud, would have remained on the losing end, out of power, especially in the Deep South, where black political strength was greatest."[5] While Confederates worked out the details of their electoral fraud within the cemeteries and other places, the cultural memory buried in cemeteries sustained the Confederate desire to usurp Republican Reconstruction and black enfranchisement. These kinds of policies reshaped the nation in provocative and controversial ways.

One way to accumulate support for these political ends was the continual expansion of the national cemetery network, which not only endured the era of Reconstruction but became a permanent feature of the commemorative landscape over the course of the nineteenth century. Southerners and Northerners thus began waging a postwar memory war through the cemetery apparatus of the cultural memory network. While the federal government built this storage system from the top down, in some ways the national cemetery system was heavily utilized from the bottom up. Veterans who formed the Grand Army of the Republic, family members who had lost loved ones to the war, ladies' memorial societies that sought to keep the memory of the dead alive, local communities that profited from the tourism but also sought to protect hallowed ground, superintendents and their staffs who sought new professional careers as caretakers, landscapers, clergymen, schoolteachers, historians, and other interested professionals—all could find in the national cemeteries a place that spoke to their individual and collective understanding of sacrifice, liberty, and nationalization. These cemetery storage systems thus guarded places where both aspects of collective memory—communicative and cultural—coexisted. Veterans who fought at these locations and family members who hoped to commune with a lost loved one at their final resting place could convene within these cemeteries and share their experiences face-to-face. But these cemeteries also became places to access relics, such as war artifacts found on the battlefield, and institute grief rituals and mourning traditions. They thus allowed people to participate in a network made up of fellow pilgrims, veterans, politicians, and tourists interested in accessing memory from the storage banks of fellow visitors. But the discursive struggle over the emerging cult of the fallen soldier also helped stunt an embryonic cult of the freedmen despite their shared centrality to dead soldiers in the Gettysburg Address. In making the soldier dead the center of cultural memory, cemeteries-as-monuments tended to cool, or at least fail to acknowledge, the civil rights claims of living African Americans.

These cemeteries nevertheless help illustrate the early postwar structural formation of cultural memory by examining the contradictory yet overlapping spheres of influence encapsulated through the ideas of sacred and desecrated, Northern and Southern, black and white, and symbolic and political. This chapter examines Marietta and Arlington National Cemeteries to explore the way grief and mourning were practiced and politicized in the early Reconstruction years as Republicans went about remaking the nation. Anguish dominated the consciousness of many Americans. Northerners and Southerners brought their heartache to these places and hoped that the language of religion and nationalism would heal their sorrow. Their willingness to participate in commemorating the dead suggests that they collaborated with government officials to build a "republic of suffering" that took Lincoln's promise seriously even while criticizing the government's role in executing the war and politicizing the grieving process.[6] These places quickly transformed into memory storage systems where Americans waged a symbolic Civil War over the meanings and intentions of the dead.

A Union sacred space in the heart of Southern soil, the national cemetery in Marietta provides an example of how the rituals of official memory surrounding the dead could influence local politics. Particularly in the South, federal officials had to collaborate with local people sympathetic to Republican attempts to redefine the republic even in the face of local resistance. Marietta was an important city because it challenged Atlanta for dominance in the region and included both a national cemetery and a Confederate cemetery within the city limits. While Atlanta had the important north/south and east/west railroad tracks running through the town, Marietta had a higher population, a military college, and the rail line connecting Atlanta to Chattanooga. In fact, Marietta played an important part in the defense of Atlanta as General Sherman's army made its way south from Chattanooga. Thus the contested national sacred space of the national cemetery overlaid the local politics of Confederate memory.

As much as Marietta was part of the Confederacy, it also included a significant pocket of Union loyalists. One such Unionist was Henry Greene Cole, a civil engineer from New York working for the Western and Atlantic Railroad. He moved to Georgia in 1838 and made his money through railroad construction and real estate. He purchased the Marietta Hotel and accumulated numerous rental properties. In building the W&A line, Cole surveyed much of the North Georgia region himself. He was connected to politicians including U.S. senator Alexander Stephens, who would serve as the vice president of the Confederate States of America. Cole also owned slaves.[7] He married into the Fletcher family, which had moved from Massachusetts to Georgia; the Coles and the Fletchers dominated much of Marietta's socioeconomic development.

Despite owning slaves and his ties to the Confederacy, Cole believed that Georgia should not have seceded. This brought scorn from fellow townspeople. His family exploited many in Marietta economically through his businesses, and his uncommitted stance to the Confederate cause produced much anxiety. In fact, some locals accused Cole of being a Union spy. Although he denied this during the war, he exuberantly claimed in front of the U.S. Claims Commission after the war that his advance knowledge of Confederate troop movements had helped Gen. George H. Thomas at Chickamauga and prevented total destruction of his Army of the Cumberland, despite defeat.[8] The Confederate Army imprisoned Cole in Atlanta for two months while troops searched his house and other properties looking for incriminating evidence. They found none. Cole demanded a trial, believing this would prove his innocence, but instead the army moved him to Charleston and suspended his writ of habeas corpus.[9] Vice President Stephens, who had known Cole since 1840 and did not believe the charge of spying, attempted to use his influence to get Cole freed. "I did all I could," claimed Stephens, "to get his release, but no heed was paid to my letters."[10]

While imprisoned in Charleston in 1864, Cole claimed his innocence. In a letter to his wife, Cole wrote, "Believe me my dearest your husband did nothing that is wrong, nothing if he has said that which was wrong, it was for no other purpose than that good might come from it in certain contingences." He alluded to the idea that he had only used his Northern contacts to protect his family and the city of Marietta should federal troops seize control on their way to Atlanta. He reminded his wife that he had spent twenty-five years constructing Marietta, saying, "There I have lived, there I wish to die and I will exert every faculty I possess to its preservation." He continued, "I know I have enemies in Marietta, unreasonable enemies. There are a great many people that I don't admire or respect, but I believe I possess a heart that bears no malice, political or personal to any human being."[11]

On May 21, 1864, Cole sat in prison fretting about the Union advance on Atlanta. Soon, he feared, federal troops would take Marietta. He worried that his wife and children lacked the means to support themselves while he was in prison, and he told his wife to make the best of a Northern invasion. Because his "unreasonable enemies" had "misinterpreted" his "friendliness" with his Northern contacts as betrayal, Cole was at a loss at what to do. "Poisoned jealousies and narrow prejudices have deprived me of doing anything for the benefit of the people." Since he could not protect Marietta, he decided he would protect his family. He told his wife, Mary, about several properties he owned. Women whose husbands served the Confederate Army lived in the houses that "have all been rent free since the war commenced," Cole wrote. Now he told her to turn out these people and "rent these to people that can pay, and sell wood, your milk, your vegetables at the high prices this would bring, it will yield you and the children a pretty good living."[12] This eviction of Confederate wives and widows certainly would not have endeared Cole's critics.

Union troops finally captured Marietta in July 1864 and settled in for the

Battle of Atlanta. Conditions worsened for the Cole family. Marietta became a principal staging ground for the Atlanta campaign. Cole's slaves, much to his dismay, left the family and fled north almost immediately. His health deteriorated, the hotel was shut down, and Union forces used his property and resources while in Marietta. Mary Cole's father, Dix Fletcher, meanwhile, appealed to Union general Benjamin Franklin Butler for Cole's release. Asking a Northern general to aid in the release of a Southern criminal held in a Charleston, South Carolina, prison demonstrated how desperate Cole had become.[13] Fletcher asked Butler to initiate a prisoner exchange—Cole for a Confederate soldier. A prisoner exchange initiated by a Union general, however, would only have supported Confederate suspicions; it would have implied that Cole was employed, or at least connected, to the U.S. military, probably as a spy. Butler did not intervene, and Cole remained in prison until he eventually received parole from the Confederate Department of South Carolina, Georgia, and Florida in January 1865. Though it was unclear why they released him, it was likely due to the overstretched Confederate prison system and economic depression. Cole signed a parole of honor in which he promised to refrain from aiding the enemies of the Confederacy.[14]

When Cole returned to Marietta, he found that the Union had destroyed most of his property, including his hotel. He told the federal Claims Commission, "It was entirely destroyed from wantonness while I was in Charleston," and he estimated the value of the hotel at $100,000. The war ended a few months after Cole's return, and he set out to reassert his economic and political influence. It seems that Cole hoped to rebuild his fortune, in part, from a revitalized postwar Northern tourist industry. Northerners often stopped there on their way to Florida. Cole and his family, including the Fletchers, even made an extended trip to Boston and New York, with a stop at Niagara Falls, to reestablish contact and secure investments from his Northern interests. While in Boston, Cole visited Alexander Stephens, gave him $100 in gold and $100 in cash, and lobbied for his release.[15] Upon returning home, he decided to donate some of his land to the City of Marietta to be used for a cemetery. He was willing to donate the land to bury the bodies of Union and Confederate soldiers who fought and died in the region. On July 22, 1866, Cole's mother-in-law noted in her journal,

He recently proffered a very eligible site to the citizens of Marietta for a Cemetery for Federal and Confederate soldiers which was rejected with scorn because they could not bury their dead with the Fed dead—he afterwards offered it to the government for a National cemetery and it has been accepted, he having been appointed Superintendent and has given employment to Mari [Dix Fletcher, Cole's father-in-law].[16]

Though Louisa Fletcher thought him "being one of the strangest kind" for this, Cole was able to secure government salaries of $100 per month for himself and $100 per month for his father-in-law, and he created a sacred site for well-to-do Northerners to tour on their travels.

Seeking a space to bury Union dead and to assert federal memory of the war, the U.S. government accepted the twenty-five acres of land in August 1866 as a "liberal and patriotic gift" from a Union loyalist in the heart of Georgia. Cole received a commendation of thanks from the secretary of war on behalf of President Andrew Johnson. It is significant to remember that the United States would never have asserted this official memory had it not been for the donation by an unofficial but very public—and contested—citizen. Thanks to Cole, the Marietta National Cemetery would include the bodies of seven thousand soldiers, white and black, who fought at almost every battle from Rome, Georgia, to Columbus, Georgia. The military also planned to close the national cemetery in Alabama and remove the bodies from there to Marietta. Work began in September; the military walled off the cemetery, built drainage ditches and interior roads, marked off the burial plots, and began burying Union dead. Among them were the remains of ten black soldiers, who were buried in graves "in the extreme South side of the [City] Cemetery" of Marietta, "none of which are marked."[17]

This federal intervention in local politics did not sit well with many in Marietta. The national cemetery was so controversial that the War Department had to secure workers from an adjacent county to perform the work.[18] Well before Cole donated his land, on the other side of town, the Memorial Burying Ground at Marietta began interring Confederates in 1863. The first man buried was physician William Miller, who had been working in a makeshift hospital in town. Several troops who died in a train collision between a troop carrier and a hospital train north of Marietta were buried near Miller. At least one cadet at the Georgia Military Institute in Marietta noted how unimpressive these burials were. In a letter to his mother, Julia, bright-eyed S. Montgomery wrote: "I have lately seen a sample how they bury dead soldiers. They dig a small hole just large enough to hold a box which contains the corpse and it is placed about two feet under the ground. The graves have no protection against hogs, dogs or anything of the kind. I think it is a shame as they have plenty of time and place for to bury them."[19]

Perhaps the ceremony was unimpressive, but the developing Confederate cemetery proved meaningful for many in Marietta. William Bosley owned the cemetery space and donated the two acres to the city. As the war continued, the cemetery continued to fill as soldiers from makeshift hospitals died. Following another train collision in which one train was carrying Atlanta troops to reinforce General Bragg at Chickamauga, the Ladies' Aid Society set out to secure more land. They persuaded Ann Moyer to donate five acres of land in 1864, and they oversaw the cemetery as it took in several hundred bodies from the Battle of Kennesaw Mountain.[20]

When Cole offered his land to the citizens of Marietta for a joint-burial cemetery, many believed he was explicitly attacking the supporters of this Confederate cemetery. Perhaps retaliating for his imprisonment, Cole hoped to dominate the reputation as well as commerce of Marietta. Drawing Northern tourists to the National Cemetery, many of whom might stay in Cole's rebuilt hotel, was interpreted by many townsfolk as economically savvy and symbolically malicious. Mariettans protested. While women of the city secured the cemetery space and managed the commemoration of dead Confederate soldiers, men of the city sent a letter to President Johnson opposing the national cemetery. The members of the Memorial Committee believed that Cole had donated the land inside the city without consulting the community; the location, they believed, would assuredly cause them "material injury." They also claimed the national cemetery constituted "an unworthy motive . . . of prejudice to the *Union* dead." Instead of the lush rolling hills that Cole donated, the committee suggested that President Johnson consider "sites more eligible" that were closer to the railroad station in the city. They proposed a site that was "out of view from the road, which could be obtained at a reasonable cost." Mariettans claimed that Cole's property would not do as a national cemetery or as a Confederate cemetery and pleaded with Johnson that it was inappropriate to accept donations from private citizens without considering the interests of the citizenry. Committee members asserted that accepting the donation "would prejudice the interests of the humblest of its citizens." They reminded Johnson finally that Congress had appropriated money for this purpose, and it would be more appropriate for the government to purchase grounds with the approval of the president. This battle over cemetery space seems to speak to how Marietta's role in the war would be remembered as either a Union staging ground or as a Confederate stronghold.[21]

The Memorial Committee certainly understood the politics of representation that were playing out in Marietta through an alliance between their chastised local villain and the victorious nation-state. They completely understood that the federal government, in conjunction with Cole, tried to coproduce the memory of the war from the Union perspective. They did not just object to the cemetery's location. Cole's land was on a small hill at the highest point in the city. Their smaller Confederate burial ground would be dwarfed by the government's cemetery, and their local funds could not match the government's treasury. They understood that this was a symbolic war over memory and they would lose it just as they had lost the actual war; thus they accused the government and Cole of exacerbating local prejudices with a national cemetery.

The citizens' complaint spawned an investigation. President Johnson passed the inquiry on to the War Department, and the quartermaster general assigned his assistant, Brevet Maj. W. A. Wainwright, to investigate. Wainwright's report concluded that there was no just cause for the complaint. He had interviewed several petitioners. When confronted, Dr. George W. Cleland, who lived on the same street as the national cemetery, rescinded his protest because he saw that the cemetery, once completed, would beautify the street and dramatically improve his property value. Wainwright reported Dr. Cleland as stating that if Cole "as a neighbor—had told him that he intended giving the land for the purpose, he would not have opposed it at first." Many who signed claimed that their friends had brought the petition to them "and rather than to get in trouble with them signed it, but it *was not* their wish that it be removed." Many signers did not own property in the city but lived in the country; many were young boys.[22]

It is difficult to assess how much passion and how much pragmatism went into the petitioners' actions. How honest were the petitioners responding to Wainwright, a Union soldier, who represented the federal presence in the city? On the one hand, they certainly did not want the cemetery reminding them of the military catastrophe, which also might remind them of their economic depression. On the other hand, many saw economic advantages to the cemetery. That protesters changed their minds suggests that they cultivated their protestations in the domain of the symbolic but had to face up to the economic reality of the city. Cole could prevent his enemies from getting jobs as much as he could help his friends with work in economically dire postwar Marietta. Wainwright's report included an update on the construction of the burial ground. He noted, "The labor is given to all as far as possible without reference to who or what they are or have been—but with a desire to help keep alive those, who must assuredly starve unless a helping hand is given them." Whether or not petitioners allowed economic reality to trump the political symbolism of the national cemetery, Wainwright believed that the protest was "one of personal and spiteful nature against Mr. Cole." Considering Cole's reputation, this cannot be separated from the politics of Marietta during the war. Wainwright's report made it to the desk of Secretary of War Edwin Stanton, who ordered that the cemetery construction continue.[23]

By the following summer of 1867, the cemetery had reached full capacity and more bodies were awaiting burial. The government needed 402 additional spaces. Cole volunteered an additional six acres, but government officials this time were reluctant to accept the gift unless it was "absolutely necessary." The land Cole was willing to donate would have cost the War Department much to develop. Cole could not use the ground because it was composed of very sandy dirt and accumulated water—this also made it bad for cemetery maintenance. The War Department would have to spend at least $6,000, "a sum entirely disproportionate to the number of bodies now reported unprovided for." Rather, Inspector of Cemeteries Brevet Col. C. W. Folsom recommended rearranging parts of the existing cemetery, including using the space between the front gate and the grave markers. Folsom believed the government only needed one acre to accommodate four hundred bodies, and it would be approximately one-sixth the cost.[24]

But Folsom had larger reservations about the government accepting additional land from Cole. Folsom suspected Cole of donating the land not out of "patriotism" but out of a "reasonable amount of self-interest."[25] One of the provisions for Cole's donation was that he and his family receive a family plot inside the national cemetery. Considering his reputation among some in Marietta, this was probably the only way to guard against desecration of Cole family tombs. Cole's position as superintendent of the cemetery and the appointment of his father-in-law to carry out the day-to-day upkeep came with salaries that were much larger than what the superintendent at Andersonville received. No doubt this income helped the Coles and the Fletchers at a time when few other business opportunities were available.

Although Folsom did not investigate his own accusations in depth—he relied heavily on the words of other officers who had spent more time in Marietta—he outlined several ways that Cole benefited from "the patriotism which he claimed." The inspector admitted that some of his points were "only matters of supposition" but others were documented. He worried that the U.S. government had expended thousands of taxpayer dollars in "ornamental improvements" and beautifying the space, which drove up the property value of Cole's adjacent home and the space bordering the cemetery, much of which Cole also owned. The cemetery could further generate revenue through a nascent pilgrimage and tourism industry for those who wanted to visit the final resting place of a loved one or for those who wanted to see the national cemetery before continuing on to Florida.[26] Although the Union Army had burnt down his Marietta Hotel, Folsom said Cole planned to rebuild it and take advantage of cemetery tourists who would need a place to stay. He added that Cole gained an economic advantage when the United States rebuilt the bridges and paved Cole Street leading to the cemetery, by his house, and by his other property. The inspector also accused Cole and his father-in-law of collecting salaries "without devoting so much of their time to the Cemetery as to hinder them from their other business." The inspector complained that Cole allegedly received compensation for helping the military contract labor resources. Perhaps this is why many who signed the protest petition recanted in person to Cole. The brevet colonel believed both men received too much money for the amount of work they did. Indeed, when Folsom inspected the cemetery, he only got to speak to Cole for a few minutes because the Georgian had been away to Atlanta for a political rally.[27]

The military inspector thus recommended that the United States should not expand the Marietta cemetery unless it was necessary because Cole held a "direct pecuniary interest" in the endeavor. Folsom concluded: "Giving him credit for a patriotic wish to see the U.S. soldiers well buried, his pleasure in seeing that is not lessened by finding that for every additional soldier buried, or every additional acre improved by the U.S., a sum far larger than the original value of the land finds its way into his own pockets." Folsom was only half-correct. For Cole, beyond any money he may have received, the cemetery was also a way to symbolically challenge those "poisoned jealousies" and "unreasonable enemies" of his who he would "do nothing to make them friends." It was Cole, nevertheless, who made possible the government's implementation of Lincoln's promise in Marietta.[28]

Those "friends" took notice of the symbolism that the U.S. government was asserting. As bodies poured into the national cemetery in 1867, the Georgia legislature voted down the Fourteenth Amendment guaranteeing equal protection of African Americans under the law. It also voted for the expenditure of monies to the Georgia Memorial Association to locate, gather, and rebury the bodies of Confederate soldiers in the Marietta Confederate Cemetery. Headed by Phoebe Pender from Rome, Mary Jan Green from Atlanta, and Mrs. Charles J. Williams from Columbus, the Georgia Memorial Association located the remains of more than two thousand soldiers at Kennesaw Mountain. The association also expanded the Confederate cemetery by securing two additional acres from Jane Porter Glover. Marietta historian Curt Ratledge claims that the association inadvertently buried some of these Confederates in the slave section of the adjoining city cemetery. He writes, "Later, when it became known—but not publicized—that this lot contained blacks—the Confederates were removed, so that no blacks were interred—in accordance with the customs of those days—next to white

Confederate soldiers." This was in stark contrast to the national cemetery where black soldiers were buried next to and among white soldiers. Funding trickled in, and it took the association almost two years to finally bury all the soldiers. They only accomplished this, claims Ratledge, with the aid of the "State-owned Western and Atlantic Railroad . . . [that] provided free transportation of the pine coffins to Marietta."[29]

The Confederate cemetery never had the financial support that the U.S. government gave the national cemetery. Although it initially demonstrated the symbolic rebellion over federal memory, the Confederate cemetery deteriorated over the years. In contrast to the beautified national cemetery with marble grave markers, a superintendent, and a staff receiving full pay, the Confederate cemetery's wooden grave markers wasted away, specific grave locations were lost, and the disarray of the cemetery demoralized Confederates. As Ratledge describes the burial ground: "It must be remembered that most of the present marble headstones were not placed until 1902, and that few—if any—mark actual graves of slain soldiers. Those sites were lost late in the last century, when the original wooden headboards were allowed to deteriorate and decay. The pattern of headstones was created to provide an attractive panorama, not to indicate specific graves."[30]

The deteriorating cemetery became a symbol of a lost cause, and its poor condition helped illustrate that the Union had won the war. Still this did not stop some former Confederates from allegedly trying to desecrate the Union cemetery. In one example, the U.S. Army believed a circulating rumor that someone in Marietta had "kept the skeleton of a deceased Union Soldier" rather than giving the remains to the government.[31] Another example was articulated by a sympathetic Confederate commentator: "The clever rebels, who, hearing that a reward was being paid for the rescue of the scattered and lost remains of deceased Federal troops, would gather up animal bones, sprinkle some uniform scraps and buttons among them and sell them to the Yankees. There can be no accurate accounting of how many pigs, cows and horses are buried in this place of honor, thanks to the enterprising larceny of these Southerners."[32]

The U.S. military never sponsored reward money for the location of dead soldiers. They used Union records to locate the bodies and officers in the quartermaster's general office and they found, identified, and reburied soldiers in the cemetery. But as time went on, this myth turned into legend, the Confederate cemetery wasted away, and this sort of story became the most effective way to "vandalize" the federal cemetery. This kind of vandalism, however, only existed within the realm of local communicative memory and could never really threaten the Marietta National Cemetery as a storage system of cultural memory.

The Marietta National Cemetery ignored the meaning of the Civil War as a fight for emancipation. Such a cemetery included the remains of blacks lying with those of whites, but these sorts of symbolic sites lost their currency in the self-aggrandizement of Henry Cole and Marietta Confederate sympathizers. The government's interest in mediating the controversy between local control of memory coupled with the War Department's inability to assert a centralized collective memory underscored the lost political potential to sculpt a usable collective memory of freedom triumphing over slavery in the early stages of Reconstruction. Had the radical Republicans and the War Department been better able to regulate the way people collectively remembered the achievements of both black and white soldiers—perhaps by placing the duty of remembering under the charge of the Freedmen's Bureau—collective memory might have included the poetics of emancipation. But local politics in Marietta subverted the cause of emancipation, and the black bodies buried among the more numerous white bodies in the national cemetery, although vaguely honored within a generic concept of national sacrifice, were reduced to oblivion within cultural memory.

This was not necessarily the case in Arlington National Cemetery. It became a contested space where government officials, particularly Secretary Stanton, eventually came to dominate the cemetery's meaning without the public interfering. Arlington became the American Valhalla, in part, because here government officials could assert interpretations of the war uncontested by spontaneous local memories. This was not always the case. The early history of Arlington suggests that storage systems of cultural memory could be built around freedmen's memories. But as Reconstruction waned and as reunification became entrenched, freedmen and freedwomen's memories dispersed.

By the time the war with Spain was over, federal officials hoped to store a new memory of the Civil War within Arlington. In this case federal officials deleted freedmen's memories, as much as possible, from cultural memory contained within the cemetery. Just as the living memory of the Gettysburg Address was homogenized into conservative interpretations at Marietta, so too did Arlington undergo a similar process. What made Arlington different was that it emerged as a space where emancipation as cultural memory lost out to conservative interpretations of reunion and reconciliation.

Robert E. Lee's wife inherited the Arlington estate from George Washington's adopted son, G. W. P. Custis. General Lee only lived in his wife's home for a few years before the war. He and his family left Arlington when hostilities broke out and Lee rejected the Union for slave-holding Virginia. In June 1862 and February 1863, Congress passed new property tax codes. George Washington Custis Lee, who actually inherited the land from his grandfather due to the fact that his mother was not legally allowed to own property, was not present to pay the property tax. The tax commissioner for Virginia seized the land, and the Treasury Department put the property up for public sale. The U.S. government paid $26,800 (well below fair market value) and handed title to the land over to the War Department. In a symbolic attack on the South and on the symbol of Lee as the quintessential Southerner, Secretary of War Stanton acquired the property, essentially seizing the plantation illegally, and turned it into Fort Whipple to defend Washington DC.

After the war G. W. C. Lee disputed this illegal purchase and won a Supreme Court decision awarding him the land. But this decision came down in 1882. By then Fort Whipple, which eventually was renamed Fort Myers, had been used as a college to instruct officers. Adjacent to Fort Whipple, a national cemetery held the bodies of those who died defending Washington DC and Alexandria, Virginia. Quartermaster General Montgomery Meigs authorized burying troops within a few yards of the house, making the home undesirable to live in. This included the first ever American tomb of the unknowns, a mass grave of 2,111 soldiers whom authorities had been unable to identify and who were buried within the long shadow of the Lee mansion. This unknown "noble army of martyrs" became a central site for Union Decoration Day ceremonies.[33] These unknowns were buried as a matter of consequence and not as a matter of spectacle and national mourning like the Unknown Soldier from the First World War. Poor bureaucratic recordkeeping, lack of soldier identification tags, and the politicization of the Lee plantation produced these unknown soldiers. Nevertheless, G. W. C. Lee could not hope to reclaim his property after the cemetery made much of the plantation worthless as agricultural land. Lee instead settled with the government for a lump sum payment of $150,000. Sequestering the Arlington plantation and turning it into a military resource was an obvious symbolic battle that Stanton won. To have so many Union dead buried in the estate once occupied by the Confederacy's single greatest symbol of masculinity—even though his wife owned the home—was Stanton's attempt at emasculating Confederate heroes and at the same time defeating the Jeffersonian agrarianism that empowered Southern aristocracy and slavery. It was an effective political use of Stanton's interpretation of Lincoln's promise.[34]

Furthering the symbolic war against the agrarian slave system, the War Department turned part of the Arlington estate into a village for former slaves. Lincoln's Emancipation Proclamation freed slaves in locations that were in rebellion against the Union. It is important to remember that this was purely a military act and not a civil law. This did not free any slaves inside the Union, but it did free slaves in the Confederacy once the federal army defeated rebel forces and conquered their territory. This proclamation also extended liberty to slaves who escaped their owners and made their way inside federal military lines; thus Washington DC became a haven for "contraband" people who escaped slavery in bordering Virginia by slipping into the heavily defended Union capital. But the military did not have the necessary training or funding to handle the escaped slaves. Throughout the war, the newly freed people depended on charitable Washingtonians and the military for food, education, and housing. For example, when the War Department seized Arlington, Secretary Stanton ordered, as early as 1862, the commanding officer of Fort Whipple to give "subsistence" to the "old and infirm negroes of the Arlington estate," several of whom were Lee's former slaves.[35]

In May 1863 Lt. Col. Elias M. Greene of the Department of Washington wrote to the chief quartermaster of a plan to eliminate "contraband" welfare. Greene proposed to turn the Arlington estate into farmland that could support "500 to 750 field hands." Greene claimed, "The force of contraband males and females, now idle in this City, and a dead weight on the Government, can be employed to very great advantage in cultivating the above lands." Although this seemed to resemble the institution of plantation slavery, Greene went to great lengths to suggest that the people would benefit through "salutary effects of good pure country air, and a return to their former healthy vocations, as 'field hands' under much happier auspices than heretofore." He also claimed, "The families need not be separated as they can still be united." While the adults farmed the land to produce corn, millet, and hay, "younger contrabands" could tend a "large vegetable garden" and "old women" could tend produce stands in the city to sell the vegetables to urban dwellers. Greene also suggested that the War Department could use the produce to help feed the troops defending the city. Freed people would receive "sanitary and moral improvement" and the government would save "an immense amount of money." The War Department accepted Greene's proposal and moved hundreds of blacks from Washington DC into the village.[36]

After the war the War Department handed this "abandoned" space over to the Freedmen's Bureau. Of course, the freedmen remained dependent on the benevolence of Washingtonians and the military. Many freedmen built homes in the village, and when they died, the U.S. military buried them near the Freedman's Village on the Arlington estate. In one of the most radical expressions of Lincoln's promise, Col. James Moore oversaw the burial of the freedpeople. If a freedman or woman died nameless or anonymous, Moore simply labeled their tombstone with the identifier "civilian" or "citizen." On the one hand, this was a remarkable transformation of the way government officials described African Americans. This can be charted through the linguistic categories used to describe former slaves; they moved from being described as "contraband" to "freedmen" to "citizen" in the space of the national cemetery within a few short years. On the other hand, the Freedman's Village represented an agrarian labor system largely dependent upon institutions operated by benevolent white people. Before the war, this space had simply been inherited agricultural land that marked the intergenerational wealth of the landed elite. Within a few short years, U.S. military officials had turned it into sacred ground and buried noble military leaders next to enslaved subalterns who had become free citizens. The existence of the Freedman's Village in Arlington served as a challenge to any narrowing of the meaning of the war and the boundaries of the nation. That is not to say that this village was egalitarian. It received insufficient financial and educational support from surrounding government agencies. A few of its residents, however, went on to become successful politicians, lawyers, and schoolteachers. These accomplishments were uneven, as many others in the village were left to fend for themselves because meager resources supplied by the War Department did not include everyone. Despite such inequality, the War Department could manipulate the symbolism of the village enough to critique Lee, his aristocratic wealth, and the slave plantation system that produced that wealth.

Just as significant, the freedmen's graves within the national cemetery produced a living memory of emancipation. French historian Pierre Nora describes this as *milieu de memoire*, where the environment surrounding the memory of the past is dynamic and interactive. People who experience living memory can do so because they experienced the past together, and they can share those experiences with others spontaneously and largely without ritual or institutional interpretation. Participating within this memory binds the individual to the group and also excludes individuals who cannot access memory because they never shared the experiences that group members shared. Freedmen at Arlington could form a dynamic group identity around their shared memories of emancipation because they experienced freedom within Arlington. But this communicative dynamic is temporary, according to Nora. As the members of the group die off or move away, the living memory ceases to function. Traces of this memory might still exist, but they can only be detected through what Nora describes as *lieu de memoire* or a site of memory. Contrary to a living memory based on experience, this kind of memory functions as a static and stagnant site. The memory can only be represented by non-group members through monuments, souvenirs, or rituals, but never through shared experiences. The Freedmen's Village at Arlington, and the adjacent freedmen's cemetery, provided a living memory of emancipation within a national site. Its existence changed the landscape of a slave plantation into a vibrant village of emancipated people. But as

Reconstruction ended and the age of imperialism began, government officials took steps to impose their own interpretations on the national cemetery. They eventually succeeded in dissolving freedmen's vital memories of emancipation by removing their living memories from the Arlington estate and leaving behind only the grave markers as sites of memory.[37]

By the late nineteenth century, controversy engulfed the village as reconciliation between Northern and Southern whites became more acceptable in national politics. The Freedmen's Village at Arlington fell under threat. G. W. C. Lee handed the property over to the government in early 1883, and Virginia relinquished its control of the property to the federal government in 1884. Ironically, the relinquishing of the Lee family's claim to their former plantation actually signaled the beginning of the end for the Freedman's Village as the War Department gained uncontested control of the burial space. The successes of the village lay primarily on the willingness of Virginians to supply free education to its inhabitants. By 1890 the local school district was no longer willing to subsidize the education of black children. The state and Alexandria County withdrew their support in part because "the United States owned the reservation and had exclusive jurisdiction over the same; and that it was the duty of the United States to keep and maintain schools for the education of the children there on." The freedmen solicited lawyer A. H. Holmes to help them appeal to the War Department to supply a school; residents signed a petition sent to the secretary of war claiming they needed a school so that "children on this reservation, so near the capital of so great a Nation, may not grow up in utter ignorance but may be able to receive that which is guaranteed to every child in the United States, a free common school education." Holmes besieged Secretary Redfield Proctor, claiming, "The citizens on that reservation are too poor to pay for private tuition," and "As things stand now we are worse off than the Indians for whose training ample provisions have been made." But Senator John W. Daniel from Lynchburg, Virginia, believed that the War Department should not provide a school. Daniel, seriously wounded at the Battle of the Wilderness as a Confederate major, believed incorrectly that some of the freedpeople had built homes on the land. (The War Department built the homes and rented them to the freedpeople. Freedpeople eventually bought the homes and made improvements on them.) Daniel called for these "squatters" to be removed so neighboring whites could open the land "to improvement."[38]

Senator Daniel's language represented just how much American memory had changed in less than thirty years. The dedicated Freedman's Village had been a model for the transition from slavery to freedom during Reconstruction. But by 1890 the people that the U.S. Army had originally called "contraband" had turned from "freedmen" and "citizens" to "squatters" with a few pen strokes of Senator Daniel's hand. Secretary Proctor from Vermont and the newly appointed quartermaster general, Richard Napoleon Batchelder from New Hampshire, did nothing to challenge the language. In fact, they embraced it. In October 1890 Batchelder responded to A. H. Holmes's request for a school and teacher. He used Senator Daniel's language in a stern warning: "You are also advised that these people are squatters on the reservation, who have no rights or privileges whatever, there, and being on the border of the reservation adjoining the Virginia line, would enjoy all the school privileges of any citizen of that state if they should remove across that line." This was cruel. It was not certain, in the days of an emerging practice of segregation, that the children of the village would be able to enroll in a school. If a school could be found, the residents would have to give up their homes in order to access the school system. But Secretary Proctor supported Batchelder's position as he authorized the removal of some residents in 1890. The destiny of the village was set. Most of the residents managed to stay on the land while they argued that they should receive compensation for their homes. In late 1899 and early 1900, the remains of soldiers who had fought and died in Cuba began arriving. War Department officials insisted that the freedmen had to leave and the village had to be dismantled.[39]

The quartermaster general in the summer of 1900 directed many of the bodies from Cuba to Arlington instead of their hometowns because "the Surgeon-General, U.S. Marine Hospital Service, has protested against the importation for delivery in the southern states of any bodies of soldiers who have died of disease in the West Indies, such shipments being dangerous to the public health." Since transportation of diseased bodies across state lines violated state laws, the War Department ordered that "any remains received at your port from the West Indies with casket marked for a point in the south ... will be forwarded with those unclaimed to this City for burial in the Arlington, Va., National Cemetery." Space was better used, argued many in the military, as a place to commemorate dead soldiers from Cuba than as a settlement for living U.S. citizens. Arlington, no longer a model of the transition from slavery to freedom, became the American Valhalla. The remains of the dead from the wars of the new imperialism were coming to Arlington, and the War Department needed more space to accommodate the bodies. The War Department decided to dissolve the Freedman's Village. In 1900, the War Department finally received a congressional appropriation to pay compensation to the remaining residents and proceeded to force them off the land and out of their own homes. The remains of the dead "citizens" and named freedmen remained inside the cemetery, but the context of their graves changed from the working living environment of the Freedmen's village to sites of American imperialism. The transition of space was remarkable. From emancipation to imperialism, the space took on new meaning as geopolitics took on a new function. Cultural memory that encapsulated the experiences of emancipation was reduced to echoes of the past precisely so that Americans could construct their national Valhalla. A living memory of imperialism now turned the graves of black "citizens" into representations of the past. Dead soldiers from America's wars for empire could be used to colonize the remains of black citizens within the national cemetery.[40]

Northern memory of the war shifted from radical and emancipatory to reformist and conservative as emancipation fell to the periphery of Lincoln's promise. Together black graves and the revolutionary idea of emancipation that they symbolized were becoming forgotten sites of memory, what historian Maria Todorova has described as *lieu d'oubli*, a site of forgetting.[41] Certainly the War Department allowed blacks soldiers to be buried in national cemeteries and even black citizens to be buried in Arlington National Cemetery. But as the politics of national sacred space and local Southern soil became mixed and contested, these gravestones defined the sacred spaces of the cemetery less and less. In fact, the politics of national cemeteries made black graves in national cemeteries vulnerable to historian Nikolai Voukav's maxim that "one forgets not by cancellation but by superimposition, not by producing absence but by multiplying presences."[42] The accumulation of identical gravestones of mostly white soldiers and the preponderance of the cult of the fallen soldier as symbols of nationalization in Marietta, Arlington, and many other national sacred spaces had the effect of multiplying presences of white nativism, Protestantism, and capitalism onto the definitions of Americanism. As issues surrounding emancipation moved to the periphery of a rapidly cooling collective memory, black graves in national cemeteries became sites of forgetting. Former Confederates, meanwhile, would be left to craft their own cultural memory of the war without regulation from the federal government or the hegemonic cultural memory network.

CHAPTER 2

The Nation, a Monument of Empire

> Imagine a society entirely absorbed in its own historicity. It would be incapable of producing historians. Living entirely under the sign of the future, it would satisfy itself with automatic self-recording processes and auto-inventory machines, postponing indefinitely the task of understanding itself.
> —Pierre Nora

In Alaska's Sitka National Cemetery, an engraved message on a headstone conveys a legend of love and loss. Lt. Samuel H. Kinney and his good friend, Lt. Benjamin W. Livermore, allegedly fell in love with the same Russian woman, Nadia. As part of the Fourth Artillery, these two officers, veterans of the Civil War, were occupying territory purchased from Russia in 1867. Sitka served as the headquarters. The men of the Fourth Artillery oversaw the geodetic survey of Alaska and tried to keep order among a diverse population of indigenous Tlingits, American gold speculators, and Russian fur traders. Nadia won the hearts of both men, but she apparently chose Lieutenant Kinney over his friend. Later Kinney and Livermore went on a hunting trip; Livermore returned a few hours later carrying Kinney's body, saying he had died in a hunting accident. The Fourth Artillery built a cemetery just outside Sitka to bury the lieutenant. Livermore then tried again to win Nadia's favor, but she rejected him a second time. The loss of his friend and his beloved was apparently too much to suffer, and Livermore killed himself. Underneath his body was a note that described Kinney's death. Livermore had challenged the lieutenant to a duel for the love of Nadia. The hunting trip was a ruse. Comrades buried Livermore in the frigid earth next to Kinney's grave and forgot them.[1] American cultural memory turned cold in the frigid Alaskan frontier.

In the United States, a sustained nation-building effort began around the time that Lincoln delivered his speech at Gettysburg's battlefield, and the federal government initiated national cemeteries across the nation. The extent of this new tradition was founded originally on the basis of slave emancipation. Was there room enough inside Lincoln's promise to include the deaths of servicemen pursuing their own jealousies in remote outposts of the American frontier well after the Civil War ended? If so, who else could gain access to this new tradition? Would African Americans who served gain special remembrance? Would Confederates somehow find room in this new tradition? This chapter examines Lincoln's promise in the rhetoric and politics of American expansion. Just as Lincoln spoke of liberty to justify sacrifices at Gettysburg, politicians and citizens supporting reunion and reconciliation used the language of freedom to heal the divisions of the Civil War and simultaneously to justify expansion into the frontier. With the dedication of battlefields and the burial of most veterans who died soon after the war, government agencies judged the work of remembering the noble dead completed. But veterans continued to serve albeit in a dramatically reduced military establishment. As congressmen in Washington DC debated extending pensions to living veterans, soldiers who died in the outpost of Sitka or in the Plains Indian Wars fought without the guarantee of being remembered. In the case of Confederate soldiers, it was understood that they would not be remembered as national heroes. Lincoln proposed to "dedicate a portion of that field [Gettysburg battlefield] as a final resting place for those who here gave their lives that that nation might live." This explicitly excluded the soldiers who died outside the context of the battle for liberty. In fact, the emerging tradition never anticipated U.S. wars fought outside the boundaries of the United States. Americans thus applied Lincoln's Gettysburg promise to martial bodies in a specific place at a specific time. War with Native Americans and Spain, however, produced occasions to widen the initially limited scope of the promise, and New Southerners were incredibly opportunistic at leveraging access to the cultural memory network by placing internal domestic Confederate cultural memories beside external imperialistic ones.

But cultural memory was beginning to change well before the United States invaded Cuba. The dominant cultural memory in the North blamed Southern culture for the malfeasance of the Civil War. Some Southerners tied to the postwar emergence of the Lost Cause movement likewise created a memory of the Civil War that resisted Reconstruction efforts by the federal government and redeemed Southern soldiers who died in the cause of the Confederacy. Southern politicians seeking this kind of "redemption" tried to outflank Reconstruction efforts by winning political offices fraudulently, implementing segregation policies through Jim Crow laws, and advocating racial violence including lynching. While these memories were emerging in the East, Americans were moving west. This migration, unlike migration in the first half of the nineteenth century, was powered by the federal government protecting private corporations and underwriting the mining and railroad speculation that brought forth new memories of U.S. expansion and empire. New titans of industry emerged, many of whom garnered their wealth from the Lincoln administration's wartime economic policies. Treasury Secretary Salmon P. Chase funded the Union war effort through the sale of government bonds to investors and issued treasury notes or greenbacks (more than $450 million) to pay federal debts especially to government contractors. "Federal contracts brought windfalls to a variety of sectors of the U.S. economy that could supply and transport the troops and that had previously been overshadowed by the wealth and prominence of export merchants and the landed gentry." People like J. Pierpont Morgan, Andrew Carnegie, and Jay Gould leveraged the wartime federal protectionism of the economy that allowed them to exploit banking, steel, and railroad industries, which required profoundly large amounts of capital investment and maintenance. In addition to remaking the economy, the Lincoln administration emerged from the war with a clear vision of the American West, one that used the federal government to award railroad companies with western lands that would help finance the creation of the transcontinental railroads in what amounted to an "unprecedented example of corporate welfare legislation and a harbinger of the priorities Republican officials would continue to support." Secretary of State William Seward, meanwhile, supported this kind of work connecting the Atlantic to the Pacific and America's Pacific to Asia. He helped the United States acquire Alaska and other Pacific way stations in the immediate aftermath of the war, which would open the door to trade with Asian countries, especially China.[2]

Standing in the way of this kind of American empire were the diverse indigenous peoples who lived in the trans-Mississippi West. The U.S. government made a series of treaties that were subsequently broken with tribes throughout the West. It moved people from their lands onto reservations and used the military to conduct wars against those who resisted the new ways in which capitalists envisioned they could exploit the West economically and geographically. Building railroads across the continent would connect the Atlantic to the Pacific, giving people on the East Coast easier access to the bounty in the Pacific, including the whaling industry, the sea otter fur trade in Alaska, and the bird guano fertilizer industry in Peru as well as continental industries on the frontier such as gold and silver, cattle, and farming.[3] Bridging the two oceans also allowed U.S. manufacturing interests, especially in the East, to access markets throughout the Pacific rim, but especially in China. Spanning the coasts came with significant costs for people who were excluded from national identity, especially for indigenous peoples pushed onto reservations and African Americans oppressed by segregation. But building this transcontinental American empire could also produce incredible wealth for those who could access American identity. All of this beckoned for new rituals and variations of cultural memory.

Northerners and Southerners standing on opposite sides of cultural memory began to think about their shared imperial interests in different ways. The Civil War disrupted their antebellum visions of an empire based on manifest destiny. Those interrupted memories could be brought back with new memories that stressed reunion and collaboration between the elites and the middle classes in the North and the South, but only if those memories acknowledged emancipation less and less. Race and gender played central roles in the reunion of Northerners and Southerners, but empire did, too. As Americans moved westward, their experiences at the edge of American empire helped them recast the way they remembered the core of the empire. As they remembered the places from which they came, they often reproduced the racial and gender categories that they learned in the metropole. Moving west was not the utopian do-over that many Americans mythologized. It was, in many ways, an attempt to reproduce the racial and gendered hierarchies of the East. This chapter charts the process of how divergent memories in the North and the South began to move closer to each other as Americans pursued their imperial interests in western spaces even before the U.S. military invaded Cuba and the Philippines in 1898.

Storage systems archived cultural memory. Decoration Day, when people decorated the graves of the Civil War dead, eventually morphed into Memorial Day and became an annual opportunity for people to access archived cultural memory in the nation's cemeteries. While Northerners developed commemorative rituals that celebrated the Union, former Confederates developed their own customs. Historian William A. Blair describes these moments in the South as opportunities that "despite having to style the rituals according to federal tastes, former Confederates still found the Cities of the Dead useful as places for resistance." Southern politicians seeking election, for example, went to cemeteries to speak at these mass gatherings while "disloyalty and resistance to Reconstruction seemed to prosper in the Cities of the Dead, fortified by memories of the war sustained through the memorial traditions."[4]

Left outside national cultural memory and openly hostile to interpretations of Lincoln's promise existed an emerging Confederate-activated Lost Cause cultural memory largely untouched by the regulatory forces of Reconstruction. Memory could be heated to stimulate transformation, but it could also help stimulate the forces of "deterioration, corruption, and decline" in what former Confederates perceived to be Reconstruction.[5] This was perhaps most fully articulated on Confederate Memorial Day in 1871 at the Magnolia Cemetery in Charleston, South Carolina. The Ladies' Memorial Association organized the disinterment of seventy-eight Confederate bodies from the Gettysburg battlefield for their reburial in

Charleston. This commemorative organization literally removed the dead from the storage system of the federal government so that they could be more accessible—and their memories more retrievable—to Confederate interpretations of the war.

This gathering was one of the many ways that Southerners tried to store cultural memory in the archives of cemeteries.[6] But on this occasion, the Rev. Dr. John Lafayette Girardeau, a descendent of Huguenot immigrants to South Carolina, marked the removal of Confederate soldiers from the ground of Gettysburg with a kind of counter-Gettysburg Address. He had spent much of his life preaching to slaves at the Zion Presbyterian Church in Charleston. During the war, he left this post to serve as a chaplain in the Confederate Army but afterward returned to Charleston and to Zion where he became a proponent of the Lost Cause mythology. He used his dedication speech to connect the Lost Cause tradition to the past. "Deep as is the grief which this occasion calls forth, we are not here simply as mourners for the dead," claimed Girardeau. "There are living issues which emerge from these graves—gigantic problems affecting our future, which starting up in the midst of these solemnities demand our earnest attention." Girardeau cast the audience's memories of the Civil War within the context of a righteous Confederacy at war with the decline of civilization. He contrasted his views of the legacy of the Lost Cause with the iniquity of the Paris Commune, which was then unfolding in France. For him the Paris Commune represented just another example of how an autocratic regime thwarted the goals of democratic liberty. This European menace, claimed Girardeau, also threatened American culture. Radical socialism certainly originated in a foreign land, but he claimed it had invaded the antebellum South.

This strange linkage between Parisian events of the early 1870s and the antebellum South served an important purpose in countering Northern memories of the Civil War. Steven Hahn suggests this "strange" linkage was not so strange at all. The historian argues that "if any part of the country approximated the image of the Paris Commune, it was the urban and rural South, most notably in an arc stretching from Virginia out to Texas." Within this arc, Hahn contends, "African Americans not only managed to invert the composition of political office holding but also struggled to construct an alternative political path, to place their own imprints on the shape of the Republic." Nowhere else did the "enormous transition in power form the propertied to the propertyless, from capital to labor—the utter reconfiguration of the Republic" occur so dramatically and robustly as it did in the "very heart of the old regime." Girardeau seemed to understand this transformation completely, and it was precisely this radical transformation of the Republic that the preacher was attempting to counterattack.[7]

As part of his counteroffensive, the Presbyterian minister constructed what historian Eviatar Zerubavel describes as a time map. Zerubavel suggests that people tend to shape their identities by imposing a continuous historical narrative over noncontiguous events of the past. This process involves using memory as an "adhesive" to mentally bridge the gap between disconnected events and disrupted chronologies. Individuals create mental maps to chart this new geography and accompanying timeline, and these "time maps" can be used to help people remember their own identity. One way to think of the Lost Cause is as a time map steeped in a counterfactual mythology of the past that artificially cuts and pastes events and chronology into a highly motivated identity. Zerubavel contends that time maps are socially constructed within cultural memory so that people can refer to it when building collective identity.[8] Girardeau attempted to impose such a time map on the Civil War by imposing a narrative of Confederate continuity onto the noncontiguous landscape of the antebellum South and the Paris Commune. By ignoring the distance and chronology between these places and events, the former Confederate chaplain could (re)define Southern identity. He used his dedication speech to construct a time map precisely so he could claim that the alleged insidious antebellum invasion of radical socialism produced "novel" social theories of race and autocratic political theories of federalism that he claimed distorted the Constitution and the natural social relations of race.[9] The speaker believed the Confederacy was the antidote to the corruptions and social decline brought on by Reconstruction and the federal government. Using this reconfigured past and connecting it to the Lost Cause heated memory enough to confront hot Northern memories of the war.

The legacy of the Civil War was assured, claimed Girardeau, when Southerners, who fought for Christianity and "were lovers of liberty, combatants for constitutional rights, and as exemplars of heroic virtue benefactors of their race," attempted to usurp this radicalism emanating from the North. Despite their efforts, the Presbyterian had to contend that these Confederate men "failed to establish a Confederacy as an independent country, and they failed to preserve the relation of slavery." But he insisted that "our brethren will not have died in vain, if we cherish in our hearts . . . the principles for which they gave their lives." Continued resistance of federalism was essential, Girardeau said, for Southerners to prevent Reconstruction efforts from turning into what he imagined as an American-styled Paris Commune. From here Girardeau began outlining a manifesto in which he articulated a sort of Lost Cause promise that seemed to lean on Lincoln's Gettysburg speech but instead committed Southerners to an altogether different social obligation. Defeated Southerners as a community, were obligated with "God's help, [to either] hold our ground, or consent to be traitors to our ancestry, our dead, our trusts for posterity, to our firesides, our social order, and our civil and religious liberties." To accomplish this, Girardeau demanded that Southerners "cling to our identity as a people!" By this he meant that Southerners should distinguish themselves from Northerners and refuse to "compromise . . . our innermost convictions." This included forming memorial associations and commemorating the Confederate dead. Confederate Southerners had yet to invent the artifices of cultural memory, like rituals and institutions or holidays. The preacher thus called for Confederates, on this day, to begin the work of building cultural memory of the Lost Cause "by enstamping on the minds of our children principles hallowed by the blood of patriots, and by leading them with uncovered heads to gaze upon the grandest monuments the South can rear to liberty—the headstones which mark the last resting-place of Southern Volunteers!" It was an obligation that Girardeau insisted the living owed to the Confederate dead.[10]

If Southerners failed in this obligation, Girardeau predicted that the last bastion of republicanism would be lost "and the last hope of a return to the noble, the glorious estate inherited from our patriotic ancestors will have gone out in the blackness of darkness." To acquiesce to the North, he believed, meant that the South would be obligated to take part in the inevitable future collapse of the North. The preacher inverted Lincoln's promise to hail the "Heroes of Gettysburg" as the "Champions of constitutional rights," to honor "Soldiers of a defeated—God grant it may not be a wholly lost—cause!" He promised the dead that "memory will keep her guard of honor over your graves," and he promised the living that remembering the dead would eventually provide the opportunity for redemption of the Lost Cause.[11]

This counter-Gettysburg Confederate address demonstrates the existence of an unreconstructed memory that relied on an alternative past—a fictive past—but a past nonetheless that could be networked together with other living Confederate communicative memories. People like Girardeau created this fictive past and used it to heat up memories of the Lost Cause while calling for resistance to the Reconstruction-dominated present. This sort of countercultural memory was replicated across the South over a long period of time on Confederate Memorial Days, in schools, with Confederate battle flags, and in cemeteries that sought to reclaim Southern bodies from federal burial grounds. Many former Confederates sought to define their own notions of citizenship and shape their own culture of the dead rather than participate in a Northern cultural memory. This alternative cultural memory operated adjacent to the dominant cultural memory but often avoided the reach of the federal government and eluded Northerners' willingness to confront it. Those who shared in the Confederate catastrophe built and dominated their own cultural memory to define identity around the Lost Cause in ways that shirked the memories of emancipation but accentuated their views of corruption and societal deterioration brought on by Reconstruction. This could be extremely dangerous as racial violence, lynching, and even the massacre in which whites pinned down and killed scores of African Americans in Colfax, Louisiana, among other parishes in the state, coexisted and seemed to take their energy from this kind of time map. But even this determined Confederate memory was conceived in a specific space and time, and it suffered serious limitations. Confederate sympathizers had to labor hard to remember their dead. No support came from the federal government, and so Confederate caretakers of the dead, often led by women's societies, had to rely on unreliable state appropriations, charity donations, and volunteers. Nevertheless, competing Northern and Lost Cause cultural memories remained alive, and they accentuated the gulf between how people in the North and South often remembered the Civil War.

Most mid-nineteenth-century Americans interpreted Lincoln's promise as a limited tradition as the state's and the citizenry's obligation seemed confined to the Civil War dead. The world of the U.S. military was quiet; indeed, civilian leadership downsized it dramatically after the war as Americans turned their attention to industrial and labor issues and the Gilded Age produced titans of industry, bust and boom cycles, and class warfare. Immigrants flowing into the country, many believed, threatened "Pure Americanism" even as migrants took jobs inside the industrial complex of the late nineteenth century that were essential to economic prosperity. Capitalists depicted foreigners as uncivilized people who brought unhealthy ideas of Catholicism, Judaism, anarchism, socialism, sex, and marriage to the United States. Middle-class Americans countered this "threat" by attempting to assimilate immigrants inside the United States and potential immigrants outside U.S. borders with Christianity, capitalism, and pure Americanism.[12] Meanwhile, segregation produced a color line that blacks could not cross under any circumstances, real or symbolic. With all these issues and no major war to fight, it was impossible to maintain a vast army in a world where the Atlantic and Pacific Oceans kept the United States isolated from European and Asian military threats. The size of the army was dictated by the needs of invading the West and controlling workers such as during the Great Railroad Strike of 1877. Without national causes to defend, soldiers' deaths and the cemeteries in which they were buried on the frontier became less and less remarkable.

This was especially true of imperialistic spaces, such as the Sitka cemetery in Alaska which, despite Seward's vision, played no real role in America's emerging ascendancy and was thus exceedingly difficult to integrate into the collective memory of Americans. Harsh winters, short growing seasons, and the presence of Tlingits as well as Russians involved in the fur trade made Alaska an uncompromising territory. Few Americans were interested in settling the region because there seemed few economic opportunities outside of the fur trade. Western Union Telegraph Company had tried and failed to build an overland telegraph line through the territory in the 1860s to connect with the Asian transcontinental telegraph system and abandoned the project when Cyrus Field's underwater transatlantic cable was completed in 1866. Without the telegraph system, companies were reluctant to invest in Alaska. Historian Walter LaFeber notes that Secretary of State Seward believed his 1867 purchase of the territory would serve to reinforce U.S. interests in the 1844 Sino-U.S. treaty, "which pledged an Open Door and equal opportunity for Americans" in China.[13] Stationing troops in Alaska, Seward believed, could help keep doors open in China while protecting U.S. settlers. But this never amounted to a successful strategy, as pioneers never came to settle the territory. Consequently, it remained a military outpost until the War Department evacuated Sitka completely and turned it over to the Treasury Department in 1877. The U.S. Navy took control of the District of Alaska from 1879 to 1884 and then turned it over to a civil government. It was during the first years of occupation under Gen. Jefferson C. Davis, who served as commander of the Department of Alaska from 1867 to 1870, that Kinney and Livermore died.[14]

General Davis infamously kicked the Russian residents out of their homes in Sitka so that Americans moving to Alaska could occupy them, but the Americans never came, and the houses remained empty. When Davis left Alaska in 1870, he went to the western United States and fought in the Modoc Indian war. The Fourth Artillery remained in Sitka to carry out the geodetic survey and keep the peace between Russians, the few remaining Americans, and Tlingits, while Washington politicians deliberated over setting up a territorial civil government. In the meantime, following the depression of 1873, the political and economic situation began to change. In 1877 troops were withdrawn from both the South, where Reconstruction came to an end, and Alaska. Although Americans had renewed their pursuit of manifest destiny in the West, few were interested in "Seward's Folly," as was noticed by the departure of the Fourth Artillery from Sitka.

In 1879, however, a Tlingit uprising forced American Sitka residents to ask a British warship to defend them. Humiliated, the United States sent a permanent warship to Sitka and turned the District over to the U.S. Navy. But troops did not return. Instead Congress passed the Organic Act of 1884, which established an appointed civil government for Alaska. Congress appointed Civil War veteran John H. Keatley as its federal judge. The Sitka military cemetery, meanwhile, began to show signs of neglect. Keatley, who had served in the Army of the Potomac, believed that Lieutenant Kinney, Lieutenant Livermore, and the others who fell while serving U.S. interests in Alaska deserved commemoration because they had earlier fought in the Civil War. The judge had just finished up his service and was about to leave Alaska in 1888 when he wrote to the quartermaster general in Washington DC about the Army cemetery: "The cemetry [sic] is not connected in any way with, nor is it in the same location with the Russian and Indian Cemeteries, but is off by itself about three-fourths of a mile east of the town proper." The judge believed the War Department should sanctify the space by turning it into a national cemetery. Keatley implicitly recognized Lincoln's Gettysburg promise to commit the state to commemorate all soldiers who fought for the Union as part of the cultural memory of the nation.[15]

But Alaska was not Gettysburg, and it was difficult to justify the national importance of the military cemetery in Sitka. Few in the War Department saw the outpost as deserving significant recognition. In fact, nobody seemed to know exactly who was buried there. Capt. J. B. Campbell of the Fourth Artillery, now stationed at Fort Warren, Mississippi, had served at Sitka during the military occupation. Campbell recalled the two officers from the Second Artillery whose remains were left in the cemetery—"Lt. Kinny [sic] was one,—I can't recall the name of the other." According to Campbell it was very difficult to maintain the cemetery even when military troops were present. "The Cemetery was enclosed with an ordinary picket fence; I had great trouble in keeping the fence up owing to the Russians and Creoles stealing pickets and rails to burn, and if no one has looked out for it since I left there, all trace of it has probably disappeared." Campbell reported that there was a record of deaths kept by the assistant quartermaster general at Sitka, but he did not know where it was. He believed military commanders sent the book to the Department of Columbia upon abandoning the Sitka post. The Department of Columbia forwarded the record to the adjutant general. But as different government agencies took control over Sitka, many names went unrecorded or neglected; some headboard inscriptions were erased by the Alaskan weather.

The poor condition of the cemetery offended Judge Keatley. "I found that no attention had been paid to this matter, because none seemed to feel the same interest in the matter as I have by reason of having been a soldier myself." He requested that the War Department give him $300 to improve the cemetery and station a salaried superintendent at the site. "There is not a civil officer here but would gladly discharge that duty. All have abundance of time to do so." Keatley felt a connection to this space because he was convinced that "some of them at least, were men who served throughout the Civil War, and are therefore entitled to as much consideration in that respect as the thousands of others whose honored remains rest in the National Cemeteries elsewhere." The quartermaster general passed the inquiry to Lt. Col. N. H. Batchelder in San Francisco. Batchelder believed that the War Department should exhume the bodies and rebury them at the national cemetery in the Presidio. But Keatley insisted that this was too expensive and that the Sitka site should be declared a national cemetery.[16]

Some repairs were needed, conceded the judge, particularly the road leading to the site, because the harsh Alaska winters froze the road and then the spring thaw turned the byway into an impassable mud bog. Keatley believed creating a road with railroad ties would eliminate this danger and allow pallbearers and mourners to easily access the burial ground. The judge claimed he could get free labor from the U.S. marshal, who oversaw the prison, and only needed to buy the planks at twenty dollars apiece. He reported the Marines had volunteered to rebuild the fence and reorganize the grounds, and the sailors of the USS *Pinta* would refurbish the headstones, which were made of wood and quickly eroding.[17] The War Department appropriated the money and commissioned Judge Keatley to supervise the work. The judge began the process of building a fence, but left in April 1889 as his service ended, without completing the work on the cemetery. He handed the project off to his successor but worried that, because his replacement was not a veteran of the Civil War, the work would remain unfinished. The cemetery quickly became dilapidated again. It was not converted into a national cemetery until 1924.[18] The Sitka cemetery reveals some of the limitations of Lincoln's promise. The War Department's reluctance to sponsor a national cemetery for Civil War veterans suggests that the military did not yet see peripheral Alaska as U.S. space. Americans did not seem to include Alaska within the cultural memory of the nation in the late nineteenth century; it sat too far out in the frontier.

But even before Judge Keatley's arrival in Alaska, other military deaths forced Americans to reconsider applying Lincoln's promise to the frontier. The controversy surrounding the commemoration of Gen. George Armstrong Custer, who died at the Battle of Little Bighorn, offers a telling narrative of how middle-class Americans and government bureaucrats began viewing the American West, unlike Alaska, as a space ripe for settlement and investment. But Sitting Bull, Crazy Horse, and a great band of Sioux, Cheyenne, and Arapaho Indians near the Little Bighorn River briefly stopped American progress in its tracks. When General Custer and his cavalry unwisely advanced on the encampment of Native Americans in the summer of 1876, they were annihilated by an unforgiving adversary.

This was not the first time the United States engaged the Sioux Indians, who had controlled vast amounts of territory where they dominated other tribes and prairie lands that provided ample trade routes and abundant buffalo herds before the Civil War. American expansion into Wisconsin and Minnesota threatened the Sioux tribes' ability to control their trading and hunting networks. Some of the Eastern Sioux tribes signed treaties with the government that allowed U.S. citizens access to huge swaths of territory in Minnesota in exchange for annuity payments, reservations, and material supplies. But the corrupt and unfair enforcement of the treaty led many Sioux leaders to risk military attacks on U.S. outposts when they believed the federal government was preoccupied with the Confederate rebellion. In response, Lincoln appointed Gen. John Pope to administer the newly formed Department of the Northwest, and Pope dealt with this Sioux rebellion with show trials and executions of thirty-eight Sioux men. Shortly after, Congress approved invalidating the treaty and revoked the annuities and the sovereignty of the reservation from these Eastern Sioux tribes. When the war was over, Gen. William Tecumseh Sherman negotiated a new treaty with leaders of the larger Sioux empire at Fort Laramie in 1868. This treaty not only confined several Sioux tribes to reservations in western South Dakota but also stipulated that Sioux leaders cease in their opposition to the construction of railroads.[19]

Some Sioux leaders, including Sitting Bull and Crazy Horse, refused to sign, and they were joined in opposition by Arapaho, Cheyenne, and other tribes that occupied the plains. Native Americans continued to wage war against the United States for as long as they could, while the Sioux who did sign refused to give up the treaty-protected sacred Black Hills region where Americans discovered large deposits of gold. These Sioux rebellions, along with Apache, Kiowa, Comanche, and others, threatened the ability of the federal government to underwrite the endeavor to bridge the Atlantic and Pacific worlds and to subsidize the huge profits that private corporations in the railroad and mining industries accumulated. Despite the Fort Laramie treaty, American citizens and corporate entities encroached on Sioux territory to mine for gold while the federal government used troops to protect miners and railroads from attacks. In similar ways that politicians in the East tried to regulate the color line through negotiations, military force if needed, and eventual segregation, the U.S. military regulated western entanglements between white settlers, private corporations, and Native Americans, often causing loss of life among indigenous peoples and also among military personnel of which perhaps the highest profile casualty was Custer, a Civil War veteran with political aspirations. His death and commemoration signaled that Americans were beginning to reevaluate Lincoln's promise as it applied to soldiers fighting to secure the frontier.

Despite the arrogance and incompetence that led to his comprehensive defeat at the Little Bighorn River, Custer became a mythical figure. His defeat happened within the context of a reeling economic collapse in 1873. Investors grew cautious as capital began drying up in the early 1870s, yet railroad tycoons continued to expand their rail empires in an increasingly risky economic environment. Native American attempts to disrupt the railroads exacerbated the financial tension. The War Department sent Custer and other military personnel to protect the investment in rail, but it was not enough. Soon after Custer's arrival, the industrywide overexpansion and inability to pay debts contaminated sectors of the national economy tied to railroads, and the nation plummeted into a severe depression that lasted for years. Much of Custer's symbolism came from his reputation as a gallant and extravagant Civil War general who reminded people of the mythology of American progress. Custer had begun the war as a lieutenant but had quickly gained promotion to brigadier general by the age of twenty-three shortly before the Battle of Gettysburg. His military action was as daring as his uniform dress was extravagant. Usually wearing a red cavalry scarf around his neck, Custer would lead reckless yet successful campaigns at Gettysburg, the Overland Campaign, and the Battle of the Wilderness among others. He was a darling of journalists, he understood politics and war, and he sacrificed his life trying to protect the mythology of progress. After his death at Little Bighorn, many viewed him as a quintessential and tragic hero. The Army originally buried him near where he fell on the frontier as they had buried the men who had died under his command. Army officials ordered the disinterment of his remains the next year, and they transported Custer's body from the distant frontier back to New York for a formal burial at West Point. They left his men buried in the plains. Organizers including his widow turned his funeral into a spectacle that even elicited the admiration of former Confederates.

Unlike the fallen subalterns, many unknown, whose graves remained scattered haphazardly in arbitrary spots across the Little Bighorn battlefield, Custer's West Point funeral was completely scripted. As historian Adam Pratt notes, after returning Custer's body to New York in the summer of 1877, his widow, Elizabeth "Libbie" Custer, postponed the burial ceremony for several weeks until enough cadets had returned from the summer break to make a suitably large audience. Libbie Custer did not passively allow the military to control her husband's legacy. After the funeral, she would go on to galvanize how Americans remembered her husband through several books and speaking tours. She was incredibly proactive and played a significant role in sculpting the memory of her husband. Custer's funeral was one of the opening moves in the effort to cultivate a heroic narrative out of her husband's embarrassing defeat. But the ceremonies at West Point did more than just redeem Custer's actions in the West; it helped heal the wounds of the Civil War. According to Pratt, Custer's funeral brought Southerners into the nationalistic fold with Northerners because they could identify with Custer as a manly white cavalier on the frontier despite having served in the Union Army during the war.[20] In the dwindling days of Reconstruction, Southerners found an early symbol of reconciliation in Custer.

But his funeral also became a distraction from another war waged on the battlefield of train depots and railroad yards known as the Great Railroad Strike of 1877. Jay Gould and other railroad owners and corporations, "faced with large fixed costs and ruinous rate wars, shored up their resources or avoided bankruptcy by slashing wages" repeatedly. In protest of yet another wage reduction, laborers went on strike, won the support of local communities, and succeeded in pulling in laborers from other industries "who saw the railroads as the embodiments of the monopolistic practices that were pressing down on them and endangering their communities." The first strikes occurred in Martinsburg, West Virginia, in July 1877, but the movement quickly expanded.

The strike ended in September after federal troops entered the fray to escort trains, disrupt workers' meetings, break up strikes, and even perform the work of running the trains when needed. Workers won concessions, too, but the strike was marred by violence from peripheral elements of the labor movement and by federal troops who sometimes used force to disperse the picketers. The confrontation brought the economy to a near standstill affecting nearly everyone in the Midwest and the trans-Mississippi West. Strikers acted collectively to challenge the monopolistic tendencies that went along with the Republican vision of empire. Wartime Republicans had reconstructed the national economy through their leveraging of finance and their protecting private corporations from carrying too much risk. Postwar corporations used this environment to accumulate vast amounts of capital and to behave as monopolies, which often crushed local communities and traditions in small towns across America almost as profoundly as they crushed Native American communities and culture in the West. Just as the spirit of the Paris Commune transformed the South, the Great Railroad Strike threatened nearly the entire nation with a revolution that would radically reconstruct the relationship between capital and labor as well as nation and empire.[21]

In late August, during the strike, organizers took Custer's remains from a vault in Poughkeepsie, New York, by ship to West Point just north of New York City. Thousands watched as pallbearers unleashed the catafalque and transported it to the chapel where it lay in state until October as Libbie Custer successfully delayed the funeral. In the meantime, the railroad strike ended, and many turned their attention to Custer's upcoming funeral to forget about the contradictions that the empire and the strike laid bare. As onlookers tried to access the chapel, sentries prevented them from entering until the designated hour at 2:00 p.m. on October 10. Only then were the chapel doors opened and Gen. John Schofield, who was commandant of West Point, "with the widow of the dead hero on his arm" led the numerous mourners who filed past the bier. Among them were Custer's father, sister, and other relatives and friends. The casket rested among "the dead chieftain's sabre and helmet," floral bouquets, a plaque that read "Seventh Cavalry," and a large American flag as well as a blue silk flag with the words in gold lettering "God and our Country."

The funeral began with a eulogy by the West Point chaplain, Dr. Forsyth, after which the "choir of cadets chanted the thirty-ninth and ninetieth psalms." After the viewing, pallbearers brought the remains out from the chapel and formed a funeral cortege that included everyone inside the chapel and the thousands who had been waiting outside while the cadets presented arms. The march from the chapel to the small cemetery began. As the pallbearers lowered the coffin, "earth was sprinkled upon it, the burial service was completed by the chaplain, and the battalion of three hundred cadets fired three volleys over the grave. The echoes reverberated from side to side of the river, flung back from cliff to cliff, and died mournfully away." The funeral mentioned nothing of Custer's calamity at Little Bighorn or the reason he was there defending the monopolies of the railroad companies. Instead it wallowed in the symbolism of religion, nationalism, and valor. It was a mourning that stubbornly ignored the lieutenant colonel's self-destructive conduct of fighting Indians.[22]

Custer's funeral was a profound commemoration that had significant implications for American cultural memory. Libbie Custer and her allies within the military deftly created a cooling system for cultural memory that helped keep Custer's present pristine from his less-than-perfect past. The commemoration of Custer's body represents this kind of moment in cultural memory. While Sitting Bull believed Custer was foolish, Custer's apologists believed he was a hero who was mercilessly killed. While some Native Americans, such as Crow medicine woman Pretty Shield, claimed Custer was found face down in the river shot in the back, supporters argued that his body was found confronting an Indian onslaught.[23] Some accused the Sioux and Cheyenne of mutilating his body while other sources claimed he was found naked in a sitting posture unmutilated.[24] Most accounts of what happened in the battle from Native Americans were articulated within the context of U.S. imperialism and stressed the injustices of Americans expanding westward. But most American accounts, including official government documents, stressed national expansion as progressive and failed to mention Custer's history of attacking Native American encampments before Little Bighorn. Like his death, Custer's funeral projected a mythology of progress that obstinately refused to acknowledge that his death occurred because he defended the interest of railroad monopolies and the federal government which sought to connect the Atlantic and Pacific even as U.S. citizens and laborers rebelled against railroad interests and attempted to disrupt railroad commerce in similar strategic ways—and for similar strategic reasons—that Native Americans used in the trans-Mississippi West. Regardless of what actually happened in the battle, Americans buried Custer with much fanfare at West Point without admitting Custer's imperialistic behavior or attitudes or acknowledging the great havoc that American progress produced at home and on the frontier.

This was a cold memory of Custer's downfall. Progress spoke to the American present, and many Americans accepted his rout within this context. The consequence of this lack of acknowledgment made the memory of Custer profoundly ambivalent. It would cast a long shadow over how Americans would remember the nation's conquest of the West going forward. The trope of progress gave Americans an explanation of how indigenous people they considered uncivilized and barbaric could temporarily defeat the U.S. military without Americans having to acknowledge that perhaps U.S. expansion was not a noble cause. Middle-class Americans and government elites, however, did not completely cool cultural memory at Custer's funeral. Questions concerning U.S. imperialism remained as symbolized by unidentified men buried at the battle site who could not be incorporated into a national cemetery—such as those Civil War veterans at Sitka—until much later. These concerns made the limitations of Lincoln's promise apparent as the state's and the citizenry's commitment to remember the martial dead did not yet seem applicable to the frontiers of the burgeoning U.S. empire. Despite the specter of an ignoble empire, Elizabeth Custer and her supporters succeeded in inserting her husband's memory into Lincoln's promise. For them he was a hero and not a conqueror. Custer's funeral thus illustrated one way Americans could expand Lincoln's promise, contour for contour, as the nation expanded. Soldiers who died for American progress could be celebrated according to the Lincolnian tradition that stressed the noble cause of liberty even for doing ignoble work in Alaska or on the western plains. While Democrats and Republicans tussled over extending benefits and pensions to Civil War veterans, the burial sites at the Battle of Little Bighorn demonstrated how vague the War Department could be when it came to commemorating men who died in defeat. Simultaneously, the commemoration of Custer's body suggests that meaningful sacrifice could be made for the nation at the edges of the empire. These sorts of commemorations imply that Americans were beginning to make rituals for a new cultural memory that could explain the imperial expansion of the nation. The hallmarks of this cultural memory laid in stressing the need for cultural continuity and social preservation by keeping the present isolated from the past. Further evidence of this shift was in the way Northerners and Southerners began finding new ways to remember the Civil War.

With America's rapidly expanding western boundaries and the lost momentum of radical Republicans signaling the end of Reconstruction, Northern attitudes toward Southerners softened as expansionists and Northern industrialists looked for new ways to harness the domestic sphere of capital and industry to the many new resources and peoples in the frontier. While New

Southerners sought to reconcile with Northern capitalists to bring industry and investment to the agrarian-dominated South, Northerners hoped to yoke Southern resources to the expansion of the American empire. Blair argues that "racism was a large part of how reunion came, but looking deeper into the political involvement of civic traditions uncovers additional factors." The historian continues, "There was a great deal more fluidity and more overlapping concerns."[25] Empire was one such concern, and this could be seen in the ways that Americans crafted imperialistic memories. As the nation's borderlands expanded, the pressure to make new memories of the Civil War was compelling for many in the North and the South. Imperialists and New Southerners needed to keep the present separated from the past in order to make a workable empire acceptable and sustainable to skeptics. Thus imperialists sought to cool the hot memories based on a fictive past found in Girardeau's counter–Gettysburg Address.

Daniel Fish, adjutant-general of the Grand Army of the Republic, delivered a Memorial Day address in 1888 at the Nashville National Cemetery in Tennessee that suggests how memories of the emerging American empire could accomplish the work of cooling memory in both the North and the South. Fish had recently completed a transcontinental journey spanning four thousand miles from the Atlantic to the Pacific. Speaking to mostly Southerners, he hoped to sanctify the "American Union, in its national aspect, as the noblest monument to its dead defenders." The incredible opportunities of this boundless empire gave the Union control from the "gateway of the Atlantic to the southwestern harbor of San Diego, where all the navies of all the seas might ride at safe anchor." Its holdings in Alaska allowed the Union empire to extend deep into the Pacific, giving Americans "unlimited choice" from the Atlantic to the Pacific to migrate, to civilize, and to industrialize at a pace so rapid "that we can catch but a glimpse of the past at best." Empire separated Americans from their memories of bygone days. It was this monument—the American empire—where Fish believed deserts and prairies would soon be civilized by the industrial know-how and agricultural production of sophisticated white Americans who commemorated the dead who perished in the Civil War. The nation they died for had become an empire. This imperial monument included valiant

Confederates who fought for conviction. Fish skillfully intertwined the Civil War dead into an imperial memory. But, he insisted, "the theory of the Confederacy was death to our national prospects." Now that the war was over, Fish contended that "as citizens of an imperial power, we take on something of the strength and dignity of the larger whole." He concluded, "These graves hide not only our dead, but our enemies as well. Let us walk from this place hand in hand. These chivalrous spirits showed themselves brave by deeds. Let their honors also be displayed by deeds."[26]

Fish's contention that an independent Confederacy would have prevented the realization of American imperial ambitions suggests that at least this high-ranking GAR official understood well how memories of union between the North and South capitulated the imperial project. Fish worked hard to cool the memory of the Civil War, describing it as a valiant struggle that led not to the freeing of millions from the bondage of slavery but to the building of an empire. But in recasting the Civil War as a prototype for imperial expansion, Fish promoted a memory of the Civil War that incited themes of reunion, not emancipation, progress, not conquest, and continuation, not transformation. Fish's commemoration address suggests that a cold cultural memory had plenty of room through which to commemorate Union, Confederate, and imperial deaths. This interpretation of cultural memory was just as advantageous for those building a cultural memory of empire as it was for those seeking to build a tradition of reunion.

This memory of the Civil War was neither continuous nor universal. But as Americans approached the precipice of a new imperial project, New Southerners, such as Robert Stiles, articulated just how much memory of the war had cooled in his dedication address of the Confederate monument at the University of Virginia in 1893. Himself a former Confederate soldier, Stiles believed that history often "led a revolt against the tyranny of results" and freed people from the "worship of success." For him, time would help people inevitably remember the noble vanquished. Stiles's kind of history was not burdened by the past. It was a history rooted in the present based on a nostalgic view of the past that Stiles believed would liberate the future. Thirty years later, Stiles suggested, history would redeem the Confederate dead. He suggested that the present trend was proof that "the world has been more just to the Confederate soldier; that is, it has been quicker to do him justice than I, for one, anticipated." Stiles claimed that nobody "hisses about 'making treason odious' or 'burying traitors in oblivion.'" Instead, Northerners "accord honor, admiration, glory, if you please—to the dead or living soldier of the Confederacy." The reason for this shift in national consciousness was an acceptance "in the minds of a majority of intelligent men" that slavery was not the cause of the war but "irreconcilable difference" between the states and the federal government.[27]

Middle-class and elite Americans looked for ways to liberate their history from the burdens of the past. The nation, many started to believe, should no longer be held back by the forces of self-criticism calling for transformation. The days of reflection were gone, and a new imperial impetus called for men of action to pursue progress. But these kinds of men and this kind of purpose created significant contradictions within the collective memory of Americans. Men of action had to bridge the rifts of the Civil War and make the frontier meaningful. Neither Americans in the East nor government officials desired to remember soldiers who died obscurely in the Alaskan frontier even if they were Civil War veterans. Location and purpose mattered when it came to fulfilling Lincoln's promise. But as Custer's death suggested, Americans were willing to reconceptualize the places and the purpose in which they should practice the rituals of Lincoln's promise. Building an empire meant making cultural memory that drew upon the present even at the expense of the past. It meant that the rituals associated with Lincoln's promise no longer needed to emphasize the sacraments of emancipation or the boundaries of the United States. In fact, the Civil War, from this cold perspective, could be remembered as a conflict that had nothing to do with freeing slaves but everything to do with preserving an imperial presence across the continent. This had serious consequences for Native Americans from the Great Plains to the Pacific seaboard who posed an impediment to the memory and practices of American progress. It also helped devotees justify stifling segregationist policies for African Americans whose blackness, many whites in the North and the South believed, was incompatible with the vision of a progressive American empire that connected the Atlantic and Pacific Oceans. Northerners and Southerners could now participate in this imperial project, and that would become especially clear when U.S. naval forces attacked the Spanish fleet in Manila and the U.S. military invaded Cuba in 1898. Cold memory would help explain American empire.

CHAPTER 3

Remembering Domestic Foreign Spaces

> Nothing gives me more satisfaction than to feel that as the President, called by the suffrages of the people, I am permitted to preside over a nation, rich with glorious memories of glorious deeds, now united in an unbroken and never-to-be-broken Union.
> —Pres. William McKinley, remarks at Milledgeville, Georgia

The need to commemorate Southerners who fought and died with Northerners in Cuba and the Philippines brought an unintended retroactive responsibility for the federal government to include in cultural memory the Southerners who died in the Civil War. Americans collectively remembered the war through their experiences of emancipation and reunion. But the reconciliation process helped cool those memories. Reunion was a gendered project, suggests Nina Silber in *The Romance of Reunion*, as Northern and Southern white men reclaimed their sense of masculinity by resolving disunion through romantic and sentimental notions of manhood as well as the historical fiction that claimed the war was a conflict to save the Union. David Blight claims in *Race and Reunion* that it was also a project of racism that made reunification possible. Lost in this nostalgic reunion movement were the harsh realities of racism and inequality. Indeed, the segregation and disenfranchisement of African Americans became the prerequisites of romantic reunion. Northern and Southern whites willingly worked together to insulate the present from the past so that they could prevent societal change and stress cultural continuity. This kind of memory did not completely dominate American cultural memory in the late nineteenth century. Indeed, cooling systems that insulated cultural memory from the past could coexist with heating systems.[1] While some like Frederick Douglass and Ida B. Wells struggled mightily to remind Americans that the story of black liberation fundamentally shaped American cultural memory and demanded that society change to embrace black equality, reunionists tried to stress continuity between the Northerners and Southerners who fought to save the Union.[2]

The consequences of these coexisting systems could be profound. Septuagenarian Henry Nelson of Edmondson, Arkansas, suggested as much when he told Irene Robertson of the Works Project Administration, "It has been a long time since I heard my parents tell about slavery. I couldn't tell you straight." Nelson was just a child when his family became free, and now he was crippled by a stroke he had suffered thirteen years earlier. His mother "talked about how the Yankees done when they come through." He recalled Yankees who "took axes and busted up good furniture. They et up and wasted the rations, then humor up the black folks like they was in their favor when they was settin' out wasting their living." Nelson noted that his parents and their fellow freedmen "wanted freedom but it wasn't like they thought it would be." He recalled, "In some ways times was better and in some ways it was worse. They had to work or starve is what they told me. That's the way I found freedom."[3] Once the experience-based communicative memory of emancipation died with his parents, Nelson's own memory of freedom grew colder. Without something to remind him of the transformative work of emancipation, the change from slavery to freedom, there seemed no real way for Nelson to reconcile the past with his current experiences of inequality. In seeking the goal of reunion, white Southerners collaborated with white Northerners to facilitate a cultural memory that reduced and displaced the memory of emancipation and equality while stressing the continuity of the republic. French historian Ernst Renan defined the nation-state as a process of citizens forgetting about a past that divided them.[4] This was fundamentally true when it came to Americans constructing a post-Reconstruction memory of the Civil War, and it had a chilling effect on cultural memory. This was neither complete nor universal, but it became the hegemonic cultural memory of white Northerners and Southerners.

Gender and race played a crucial role in the reunion movement, and so did empire. While many Americans worked to moderate cultural memory of the Civil War, U.S. officials sought ways to justify their imperial pursuits. The intersection of reunion and empire offers an opportunity to examine how America's quest for empire and New Southerners' strategies to transform cultural memory converged and thrived within a collective amnesia. If commemoration of soldiers in the pursuit of empire could effectively extend the meaning of Lincoln's promise beyond the boundaries of Civil War battlefields and the definitions of emancipation, then Confederate dead could well be covered by the promise (as long as they were able to justify their commitment to nation and empire). New Southerners, federal officials, members of the Grand Army of the Republic (GAR), and supporters of the United Confederate Veterans (UCV) collaborated to construct new cultural memories of the Civil War. In exchange for U.S. recognition of Confederates as national heroes, Southern politicians would support the expansion of the American nation, and they would work hard to embed the domestic racial politics so dominant in the South into this expansion. These sorts of groups attempted to silence the past, keeping it out of the discourse of reconciliation and reunion that now dominated the present renegotiation of the memory of the Civil War.

GAR and UCV officials, together with government leaders and citizens, collaborated to connect dead bodies with reified memories that helped hide the emancipatory meaning of the war. This occurred at the precise moment that Republicans gave up their leadership on civil rights. Many lawmakers capitulated on the race question and turned their attention to the sectional problem between Northerners and Southerners. Together these groups helped produce a cultural memory that was reconciliatory, Anglo-Saxon, and imperialist. Reconciliation as the dominant cultural memory helped stifle memories of emancipation that continually threatened to rise to the surface. Jim Crow laws proliferated and even gained federal protection through the U.S. Supreme Court in 1896. Protestant capitalists struggled to synchronize memories of reconciliation and empire with the rhetoric of democracy and constantly feared that cultural memory might spin out of control. By examining the fitful commemorations of veterans who died at the edge of empire, on the hills of Santiago, Cuba, or in the suburbs of Manila in the Philippines, and comparing them to the retroactive commemorations of Confederates who died during the Civil War, this chapter suggests that Americans reformed Lincoln's promise to bound the state and the citizenry to a project of cultural memory that simultaneously justified reunion and American expansion.

As the nation turned more toward global empire, cooling cultural memory became more important to politicians, nativists, Protestants, and capitalists in the North and the South. The Spanish-American War in 1898 required a new ambiguous understanding of American memory. This was especially so as the United States' objectives in this war in Cuba seemed unclear to many.[5] The sudden and ascendant global presence of the United States prompted a reevaluation of the Civil War dead alongside the war dead from Cuba, and reunionists boldly took advantage of the moment. Union Maj. Myron E. Dunlap used his Memorial Day address at the Confederate cemetery near Appomattox Courthouse in Virginia in 1898—just five days after Congress declared war on Spain—as a call to "cover them with flowers! the Blue and the Gray alike. Sleep! brave men sleep!" He continued, "As evidence of our unity and fraternity, see yonder!" as "veterans are now marching elbow to elbow and tenting together."[6]

Veterans from both wars were now to be remembered in an imperial context as the dead became one way to commemorate and celebrate the arrival of Americanness onto the global scene. An active will was needed to separate the past conflicts of the Civil War from the present conflicts abroad. Dunlap explicitly acknowledged this changing role in the United States, admonishing that Southerners were the last "great body of American patriots" due to the "foreign emigration [that] has deluged the North and the West." "Standing here upon the threshold of a new century, in the presence of the heroic dead; with all our past differences reconciled," Dunlap encouraged his audience to "pledge to each other our lives, our fortunes, and our sacred honor."[7]

America's emerging global influence and the new nationalization that accompanied it helped transform the meaning of Lincoln's promise and contributed more generally to what historian Jackson Lears describes as the rebirth of the nation.[8] People who sympathized with the Confederate cause saw the emerging American ascendancy in the world system as an opportunity to further ensconce cold memory into American culture. Southern men had played just as important a part in waging war abroad as Northern men did; they sacrificed their lives, in part, so that Northern industrial corporations could generate more wealth.

Many Southerners seemed to agree with Major Dunlap's sentiments. In July 1898 before the war in Cuba had ended, ten thousand Confederate veterans descended on Piedmont Park in Atlanta, Georgia, at the United Confederate Veterans' annual reunion. When Gen. John Gordon, the main speaker, "entered the hall[,] the applause and cheering were deafening." With his former adversary, ex-governor Rufus Bullock in attendance, the crowd "began to shout, 'Gordon! Gordon!' From all parts of the building the name was taken up, and the greeting was assuming vociferous proportions when the General rose and lifted his hand. The audience was stilled instantly."

Bullock, a Republican, defeated Gordon in the 1868 gubernatorial election in Georgia. The Ku Klux Klan, which Gordon led, forced Bullock from office before the end of his term in 1870. Bullock eventually returned to Atlanta where he became a businessmen and member of the Piedmont Driving Club. His presence in an audience that so clamored for Gordon, his onetime political rival, demonstrated just how much reconciliation was at its height in Georgia. Gordon's friend and ally Henry Grady, the Atlanta journalist, had spoken of a "New South," and Northern industrialists were resigned to allowing white Southern elites to deal with the "race problem," particularly if it meant that they could exploit the industrialization of the South for their own profit. Gordon used the opportunity of the UCV reunion to redress criticism that such reunions were evidence of Southern disloyalty. He called for reconciliation with the federal government. He argued that "the protection of the Negro by Southern courts, his reliance for security upon Southern sentiment, and his education through white taxation in Southern schools" was evidence that Southern states accepted the verdict of the Civil War on the issue of slavery. Of course, by the time Gordon delivered this speech, Georgia legislators had segregated schools, railroads, streetcars, and prisons while the U.S. Supreme Court had overturned the Enforcement Act of 1871, which allowed officials to try members of the Ku Klux Klan or the Redshirts in federal court, and reversed the Civil Rights Act of 1875, which barred discrimination in public places. Gordon contended that Southerners showed their loyalty to the Union by the "presence and prowess of her heroic sons at the front in the war with Spain." He added:

> Many of you assembled here would have been there but for impaired health and failing strength. But our sons and grandsons are there. Among the great ends to be attained in this conflict with Spain—the freedom of oppressed islands in both oceans, the wider influence of America in the councils of the nations, the increased respect for their power on land and sea—there is still another achievement to be attained, no less glorious and far-reaching, namely, the obliteration of all traces of distrust among ourselves and the complete and too long delayed unification of the American people.

This was a perceptive and astounding Southern critique of the dominant terms of American cultural memory.[9]

Perhaps no one but Gordon, a long-serving member of the Ku Klux Klan in Georgia, first commander in chief of the United Confederate Veterans, Reconstruction resister, proponent of the New South, former Georgia governor, and U.S. senator to go along with his military accolades during the Civil War, could challenge the Confederate hard-liners such as John Girardeau, who demanded absolute commitment to the memories of the Confederate dead and absolute resistance to Northern cultural memory. New Southerners such as Gordon took their opportunities to invent a new memory, muddled up with suggestions that Southern leaders such as Gordon actually supported black freedom as much as he supported the liberation of Cuba and the Philippines. The Spanish-American War created an opportunity to redraw the boundaries of American identity and reduce the power of the North to dictate cultural memory. After his speech, Gordon reviewed a massive parade of United Confederate Veterans down Peachtree Street in the pouring rain.

Not everyone agreed with this kind of memory that undergirded reunion and empire. University of Chicago president William R. Harper invited Booker T. Washington to speak at the Chicago Peace Jubilee on October 16. During a heated and nearly omnipresent national debate about the imperial and republican contradictions of waging war abroad and potentially annexing new peoples and territories, Washington accepted the invitation and delivered a speech in the Chicago auditorium to an estimated crowd of sixteen thousand.[10] President McKinley, many members of his cabinet, and military personnel attended and heard Washington deliver "one of the most eloquent tributes ever paid to the loyalty and valor of the colored race, and at the same time, one of the most powerful appeals for justice to a race which has always chosen the better part."[11]

Washington succinctly traced African American experiences within the context of U.S. history, highlighting how black men and women always "chose the better part." This was true when it came to submitting "to slavery or choos[ing] death and extinction," choosing the Americans over the British in the Revolutionary War, choosing patriotism and loyalty during the War of 1812, and the serving the "better part" during the Civil War. The same was true, suggested Washington, in the war with Spain when black soldiers helped take San Juan Hill and secure the city of Santiago. Washington asked his audience to consider these events and the loyalty of African Americans to the United States, "then decide within yourselves whether a race that is thus willing to die for its country should not be given the highest opportunity to live for its country." Washington went on to praise the United States as being victorious in every single conflict of its history save one.

> We have succeeded in every conflict, except the effort to conquer ourselves in the blotting out of racial prejudices. We can celebrate the era of peace in no more effectual way than by a firm resolve on the part of Northern and Southern men, black men and white men, that the trenches which we together dug around Santiago shall be the eternal burial place of all that which separates us in our business and civil relations. Let us be as generous in peace as we have been brave in battle. Until we thus conquer ourselves, I make no empty statement when I say that we shall

have, especially in the Southern part of our country, a cancer gnawing at the heart of the Republic, that shall one day prove as dangerous as an attack from an army without or within.[12]

Washington insisted that white Americans in the North and South remember the past. In fact, it was the past that contextualized his call to transform the present. It was a critical attempt to heat up cultural memory by recounting fundamental African American contributions in the historical past that contextualized the way Americans should remember the Spanish-American War. Using the past to contextualize the present allowed Washington to call for social change in the presence of some of the most powerful men holding national office. But it also allowed the former slave to issue a warning to those powerful men that failure to initiate racial and social change within the Republic would spread a cancer throughout the nation that threatened the very existence of the American Republic.

About the time in October when Washington delivered his Chicago address, newspapers reported that President McKinley planned to attend the Atlanta Peace Jubilee later in the year. This was part of a southern swing in which McKinley hoped for "reconciliation of the sectional heart" and "consolidation of southern support for overseas expansion."[13] Washington hoped to invite a sitting president to tour his institute in Tuskegee, Alabama, and McKinley's visit to Atlanta provided just such an opportunity. The educator set off to Washington to invite McKinley to tour Tuskegee after the Atlanta Jubilee. It took Washington several visits to the nation's capital and the help of several of his white allies to finally secure the president's acceptance. In every meeting, Washington found McKinley "kind, patient and most cordial, apparently forgetful of the differences in our history." Washington was being polite and respectful, but this statement also rang with irony. Washington described his final visit in November, the one that secured finally the hesitant president's acceptance within the context "a few days after the election riots of that year in North and South Carolina, when the colored people throughout the country were feeling gloomy and discouraged."[14] Washington was referring to the race riots that ensnared the November election of 1898. In Wilmington, North Carolina, white Democrats rigged the election and voted out Fusionist politicians—a political alliance between black Republicans and white Populists—who had unseated Democrats earlier in the decade. Democrats succeeded by stuffing ballot boxes and intimidating voters to suppress Fusionist turnout. Democrats won in Wilmington and throughout North Carolina, but in Wilmington white Democrats initiated a riot in the wake of their victory that became the backdrop for an immediate coup d'état of city government. The riots included gunning down blacks in the street, burning down black-owned homes, and banishing black business owners and white Fusionists and Populists forever from the city. The riots turned Wilmington from a majority black city to a majority white city.

McKinley, a Republican, did little to prevent the violence or to hold the organizers of the coup accountable despite receiving many such requests. Harry Jones of Denver, Colorado, noticed what happened in Wilmington and feared such violence might spread westward. He pleaded with McKinley, "In the name of God and humanity lend us a helping hand! Give us some protection or one kind word through the press." A Wilmington woman sent a letter with her name withheld because "I cannot sign my name and live." She shamed the president's inaction, asking, "Can we call on any other Nation for help? Why do you forsake the Negro?" She added, "The Grand and Noble Nation who flies to the help of suffering humanity of another Nation? And leave the Secessionists and born Rioters to slay us." She begged McKinley, "For Humanity's sake help us. For Christ sake do. We the Negro can do nothing but pray. There seems to be no help for us."[15] McKinley offered neither to help nor to speak out against the violence.

This was the state of things when Washington made his last visit, finally persuading the president to accept his invitation. McKinley clearly was looking for an opportunity to control the damage from his administration's inaction, especially with African Americans. Washington gave McKinley the opportunity for "reclamation of his reputation in racial affairs."[16] Washington noted that many people were there to see the president, yet "he detained me some twenty minutes, discussing the condition and needs of my race in the South." Washington told the president, "I thought a visit from the President of the United States at this time to a Negro institution would do more than anything else to encourage the race and show to the world in what esteem he held the race." McKinley accepted the invitation, saying he was motivated to show interest "by acts rather than by mere words," and if touring Tuskegee "would permanently help the race and the institution," then he "would most gladly give up one day of his administration to visit Tuskegee" after he attended the Atlanta Peace Jubilee.[17]

But words do matter, and the political facts were that President McKinley needed speeches more like Gordon's in Atlanta, not Washington's in Chicago, to shore up the political weaknesses that McKinley obsessed over. Touring Tuskegee, the president hoped, would not only show his support of African American institutions of education but would also allow him to respond to Washington's critique in Chicago. The "cancer" of racism was clearly spreading through violence in North and South Carolina. McKinley could address this at Tuskegee. In planning his southern trip, he also hoped to motivate support, especially in anti-imperialist Democratic strongholds in the South, for his imperialist designs in the wake of the U.S. military's "splendid little war" in Cuba. Third, the conflicts in Cuba and the Philippines saw Northerners and Southerners fight side by side, and like Gordon, McKinley was looking for reconciliation opportunities. The president too had soldiered in the Civil War, rising to the rank of captain. After the war he entered politics and became a Republican congressman from Ohio and then governor of the state before winning the presidential election of 1896. Of course McKinley had carried the single southern state of Kentucky in his 1896 election against Democratic candidate and anti-imperialist William Jennings Bryan, and it was important that the McKinley administration gain support for the upcoming negotiations with Spain at the Treaty of Paris. By the time he came to Atlanta for the Peace Jubilee, which commemorated the end of the Spanish-American War, nearly six months after the Confederate reunion in Piedmont Park, the president was looking for support not only for his continued policy in Cuba but also for his policy of annexing the Philippines. On the eve of the Jubilee, the president entered the Capitol and delivered his speech to the Georgia legislature after the Spanish-American War had ended in Cuba but before events in the Philippines had turned dire. Here he articulated a compromise—amending Lincoln's promise—that gave

Confederate dead official access to national cemeteries. McKinley largely offered this compromise in exchange for Southern political support at least in terms of negotiating peace with Spain and annexing the Philippines.

To boisterous cheering from Georgian legislators, many of whom had fought in the Civil War or served in the Confederacy, McKinley insisted, "Fraternity is the national anthem," and "the Union is once more the common altar of our love and loyalty, our devotion and sacrifice." Referring to the invasion of Cuba, he noted, "The old flag again waves over us in peace with new glories, which your sons and ours in this year added to its sacred folds." He reminded the audience that "the memory of the dead will be a precious legacy . . . what an array of silent sentinels we have, and with what loving care their graves are kept!" Then the president segued from the Spanish War to the Civil War:

> Every soldier's grave made during our unfortunate Civil War is a tribute to American valor . . . the time has now come, in the evolution of sentiment and feeling under the providence of God, when in the spirit of fraternity we should share with you in the care of the graves of the Confederate soldiers. . . . if it needed further justification, it is found in the gallant loyalty to the Union and the flag so conspicuously shown in the year just past by the sons and grandsons of these heroic dead.[18]

Similarly, in his Memorial Day speech in 1900 at the Antietam battlefield and adjacent national cemetery, McKinley was "glad that the Union was saved by the honorable terms made between Grant and Lee under the famous apple-tree; and there is one glorious fact that must be gratifying to all of us—American soldiers never surrendered but to Americans!" He praised Union and Confederate troops, saying, "The valor of the one or the other, the valor of both, is the common heritage of us all." He concluded: "The followers of the Confederate generals with the followers of the Federal generals fought side by side in Cuba, in Porto Rico, and in the Philippines, and together in those far-off islands are standing to-day fighting and dying for the flag they love."[19] The applause and cheers from the attendants underscored the firing of new collective imagination, one that now included white Southerners and silently consigned African Americans to oblivion past and present.

This was McKinley's promise to former Confederates, and it borrowed from the obligations of citizenship embedded in Lincoln's promise. In fact, McKinley's Atlanta speech serves as a rhetorical prism through which to measure the distance between the meaning and reasoning of this new Lincolnian tradition emanating out of Lincoln's Gettysburg Address. Lincoln's speech dedicated space to those who died "that [the] nation might live," and gave resolve that the nation "should have a new birth of freedom." In a manifestation of cultural memory, Lincoln borrowed the religious understanding of the Good Death in the world of Victorian Christianity to explain the recent deaths of soldiers on the battlefield. They may not have died a peaceful death in the presence of their family, and they may not have received assurances that their souls would reach heaven, but Lincoln guaranteed that their deaths for liberty were purposeful and that souls reached the Valhalla of the nation. McKinley, whose eulogizers controversially would insist that he had inherited Lincoln's legacy as an assassinated Republican president, dramatically opened new commemorative spaces by extending a belated Good Death to those who fought against the nation and that new birth of freedom. These Confederate bodies completely obscured the memory of the Civil War as a conflict fought over emancipation and thus signified the political transformation of American cultural memory. This permitted the president to argue that North and South, no longer divided by the memory of the Civil War, could look forward to the new noble cause of American overseas imperialism. He offered Southerners recognition of the bodies of Confederate soldiers in exchange for their support of the global rise of the United States. Remembering the Civil War as a necessary war to "save the union" and as a "fight amongst 'brothers'" gained momentum in a world where Americans were reopening doors in Asia and acquiring colonies in the Caribbean and the Pacific. To sustain this imperial project, government officials were now prepared to incorporate Confederate memories still surrounding the Civil War dead into cultural memory. This also bound Southerners to the obligation to remember the dead through the discourse of the national imagined community, but it did not commit them to commemorate the discourse of emancipation; rather, McKinley made his promise to them, obliging Southerners only to honor the discourse of reconciliation and progress.

After his speech to the Georgia legislature, McKinley reiterated his policy of reconciliation with several speeches delivered the next day as part of the Atlanta Jubilee celebration marking the successful end of the Spanish-American War and the return of American soldiers. Most major cities performed similar jubilee celebrations, but McKinley chose to attend Atlanta's. He headed the parade that went along Peachtree Street from downtown north to Ponce de Leon Avenue, retracing the steps in reverse of General Gordon and the United Confederate Veterans just a few months prior. Earlier in the day Georgia legislators passed resolutions praising McKinley's speech. Crowds lining both sides of Peachtree Street cheered as the president made his way along the route. After the parade, McKinley and his entourage were hosted at Piedmont Park by the Piedmont Driving Club, and he spoke to a capacity audience in the same 10,000-seat auditorium that General Gordon had addressed six months earlier. He stated: "Under hostile fire on a foreign soil, fighting in a common cause, the memory of old disagreements had faded into history. For this result every American patriot will forever rejoice. It is no small indemnity for the cost of the war. This government has proved itself invincible in the recent war and out of it has come a Nation which will remain indivisible forevermore." McKinley used practically the same words as Gordon while standing in the same spot. This was not "a crusade of conquest," argued the president, but the "reward of temperate, faithful, and fearless response to the call of the conscience, which could not be disregarded by a liberty-loving and Christian people."[20]

The successes in Cuba did not mean that the struggle had ended. Despite the martial victories, the president announced that his administration intended to occupy Cuba and the Philippines. He reminded his audience in Piedmont Park that "the task is not fulfilled. Indeed, it is only just begun. The most serious work is still before us, and every energy of heart and mind must be bent and the impulses of partisanship subordinated to its faithful execution." To this end, McKinley imposed his own time map justifying empire by beckoning to the memory of Bunker Hill and Gettysburg. "At Bunker Hill liberty was at stake; at Gettysburg the Union was the issue; before Manila and Santiago our armies fought not for gain or revenge but for human rights." In a way this was a strange comparison. The president compared the acts of the revolutionary generation at Bunker Hill, who fought against an empire, to the sacrifice of soldiers at Gettysburg, who fought for a new birth of freedom, to soldiers who fought in the Philippines and in Cuba, who transformed the American republic into an actual empire. But McKinley's time map glossed over the historical inconsistencies that underscored his view of the American empire as having a relatively pastless present. He continued, "Thus far we have done our supreme duty. Shall we now, when the victory won in war is written in the treaty of peace and the civilized world applauds and waits in expectation, turn timidly away from the duties imposed upon the country by its own great deeds?" Three cheers for McKinley marked the end of his speech. The "ancient wounds" of the Civil War that were slipping from memory to mythology needed to heal if McKinley was to gain support for his plans in Cuba and the Philippines.[21]

Later that night at the Jubilee banquet, McKinley again had a chance to address prominent Atlantans. The editor of the *Atlanta Constitution*, Clark Howell, served as toastmaster for an evening attended by Governor Allen Candler, Governor Johnston, Governor Voorhees of New Jersey, and former governor Rufus Bullock. Treasury Secretary Lyman Gage, Secretary of the Navy J. D. Long, Postmaster General Charles Smith, Secretary of Agriculture James Wilson, Secretary of War R. Alger, as well as Generals W. R. Shafter, Joseph Wheeler, and A. C. M. Pennington were all present. Howell introduced the evening with an invocation: "In the presence of God, with uncovered head and bowing reverently in acknowledgement of divine leadership, a Nation stands to-day upon the threshold of a new century, content in and conscious of the performance of a duty well done in His name." Howell acknowledged that "the central figure of the story is the Chief Executive of this great nation." McKinley then rose to boisterous applause. At the banquet he announced: "Reunited! One country again and one country forever! Proclaim it from the press and pulpit, teach it in the schools, write it across the skies! The world sees and feels it; it cheers every heart, North and South, and brightens the life of every American home. Let nothing ever strain it again. At peace with all the world and with each other, what can stand in the pathway of our progress and prosperity?" McKinley identified himself as a patriot who could lead reconciliation efforts between

North and South. It was a significant break with his party's tradition of "waving the bloody shirt," and it pandered to a New South audience whose support he would need while conducting forthcoming military and nation-building operations in the Philippines.[22]

Navy Secretary Long toasted the crowd immediately after McKinley's speech and reminded the audience that soldiers, "pushing from day to day on to Santiago through the tropical jungles under a tropical sun, wet with tropical rains, exposed to unknown diseases, and only the coarsest fare to eat, you would agree with me that the typical hero is the American regular." Long added, "He [the American soldier] is entitled to all the love and gratitude that a great and generous Nation can bestow upon him." George Peck of Chicago toasted the shared revolutionary heritage of Northerners and Southerners during the Civil War. Borrowing from McKinley's time map, which conflated Bunker Hill, Gettysburg, Manila, and Santiago, Peck recalled that "there was a time when some who are here to-night did not love each other overmuch, and yet when the stress was fiercest and the fire seemed ready to consume, neither side gave up its memory of Lexington and Yorktown." Peck added, "Tradition, language, literature, common hopes and common interests make a nation; and these are a thousand times stronger than the sanctions of written charters, or the authority of blood." Peck than tied this new unity to the task that lay ahead. "Gentlemen, the flag cannot come down. The institutions and the policy of a free republic are equal to new conditions or they are worthless." He concluded, "The new Union, which war has welded more firmly together, summons us and leads us forward." Other speakers addressed similar themes. The editor of the *Boston Globe* responded to the toast "Santiago, the Plymouth Rock of Cuban Freedom," while General Wheeler responded to "The South's part in the war," and Postmaster General Smith addressed, "The War as an Echo of Independence Hall." Practically everyone in attendance shared McKinley's view that the Spanish-American War gave birth to a new Union and that tougher work lay ahead in civilizing Cubans and Filipinos.[23]

Elite men during the Atlanta Jubilee drew a time map that tied disconnected themes of American history together unnaturally. Unlike Girardeau's time map that drew upon a fictive past to contextualize resistance to

Reconstruction and change to the present, this Jubilee time map reflected a cold memory. These memories of American history did not bring the past into the present. Rather, speakers made sure that the present provided the context through which they recalled events of the past. They crafted a memory that made the past subservient to the present. The toasts at the Jubilee banquet sought to preserve the present by pretending that continuity existed between the present actions of U.S. invaders in Santiago and actors of U.S. history such as the Pilgrim settlers and the signers of the Declaration of Independence. Events like the Atlanta Jubilee marked just how much Northern and Southern cultural memories had moved from resentment to reunion. If there was ever any doubt about America's involvement in global politics, events like the Confederate reunion and the Atlanta Jubilee were quickly putting these doubts to rest.[24]

The next morning, McKinley and his entourage of military generals and Alabama state officials, including the governor and much of the state legislature, arrived by special train to tour the Tuskegee Institute in Alabama. Faculty and students performed a parade, Washington escorted the visitors on a tour of the campus, and many officials gave speeches in the chapel. McKinley's speech was no "Atlanta Speech" to the Georgia state legislature, and he offered the students and faculty no comparable place in American cultural memory as he did to white Southerners. McKinley was impressed with the buildings and the grounds, and he praised all who worked and went to Tuskegee. He noted, "No country, epoch or race has a monopoly upon knowledge. Some have easier but not necessarily better opportunities for self-development." Education could transform lives, echoed the president, "no man who has them ever gets into the police court or before the grand jury or in the workhouse or the chain gang. They give one moral and material power. They will bring you a comfortable living, make you respect yourself and command the respect of your fellows." He admonished the students, "Whatever you do, do with all your might, with will and purpose, not of the selfish kind, but looking to benefit your race and your country." The president reminded them that "in comparing the past with the present you should be especially grateful that it has been your good fortune to come within the influences of such an institution as that of Tuskegee." Such an admonishment from the president of the United States must have been inspiring and compelling for many in the audience. To be recognized by such dignitaries probably encouraged many to continue enthusiastically with their work. But unlike his speech to Georgia politicians, McKinley offered no federal assistance to Tuskegee in terms of materialism or cultural memory. In fact he offered the Confederate dead more financial commitments from the federal government than the living students of Tuskegee.[25] Blair describes McKinley's success on his southern trip as rather mixed. The historian claims the president succeeded in reconciling white Northerners and Southerners, but he largely failed in getting Southern Democrats to support his plans to annex the Philippines. On top of this, racial violence continued.[26]

McKinley's Southern trip to Atlanta and Tuskegee exposes the interconnections of domestic empire and empire abroad. McKinley tried to persuade Southerners in Atlanta to embrace a policy toward imperialistic treatment of exotic brown-skinned non-Protestants in Cuba and the Philippines, while in Tuskegee McKinley tried to sweep white Protestant treatment of black-skinned Americans in Wilmington and other Southern places under the rug. The trip itself became an expression of comparing foreign and domestic experiences of imperialism. It took the perceived discontiguous relationship of space between faraway lands and the domestic front and made them contiguous for the purposes of enacting an imperialistic federal policy that treated citizens and subjects alike who could not find their way into the definitions of American memory. In this way, McKinley could consider his trip as a success in fully transforming Lincoln's promise from mobilizing to tempering American cultural memory. The trip can be seen as verification that many elites in the North and the South believed that the past was not really present in the present, creating new ways to conflate the Civil War with America's wars for empire.

As a down payment on his promise to include the Confederate dead in the Lincolnian tradition, McKinley agreed to support the reburial of Confederate bodies in Arlington National Cemetery. General Gordon and UCV leadership worked with Senator Joseph Hawley of Connecticut, who proposed a bill that appropriated $2,500 for the disinterment of 128 Confederate dead from the Washington DC Soldiers' Home Cemetery and 136 dead already inside the gates of Arlington with badly dilapidated gravesites. They would be moved into their own Confederate section. The bill easily won congressional approval, and McKinley signed it on June 6, 1900. Thus at about the same time that the War Department pushed the last African Americans out of the Freedman's Village at Arlington, Southerners were laying out a new section at the top of the nearby hill to deposit Confederate remains with brand-new white marble tombstones. Many of the Confederate dead already buried in Arlington were "scattered about the cemetery" with "absolutely no way to distinguish the grave of a Confederate soldier from that of a Quartermaster's employé, a citizen, or a negro contraband. The same style of headstone marks all alike, bearing only the number of the grave and the name of the individual." Removing Confederate dead from this democratic obscurity of the cemetery would elevate the commemoration of the Confederate dead above that of the freedmen's graves. To secure this commemorative promotion, the local United Daughters of the Confederacy began fund-raising for a monument to be sculpted by former Confederate soldier Moses Ezekiel. In 1903, for the first time, Confederate dead were neatly buried in the Confederate section and former Confederates still living were included in the Memorial Day services.[27]

UCV leaders, particularly Gen. John Gordon, supported reconciliation on Southern terms. Many women's societies also signed on for the project of incorporating Confederate dead into the Valhalla that dominated American cultural memory. But not all Confederates were happy about this sort of inclusion. Women's memorial groups traditionally commemorated the Confederate dead, argues Caroline Janney in *Burying the Dead but Not the Past*. Many women's memorial associations in Virginia gave their members access to the public sphere, where they developed their own mourning traditions, and Janney claims that these traditions were often connected to the revanchist Lost Cause movement.[28] Marginalized by their femininity during wartime, yet bearing the conflict's costs as mothers, wives, and daughters of the dead, these women were often more committed to the Lost Cause than the surviving men who could bond with their former enemies. The expansion of Lincoln's promise, in concert with the movement for reconciliation and reunion, challenged women's control of Southern cultural memory. Many women understood that incorporating the Confederate dead into a variation of the Lincolnian tradition, even if stripped of its memories of emancipation, would make the hot memories of the Lost Cause much weaker. Some women's groups resisted UCV male leaders who, they believed, were giving up on what had been a Confederate promise to the dead as Reverend Girardeau had argued on Confederate Memorial Day. For them, efforts by male UCV leadership to bury Confederates in Arlington was a compromise too far that replaced the traditional commemorative role of Southern women with the rituals of the federal government. These women rejected visions of the New South, and many UCV leaders overseeing the reburial of Confederate dead in Arlington National Cemetery grew concerned by their objections. Although the Ladies' Southern Relief Society of the District of Columbia and the Ladies' Memorial Association of Montgomery, Alabama, supported the reburial project, many Southern women broke away from these groups to form new organizations hoping to persuade the War Department not to implement the law. Representatives from these newly formed groups wrote to the secretary of war and asked him to remove the Confederate dead to Hollywood Cemetery in Richmond, Virginia, instead of Arlington.

UCV men were clearly frustrated by this protest and openly questioned the women's group: "They seem to forget that we are Southern as well as they." They continued, "We would view with great sorrow the carrying out of the plan proposed by the organization above referred to; would deem it a desecration, a great wrong to our revered dead comrades." Instead, it was the "earnest desire" of UCV organizers "that these dead comrades remain in the care of the United States government." Hilary A. Herbert, secretary of the UCV, colonel in the Confederate Army, and former secretary of the U.S. Navy, felt that "if the bodies of the Confederate dead . . . are taken up and carried South, this would be giving up the Capital of what is now our common country entirely to the Union dead." Herbert added, "The Confederate dead will have no interest and no memorial telling them of their deeds anywhere within the reach of the city that was named for George Washington, the greatest of American rebels!" Instead, he believed Arlington would serve the Confederate cause better, as it would be visited by "generations yet unborn" and would "direct the attention of every visitor" to the "respect and admiration for the Southern soldier entertained by his former foes." Commander in Chief Gordon claimed, "It is not practicable for our ladies to carefully protect and keep in perfect condition all Confederate graves in the entire country, North and South." Gordon insisted that Secretary Herbert should do his best to convince the secretary of war not to consider the protests of the women's groups. Gen. Stephen D. Lee, head of the Mississippi Historical Society, asked the secretary of war to act speedily to rebury the dead so as to mitigate still lingering sectionalism. "Those of us who want to see all sectional feeling and bad blood resulting from the war removed should act always in the spirit manifested on all occasions by President McKinley whenever he touches on the war."[29]

McKinley's Atlanta speech and the reburial of Confederate dead in Arlington borrowed from the traditions first uttered by Lincoln at Gettysburg. But these moments inverted the tradition in profound ways. The emergence of the formal American empire in the Caribbean had consequences for how Americans remembered the past. This imperial memory bestowed upon the Confederate dead the ability for Southerners to access the cemeteries as well as the cultural memory of the nation. While Kinney and Livermore, Union veterans of the Civil War, lay buried in Alaskan obscurity, and while freedmen were being cast out of a living monument to emancipation in Arlington, those who fought against the liberation of slaves could now be fully incorporated into Arlington National Cemetery and cultural memory. Senator Joseph Foraker of Ohio sponsored the bill that marked the legislative implementation of McKinley's Atlanta address. The 1906 Foraker Bill authorized the War Department to create the Office of Commissioner for Marking Graves of Confederate Dead under the authority of the quartermaster general. This was a position appointed by the president. William Elliott was from South Carolina and fought for the Confederacy. After the war, he served as a congressman from South Carolina. President Theodore Roosevelt appointed him to the position in 1906. When Elliott died in 1907, Roosevelt appointed Gen. William C. Oates of Alabama. Oates fought for the Confederacy as well and lost an arm during the war; President McKinley awarded him a position of brigadier general during the Spanish-American War. In between the Civil War and the war with Spain, Oates became a Democrat, a U.S. congressman, and then a governor of Alabama. When Oates died in 1910, President William Howard Taft appointed James Berry, who also served in the Confederate Army and was a former governor and U.S. senator of Arkansas. Commissioners thus were older Southern men who perhaps could be trusted not to stir up too much controversy but who played an important part in commemorating the cause for which they had fought; they were themselves symbolic of reunification efforts and the cool memory that went along with their work.

The end of Reconstruction and the downsizing of the U.S. Army after the Civil War accompanied a memory boom. While black leaders such as Frederick Douglass, Ida B. Wells, and Booker T. Washington were attempting to build a network to cultivate a hot memory of emancipation through speaking tours and media outlets, Southern whites along with Northern whites who had lost the will to pursue civil rights were supporting a storage and retrieval system that stressed reunion and reconciliation over emancipation. They built their network around Memorial Day, Confederate Memorial Day, and national cemeteries as well as the local control of schools where Americans of all ages but not backgrounds could easily retrieve cultural memory. Government officials and expansionists meanwhile hoped to expand the nation's borders and scale up its industrial capacity. They sought to negotiate with citizens to build a cultural memory network based on consensus of white Northerners and Southerners. The rituals of national mourning stored in the national cemetery network became opportunities to retrieve and communicate memories of reconciliation. Symbols of the old Confederacy gained storage space while symbols of freedmen and emancipation lost space in the cultural memory of post-Reconstruction Americans. As American imperial projects unfolded, those with less space had a harder time retrieving cultural memory. Reunification also brought a greater role to the federal government. The War Department took an increasingly active role in the reconciliatory memory-making process. The reburial of Confederate bodies in Arlington relied on congressional appropriations and War Department cooperation as much as it needed UCV management. This would have significant impact on the cultural memory of Americans as the Civil War generation—and the memories that they experienced—began dying off in the twentieth century. As the cultural memory shifted, the absence of memorials, gravesites, and commemorative traditions meant that there would be no physical artifacts or ritual practices to remind succeeding generations of the importance of emancipation. It would be erased and forgotten were it not for the innovative alternative memory networks built by African Americans such as Paul Laurence Dunbar, Frederick Douglass, Ida Wells, Booker T. Washington, W. E. B. Du Bois, and countless other people who preserved the past in memory through poems, literature, black colleges, and everyday conversations. Over time these oppressed memories would warm and thaw American cultural memory again, but not until the middle of the twentieth century. If the cornerstone of nation-building was actively forgetting, then the ascendancy of the United States as an industrial and imperial global power was realized out of the racialized context of forgetting the emancipatory meanings of the Civil War. American cultural memory had grown cold, and it would not be completely warmed again until the generation of the civil rights movement drew upon the past to challenge racist Jim Crow laws that proliferated within the cold memories of American empire.

In exchange for consensus with government and War Department officials, Confederates gained access to the cultural memory network that had once been off-limits. This admittance helped legitimize Confederate and New Southern interpretations of the war. This came at a cost, however, because the War Department, as the keeper of the dead and the protector of the American empire, retained control over cemeteries. As a private organization, UDC strategies were not as effective as the strategies of the UCV. New Southern businessmen who joined the UCV let the government help them reinterpret the Confederate graves, and in exchange, government officials legitimized their lingering racialized interpretations of the war. They found a way to incorporate Confederate dead into American cultural memory as symbols of reconciliation and imperial cooperation. This allowed UCV officials to play a significant role in how the government maintained the cemetery. This new path involved a move away from the local and factional understandings of the Civil War dead and toward a federalized and imperial meaning. Commemorating the Confederate dead in Arlington cemetery would not have materialized had President McKinley not used the Spanish-American War to invert the Lincolnian tradition, which now provided an effective system to cool the cultural memory of the Civil War. Memories of American empire could be stored within Confederate and national cemeteries where people came annually to fulfill the ritualized obligation between the state and the citizenry to remember the dead. This kind of reconciliation was happening along with the multiplying of Jim Crow laws and state-sanctioned racial discrimination. These kinds of cemeteries became repositories of cultural memory that stressed white dominance, and the ritual performed in these places shaped the cultural memory of Americans at home and of the way citizens imagined American identity abroad.

PART 2

Retrieval

On Thursday, November 10, 1898, two days after Election Day and about three months after the armistice of the Spanish-Cuban-American War, Spanish war volunteers of Company K of the Second North Carolina Volunteer Infantry who also served in the Wilmington Light Infantry (WLI) joined with members of Wilmington's Naval Reserves in downtown Wilmington. They were met by politicians of the White Government Union (WGU) financed by the Democratic Party apparatus, Democratic politicians, and Red Shirts—terrorists who supported the Democratic Party, wore red shirts, and who often referred to themselves as Rough Riders, probably as an emulation of Theodore Roosevelt's famous cavalry unit. It was 8:15 a.m., and these men were waiting for Alfred Moore Waddell (Democrat, former Confederate, and former U.S. congressmen) to arrive at the WLI armory. The night before, Waddell and members of the WGU proposed to black community leaders of Wilmington a "White Declaration of Independence" from the city government. Waddell's declaration received 445 signatures; it called for the forced resignations of the mayor and the chief of police and the silencing of the *Daily Record*, the state's only daily black newspaper, owned and operated by Alexander Manly. White Wilmingtonians threatened violence if the black leaders failed to respond to their demands by 8:00 a.m. on November 10. Waddell showed up at 8:15 a.m. and told the assembled mob that he had received no response from black leaders. The Rough Riders then led a parade of men through town in military formation to the offices of the *Daily Record*, while the WLI and the Naval Reserves remained at the armory. WGU men and Red Shirts targeted Manly's newspaper because Manly had printed a critical editorial responding to Wilmington's Democratic newspaper, *Morning Star*, which reprinted a speech that Rebecca L. Fenton had given a year earlier in Georgia in which she defended lynching as a necessary bulwark of Southern society. As the procession neared Manly's property, the crowd grew in number, reaching nearly 1,000 people. It took an hour for all of the marchers to reach their destination, and when they reached the *Record* offices, men from the Red Shirts stormed the building and set it on fire.[1]

These men were acting on the overwhelming (and rigged) Democratic victory of the 1898 election that had happened two days earlier. Previous elections saw Fusionists—an alliance between black Republicans and white Populists—come to control most of North Carolina. Fusionists gained the state legislature, the governor's office, a U.S. Senate seat, and many local governments throughout the state by funding public education, reforming corrupt polling laws, and increasing the number of black officeholders and registered voters throughout the state. In the lead-up to the 1898 election, WGU and Democratic officials sought to eliminate Fusion politicians who operated what the WGU claimed was a black government, particularly in their stronghold of Wilmington, which was the largest city in the state at the time, home to a black majority, and governed by a majority of white officials. Democratic tactics for winning the 1898 election amounted to voter fraud and intimidation. Red Shirts rode armed through towns and countryside to intimidate Fusionists. Perhaps they imagined themselves as doing similar work as the famous cavalry unit of white soldiers who charged through the hills and valleys of Cuba defeating brown bodies of the Caribbean. Meanwhile Democratic politicians and pundits constantly published incendiary stories and political cartoons meant to racialize the looming election and suppress voter turnout. On November 8, Election Day, the Rough Riders continued their intimidation tactics while WGU officials stuffed ballot boxes statewide. The election restored the Democrats to the state legislature and the contested U.S. Senate seat and to many local governments including a crushing victory in Wilmington. Despite the victory, Democrats, the WGU, and Red Shirts immediately set into action what became the opening moments of a coup d'état.[2]

Waddell led the Rough Riders on November 10. After leaving the charred remains of the *Record* building, some Rough Riders, buoyed by the violence, ventured into the Brooklyn neighborhood of Wilmington, a community of black and mixed-race citizens, to suppress any potential reprisals. Gunfire soon erupted between whites and blacks. Word reached the governor in Raleigh, who then sent a telegram to the armory ordering the WLI and the Naval Reserves to restore order. Neither members of Company K serving in the WLI nor members of the Naval Reserves actually saw action in Cuba during the war. Both groups had been held in reserve in port or on base for the duration of the short conflict. This was the first action they had seen. The WLI ventured into Brooklyn with a Colt machine gun capable of firing 420 rounds per minute while the Naval Reserve had a Hotchkiss rapid firing gun. Walker Taylor, who commanded the WLI, declared martial law and proceeded to shoot and kill black men whom he found in violation of his command. They shot men in the back on the street, they shot men who returned fire, they burned houses, and they gunned down as many as twenty-five men as violence ripped through the town into the evening.[3]

Some of the Red Shirts blamed Daniel Wright, a black citizen, for instigating the violence, accusing him of shooting two white men in Brooklyn. Some in the WLI found him hiding in his home. Witnesses said that he shot into the crowd from inside the home. Members of the WLI burned his house down to force him out, and when he tried to escape, they captured him. Someone came from behind and hit his head with a gas pipe. Another person went to look for a rope to lynch him. In the meantime, someone decided to let him make a run for it. They let him run several yards before opening fire. He was left to die in the street, but he remained alive. No one took him to the hospital until later in the afternoon, where he died the next day from his thirteen gunshot wounds. One eyewitness claimed that a group of whites entered another man's house, "he sitting at the fire, they thought he fired a shot; he ran, they shot him down, then took up a stick of wood and bursted his brains out." One related an account of "a black policeman named Perkins [who] was killed as he left his home in the Dry Pond area by a Red Shirt who claimed he had waited four days to do the shooting."

Many of the dead and wounded lay unrecovered for a day or more. Whites refused to let blacks attend to the dead and wounded. The black coroner, David Jacobs, tried to recover some of the bodies and begin an inquest, but his efforts were stymied. Many black men and women fled their homes and took refuge in the woods and swamps surrounding the city. Rev. J. Allen Kirk, pastor of the Central Baptist Church, took refuge in a cemetery, claiming that "thousands of women, children, and men rushed to the swamps and there lay upon the earth in the cold to freeze and starve. The woods were filled with colored people. The streets were dotted with their dead bodies." Many families could only recover and bury their loved ones at night, and many dead remained unidentified in unmarked graves, making the actual number of dead unknowable. There was no Lincolnian tradition here.[4]

Meanwhile, Waddell and his closest Democratic associates forced Mayor Silas P. Wright and his administration, the chief of police, and the members of the board of aldermen to resign. As many as two hundred armed men lined the corridors of city hall as each man, democratically elected to his position, reluctantly signed resignation papers as gunfire could be heard in the streets. After securing their resignations, the Democrats immediately elected Waddell as mayor, and he and his appointed cabinet straightaway implemented a banishment campaign where they forced key Populists and Republicans, both white and black, to leave the city forever. WLI members escorted these former city leaders to the train station and gave them tickets for a destination out of state. Members of the WLI continued the banishment campaign, acting on many personal grudges, and of course thousands of black Wilmingtonians voluntarily departed. Political leaders, property owners, successful businessmen, laborers, men, women, and children forcibly and voluntarily left the city, which would severely limit Wilmington's economy in the coming years. Within a matter of days, Wilmington went from a city with a black majority to white majority and from Republican and Populist control to Democratic control. Democrats, now in power, secured their political legacy by quickly implementing Jim Crow voting laws and gerrymandering districts within the city. Democrats throughout the state were inspired to impose segregation laws in the wake of the Wilmington coup.

Nearly three months later, on the other side of the Pacific Ocean, white Americans again took up arms against brown bodies to impose white rule in the Philippines. The United States began sweeping Filipino forces under the control of President Emilio Aguinaldo out of metropolitan Manila and into suburban areas. Supported by Adm. George Dewey's gunboats, which shelled the area from Manila Bay, U.S. forces soon overcame Filipino resistance. Within a few days, the Americans controlled the Pasig River and various strategic locations surrounding Manila. On February 10 U.S. regiments began their assault on the suburbs of Caloocan where Aguinaldo had been sending reinforcements. John Bass, correspondent for *Harper's Weekly* and embedded with the Twentieth Kansas Regiment, related how these Americans fought their way through Caloocan in February 1899. Taking Caloocan proved difficult because the Americans had to negotiate a narrow strip of land leading into a wooded area that then opened up into a series of rice fields. Navy ships shelled the town as the Twentieth Kansas began its assault. Bass likened it to a holiday. "It was like a great Fourth of July to hear the distant boom of the guns of the *Monadnock*, and the rushing shells cutting through the woods until they exploded with a thundering roar." He went on to describe the battle in glowing terms despite the tragedy unfolding in front of him: "It certainly was a stirring sight to see our line advancing in the open, driving the insurgents at every point, and gradually closing in on the doomed town." When an American soldier fell near him, Bass noted, "He fell, not as we read of in books, throwing up his arms and clutching at his coat, but sinking in a limp heap."[5]

Bass's report was eerily similar to depictions of violence used in Wilmington to overthrow the democratically elected government there. Once the advance reached Caloocan, Bass met up again with the Twentieth Kansas as the men went "from house to house to clear out the remaining insurgents." He reported, "There was a rush for the church, and with a cheer, up went the American flag. In the road dead Filipinos lay here and there like great disfigured dolls thrown away by some petulant child." But the Filipinos continued to fight, and the Americans pushed on through Caloocan all the way to nearby Malabon where the fighting stopped for the day. Heading back to Caloocan, Bass observed that Filipino sharpshooters had "lodged in the houses," and consequently "the town had to be burned." He described the horrible scene somewhat nostalgically:

> In the fading light of day the dry nipa huts, set afire, shot great gothic spires of flame into the sky. The main street of the town was roasting hot, and we rode through on a gallop. The Bambook huts bursting with flame crackled like musketry fire. . . . As we rode back to town over the battle-field, the doctors were still wandering about in the darkness, calling into the night from time to time to make sure that they had left no wounded on the field.

It was a desolate scene that seemed to communicate the achievements of the Twentieth Kansas.[6] Those achievements, however, snuffed the life out of the Philippine Declaration of Independence from Spain and the fledgling Filipino republic under the Malolos Constitution.

Comparing the actions of Americans in Wilmington and in Manila provides a contrast through which to think about the relationship between the homeland, the frontier, and cultural memory. It matters where memories are made. "Memory needs places and tends towards spatialization," suggests historian Jan Assmann, not only "to provide a setting for its [group member] interactions but also to symbolize its [group] identity and to provide points of reference for its [members'] memories." These "spatial frames for memories" include "what the house is to a family, village and land are to a farmer," or what the color line is to segregationists and frontier landscapes are for imperialists. Assmann suggests that these spatial frames can be linked together to make a "memory landscape."[7] Americans made cultural memory in the landscape of Wilmington in late 1898 and again in the landscape of the Philippines in 1899. The memories were eerily similar. American identity could be shaped in contradistinction from Filipinos and Spaniards at the edge of empire as much as it could be shaped by whites in contradistinction from blacks in the very heart of the homeland. Not only did identity matter in opposition to "the other," but just as important was the landscape in which people created those identities. Americans made cultural memory in Wilmington that was powerful enough to remind blacks of the brutal nature of white nationalism. Americans produced cultural memory in the Philippines, too, and demonstrated the power of imperialism. Together these demonstrations of memory and power illustrate how homeland and frontier could be connected as a memory landscape.

Memories of power can be extended over acquired spaces to impose a repertoire of imperial power, write Jane Burbank and Frederick Cooper in *Empires in World History*. "The nation-state proclaims the commonality of its people," while the "empire-state declares the non-equivalence of multiple populations." While "the nation-state tends to homogenize those inside its borders and exclude those who do not belong," the empire-state "reaches outward and draws, usually coercively, peoples whose difference is made explicit under its rule." Burbank and Cooper claim that this description of empire presupposes that "different people within the polity will be governed differently." While difference may exist within the polity, similarity may exist for people who reside domestically or abroad but whose existence lies external to the polity. For example, Burbank and Cooper suggest that "many empires used difference as a tool of rule, making sure that the ties of elites and groups to the sovereign were stronger than the linkages of imperial subjects to each other." They suggest that while nations are distinct from empires, they usually share coinciding spaces overlapping and intertwining in intimate and violent ways. These shared places might form a memory landscape of internal and external colonial geography where similar colonial strategies of control are practiced both within and beyond the boundaries of the nation.[8]

Cemeteries from America's Civil War stored the shared memories of racial oppression, especially after McKinley inverted Lincoln's promise in the lead-up to the Philippine-American War. Commemorating the dead thus also created opportunities for retrieving stored cultural memory that helped white Americans in Wilmington and in the Philippines remember the racial oppressions of home and empire as they governed nonwhites within the nation and within the empire. These kinds of memories could be retrieved from the stored memories of the Civil War and Reconstruction and be extended to reinforce racial color lines at home and on the frontier.

Examining how Americans retrieved cultural memory at home and abroad can highlight the role of cultural memory within the American imperial repertoire of power. Key mechanisms of this repertoire were the color line at home and Orientalism at the frontier, which were both usually invisible, although nearly everyone knew their locations.[9] Their relative invisibility made it easier to obscure the American imperial project at home and abroad. If nation-states and empires occupy overlapping spaces, then mapping the color line and Orientalism in places like Wilmington and Manila can help people visualize the memory landscape in which the American colonial repertoire of power functioned. Commemorating the war dead has long served a useful political purpose of mitigating the national disgrace of war. Understanding the geographic relationship between disgrace and commemoration can help make clear the way that Americans retrieved memory as a way to negotiate the overlapping imperial and domestic places. Locating black and brown dead bodies produced at home and abroad and comparing them can help scholars triangulate the tricky and sometimes uneasy memory landscape of republicanism, Jim Crow, and Orientalism.

CHAPTER 4

Retrieve the *Maine*!

None but the dead have free speech. None but the dead are permitted to speak the truth.
—Mark Twain, *Mark Twain's Notebook*

Justifying imperialism by nationalizing dead bodies from a war of empire helped bend cultural memory and national identity for Americans. The war dead played an important role in helping justify what Cuban historian Louis A. Pérez Jr. describes as a "moral source of United States hegemony in Cuba." Pérez views this moral righteousness as "simultaneously a source of moral entitlement and means of social control by which to transact assumptions of domination" among Cubans.[1] Americans expected Cubans to be grateful for the sacrifices that U.S. soldiers made to liberate the island from Spanish colonial rule. As Pérez and others suggest, this was an American cultural memory of the war rooted in the politics of gaining support for America's involvement in Cuba. It incorporated Confederate memories of the Civil War while obscuring the Cuban, Puerto Rican, and Filipino memories of independence. Government officials in the United States and in Cuba flooded the cultural memory of the war with monuments, gravesites, and artifacts useful for storing and retrieving republican interpretations of U.S. involvement and dissipating imperialistic interpretations. Americans began envisioning the United States as a reunified nation with a global mission.

They began seeing themselves after the Spanish-Cuban-American War as new players on the global scene, and they communicated these memories of the war in Cuba well into the twentieth century. The cultural memory of death became a key network in identifying where Americans could locate the nation's boundaries and determine who were and were not citizens of the nation. The memories expansionists held of their domestic homelands would thus play a crucial part in shaping newly forming memories in places of expansion. Likewise, new memories would produce a feedback loop—through cultural memory—that could validate people's memories of home. This feedback loop produced a memory of empire that pinioned memories of home and abroad together in ways that defined citizenship. Retrieving cultural memory thus became a crucial act through which Americans claimed rites of citizenship and understood U.S. identity in the world. It demonstrated an ability, as Jan Assmann describes, that "conveys a sense of belonging that is something very different from a natural, ethnocultural awareness. A consciously communicated and acquired sense of belonging connects with a different consciousness than the sense of belonging into which one is born." This was a crucial technique that Americans learned and developed in the invasion of Cuba in 1898. "Culture produces identity internally," suggests Assmann, and "it also produces alienation externally."[2]

Cultural memory retrieval became a necessary test of American citizenship as the reality of expansionism threatened the authenticity of republicanism. Americans did not make these national identities necessarily in the storage of cultural memory. More often than not, they made them when they retrieved cultural memory from storage. This cultural practice mimicked a biological process. "Recall of memory is a creative process," claims neuroscientist Eric R. Kandel. In the internal biological memories of humans, retrieval plays an important role in shaping identity. Often stimulated by an outside source, neurons deliver the uninterrupted stimulus to the brain. Once received, the mind interprets this stimulus, in part, based on saved memories already in storage. Kandel suggests, "What the brain stores is thought to be only a core memory. Upon recall, this core memory is then elaborated upon and reconstructed, with subtractions, additions, elaborations, and distortions."[3] When humans engage in memory recall, they are incapable of retrieving memories as they actually happened. Their retrieved memories of past events are filtered and interpreted to help each individual shape an identity in the present. Thus memories of the past are socially constructed, evolving over time, and humans use this evolutionary process to help them interpret and even shape the present. It is an essential coping mechanism for identity-making. Yet "cultural memory is not biologically transmitted, it has to be kept alive through the sequence of generations," claims Assmann. "The difference is that the group memory has no neurological basis. This is replaced by culture."[4] When individuals within a group share their retrieved memories of the dead, they bring a communicative retrieval process that is spontaneous, evolutionary, particular, and profane into dialogue with a cultural memory retrieval process that is interpretive, institutionalized, ritualized, and sacred. At moments when communicative and cultural memory intersect, usually on occasions when the living interact with the dead, collective memory can be transformed, because anyone within the group can make additions, subtractions, elaborations, and distortions that affect cultural memory. It is a moment when experience-based memory and ritual-based memory can inform and transform each other to produce a new memory. Yet these adaptations are a necessary strategy to communicate memory to successive generations. "The meaning of the texts," suggests Assmann—in this case the dead—"must be kept alive by constant adaptation to changing circumstances; otherwise this meaning gets lost within the three or four generations of communicative memory." In order to fulfill Lincoln's promise to remember the dead, the interpretation of the dead had to change over time. It is a necessary evolutionary and adaptive process that is simultaneously embedded in the traditions and rituals of commemoration. This was what Lincoln accomplished at Gettysburg and what McKinley inverted in Atlanta. It is an example of how memory retrieval works culturally and what must be done to keep the memory of the dead alive.

This (re)presentation could only be made in the wake of a wildly successful war. Perhaps inauthentic, perhaps ostentatious, the recovery of the dead from Cuba nevertheless allowed millions of Americans to participate in retrieval of cultural memory surrounding the Lincolnian tradition. In the wake of the war in Cuba, the United States became the dominant power in the Western Hemisphere and began its rise to hegemonic power in the world system. The United States joined the overseas imperialist community in the late nineteenth century and was in competition to replace a deteriorating British empire. Americans looked back on the easy victory over Spain as evidence of national greatness. Retrieving memory of the war through a creative process added as much as it subtracted and distorted as much as it reconstructed.

The call to "Remember the *Maine*" came to describe how Americans retrieved and communicated memory of the war. People associated the war with a thing, in this case a wrecked battleship. As Assmann reminds, "Objects reflect ourselves" and the "world of things in which we live has a time index that refers to our present but also, and simultaneously, to different phases and levels of our past."[5] The raising and resinking of the USS *Maine* in 1912 provides a key opportunity to examine how Americans understood themselves and communicated their imperial memories to each other because they devoted so much energy and passion to remembering what they considered *the* material object of the war. A symbol of the American steel industry, gunboat diplomacy, reunification, and imperial power, the *Maine* gave McKinley the excuse to invade Cuba after a military commission investigated the wreckage and determined that the Spanish had sabotaged the gunboat on February 15, 1898.

Of the 355 U.S. officers, crew, and marines on board, 261 died when the ship exploded. Seven crewman and an officer died later from injuries. Only 165 bodies were recovered. The remaining 96 were either buried in the wreckage or lost in the harbor forever. Politicians, historians, and popular sentiment, claims Pérez, saw the *Maine* as the single overarching cause of the war with Spain. "The destruction of the *Maine* served to arouse public wrath, thereby creating a climate of opinion in which war became an acceptable if not inevitable course of action." The problem with this association, asserts Pérez, is that it paints the whole American invasion of Cuba—and American empire—as an accident of history, a war of destiny rather than imperial design. This produced the message that "newly acquired colonial territories are portrayed as an incidental and wholly fortuitous outcome of this accident—not the product of policy calculations, and certainly not the continuation of political relations by other means." But so many people in 1898—and Pérez insists this carries over into the twenty-first century—accepted the idea that the war with Cuba was an accident sparked by Spanish saboteurs sinking the *Maine* because it allowed people to connect their nationalistic and republican impulses to the gunboat to make sense of an ambiguous war of empire. This was why people tried to "Remember the *Maine*" and why its raising and resinking posed such a universal public response. "The *Maine* is thus refractory," suggests Pérez of its first sinking, "a convenient means through which to create a usable past that serves at once to reflect and reinforce generally shared assumptions about the beneficence of the American purpose." This could also be said of its recovery and second sinking. As the Army Corps of Engineers retrieved the wreckage from the bottom of Havana Harbor, Americans participated in the retrieval and communication of the cultural memory that they made from the wreckage.[6]

The hulk lay at the bottom of the shallow Havana Harbor for fourteen years and made the harbor difficult to navigate, but it also created a rallying site for Americans living in Havana. Portions of the bridge and mast rose out of the water as a reminder to the U.S. presence in Cuba and the larger Caribbean. "The U.S. government and American community in Havana," historian John Marshall Klein writes, "sought to craft the ship's story into one of sacrifice and noblesse oblige that could legitimize American influence in Cuba."[7] But by 1910 this mythology was increasingly difficult to maintain. Cuba "received" its independence from the United States in 1901, but in name only. Cuba then elected American-friendly Tomás Estrada Palma as its first president. Originally a revolutionary against Spanish colonialism, Palma secured his presidency after winning the election and signing the Cuban-American Treaty that included the Platt Amendment. This amendment allowed the United States to occupy Guantanamo Bay with U.S. troops and intervene in Cuban affairs whenever deemed necessary. In 1906 Cuban revolutionaries who were not happy with Palma's pro-American stance challenged his reelection bid. His relaxation of a tariff on U.S. goods brought much business and investment to Cuba, but little of it helped the Cuban economy. When the revolutionaries threatened to depose Palma, the United States sent troops stationed at Guantanamo Bay into the country again.[8]

In the aftermath, President Roosevelt appointed Charles Edward Magoon as provisional governor of Cuba. Fresh off his position as governor-general of the Panama Canal Zone, Magoon claimed to support the Cuban republic and proceeded to crush the revolutionaries. He became wildly unpopular among Cubans because he continued to allow American companies to exploit Cuban resources. The *Maine* was an important site of memory for Magoon that he and his compatriots in Cuba used to remind Cubans of the American sacrifice during the war. Once Magoon eliminated any threats to U.S. interests in Cuba and opposition to conservative Cuban politicians, new elections were held in 1908, and José Miguel Gómez won.

Unlike in the Philippines where the United States had instituted a formal colonial government and could impose its will through brute force, America did not "own" Cuba, and tensions would always be present. The invasion of 1898, the invasion of 1906, the race war of 1912 in which President Gómez had sanctioned the killing of thousands of black Cubans, many of whom had formed the Partido Independiente de Color, were a few of the most troubling moments for American neophyte imperialists attempting to operate an informal empire in Cuba. Thus the *Maine* as a symbol of U.S. benevolence was fast becoming a symbol of tense relations between the United States and Cuba. The wreckage not only blocked off part of Havana Harbor but it also reminded many Cubans of the continuing saga of an informal empire that consistently reopened the wounds of the Platt Amendment.

In 1910 Congress approved and appropriated money to raise the ship, to recover the bodies still inside, to remove the wreckage from the harbor, and to reinvestigate the initial commission's findings as to the cause of the ship's sinking. But this appropriation threatened to undermine the fragile republican concealment of imperial memory. The recovery signaled a retreat of informal empire based on gunboat diplomacy. It was an admission that Cuban-U.S. relations had deteriorated, that Cuba was not part of the formal U.S. empire, and that many Cubans were not grateful for America's role in their affairs. Although U.S. officials believed that the recovery would surely validate the cause of war, the whole episode brought to life intense patriotism and scrutiny in the United States, Cuba, and Spain. Many people believed raising the ship would further reinforce U.S. actions in Cuba. Others had their doubts. Many Americans and pro-American Cubans feared that raising the ship and examining it in broad daylight would show that no mine exploded it and that the United States had invaded Cuba without cause. The very symbol of U.S. power in the Caribbean—made with U.S. steel and manned by U.S. sailors—carried with it deep anxiety over the moral righteousness of Americanness and the ability to become a leader in the world system. Government officials and U.S. citizens had to create memories of the war anew in order to maintain the cultural memory that U.S. intervention was based on republicanism and not imperialism. Thus the whole process of recovering the battleship threatened to transform cultural memory.

There was no precedent in raising a ship this size. The Army Corps of Engineers began the work with a $300,000 appropriation from Congress. They took proposals from private companies to do the actual raising. Several companies submitted ideas including one from the Arbuckle Company using compressed air. The corps rejected the Arbuckle plan because the compressed air would distort the structural analysis of the wreckage. The O'Rourke Construction Company proposed building a wharf out to the ship and then tunneling beneath the ship to put slings around it. The idea was then to slowly raise the ship out of the water. But this plan, claimed corps officials, was too expensive and time-consuming. Another company proposed taking the ship apart with the use of dynamite, but this was "discarded as opposed to the sentiment of the nation." Most Americans viewed the wreckage as an important object of memory, and destroying it piece by piece seemed like sacrilege. A fourth option submitted by the Lackawanna Steel Company called for building a cofferdam around the wreckage and pumping the water out so that investigators could examine the hulk. The U.S. Navy suggested using floating docks and hydraulic mining to sever the ship from the harbor floor. The War Department eventually chose the cofferdam option, as it was the least expensive and best able to preserve the wreckage.[9]

The War Department wanted control of the investigation without outside or independent oversight. Although the ship rested in Cuban waters, it was U.S. property, and therefore the U.S. Army wanted territorial rights and exclusive access to the ship. Cuba ceded those rights temporarily to U.S. engineers. Cuban president Gómez agreed to "admit, free of all duty, all materials and supplies required by the United States and the agents or agencies employed by it on this work." He also granted the U.S. "extra-territorial jurisdiction over such a portion of the waters of Havana Harbor as are, or will be, occupied by the *Maine* and the necessary engineering constructions, fixed or floating, required in the proposed work." This included "extra-territorial" control over docks, wharfs, and warehouses.[10] Gómez agreed to aid the United States because he too wanted the harbor cleared. He had received his presidency, in part, because of U.S. involvement in Cuba, and he wanted to remove a monument used by Americans to justify the occupation in 1906.

The War Department had control of the waters around the hulk and wanted to have control of labor as well. Chief of Engineers William H. Bixby recommended from Washington DC that "it is *very essential that, when work is once started, the officer in charge shall be free from all interference* by outside contractors and houses supplying material, and that he shall be *free to direct labor and use* any and all *plant* within reach *without* necessity of *formal contracts*." Bixby recommended that the congressional appropriation was not enough to complete the work. He suggested that Congress levy another $200,000. Completing the project within budget meant completing it on time. The only way to accomplish this was to allow the officer in charge full control of labor. In addition, Bixby wanted Cuba to supply most of the machinery—steam hoisters, dredges, pile-drivers, and pumping machines—free of charge.[11] The War Department expected to have control over this process with as little influence from the press or labor unions as possible.

Bixby and his fellow planners quickly learned that they would not have as much control as they hoped. Criticisms about the project plan and labor policies came from a variety of interested parties. Spanish-American War veterans voiced one concern over Bixby's labor practices. Joseph Jacoby, commander in chief of the United Spanish War Veterans, became very nervous about the Corps of Engineers' use of manpower. Jacoby had learned that private contractors had won the diving contracts to explore the ship and had found forty-five bodies already. Jacoby wrote to the secretary of war, "I know it has been a customary thing in Cuba to gather up the bones of the dead in a sort of promiscuous pile, and am sure you will agree with me that no such fate should overtake the remains of our beloved boys who went down with the *Maine*."[12] Jacoby, as a veteran, was insinuating that the War Department did not care enough about the preservation of the remains of his fellow soldiers. Col. William M. Black of the Army Corps of Engineers headed the project of raising the *Maine*, and he made clear that "there are no contractors engaged in the work of removing the wreck." He added that the Army planned, "as the unwatering" proceeded, to "prevent the occurrence of any wilful [*sic*] or inadvertent action which might throw a doubt on the findings" of the cause of the sinking. Black added, "No one should be permitted on the wreck excepting persons directly connected with the work of its removal."[13] These sorts of letters reminded War Department personnel that although they had charge of raising the ship and recovering the remains of the dead, they had to accomplish their tasks in ways that honored the dead and appeased the sentiments of veterans.

A more serious problem arose. The project team had completely underestimated the cost. By the spring of 1911, the original $300,000 appropriation had been exhausted. Colonel Black ran the project from his office in New York, but the officer under Black overseeing the actual work in Havana was Lt. Col. Mason M. Patrick. Patrick reported in late January that there had been huge delays in work for a number of reasons. Weather was abysmal, and rain and wind had forced Patrick to stop work for the safety of the workers. Equipment did not work properly. Patrick complained about the dredge boat *Sauga* being "good-looking" but "badly designed." But the biggest problem was due to the cofferdam. Patrick reported that the workers had no experience with pile-driving. "Three shifts of green men were put on each machine, and ... their efforts were ineffective, with resulting heavy expenditures of money and a very inadequate return." Quickly running out of funds, Patrick and Black considered a yearlong work stoppage until Congress approved further funds, but they were very concerned about people stealing souvenirs from the *Maine* and materials from the worksite. Black suggested that they send U.S. troops to guard the site, but Patrick claimed the U.S. minister in Cuba recommended against it.[14] The wounds from the intervention of 1906 seemed too fresh in the minds of many. Instead Patrick would have to hire local watchmen while Congress pondered an additional $700,000 appropriation submitted by the War Department to complete the project. This more than doubled the original appropriation and brought the total cost to $1 million.[15]

Congress eventually appropriated and disbursed the money, but this did not necessarily help speed up the project. Building the cofferdam was more difficult than the engineers had imagined. The bottom of Havana Harbor was very hard, and workers often bent the interlocking steel beams and sheet metal as they pounded them into the harbor. Workers had to drive 3,200 piles in total to make the cofferdam work, yet pile driver crews could only average 13 piles driven per eight-hour shift due to the difficult terrain.[16] As the months went by, the work crews gained more experience with the work, and they became more efficient. But early cylinders were often very low quality and began leaking. Newspapers began criticizing the entire project. One editor claimed, "A complete failure of the effort to raise the Maine is now generally predicted." He claimed that workmen drove the cylinders too low and the outside water would wash over the dam at high tide. This report prompted William Ellis, a foreman working on the cofferdam who had recently been relieved of his duties, to write to the secretary of war. Ellis claimed the work on the dam was woefully inadequate: "In my thirty years experience, I have never witnessed a more disgraceful state of affairs than that which has been practiced on the Maine Cofferdam work." Ellis forecast that the water would eventually break the dam and "bury the Maine in mud."[17]

In July 1911 Patrick discovered that cylinder F was leaking. He reported, "On investigation it was found that in the process of driving the piles some of the bolts of the fish plates joining the individual pile sections had fallen out, permitting the entrance of water."[18] Although these leaks were plugged and the cofferdam was braced, the press reports became so negative about the construction of the cofferdam that John Arbuckle, whose bid to use compressed air to raise the ship had been turned down, resubmitted an informal request for the secretary of war to consider. Arbuckle wrote, "I am informed that the most eminent engineers say when the water and mud is removed, the sheet piling will collapse." To prevent this, the engineers reinforced the interior of the dam with stone and dirt. But Arbuckle claimed his associate had made two trips to the site and had photographic evidence of "human bones under the stones dumped to strengthen sheet piling." Secretary Stimson was intrigued enough to inquire about Arbuckle's proposal, but he decided to remain with the cofferdam method.[19]

Even the workmen came under scrutiny from some observers. The recommended length of a dive at the time was no more than four hours, and one diver, Theodore McMahon, complained of temporary paralysis because Army officials required him to dive for more than four hours. When Colonel Williard wrote Bixby about the matter, Bixby assured him that if McMahon had been on dives longer than four hours, it was due not to the Army but to his own decision to remain underwater for that long. Bixby contended that McMahon worked as long as the other men but spent less than four hours underwater. He hoped that the diver would get over his illness, but claimed it was no fault of the Army Corps of Engineers. McMahon's problems were symptomatic of the labor policy governing the project. The War Department had complete control over labor, but this control brought with it responsibility for any untoward consequences. Engineers had no real experience in raising a ship of this size. Their trial and error method of driving piles and reinforcing cylinders was necessary, and engineers overcame most of the setbacks that crews encountered. These sorts of policies and practices, however, detracted from the sacredness of the project in the minds of many critics.

Besides unblocking the harbor, the two main rationales for raising the ship were to recover the remains of those who went down with the ship and to reaffirm the *casus belli* of the U.S. invasion of Cuba. The cofferdam method that the Army Corps of Engineers chose now threatened to undermine these projects. It affected memories of Americans who had connected the "accidental" U.S. empire to the *Maine* and its destruction by an external explosion. The War Department's control and consequent lack of transparency produced anxiety among people who considered the *Maine* a thing of cultural memory. This was reflected in the rehashing of the causes of the sinking and the debate over the Corps of Engineers' plan to dispose of the wreckage. The editors of the *American Marine Engineer* in New York City argued that the army should "Raise, Not Sink, the *Maine*." They noted:

> This nation wants the *Maine* raised, as nearly intact as possible, in order that its condition may be seen by all men, in order that all possible light may be thrown upon the origin and nature of the catastrophe of 1898, in order—as we hope and expect—that the contentions and reports of our officers concerning it may be proved correct, but in order, above all else and in any contingency, that the good faith and moral courage of the American government and nation may be vindicated. In a deliberate and persistent suppression of the facts, or avoidance of their exposition, there would be a dishonor which we would not willingly see America incur.[20]

Much was at stake in raising the wreckage. The Corps of Engineers responded to the accusations, agreeing that the "wreck should be seen just as it lies, before any part of it has been disturbed in any matter what-ever." But the corps rejected the idea of not resinking the *Maine*. It was an obsolete class of ship and could not be recommissioned. The War Department expressed no interest in using it as a memorial because "it would be but a gruesome exhibit, an object of curiosity, a reminder of a national tragedy." Examining the wreckage was important to military officials, but they did not believe it a suitable tool of cultural memory. The War Department thus planned, "with appropriate ceremonies, [to] give it honorable burial beneath the waves."[21]

The anxiety over the *Maine* reached a fever pitch after engineers drained the cofferdam and inspectors investigated the wreckage. The initial findings of 1898 were called into question, for it was clear from the wreckage that the explosion had been internal not external. The keel and other parts of the structure bent outwards, not inwards. The *Morning Star* of Newark reported Bixby's astounding admission that "the secret will never be known." Bixby continued, "It has been clearly established that there was an internal explosion. But this does not disprove the theory of a mine or torpedo placed outside."[22] In addition, Bixby claimed that recovery teams had only found between forty and fifty bodies, and the rest were lost forever. Bixby's comments set off a tidal wave of criticism as he undermined the two most important reasons for recovering the *Maine*. The ship as a "useable past" to describe the "beneficence of the American purpose" fell under attack with Bixby's candid statements. The *Inter-Ocean* newspaper of Chicago claimed, "General William H. Bixby, U.S.A., does little credit to his uniform by the manner in which he states his conclusions." Bixby asserted the explosion came from inside the ship's magazine, but he did not rule out completely that an outside force could have triggered the internal explosion, although he doubted the external theory. The editor admitted, "All of which may be technically true. Yet, put as General Bixby puts it, the statement is one which disgraces its maker by propagating a falsehood and by giving aid and comfort to his country's enemies, within and without her borders." The editor then reiterated the mine/torpedo theory of the explosion and accused "Americans who are never so happy as in reviling their own country [have] sought then and ever since to blink the facts or lie out of them, with intent to make the American people feel ashamed of the righteous wrath."[23]

Bixby's comments seemed to challenge the memory of American empire. By suggesting an internal explosion occurred, Bixby articulated a memory of the *Maine* and the U.S. invasion of Cuba that was considerably warmer than many Americans accepted. The ship provided evidence of the past that suggested America's invasion was not accidental at all but rather opportunistic. This insinuated that the U.S. invasion was one of design that seemingly contradicted the republican desire to free Cubans from Spanish colonialism. Bixby's analysis, perhaps inadvertently, thawed American cultural memory just enough to expose the canard that American empire was republican in nature. Even more damning, in the editor's eyes, Bixby's remarks undermined the glorious cause of the war:

> As for the wreck of the *Maine*, here is what should be done with it: erect thereon a worthy monument to the 266 American citizens there treacherously slain. Let that monument be a perpetual witness to the tale of how the *Maine* was avenged and Cuba freed, that devoted Americans may tell their sons a hundred years hence and that these sons may know how to love their country and how to die for her honor![24]

This was a call to mark Havana Harbor forever as a symbolic boundary of an "accidental" U.S. empire. And although the War Department remained uncommitted to this sort of symbolic value, others were supportive. John Harvey sent the above newspaper clipping to Secretary Stimson and handwrote, "I fought through the war of the rebellion with a gun—it seems now our officers want to do all the fighting with their mouths—is it not about time for another reprimand?"[25]

Despite evidence to the contrary, such as the outwardly bent keel, which suggested an internal explosion happened, and Bixby's own analysis, the 1911 military investigation panel decided that an external detonation caused the internal explosion. Many accepted this decision because it eased their anxiety over remembering the war. With the cause of the explosion blamed on sabotage, the wisdom of invasion could be justified. Work on the hulk continued slowly as workers painstakingly washed the mud that encased the emerging wreckage through wire screens searching for human remains and personal belongings.[26] As workers discovered bodies from the wreckage, they took the remains to the shore and placed them in coffins stored in Cuban warehouses. There the dead remained until the wreck was ready to be removed. Sixty-five sets of remains were eventually reclaimed. After salvaging the still useful parts and relics from the wreckage, engineers patched up the ship. The wreckage had finally been investigated and repaired, at least enough to float, by March 1912. To separate the wreckage from the mud-seal at the bottom of the cofferdam, engineers drilled "twenty-nine two-inch holes" in the bottom of the wreck and connected them to pipes. Engineers then forced water through the pipes by a pump which weakened the seal enough that flooding the dam would raise the ship. The plan worked, and the repaired hulk floated.[27] Engineers placed an official U.S. flag on the ship after flooding the dam. After final repairs, the workmen dismantled a section of the cofferdam and pulled the floating wreckage out of the enclosure.

What remained in Havana was the general cleanup of the worksite. The engineer corps began removing the cofferdam one pile at a time. After removing the dam, the engineers contracted with the Cuban government to dredge 75,000 cubic yards of the harbor at forty cents per yard. Additional dredging cost Cuba eleven cents per yard. This included sinking the leftover wreckage of the *Maine* into the mud. More than 200 tons remained; part of the bow remained because "it was jammed in close to the cylinders" of the dam. Colonel Black had the workers cut up the remaining wreckage, "shackled and buoyed, so that it ought not to be difficult to remove." Additionally the starboard turret remained in the mud. The only solution was "very deep dredging around the turret" to sink it further into the mud and free up the harbor for navigation. Once the piles were finally removed, the steel was returned to the Lackawanna Steel Company.[28] In addition to paying for the dredging of the harbor, the president of Cuba wanted to cement the reciprocal relationship between his government and the United States. Gómez opened the Cuban Congress in April 1912 and reminded the legislators that "I do not wish to conclude this message without recording an event that has demonstrated to the entire world the close ties of affection which bind us to the American people." He concluded, "Our Government and the American Government consociated in this act and inspired by a common sentiment fulfilled a pious duty."[29]

The logistics of raising the *Maine* spoke to the difficulty in the building of an informal empire. The very symbol that Americans and sympathetic Cubans hoped would bolster relations was dug up and resunk in international waters. It was suggestive that American officials had learned in the years between 1898 and 1912 that they would not be able to control Cuba the way empires of Europe had controlled their colonial possessions. Americans, as neophyte imperialists, had to pursue their interests in Cuba in much more innovative and informal ways. The raising of the *Maine* was reflective of just how much the Americans had learned about operating an informal empire in the years since the war with Spain. Just as there were plenty of mistakes and mishandling of the *Maine* project, U.S. officials also made mistakes in their heavy-handed trial and error interventions in Cuba. Government and War Department officials were stretched just as the Army Corps of Engineers were overextended in the logistics of raising the wreckage.

When it came to the memory of the *Maine*, the War Department likewise planned to have complete control without influence from veterans or the general public. But sinking the ship deep in international waters and beyond the reach of veterans and citizens threatened to distort cultural memory.

The War Department did not gain complete control as officials had hoped; Americans began voicing their opinions on the reclamation project, revealing just how much they connected their memories of the war to the destroyed ship. The *Maine* still mattered. They saw in the retrieval of the battleship a retrieval of cultural memory that they wanted to access and communicate. What was at stake was the clashing of two polar interpretations of memory. American officials were interested in disposing of a symbol that made relations with the Cuban semi-colony tense while citizens embraced the myth that the empire was temporary and that it would not enlarge. For them the tragedy of the *Maine* was a potent symbol of American benevolence.

Unlike the Civil War where the dead could be buried in proximity to their families, most of the work of commemoration in Cuba and the Philippines took place overseas. Thus although the War Department had sought to transform the wreckage into a site of memory, too many Americans resisted these wishes. As public-spirited citizens, they too wanted a say in how the ship would be memorialized. In what can be seen as little criticisms of the recovery project, people sent thousands of letters voicing their concerns. Some of the public sentiment was incredibly personal and saw in the raising of the hulk a chance to recover personal belongings of loved ones who had perished while on board. For example, Isaac Auchenbach asked Secretary of War Henry Stimson if the engineers had found his brother Harry's gold ring. "I am very anxious to recover my brother's ring, as it would certainly be a most notable trinket to possess, both as to the memory of my brother, and as to the manner and circumstances under which the ring was returned to me."[30] Assistant Engineer Darwin Merritt died in the explosion, and divers discovered his body near the position where he was last seen alive. His father, a minister in Red Oak, Iowa, asked for his son's class ring. But only an "officers uniform and cap and buttons [were] found with [his] remains." His class ring was nowhere to be found and was listed as "probably stolen by workmen." Shortly thereafter the Cuban newspaper *El Mundo* came into possession of the ring and turned it over to U.S. authorities who forwarded it to Mr. Merritt in Iowa.[31] The retrieval of these sorts of personal objects demonstrates how the sunken hulk still powered a living memory for those who had lost their loved ones in the explosion no matter how much the government intervened.

Letters flooded in from all over the country asking the government for a *Maine* relic. William Ludwig, a jeweler and silversmith from Chamberburg, Pennsylvania, had no relatives on board the ship but asked his congressman, Benjamin K. Focht, to "aid me in the effort to get a piece of 'The *Maine*,' now being raised in Havana harbor. Want something from her—a nail—piece of iron—wood—anything. Will pay all expenses and reward you too."[32] Eberhard Faber requested that the recovery effort send his pencil company all the rubber bands and lead pencils recovered from the wreck.[33] The cities of Moline and Rock Island, Illinois, requested pieces of the ship for their citizens.[34] The Order of the Knights of Pythion, San Diego, California, chapter requested relics from the ship.[35] The National Museum of Cuba petitioned the War Department for the rapid fire gun removed from the wreckage.[36] The Borough of Pompton Lakes, New Jersey, requested the thirty-inch ventilator from the ship to place in the city's square. Already sanctioned by the New Jersey Historical Society, the square was one of George Washington's headquarters and the city already had a field artillery piece from the Wilderness campaign of the Civil War and shells from the Petersburg siege.[37] The city of South Bend, Indiana, requested some bronze from the ship so that the city's Polish Falcons fraternal order could produce a "memorial tablet."[38] Officials from Ohio asked for mementos to be displayed at the Ohio State Fair.[39] The secretary of the Navy requested the ship's instruments for the Naval Academy Museum. Cuban authorities asked for a steel cupola from the conning tower. The Military Service Institution of the United States wanted the mast not destined for Arlington Cemetery. The mast was already stored at Casa Blanca, and the War Department hired watchmen to "prevent the cutting off and carrying away of detached portions of the mast."[40] Part of the congressional legislation allowed for the War Department to disperse unneeded artifacts. So many requests came in from around the country that the War Department had to appoint a special board to determine who was most qualified to receive the relics. The board included an officer of the Navy and an officer of the Corps of Engineers. Together they decided where the pieces of the *Maine* should end up. Although the War Department retained much of the power as to who could access these relics, they also opened up the possibility for

Americans and Cubans to participate in the retrieval and communication of cultural memory.

These requests demonstrated that the War Department would not be able to control the commemorations surrounding the sunken ship. For example, some saw in the wreck an opportunity to spread patriotic pride to American schoolchildren. Money was running short for the recovery project in 1911. But Dr. George Maines of New York wrote to President Taft and every governor in the United States in hopes of raising $250,000 for the effort. He wrote, "I would like to see the schoolchildren of this country contribute the desired amount. If each one would give one penny, plenty of money would be forthcoming." Maines added, "Not only would a great good be accomplished but it will tend to arouse the spirit of patriotism which is so freely evinced in 'young America.'" He suggested that each state governor open an account for the purpose. Children could bring their pennies to their teachers, who would then give them to their superintendent, who would deposit them in the bank account. "With the aid of the associated press and the public dailies throughout the country this plan can be quickly and successfully launched." Despite the War Department refusing the proposal, claiming that officials could accept the schoolchildren fund only after receiving congressional approval, this was an attempt to get a new generation to participate in the cultural memory of empire.[41]

Others criticized the War Department's plan to raise and resink the wreck because some believed it reflected the continued Northern interpretation of memory that trampled on Southern identity. "A Patriot" believed that the dead should remain with the ship and the hulk should remain in the harbor. "Were I a sailor," A Patriot wrote, "I should prefer, when dead, to rest anywhere but in Arlington. To me Arlington stands as a persistent disgrace to the nation, a confiscated property of a great gentleman and a forcible robbery of his ancestral lands." Although reflecting the flickering remnants of men and women who continued to see Northern oppression in the new traditions of cultural memory, A Patriot's position was willing to commemorate the sailors who died on the *Maine*, no matter how untrustworthy he found the federal government. The *Maine* could accomplish for some people what Arlington National Cemetery could not—provide a memory of reconciliation albeit qualified. The critic's comments reflected an individual who did not want to simply forget the Southern identity constructed out of the Lost Cause movement and overrun by government bureaucracy. It was a memory of the *Maine* as a symbol of reconciliation that reintegrated Southern identity into cultural memory.[42]

The War Department also had to adapt to the concerns of veterans. Every year the United Spanish War Veterans traveled to Havana and held a dedication ceremony to the victims of the *Maine* on February 15. Historian Jon Bodnar describes this sort of memory-making as "vernacular memory." Bodnar suggests that these kinds of unofficial acts created moments when citizens and other unofficial people asserted their own remembrances. For veterans, this annual ceremony proved a powerful way of reliving memories of service and commemorating lost comrades. The *Maine* provided an exceptional opportunity for former soldiers, even those who had never served on the ship, to retrieve cultural memory. Commander in chief Joseph Jacoby and his fellow veterans planned the dedication ceremony for 1911 while the military continued work on the ship's recovery. Usually attendees would hold memorial ceremonies on land, and some would venture out to the sunken hulk to leave wreaths and other commemorative memorabilia onboard. But the tight control that Colonel Black held over the *Maine* made this impossible. Jacoby was not pleased. He wanted to "place a small bronze tablet on the mast, bearing a fitting epitaph, to be left on the mast when it is removed to Arlington Cemetery."[43] But Black did not support this effort. He claimed a memorial service would unnecessarily hold up work, and the bronze plaque went against the congressional decree to take the mast to Arlington. Here Bodnar's description of "official memory" is useful to illustrate the tension of memory that government officials held over the site and how it countered the vernacular memories of the Spanish-American War Veterans. Government officials even tried to prohibit them from enacting their own memories of the USS *Maine*. Black used the weather as an excuse, noting, "The weather conditions continue to be abnormally bad and that heavy rains, which are almost unknown at this time of the year in Havana, continue to impede the work." He continued, "I would not desire to do anything which would offend any large body of our citizens in its wish to do a patriotic act, but I do not feel at all sure that either the personality or the methods of the petitioner are beyond question."[44]

William Bixby agreed. But Jacoby persisted, and Bixby finally compromised with the commander in chief. Bixby did not object to the veterans group holding memorial services on shore. But he feared that going out to the ship would cause a loss in labor and resources. Additionally, he argued, "It will be difficult to prevent the wreck from being overrun by visitors if any exceptions at all be made to the already adopted and necessary rule that no visitors are to be admitted."[45] The War Department permitted the veterans to hold their annual ceremony, but refused to allow Jacoby to fasten the plaque to the mast.[46] Veterans and government officials mediated the tensions of vernacular and official memory by reaching a compromise. This compromise gave the Spanish-American War Veterans access to the wreck over the initial objections of the War Department and showed that the secretary of war and other officials, despite their efforts, did not have complete control over the memory-making process.

Many interpreted the wreckage as a justification for America's involvement in Cuba and a sanctification of American benevolence. For many, the commemoration of the *Maine* was less personal, less about comrades, and more about republicanism. They too sought access to the wreckage. William Maybury, an "expert on oils and oil and water lands" from Los Angeles, sent President Taft a poem to display at the base of the mast that was to be erected in Arlington National Cemetery. He wrote "Remember the *Maine*" in March 1898, but the recovery of the *Maine* convinced him to submit it to the government in 1911. He penned:

> She lies in the mud, mates / all tattred an torn / though the treacherous Spaniard / not far from her home / her mission was mercy / her friendship humane / that beautiful ship / they called her the *Maine*. / Her crew noble heroes / to the bottom have gone / through the mean dirty treachery / of that Spaniard, the Don.[47]

This excerpt from the much longer poem underscored Maybury's belief that the United States was a benevolent power that was involved in Cuba because of destiny rather than design. The "beautiful ship" sullied by "dirty treachery of that Spaniard, the Don," who delighted in "murder" and "torture," demonstrated how easily Americans could cover over the tensions of informal empire.

Others were not so willing to obscure American imperial interests. Some Cubans critical of the American presence claimed that the U.S. government blew up the ship in order to pursue its imperialistic agenda and thus Cubans owed Americans no gratitude.[48] Spaniards in Madrid likewise posited theories. A monthly magazine from Spain, *El Hogar Espanol*, argued that someone not of Spanish extraction destroyed the ship, and the raising of the *Maine* would prove it. Henry Clay Ide, governor-general of the Philippines in 1906–7 and current ambassador to Spain, sent a translated copy of the article ironically titled "Remember the *Maine*" to the secretary of state and assured the War Department that all the daily newspapers in Madrid included similar stories.[49] The author of the article wrote, "Most certainly there has not been in the whole of Spain a single person that ever suspected that the catastrophy of the '*Maine*' was the work of a Spaniard." The author also claimed that when the peace treaty was signed, Spanish authorities proposed a joint American-Spanish investigation into the explosion, which "the North-American Commissioners decidedly rejected . . . undoubtedly because it did not suit their Government that this point should be cleared up." The author reported that exposing the wreck to sunlight for all to see "forced" American officials "to publicly declare before the world, that the blowing up was caused by an explosion in the magazine." He concluded, "One is justified in thinking what would have happened had matters occurred in a reverse order, how many millions would that Government have claimed as a compensation for the injuries experienced?" Just like Americans, Spaniards were invested in memories of the sinking of the warship and its consequences for their country and empire. But these Spanish memories posed a potential threat to the imperial cultural memory that many Americans used.[50]

Some Cubans were likewise invested in the wreck. As Klein suggests, "The most common Cuban reactions encompassed a spectrum of attitudes that can be characterized as open embrace, official ingratiation, tactical manipulation, veiled opposition, and outright hostility." The mayor of Matanzas, Cuba, Isidoro Ojeda, wanted American authorities to turn the cofferdam into an island once the wreckage had been cleared. It would be called Maine Island and serve as a permanent reminder to Cubans. The mayor claimed,

> The spot where these men were massacred they bought with their lives. There their bones have been resting for thirteen years and therefore it is a sanctuary, a sacred place, a consecrated spot, a holy and inviolable site that the United States has inherited from the victims and we must keep it forever, not allowing the place to be profaned in any time.[51]

Ojeda followed this up with a letter written directly to Secretary Stimson, claiming these sentiments were "genuine expressions of my feelings toward those sacred victims who lost their life in the sad catastrophe." He reminded Stimson that thousands of Americans who came to Cuba made their first trip to the wreckage site "as a first duty to go as on a pilgrimage to visit the holy place." He claimed that it was not a burden in the harbor and that everyone who passed by the wreckage was respectful.[52] When Bixby passed on the proposal, he suggested that legislative approval in both the United States and Cuba would be necessary before it could be acted upon.[53]

"Remember the *Maine*" as a metaphor to go along with the drumbeat of war was reinvigorated and reinterpreted with every inch of water pumped out of the cofferdam. The U.S. government lost its monopoly of the wreckage as a carefully guarded site of memory. Harry Gradel, a druggist from Cincinnati, likened "Remember the *Maine*" to "the battlecry of the Texans' 'Remember the Alamo' which carried them to victory over Santa Ana at San Jacinto." In response to the plan to sink the *Maine* in deep water, which Gradel did not support, he asked, "Would the Texans demolish the Alamo?"[54] Others saw in the wreckage a symbol that reflected the foundations of American republicanism. After reading General Bixby's critical remarks, comments from other government officials, and numerous newspaper accounts that claimed the ship blew up from an internal boiler and few remains would be found, James Wolferdern of Lamar Township in Clinton County, Pennsylvania, suggested that these "truths" would "cause a greater downward trend of American character." "Greater publicity" of the real cause would "aid the moral reform of the Republic. Let Truth be Known on cause of blowing up battleship *Maine* for humanity Sake," wrote Wolferdern. His anxiety marked how much he had invested himself in the *Maine* disaster and the American republic.[55]

Others had less traditional but just as anxious memories of the sinking of the ship. One of these individuals was Mrs. Helen Temple of Mexico, New York, who wrote General Bixby that she had special knowledge concerning the cause of the explosion. Temple stated that her correspondence with Bixby remained private as she was "not a public person." She wrote that she had a lifetime of experiences of dealing with people "from the other side of the river." Accompanying Temple's letter was a newspaper article that included an update on the recovery operation. The article mentioned that Lt. Friend W. Jenkins had died in the explosion and divers recovered his body in 1898 from the torpedo chamber. After reading detailed news reports of the recovery operation in June 1911, she claimed that she had met the ghost of Lieutenant Jenkins while in her home. She informed Bixby that once she recognized Jenkins, she asked him, "Who destroyed the Main[e]?" The spirit replied, "The damn Spaniards placing explosives under the bow of the boat." She reminded Bixby that she and the ghost would help in any matter "which may help in the effort to raise the *Boat*." Temple's was a metaphysical remembrance of the ship, but it was no less filled with anxiety over what the engineers would discover in relation to the explosion. It was a peculiar expression of cultural memory, offering access to the "authentic" experiences of those who had perished during the explosion and sinking of the ship.[56]

People still cared about the *Maine* after fourteen years. Early on people wanted relics, but as the ship gradually emerged from the water, many began calling for a proper memorial to the dead and the wrecked hulk. The Comet Film Company of New York wanted to film it.[57] Edwin Ray of Tacoma, Washington, suggested that the ship "be covered with dredged material with a view to forming an island within the present cofferdam and the erection thereon of a monument to the memory of the men who lost their lives."[58] Charles Julius Funck, a former classmate of President Taft, claimed that sinking the wreckage "was not the sentiment of the American people towards the ship, an object of reverence equal to the battlefields of Gettysburg, Shiloh, Chickamauga, or the melancholy site of Andersonville." To "Remember the *Maine*" was to remember "the South vindicating its reunion with the North," contended Funck, asserting that the ship was "the symbol of the restored Union. Now to sink the ship forever from sight would be equivalent to sink all the monuments of the Revolutionary War and the War Between the States likewise into the ocean and obliterate them forever all but a dim recollection of them." He asked Taft to reconsider the "hasty ill-considered consummation" and instead to make the *Maine* an "ever present beacon of fidelity to the flag, the Union and the principle for which the Revolutionary War was fought, applied to Cuban independence."[59]

Although government and military officials wanted to control the wreckage, they were sensitive to popular opinion. The entire project exposed the myth of Spanish sabotage and showed that American benevolence was not an act of permanent presence and empire building. The public was demanding that the *Maine* be commemorated in the Lincolnian tradition. American officials were also sensitive to the difficulties of the Cuban semi-colony and the symbolism that the wreckage projected onto the informal empire. War Department officials navigated these disparate narratives by appeasing people's desire to participate in the collective memory surrounding the wreckage. But they also hesitated to turn the *Maine* into a national monument, fearing that it would exacerbate the already tense Cuban-American relationship. The *Maine* had clearly dredged up people's memories. Thus in 1912 War Department officials discovered that they could enlist the popular will to further institutionalize disguised imperial memories by creating a memorial ceremony that would both minimize criticism and appease the people. They set out to produce an elaborate recovery and resinking ceremony that would end speculation about the cause of the war and justify it as a war of Cuban liberation rather than a war of empire.

Despite numerous attempts by citizens to participate in the official commemoration of the *Maine*, government officials rejected them all. It fell to Beekman Winthrop, former governor-general of the Philippines and former governor of Puerto Rico, to make the final decision as to the disposal of the *Maine*. As acting secretary of the Navy, Winthrop advocated the "propriety of towing the wreck out to sea beyond the three mile limit before sinking it, if this be practicable, in order that it may not find its last resting place within the territorial waters of a foreign country."[60] Congress approved and provided funds for the War Department to dispose of the wreck with appropriate funeral honors. Despite the wishes of the public, government officials would not allow the wreckage to become a source of perpetual controversy and perhaps in the future a criticism of American empire building and war making.

This included bringing the remains of the dead home from beyond the borders of the United States. President Taft demanded that the War Department "make the transportation of these remains one of dignity, befitting the fact that they lost their lives for their country."[61] But even returning the dead was wrought with difficulties. The transfer of the bodies from Cuban land to an American ship caused a diplomatic dilemma. At first the War Department planned to land an armed military force in Havana to retrieve the bodies from the warehouse. But diplomats in Cuba, including the U.S. ambassador, Arthur M. Beaupré, feared that this would remind many in Cuba of the wounds from the two previous U.S. invasions. The transfer of the dead and the larger memorial ceremony were also difficult on President Gómez's administration. Gómez faced reelection in 1912 and had to undertake a difficult political triangulation. Klein suggests, "His need to ingratiate himself to the U.S. government, promote his credentials as a Cuban nationalist, and satisfy Spanish community financial backers [from whom he had taken numerous campaign contributions] were not easy to reconcile."[62] He defended American interests in Cuba and worked closely to preserve the American symbolism in the USS *Maine*. Gómez viewed the *Maine* as symbolic of a "fate [that] is so closely connected with the history of the Independence of Cuba." The Cuban president even requested a part of the ship for use in a monument "that will forever recall the union in love between the Great Republic of the United States and the Republic of Cuba."[63]

Instead of Americans taking the remains, the Cuban president offered to have Cuban troops carry the caskets out to the anchored transport. But the Navy regarded the boarding of an American battleship by armed foreign troops as unacceptable. Eventually diplomats overcame the impasse by allowing a small armed U.S. force to come ashore. Their presence was only in relation to guarding the dead. In preparation for the handover, the

Cuban government moved the dead bodies from the warehouse to Havana's city hall, where they laid in state. Cuban navy and army men along with national police lined the route. With "proper honors," they oversaw a U.S. armed force escort the bodies through the streets of Havana. Once at the dock, the Cuban navy officially handed over the remains to the USS *North Carolina*, and the U.S. force loaded them.[64] President Gómez did not attend the ceremony, but he ordered public buildings in Havana to lower their flags to half-mast.[65] He also ordered cannon fired every half hour from sunrise to sunset. The *North Carolina* and the USS *Birmingham* then escorted tugboats as they pulled the *Maine* wreckage out of the cofferdam. The *North Carolina*, escorted by the *Birmingham*, moved out of the harbor escorted by the Cuban navy. Upon leaving the harbor, the Cubans fired a salute of "21-minute guns" and all the soldiers on land stood at attention while a funeral march played until the two ships passed completely out of the harbor. The two battleships fired a salute of twenty-one minute guns in response to the salute fired from the Cuban shore and then escorted the wreckage of the USS *Maine* to deep waters.

The Cuban navy escorted the hulk to international waters alongside the U.S. naval vessels. The flagship of the Cuban navy carried Cuban politicians and military personal who stood at attention as the band played "American and Cuban national airs." Once they reached the three-mile international water mark, the Army Corps of Engineers sent a boarding party to resink the now floating wreck. They had rigged explosives in the hull to blow out the bulkhead should opening the valves not work properly. Colonel Black made sure that the use of dynamite was "proportioned as to open up the bulkhead with certainty while doing as little damage to the rest of the hulk as practicable, especially since the Navy proposes to have a number of moving pictures taken showing the operation of sinking." Black warned, "There should be as little spectacular business about this as possible."[66] But the boarding party did not have to detonate the dynamite. After they boarded, they took nine minutes to open the valves and gates in the bulkhead. Water spread throughout the hulk for a second time, and the ship disappeared beneath the surface after forty-one minutes with the previously fastened U.S. flag one of the last parts of the wreck to disappear beneath the water.

As the ship began sinking, the U.S. military personnel, all in white uniforms, stood "at quarters, with guard paraded," and played a funeral march, then taps, and finally fired three volleys. Cold water interred the wreckage from public criticism, and cold memory entombed the wreckage from the past. The wreckage came to rest, according to Army Corps of Engineers estimates, about 620 fathoms below the surface, finally obscuring one of the most imperialistic icons of the Spanish-Cuban-American War.[67]

After resinking the *Maine*, the *North Carolina* and the *Birmingham*, with flags at half-mast, sailed up the southeastern seaboard of the United States to Hampton Roads, Virginia. The remains of the men were then transferred from the *North Carolina* to the smaller *Birmingham* and taken upriver to the Navy Yard at Washington DC. Here a special detail unloaded the bodies and transported them to Arlington National Cemetery. Once in the federal district, U.S. officials performed a memorial for the remains. A battalion of seamen escorted the caskets to the south side of the State, War, and Navy Department Building at 2:15 p.m. on March 23. The service began at 2:30 p.m. and concluded at 3:15 p.m. President Taft and Father John P. Chidwick, who served as the chaplain on the *Maine*, delivered addresses. Flags on all public buildings were lowered to half-mast for the entire day. The *Birmingham* fired a twenty-one-gun salute. After the memorial service, the funeral procession moved back to Arlington. The procession included a police escort followed by an Army escort, which included a band, a squadron of cavalry, and a battalion of engineers. A naval escort followed made up of the Marine Band, a battalion of marines, a battalion of sailors, the Naval Band, and another battalion of sailors. After them came the clergy followed by the caissons carried by Navy men followed by honorary pallbearers made up of the United Spanish War Veterans. After this came the mourners, including family members, President Taft, the secretary and assistant secretary of war, the secretary of the Navy, and members of Taft's cabinet. Aides, members of interested societies, foreign officers, and citizens concluded the procession. At the grave site, the Navy chaplain Bayard, Father Chidwick, and the United Spanish War Veterans conducted a second memorial service. After this, the bands played taps, and the Marine battalion fired three volleys of muskets. Finally the Army battery fired a twenty-one-gun salute.[68]

Human remains and scrap metal became the relics of American memory in the context of expansion in the early twentieth century. Engineers from the army investigated, authenticated, and imbued these relics with an aura that was magnified by the resinking of the ship and the burial of human bones in Arlington. This coupled with the Cuban government's compliance in producing a memory of redemption and justification further demonstrated the Cuban-American alliance in the face of Old European colonialism. But American officials were also experimenting with imperialism in the Caribbean and in the Pacific during the first two decades of the twentieth century. The relics of the *Maine* helped people imagine and communicate U.S. identity to each other. They formed a network of cultural memory that encouraged people to remember that the reason behind government officials' desire to expand the nation-state was not to oppress others but to free them.

This served the immediate agenda of attempting to gather support of American actions in the frontier, but it also served a longer process of cooling cultural memory. Northerners and Southerners had finally come together, at the exclusion of African Americans, immigrants, Native Americans, and now Cubans, to see themselves as having a common cultural memory. Government officials built and used cultural memory to explain the necessity of the war, to justify the expansion of the bureaucratized state beyond its borders, and to forget the Cuba Libre movement. The negotiation between the government bureaucracy and the American public demonstrates that this collective impetus to "Remember the *Maine*" was coproduced. The memory of emancipation expressed through Lincoln's promise had shifted and now stifled Cuban liberty. Dead bodies of the empire—represented to an American public dubious of the effectiveness that the imperial frontier had on their own lives—became effective places to retrieve a cultural memory that described the Civil War as a conflict that saved the Union, reunited former domestic enemies, and justified imperialist adventure in places where few welcomed the expansion of the U.S. frontier. This was representative of how dire American neophyte imperialists were at operating an informal empire. Had they been able to leave the *Maine* or American bodies in Cuba, they might have had tighter relations with Cubans in the long term. Instead, the retrieval of American imperial cultural memory from

Cuba, represented in the retrieval of important national relics and American bodies from Cuban spaces, demonstrated the limitations of American empire. Politicians and War Department officials symbolically dismantled gunboat diplomacy in Havana Harbor. Military officials buried bodies from the explosion in Arlington National Cemetery along with the aft mast of the ship. They moved the foremast to the U.S. Naval Academy in Annapolis, Maryland, and disinterred the seven sailors buried in the Florida Keys who had died in hospital from injuries received in the explosion and reburied them in Arlington as well. This symbolic remarking of the Cuban-American boundaries foreshadowed the onset of a more sophisticated informal empire based on dollar diplomacy combined with symbolic and diplomatic cover. U.S. officials' strategy to focus on the *Maine* rather than geopolitics of the war critically helped explain to the U.S. public the righteousness of the United States in a new global and imperial age. To protect this memory, the War Department found it necessary to raise up and resink the USS *Maine* in deep international waters, simultaneously revealing and obscuring an ambiguous symbol of American imperial power.

CHAPTER 5

Memories of a Foreign Land

If the Administration has led us into policies which cannot bear discussion in the light of the Declaration of Independence, of the Constitution of the United States, and the teachings of George Washington and Abraham Lincoln, must we bury the Declaration of Independence and the Constitution and Washington's and Lincoln's teachings out of sight, so that they may not interfere with the ambitions and schemes of our rulers? Is it not rather high time to bury such policies so that the great American republic may dare to be itself again?
—Carl Schurz

Following the successful military campaigns in Cuba, McKinley extended the Lincolnian tradition to all white American men regardless of the divided legacy of the Civil War. But the ongoing U.S. occupation of the Philippines complicated the meaning of liberty embedded in Lincoln's promise, for Filipino resistance sundered the connection between individual sacrifice and a "new birth of freedom" for the nation. Stuart Creighton Miller reveals the inconsistencies with the American occupation of the Philippines, while Paul A. Kramer calls the occupation a race war, which utilized the designs of "otherness" to mold American identity in opposition to an invented "Filipino" nationality where no such identity previously existed.[1] These notions of race and empire fashioned in the frontier became the cornerstone of officials' ability to secure the United States' position as a Pacific nation within the

Western Hemisphere. The eventual downturn in violence in the Philippines after 1903 allowed Presidents Theodore Roosevelt, William Howard Taft, and Woodrow Wilson to turn their attention to safeguarding the U.S. empire closer to home. The stakes were high. Cotton producers had open markets in China, and steel magnates had strong business connections with Russia because the tsar needed steel to build the Trans-Siberian Railway. Russia and Germany also posed formidable competition in Asia.

The construction of the Panama Canal formed the centerpiece of the U.S. Atlantic and Pacific naval power and the Roosevelt Corollary to the Monroe Doctrine allowed the United States to invade Caribbean countries whenever the security of the canal or the United States was threatened. The gunboat diplomacy symbolized by the 1906 cruise of the Great White Fleet, dollar diplomacy, and a willingness to send the marines into Central American and Caribbean trouble spots served to strengthen the United States' ascendant position in the Western Hemisphere. The stage was set for a global competition where the United States had nearly total control of the Western Hemisphere and key sea lanes throughout the Pacific Rim to enact the vision of a new kind of empire based on trade agreements and global marketplaces. This kind of empire differed greatly from European-style empires that relied on territorial conquest of foreign lands. Instead, the American empire built semi-colonies that harnessed the power of private investors and protected these interests with the U.S. military without having to territorially occupy distant lands.[2] Domestic unity between the North and the South coincided with the rise to world power. Presidential rhetoric notwithstanding, empire building always came with costs and risks. By examining the organizational, logistical, and even diplomatic difficulties that attended the retrieval of the dead from conflicts in the Philippines, this chapter seeks to illustrate the imperial memories of power that made American empire possible.

This chapter also examines the changed Lincolnian tradition in the light of the less than magnificent campaigns in the Philippines and compares them with domestic disgraces of violence within the boundaries of the nation-state. It suggests that Americans at the beginning of the republic's age of empire could extend or retract Lincoln's promise to specific dead bodies as a way of projecting the memory of American power. These episodes point to the limits of empire building in the early twentieth century before the U.S. entry into the Great War in Europe. Retrieving the dead in hostile surroundings proved a very different experience from the recovery operations after a victorious war in Cuba. These bodies as sites of memory often permitted people to think about the nation and the empire in conflicting ways. On the one hand, the dead demonstrated the limits of empire and the meaninglessness of fighting in foreign lands. On the other hand, the dead became a substitute for the empire by justifying continued military action in order that soldiers not die in vain. Regardless of the interpretation, dead bodies were not meant to represent what actually happened in the Philippines or at home. Rather, they were supposed to represent the layer of U.S. republicanism that overlaid and obscured the reality of U.S. imperialism.

The depression of 1893 demonstrated the instability of the rapidly industrializing U.S. economy. Overproduction, many believed, stymied the efforts of corporate administrators to recoup profits from their industries, which required immense front-end fixed investment that had to be carried for months or years into the process of mass production before they could extract profits from their enterprises. Many looked to the marketplaces in Latin America and Asia to export the surplus brought on by overproduction.[3] Americans voted for Ohio Republican William McKinley in 1896 largely because he promised everyone a "Full Dinner Pail." One way McKinley and his advisors, especially campaign manager and future senator Mark Hanna, sought to fulfill this promise was to engage in overseas expansion in Cuba, Puerto Rico, Hawaii, Guam, and the Philippines. After the United States defeated Spain in Cuba, it bought Spain's colonial possessions in the Philippines for $20 million. In a hotly contested debate in which the languages of social Darwinism, racism, anti-imperialism, and imperialism were used on both sides of the aisle, Congress narrowly voted to annex the Philippines as a colony. This provided the United States with a military presence in the Pacific from which they could more easily keep the "Open Door" in China from shutting as well as completing a Trans-Pacific shipping and distribution network, complete with naval presence and coaling stations, that connected American industries to the doorstep of Asian markets. Emilio Aguinaldo and other Filipino anticolonial activists sought self-determination and democratic government instead. These two narratives intersected on the battlefield as the U.S. military transformed almost overnight from a liberating force to an occupying force designed to bring "benevolent assimilation" to what Governor-General William Howard Taft described as America's "little brown brothers." The program of benevolent assimilation outlined by President McKinley called for Filipino cooperation in exchange for U.S. military protection. The agreement promised Filipinos security in exchange for subjugation to American power. Filipinos initially resisted the occupation, using conventional methods of warfare that doomed them. Aguinaldo, a major general in the Filipino anticolonial movement, quickly shifted his strategy to guerrilla warfare. Unable to overcome American forces, he hoped harassing operations would demoralize U.S. soldiers and U.S. voters as the election of 1900 pitted McKinley against Democrat William Jennings Bryan, who promised to end U.S. imperialism in the Philippines.

Anti-imperialists relied on heating cultural memory as a strategy for undermining the imperialism of the McKinley administration. They relied heavily on a strategy of using the past to call for dramatic change in the presidency, in foreign policy of anti-imperialism, and domestic policies in the way Americans regulated corporations, banking, and currency. Key to this strategy was contrasting the American republic with the American empire. How could a country that revolted out of an empire in the previous century allow itself to acquire colonies? It seemed anathema to republicanism. Perhaps the Princeton graduate and pastor of the Brick Church in New York City, Henry van Dyke, most clearly illustrated this controversy in his Thanksgiving Day sermon in 1898. "Have we lost our own faith in freedom? Are we now ready to sell the American birthright for a mess of pottage in the Philippines?" This allusion to the biblical Esau selling his birthright to his brother Jacob had consequences for the United States, especially since Americans already had a difficult time at home. Here van Dyke located the American empire in the Philippines in close proximity to domestic places to justify his anti-imperialist position. "Is our success in treating the Chinese problem and the Negro problem so notorious that we must attempt to repeat it on a magnified scale eight thousand miles away?" The pastor described the pursuit of empire as a mess of pottage in which he prophesied that the racial violence in Wilmington after the 1898 election represented "the joyous salutes that herald our advance to rule eight millions more of black and yellow people in the islands of the Pacific Ocean." Van Dyke was no racial egalitarian, but such critical memories of the republican America used the past to highlight the close racial connections between home and the frontier.[4]

Republican Carl Schurz likewise hoped to insert the past into cultural memory in his critique of imperialism. His "For the Republic," a speech he delivered at the Philadelphia conference of the Anti-Imperialist Leagues, described the McKinley administration as betraying the republican values of Washington and Lincoln. He also suggested that the imperialists were forfeiting the meaning of the Declaration of Independence. He likened the war in the Philippines to the Civil War, in which Schurz served as a major general, claiming that "the real firing line is not in the suburbs of Manila. The foe is in our own household. The attempt of 1861 was to divide the country. That of 1899 is to destroy its fundamental principles and noblest ideals." Linking wars of the past to the present, the former secretary of the interior also linked the places of the frontier and the homeland together. Schurz, who supported fellow Republican William McKinley in 1896 but now opposed him, went on to liken the debate that grabbed hold of Americans in Washington DC and around the country surrounding annexation of the Philippines to the debate surrounding the Compromise of 1850. Schurz argued that annexation was an equivalent moral question to ending slavery. He consistently tied the anti-imperialist position to the legacy of Washington, quoting the first president often while also associating the memory of Lincoln and the Civil War to a moment in the past that imperialists of the present had forgotten. Slavery at home, like imperial governance abroad, had betrayed American values, Schurz said. He continued tying domestic places to the frontier by accusing the imperialists of taking the fight to Filipinos by declaring that U.S. generals believed the Filipinos "had become 'abusive,' and 'insulting,' and 'defiant,'" words often used by whites to control blacks in domestic spaces.[5]

Filipino nationalists such as Felipe Agoncillo used parallel arguments to argue for Filipino independence. His *To the American People* compared the story of Philippine independence and the narrative of American independence, likening their war against Spain to America's revolution against Great Britain. Agoncillo concluded that "if your sacred *Declaration of Independence* is still existing and respected and honored by all American citizens, the Philippine people ask you for its due accomplishment." This was a deft use of memory deploying America's past accomplishments to critique imperialists, but American officials would neither listen nor meet with Agoncillo before, during, or after the Paris peace conference in which they secured the Philippines from Spain.[6]

Anti-imperialists often linked the U.S. subjugation of Filipinos to slavery while failing to recognize the lack of equality and civil rights for African Americans. But not all did. Some understood the intimate and violent connections between empire and Jim Crow. If Schurz's comparison alluded to the way white Americans treated African Americans, anti-imperialist, poet, and Unitarian minister John White Chadwick was explicit in using the past to compare the repertoire of imperial power in its domestic and foreign expressions. Like Schurz, Chadwick used the past to critique American imperial memory. The Massachusetts-born Unitarian associated Emilio Aguinaldo with Samuel Adams and the Filipino fight against the United States with the American Revolution. But Chadwick also likened the Philippines to events closer to home. Many imperialists claimed Aguinaldo did not represent Filipinos and only came to power through military dictatorship. Chadwick countered this claim: "The method of Aguinaldo's election to the presidency was more fair than that in half a dozen of our own Southern States during the last thirty years." The graduate of Harvard Divinity School elaborated, "We do not have to go to Luzon for American barbarities. We have them nearer home. We have them in North Carolina, in South Carolina, in Ohio, in Texas, in Georgia." Chadwick turned his attention to a recent lynching, which was probably that of Sam Hose (also known as Tom Wilkes) in Newnan, Georgia, just outside Atlanta. Many from Atlanta heard of Hose's capture—he had been accused of killing his white employer—and Atlantans traveled to Newnan by train to witness what everyone knew would be his premeditated murder. Hose's death was indeed brutal. It was witnessed by more than two thousand people as whites mutilated and cut off parts of his body, burned him alive, and then sold his body parts for souvenirs. Chadwick asserted, "We have heard nothing of the Filipinos that approaches its infernal wickedness."[7]

Here Chadwick's connection became explicit. "Why have I lugged this Georgia lynching into a sermon on the present distress? Because the Georgia lynching is part of it." And then he made his anti-imperialist argument as explicit as he could. "We have a race problem here at home in our 'parochial politics' so vast that we should not be greedy of another in the Philippines." The lynching in Georgia, contended Chadwick, "conveys a needed lesson, viz., that *race antipathy* is a social factor of immense importance." He pointed out that "the long catalogue of lynchings . . . is so much extended that the irony of our setting out to civilize some millions of Filipinos must be apparent to anyone who has a grin of humor as big as a hypothetic atom." He could clearly see how race layered the overlapping geography of empire and nation, bringing two places together that were separated by the Pacific Ocean. He believed that white people should leave Filipinos and the Philippines alone. "It cannot be that this great nation, which has done such glorious things for freedom and humanity, will persist in doing that which must affront the common justice of mankind."[8] Chadwick demanded change, and he injected a white hot memory into the cultural memory of America's involvement in the Philippines.

Imperialists, however determined to prevent change in political leadership and transformation of cultural memory, kept using techniques to cool cultural memory in their pursuit of empire. William Howard Taft, the governor-general of the Philippines, asked Americans to stay on course and invest financially in the Philippines. He suggested that the Declaration of Independence was "forgotten" in the Philippines and that anti-imperialists had misrepresented "their legitimate aspirations based upon their independence." Filipinos were not "satisfied," claimed Taft, in part because they had not been "yet pacified." Here and throughout his address to Union Reading College, Taft suggested that Filipino claims for independence were illegitimate because they had not yet created investment, infrastructure, and a legitimate government. Only American corporations could produce the investment needed to establish an independent Philippines, and Taft promised investors that they would receive handsome rewards for their troubles, especially if Congress stayed the course by reducing the tariff on tobacco and sugar, which the McKinley administration supported. Investment was "the only method that I see by which the American trade in these islands can be made profitable and the American merchants who have ventured here can be made rich." He did not ask investors to act out of altruism or patriotism. "It is most fortunate that we find moving toward the same end both honor and profit."[9]

Secretary of War Elihu Root, campaigning for McKinley's reelection, was more direct in his belief in the illegitimacy of Philippine claims for independence. Root described Aguinaldo in racial terms as a "Chinese half-breed" who instigated true "Oriental treachery" when Filipinos turned on their U.S. allies in February 1899. Aguinaldo betrayed his countrymen and the sentiments in the Declaration of Independence, said Root, because "the people of the Philippine Islands never consented to that [Malolos Constitution] government." He also accused anti-imperialists of denigrating the troops when they criticized the war. Root blamed Bryan and his supporters if troops had low morale, and he stopped just short of accusing them of traitorous collaboration with the Aguinaldo government, which, like the anti-imperialists, desired an American retreat from the Philippines. Root leveled a stinging critique of McKinley's critics. The secretary of state, in fact, denied that American involvement in the Philippines could be characterized as imperialism. When attacking an anti-imperialist sticking point that empire would change the nature of the U.S. republic, Root clearly illustrated his understanding of how domestic places inside the United States influenced the frontier, especially in places like the Pacific archipelago. "The government of the Philippine Islands will not affect the character of our institutions, but the character of our institutions will determine and mould the government of the Philippine islands." He continued his attack by questioning Bryan's sincerity in the campaign, pointing out how duplicitous the Democrats were when it came to anti-imperialism abroad in contrast with their enforcement of the color line and Jim Crow laws domestically. "Is the party which is governing and avows its intention to still govern ten millions of black citizens in the South, without their consent, whether by law or fraud or force, really disturbed about imperialism and the Declaration of Independence?"[10]

Root continued this line of attack mercilessly, declaring that U.S. involvement in the Philippines would not change the "character of this republic," even if inside the United States, "the party which governs the city of New York, the party which governs Mississippi and North Carolina, with their class of hereditary voters, may distrust its capacity to maintain its virtue while it governs others." But Root claimed that "American love and liberty and justice" would sustain the republic "as a living force" in the Philippines just as it had along the "Atlantic and the Lakes and plains of our own land." He understood where the overlapping places of nation and empire existed within the U.S. empire. He attempted to make these places "contiguous" to illustrate his accusations that anti-imperialists, and specifically William Jennings Bryan, were disingenuous in their claims. To secure the authenticity of the McKinley administration's war in the Philippines, the secretary embraced the military dead from the Philippines to justify why Americans voters should reelect McKinley in 1900. "The bodies of our men who fell during that dreadful night and the days of conflict which followed have been brought back reverently across the Pacific and laid in honored graves among their countrymen," said Root. And he asserted that their work was not yet done. "But, not yet—not yet had the soil stained by their blood been surrendered to their slayers. Not yet has the treacherous and wicked attack, which they died to defeat, been turned into victory by the act of an American President." Root's political campaign speech deployed the memory of a conflict that shielded the past and resisted change, especially the political change that anti-imperialists were hoping to make. Root's memory was cold. Whether hot or cold, anti-imperialists and imperialists unmistakably understood how the "contiguous" if not shared places of empire and nation made cultural memory and how the debate about empire in the Philippines was just as much about American identity at home.

McKinley won the election of 1900, and he continued to miscalculate and mishandle the Philippine war. McKinley's victory thwarted Aguinaldo's strategy, but the unequal contest between Americans and Filipinos continued until 1913. McKinley failed to keep his campaign promise to end the war in sixty days, knowing that the United States needed to control Manila if it wanted to influence events in Asia.[11] McKinley had placed military and civil power in the hands of Gen. Wesley Merritt and later Gen. Elwell Stephen Otis. This was a disaster, as these generals disregarded local and cultural customs and lacked the diplomatic and negotiation skills needed to assimilate colonized Filipinos. This kind of martial power signified the beginning of a much longer imperial process described by historian Paul Kramer in which American colonizers "invented Filipinos" by reacting to "barbaric" Muslim resisters and producing a transnational empire of race and brutality.[12] McKinley eventually replaced Otis with Gen. Arthur MacArthur and appointed Taft to establish a civil government in the Philippines. This proved disastrous as well; Taft and MacArthur infamously failed to cooperate with one another. The death of hundreds of thousands of Filipinos and thousands of American soldiers ensued. First General Otis and then General MacArthur ordered and oversaw horrific military practices to counter Aguinaldo's guerrilla strategy. The military leadership then tried to censor journalists, only giving access to those who would distort the information that Americans received through press outlets.

For a while the propaganda was largely successful and even managed to help mitigate calls by the Anti-Imperialist League to end the violence. But eventually the war became a public relations disaster, and news of atrocities began leaking into public consciousness. By 1901 McKinley again had to correct the U.S. occupational strategy. He first split military from civil responsibilities. Then he replaced MacArthur with Maj. Gen. Adna Chafee. This strategic victory for Taft enhanced his position, and after McKinley's death, President Theodore Roosevelt handed all civil authority to him and appointed him governor-general of the Philippines. But this did little to change the circumstances on the ground. The split responsibilities actually produced tension between civil and military officials seeking authority to control the Philippines. Taft and Chafee cooperated worse than Taft and MacArthur had. And Chafee responded to Filipino insurrection with even greater vindictiveness than had MacArthur. Chafee unleashed a whole series of punitive measures that directly ignored Order Number 100 issued in 1863, which had set forth U.S. rules of war. Chafee authorized the "water cure" to obtain information about Filipino forces, implemented scorched earth tactics that razed entire villages as punishment for defying U.S. "authority," and constructed concentration camps that were responsible for the deaths of some of the guilty and many of the innocents.[13]

This sort of war of imperialism called for a remembrance that was significantly different from the commemoration of the Civil War dead. Places like Manila, Balingiga, and Caloocan could not commemorate the dead the way that Gettysburg, Antietam, or Andersonville sanctified the spaces where the soldiers actually fought and died. Commemorations by American soldiers over the Balingiga dead on the island of Samar in September 1901 offered one example of how soldiers could apply a vulgar version of Lincoln's promise to the confusing violence that accompanied overseas empire building. Inhabitants of the town of Balingiga planned to attack Company C of the Ninth U.S. Infantry, who occupied the town. Townsfolk smuggled men and machetes into a church on the night of September 26 by hiding them in coffins and feigning a funeral for cholera victims.[14] The next morning, Balingiga's police chief, Valeriano Abanador, approached Company C's sentry guard and began talking to him. In an instant he grabbed the guard's gun and shot him. In another moment, bolomen rushed out of the church and into Company C's camp. In the fighting that followed, all but six men of the company were either killed or wounded. The six escaped by boat and made it to the closest U.S. garrison at Basey, commanded by Capt. Edwin Bookmiller. Shocked by their report, Bookmiller and fifty-five men of his Company G, along with the six survivors of Company C, picked up weapons, secured a boat, and returned to Balingiga.

When they made shore and entered the camp, the soldiers were stunned. They saw their comrades' bodies had been mutilated. "Bodies were split open and stuffed with flour, jam, coffee, and molasses." Even the company's dog had been killed and mutilated. Bookmiller and his men were searching for perpetrators when they stumbled upon a Filipino funeral service commemorating the twenty-eight Filipinos who had died in the morning's raid. Their bodies lay in a trench. Bookmiller stopped the funeral and decided to replace it with a spontaneous memorial service of his own. His men found the twenty Filipino gravediggers who were hiding in the bush. The captain forced the gravediggers to pull all the dead Filipinos out of the trench and stack them in a pile. Then he coerced them at gunpoint to gather the U.S. dead and put the mutilated carcasses into the trench. Bookmiller, who upon his own death in 1946 would be buried in Arlington National Cemetery, began reading scriptures as a memorial service. He ordered the Filipinos to fill the trench with dirt while his bugler played taps. Afterwards, the company soaked the dead Filipinos with kerosene and set the pile of flesh alight. As the flames consumed the bodies, Bookmiller handed the twenty gravediggers over to the six survivors of Company C, who executed them. Then Bookmiller ordered his men to burn the village of Balingiga. The somber bugler played taps as they executed and burned—a striking juxtaposition that foreshadowed the atrocities committed by some U.S. forces sixty years later in Vietnam. Certainly, as the press claimed, Balingiga "was the worst disaster for the United States Army since Custer's fate at Little Big Horn."[15] But what was more striking than the military defeat of Company C was the way the Americans treated the dead. Bookmiller's funeral service was a perverse enactment of Lincoln's promise. He extended the state's commitment to commemorate members of the fallen community, but he achieved this by simultaneously desecrating Filipinos. This gave an additional brutal meaning to the Lincolnian tradition in the context of overseas imperialism.[16]

Even when Americans respected Filipino sacred spaces, it became very difficult to overlay the symbolism of "benevolent assimilation" on the places of Filipino memory. For example, Americans found it difficult to sanctify the space of colonial occupation in Paco Cemetery in the heart of Manila. Spanish colonizers originally built it for Spanish citizens. It had an octagonal shape with an inner circle and a Roman Catholic chapel dedicated to St. Pancratius, a fourteen-year-old martyr of ancient Rome. But in 1820 a cholera outbreak forced its rushed completion, and many Filipino families got access to the cemetery and buried their dead in this colonial space. They placed cholera victims in tombs in the walls of the cemetery. By the end of the century, the cemetery was a fitting place to challenge Spanish occupation and produce anticolonial unity. It was also the initial burial spot of the politician, poet, and nonviolent anticolonial José Rizal. The Spanish executed Rizal in 1896, which made him a martyr and helped set off the Philippine revolutionary movement. Rizal's nonviolent anticolonialism became a powerful weapon against the Spanish empire. In a pathetic attempt to erase the memory of Rizal and keep his burial space from becoming a shrine for protesters, the Spanish refused to hand over his body to his family and secretly buried Rizal in Paco Cemetery. His sister, however, apparently located the spot after searching for several days and paying off Spanish guards.

When the United States became the occupying power in Manila in 1898, empire builders sought to differentiate their presence and purpose from that of Spanish colonial rulers. The Americans formally recognized Rizal's burial space and allowed his family to reclaim his remains. Rizal's family took his body but marked his burial space in Paco Cemetery with a monument; it became nationalistic sacred space. But this produced numerous awkward tensions. Perhaps this was most evident in a burial ceremony conducted by U.S. soldiers on November 1, 1898, All Saints Day, a few months after the Spanish had surrendered and the Spanish-American War had ended, a few days before the violence in Wilmington erupted, and three months before U.S. soldiers attacked Manila and Caloocan. A special correspondent to *Harper's Weekly*, John Bass, reported on Paco Cemetery as part of the sights and sounds of Manila after the war. Bass chose to spend part of All Saints Day in the cemetery in part because the religious nature of the day brought many Catholic Filipinos there to attend Mass and light candles by the graves of loved ones. Bass mentioned the religiosity of the place, briefly reporting that "the two concentric rings of walls blaze with the light of thousands of candles and small lamps," with people milling about in conversation and commemoration of lost loved ones. But overall he chose not to describe the religious nature of the burial ground; rather, he related the fashions of the people in ways reminiscent of how Edward Said described Orientalism.

> I never knew before what became of all the Derby hats of bygone years, but now I know that they are sent out to the Philippines. Little native men in spick and span shirts with the tails floating to the wind, wear Derbys

of every conceivable shapes, some perched on the top of their heads after the fashion of the Irish music-hall comedian.... Little Philippine women with stiff clean piña dresses and black gauze veils over their heads, looking neat and wholesome, swing along with that peculiar undulatory motion of the body which reminds one a little of the snake. Mestiza girls in costumes not quite Philippine, and certainly not European, hold their heads high and stiff at the common people as befits their superior caste. Spanish women, in dresses after the Paris fashions in the sixties, hang indolently on the arms of gallant Spanish officers who carry themselves with the haughty pride of conquerors. And, finally, Jimmy Green, in an ill-fitting brown duck suit with a flannel shirt and a campaign hat, slouches along to see the sights.

This strange depiction of the people and the cemetery of Catholic and colonial Manila set the stage for what happened next.

Unexpectedly the familiar sound of the old hymn "Nearer, my God, to Thee" swelled through the cemetery. We hurried to the spot. There about a grave half filled with water stood a company of big American soldiers, singing, hat in hand, the last hymn over the grave of their comrade. To one side, rifle in hand, a squad of men awaited the moment to fire the last salute. In the uncertain light of the coming night, touched with the distant sheen of many candles, surrounded by strange people in a strange land, they let the coffin down with a splash into the grave. The volley startled the Spaniards and Filipinos, and when the trumpeter sounded taps a dense crowd had gathered around the soldier's grave.

Bass noted how surreal the ceremony was. The juxtaposition of the two cultural views of death depicted the Americans implementing Lincoln's promise to commemorate the dead in the middle of an exotic scene. Even Bass was surprised. He seemed to relate that the dead American was out of place in the cemetery. How could Americans bury the noble dead in a shallow water-filled grave surrounded by boneyards and irreverent behavior?[17]

This uncomfortable juxtaposition was even more evident in 1899, when U.S. forces became official colonial overseers and the military needed to quickly bury the men who had died in the fighting against General Aguinaldo's forces on the outskirts of Manila. Perhaps U.S. representatives sought to overlap the sacredness of Rizal's martyrdom with dead soldiers in Paco Cemetery in the early days before U.S. annexation. Just as Rizal had died a martyr to Spanish colonialism, so too, believed U.S. officials, had Americans died in liberating Manila. But in time, most of the American dead buried there had perished while fighting Aguinaldo. A leader of the Filipino independence movement, Aguinaldo and fellow Ilustrados had helped establish the Katipunan Society for a revolutionary movement out of the remains of Rizal's own organization, La Liga Filipina. This, among other connections of class, ethnicity, and education, somewhat tied Aguinaldo to Rizal, although they differed significantly in their anticolonial strategies.[18] The U.S. Army's symbolic attempt to fuse the revolutionary spirit of Rizal with the benevolent assimilation symbolized by dead U.S. soldiers in Paco Cemetery simply did not work.[19] The cemetery filled with dead Americans became instead a site commemorating the occupation of the Philippines. It formed an anticolonial space that U.S. presence could not sanctify. Thus military officials had to reinterpret cultural memory of the war by retrieving bodies and returning them to the United States where Americans could control their symbolic meaning without the threat of Filipinos critiquing American relics. Just as in Cuba, retrieving dead bodies became an important aspect of how Americans retrieved and communicated cultural memory of the conflict.

Of the nearly 125,000 troops, more than 4,000 died and another 3,000 were wounded. More died from disease than in battle. The military authorized initially two recovery missions to the Philippines. The burial party superintendent was David. H. Rhodes, who had previously served as a landscape gardener at Arlington National Cemetery, an inspector of national cemeteries, and a register of marking American graves in Cuba. F. S. Croggon took over from Rhodes the following year. Unlike the Civil War, when thousands of soldiers died as unknowns, these contractors vastly improved the ability to identify the dead by painstakingly documenting evidence and recommending new uniform policies that the U.S. military would later implement. Their reports detail how they located, recovered, and returned the dead to the United States. In repatriating the bodies, the U.S. Army signified that the soil of the Philippines, like Cuba, could not adequately serve as a final resting place. The War Department did not propose an American cemetery in the Philippines and would not dedicate one until 1960.

The enormous distance between battlefield and military cemetery was an indication of the difference between the Civil War and a colonial war. The hundreds of U.S. outposts throughout the Philippine islands made it difficult to recover the bodies. Before the days of identification tags, or "dog tags," the U.S. Army buried men with a sealed bottle. This began a new way of identifying the dead, an improvement over the methods used during the Civil War. Inside the bottle, a piece of paper identified the body. But sometimes the writing on the paper faded or the cork did not seal properly, destroying identification information. This was not a uniform process either; some units did not have bottles to bury and had to find other means of identifying the grave. Sometimes graves went unmarked or were disturbed by people or animals. On top of this, the mix of volunteer soldiers and regular army men coupled with the friction between military officers and civilian contractors brought confusion and uncertainty to the process. Both Rhodes and Croggon complained numerous times about the uncooperative spirit of many post commanders and the complete lack of professionalism in taking care of the dead.[20]

To make matters worse, Rhodes and Croggon took their directives from officers in Washington DC, and these often seemed impractical to execute. For example, the adjutant general's office in Washington DC provided the list of the dead and the location of the buried, but this report had many errors. Uniform measures for reporting the whereabouts of the dead did not exist. Volunteer units and regulars differed in the way that they marked the spaces of the dead. Some towns on the list did not exist, while other locations where graves existed sometimes were not mentioned. It made it difficult for the superintendents to untangle the whereabouts of many graves. When they could not locate a town that was supposed to exist, they could do nothing but move on to the next location. When they found a grave, sometimes it was empty. Some areas with abandoned posts, meanwhile, remained hostile. Rhodes often required a military escort to protect his men from enemy fire while they did their recovery work, but sometimes this was

FIG. 1. Photo of the Paco Cemetery boneyard in Manila. This was part of the scene journalist John Bass described on All Saints Day in Manila. From *Scenes Taken in the Philippines, Japan, and on the Pacific Relating to Soldiers* by J. D. Givens (privately published, 1914). Courtesy of the Huntington Library, San Marino CA.

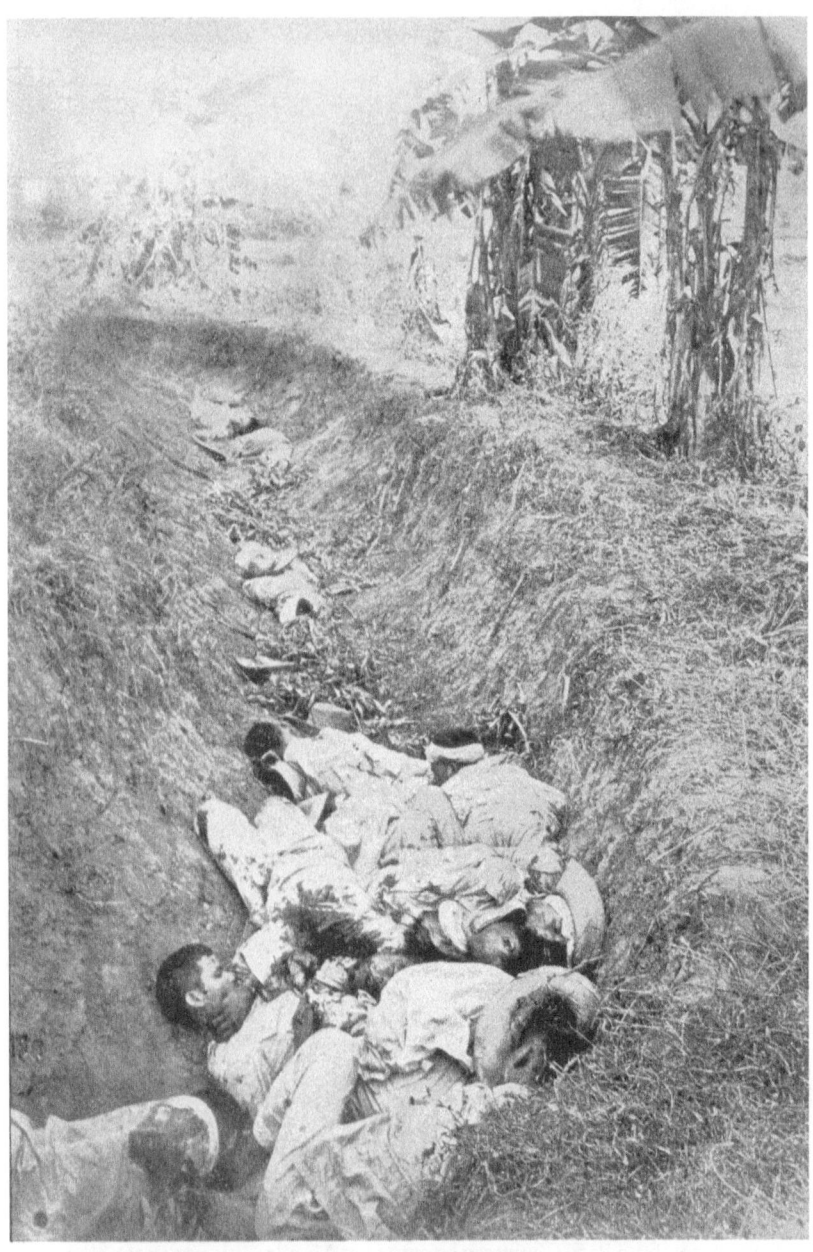

FIG. 2. Trench filled with dead Filipino combat soldiers. From *Scenes Taken in the Philippines, Japan, and on the Pacific Relating to Soldiers* by J. D. Givens (privately published, 1914). Courtesy of the Huntington Library, San Marino CA.

FIG. 3. Dead along the road to Caloocan outside of Manila. From *Harper's Pictorial History of the War with Spain*. Courtesy of the Huntington Library, San Marino CA.

FIG. 4. The USS *Maine* wreckage lying in Havana Harbor taken ca. 1900. Sailors' bones remained in the hulk until the Army Corps of Engineers retrieved them a decade later. Library of Congress American Memory Project, https://cdn.loc.gov/service/pnp/det/4a30000/4a31000/4a31800/4a31863r.jpg.

FIG. 5. A panoramic view of the wreckage near the bottom of the cofferdam, June 21, 1911. Engineers built the cofferdam around the wreck and then pumped water out of the dam, slowly revealing the sunken ship. Library of Congress American Memory Project, http://lcweb2.loc.gov/pnp/pan/6a23000/6a23400/6a23443r.jpg.

FIG. 6. A panoramic view of the wreckage inside the cofferdam. Notice the rock piles along the inside of the cofferdam. This was to stop leaking due to the difficulty in constructing the dam and may have hindered recovering some of the material objects of the wreckage. Library of Congress American Memory Project, July 18, 1911, https://www.loc.gov/resource/pan.6a22694/.

FIG. 7. A panoramic view of the cofferdam just before the Army Corps of Engineers began draining it. National Archives and Records Administration, "Wreck of the U.S.S. Maine, 16 June 1911," http://www.archives.gov/exhibits/panoramic_photography/images/wreck_uss_maine.html.

FIG. 8. A panoramic view of the Spanish-American War veterans group commemorating the sinking of the ship entitled "13th anniversary, destruction of the USS *Maine*, Havana Harbor, 15 February 1911." The cofferdam is still under construction. Library of Congress American Memory Project, https://www.loc.gov/resource/pan.6a22663/.

FIG. 9. At five-foot-nine and 186 pounds, Bluethenthal played center for the Princeton Tigers and received All-America honors from several rating agencies in 1911 and 1912. Princeton went undefeated in 1911, the season Bluethenthal was named a second-team All-American, with a record of 8–0–2. The Princeton 1911 team was retroactively named the National Champions for 1911 by several rating agencies. Courtesy of Cape Fear Museum of History and Science, Wilmington NC.

FIG. 10. Arthur Bluethenthal at a writing desk composing a letter, somewhere in Serbia near Monastir. Most of his letters were handwritten, but his letter to friends Arthur and Davey was typewritten. Courtesy of Cape Fear Museum of History and Science, Wilmington NC.

FIG. 11. Arthur and his friends probably at his father's beach house on Wrightsville Beach near Wilmington. Arthur is on the far right holding an oar and dressed in women's swimming attire. Arthur's friends share the slightly out-of-focus frame, but it is not known whether his friends Arthur, Davey, and "Nuts" are in the photograph. Courtesy of Cape Fear Museum of History and Science, Wilmington NC.

FIG. 12. Arthur Bluethenthal took this photo of a man picking up the body parts of his granddaughter killed by a Bulgarian artillery shell in Monastir moments after the child's horrific death. Courtesy of Cape Fear Museum of History and Science, Wilmington NC.

FIG. 13. Formal military photograph of Robert Burton House, future collector of war records and chancellor of the University of North Carolina at Chapel Hill. North Carolina State Archives, Raleigh NC.

FIG. 14. Kiffin Yates Rockwell and his airplane in France. North Carolina State Archives, Raleigh NC.

FIG. 15. Nurses of Hospital No. 65 in North Carolina just before leaving for duty in France. North Carolina State Archives, Raleigh NC.

FIG. 16. Nurses of Hospital No. 65 just one month before Ione Bain returned to North Carolina. North Carolina State Archives, Raleigh NC.

FIG. 17. Base Camp Hospital No. 65 in Kerhoun, France, where Ione Bain and Irene Brewster worked. North Carolina State Archives, Raleigh NC.

FIG. 18. Formal military photograph of Thomas J. Bullock sent to the archives by his widow, Cleopatra. North Carolina State Archives, Raleigh NC.

FIG. 19. The work of chaplains and the Graves Registration Service. On each cross is the tin square identifying the dead. The cross on the right has a dog tag affixed to the cross above the tintype. North Carolina State Archives, Raleigh NC.

FIG. 20. An example of an early temporary American military cemetery in France. Graves Registration Service tintypes are visible on these wooden crosses. These bodies would be removed and reburied at least once more before receiving a final burial in France or in the United States. North Carolina State Archives, Raleigh NC.

FIG. 21. North Carolina officers viewing a temporary cemetery. These transitory burial grounds maintain the identification information in the form of tintypes on the front of the wooden cross and the soldiers' dog tags on the back of the crosses in the foreground. North Carolina State Archives, Raleigh NC.

FIG. 22. A view of the landscape in which Graves Registration Service personnel had to operate. This difficult terrain marked by rifles, helmets, and personal gear made it difficult for GRS agents to always identify bodies reliably. North Carolina State Archives, Raleigh NC.

FIG. 23. U.S. soldiers visit the grave of a fallen comrade in a cemetery in Hurbache, France. The GRS had to consolidate the dead from thousands of burial sites in France, many of which were in the cemeteries of small French communities like the one pictured above. North Carolina State Archives, Raleigh NC.

FIG. 24. U.S. soldiers visiting a temporary gravesite of fallen comrades in its early phase of construction. North Carolina State Archives, Raleigh NC.

FIG. 25. A twilight service given by Chaplain Vaughn at the cemetery in Moranville, France, on November 12, 1918. North Carolina State Archives, Raleigh NC.

FIG. 26. Warren Harding using a microphone, which was placed just beyond the small podium, at the dedication speech of the Unknown Soldier at the Arlington amphitheater. Library of Congress, American Memory Project, http://www.loc.gov/pictures/resource/npcc.22389/.

FIG. 27. The crowd assembled behind the amphitheater at the dedication of the Tomb of the Unknown Soldier in Arlington National Cemetery on November 21, 1921. The microphone can be seen next to the stairs leading up to the crypt. Library of Congress American Memory Project, http://www.loc.gov/pictures/resource/npcc.22393/.

FIG. 28. Santiago Surrender Tree in Cuba. Caption: "The Surrender Tree Site is one of the 'musts' on tours for American Tourists visiting Santiago de Cuba. The Spanish Commander surrendered the city of Santiago de Cuba on July 17, 1898, to the United States Army under General William Shafter on terms agreed upon at this Tree and virtually ended the Spanish-American War. The Surrender Tree Site is maintained by the United States Government." Photographed January 1957 by Oscar H. Guerra, American consul. National Archives and Records Administration, College Park MD.

impossible to secure. Recovering bodies in the Philippines and returning them across the Pacific to the United States was difficult and wracked with poor military planning and neglect.[21]

After receiving his orders, Rhodes left Washington DC on September 20, 1900, assembled his fifteen assistants, secured supplies in San Francisco, and left California on board the *Hancock*. They arrived in Manila on October 29, 1900. The war had been raging for nearly two years. Rhodes unloaded coffins, tools, and supplies from the *Hancock*. On November 14, his crew began their mission, concentrating on cemeteries around Manila. They secured 275 bodies at Malate and 89 from Paco Cemetery. For the rest of the year, the burial party worked in Manila and the Laguna Bay area. It was tedious work made more difficult by the ambivalence of U.S. officers in the field. For example, Rhodes sent a letter in late November to the naval commandant at Cavite, asking for a list of sailors and marines buried in the naval cemetery. He received no response. On December 4, Rhodes took two assistants and went to Cavite and met with Commandant Captain Freemont. The captain turned the men over to a surgeon, Dr. Wagner, who was supposed to keep the burial records. But Wagner did not have them, as his "responsibility ended when a body left the door of the hospital." Incensed, Rhodes went back to Freemont, who sent him to Master-at-Arms J. S. Eckstrom, "who had charge of the graves." Freemont gave Rhodes a list of fifteen dead men. When Rhodes arrived at the cemetery with Eckstrom, there were thirty graves, and Eckstrom had no idea which gravesite went with which name. The Master-at-Arms had other duties to perform, and sometimes burials were completed without Eckstrom's knowledge, and he would only find out about them much later.

Rhodes made sketches of the graves and left. He returned two days later with the corps and coffins to reclaim the dead. When he asked Freemont again for the burial records to confirm the names of the dead, the captain claimed he "knew nothing about graves, nor about the Marines, nor did he want to know anything about them." Rhodes opened the thirty-one graves, but only twenty-four had bodies in them. After much work and cross-referencing, he was able to identify most of the bodies, but his experiences at Cavite caused him to report that "it will be observed that nothing short of gross carelessness or rank stupidity had had full sway with respect to the matter of the graves of the dead at this Naval Cemetery, during the past two years." The quartermaster general noted in the margin of Rhodes's report next to this passage the word "omit." This critique did not appear in the official report to the secretary of war and thus never made it into public record. Consequently, there was never any official inquiry to investigate the matter. But in his September 30, 1901, report to the quartermaster general, Rhodes continued to level heavy criticism against Freemont and Wagner. "Common respect and decency, both for the dead and their relatives and friends, demands better treatment." The conditions at Cavite for reclaiming the bodies and the memory of the soldiers were "a disgrace to all concerned." Rhodes requested that the quartermaster general forward this section of his report to the secretary of the Navy, but again it was omitted from the quartermaster general's report, and no investigation was initiated.

Rhodes diligently and efficiently carried out his duties, and despite setbacks, he kept his schedule fairly well. Around Manila, railroads accessed much of Luzon. Rhodes and the corps would travel by train. Before they left, Rhodes organized shipments of caskets by rail to intermittent locations along the railroad concluding at Dagupan-Pang terminus. The corps went to Dagupan, picked up the waiting caskets, and ventured to the interior to retrieve bodies. They brought the full caskets back to the train for delivery to Manila and eventual shipment to the United States. Many would go to Arlington, but most would be sent to the soldiers' home towns. The corps made their way back to Manila, likewise recovering bodies along the way. Again Rhodes complained about the field officers' lack of urgency in keeping burial records. On January 28, 1901, Rhodes went to Tarlac on Luzon to investigate rumors of buried soldiers there, even though he had received telegrams claiming there were no bodies. Eventually he discovered two bodies: "One was found in a lately-plowed field about half a mile out of town, and the other in the native Cemetery, covered up by deposits of sand washed from adjacent roadways. Neither grave was marked in any way." Rhodes believed that "'Post Records,' if there be any, are taken away with them to some other point." This made it extremely difficult to recover men who had died while one company controlled a garrison but were forgotten when another company relieved it. The corps nevertheless continued its work and returned to Manila on February 26 to prepare for the next segment of their mission.

From this point Rhodes's burial party would completely utilize water transportation, as no rail lines existed linking the islands of Samar, Mindanao, Luzon, Leyte, Cebu, and Negros. The problem for Rhodes was that he could not obtain a suitable transport. The only available U.S. vessel, the *Sacramento*, was undergoing repairs in dry dock. He could find no other ship, so Rhodes secured a local private vessel, *El Cano*, from the Compania Maritima Line. The corps left Manila on *El Cano* on March 27, 1901. This posed a different logistical problem than the railroads of Luzon; they had to carry all the caskets and all the tools and supplies with them on the ship and recovered bodies would remain in the ship's hold until they returned to Manila. On April 21, the group had to secure small boats to get to shore in the shallow harbor of Antimonan. The *El Cano* had to anchor in deeper water. Upon their return with filled caskets, they "encountered a rough sea and a heavy ground swell which nearly swamped the small boats used, but they finally arrived at the ship with the bodies and the men on board." This also posed difficulties when Rhodes wanted a military escort to help him reach dangerous areas still under fire. The next day, the corps requested the help of the commanding officer at Mauban to supply troops for a two-day tour of hot spots at Binangonan and Baler. Troops arrived on board *El Cano* fully supplied, but the ship had to wait several hours for a commissioned officer to report and take command of the military escort. In the meantime, the commanding officer at the base changed his mind and recalled the troops because "he was expecting an attack by insurgents, and would need his men." The troops disembarked from the ship, and Rhodes was forced to skip Binangonan because "it was absolutely unsafe to attempt to visit it without a strong escort."[22]

In light of these kinds of difficulties, a typical day for the expedition included treacherous travel, hard work, and lots of downtime in between stops. The ship would leave port in the evening and sail to the next destination. Rhodes would have his laborers on shore by 6:00 or 7:00 a.m., but sometimes they made land before 5:00 a.m. Rhodes would try to secure

Army carts and horses, but he usually had to commandeer local bull carts to carry the coffins and tools to the gravesite. Occasionally locals did not have bull carts, and so the laborers would carry the tools and empty coffins to the interior by hand, locate the graves, disinter and disinfect the bodies, place the remains in the coffin, and carry the full coffins back to the ship. Sometimes the burial spaces were near the shore or in the town. Often the shallow harbors required the ship to anchor a mile or two away from shore, and the corps would have to row their launches full of coffins and supplies from the ship to the shore. Most of the time the bodies were buried in the interior, and the corps would have to march ten, twenty, as many as thirty-six miles into the interior negotiating incredibly rough terrain, monsoons, typhoons, mudslides, and the threat of attack before venturing back along the same route with the recovered bodies. When multiple locations were within several miles of each other, Rhodes split his corps into two or three groups and sent them out to the different sites. At times, no roads led to the locations, and the corps would have to use flat-bottomed boats made by locals to navigate upstream. There was always the threat of capsizing from the hard-flowing currents. It was a daunting expedition, but according to his reports, Rhodes remained disciplined, resourceful, and persistent.

Despite every effort, retrieval and identification remained difficult goals for the burial party to accomplish. On April 27 the *El Cano* returned to Manila to unload the 212 recovered bodies, took on 425 more caskets, and began the tour of the Southern Islands. At Torrijos, Marinduque, the corps recovered three of the four bodies they were looking for. They could not identify any of them, however, and so Rhodes placed the remains of the three men in a single coffin. At the next location on Masbate, Rhodes did not disinter two soldiers "by request of the officers present" because the deceased were "deserters." These dead soldiers received no investigation and had no court-martial while alive, and even after death, instead of being commemorated, they remained buried and forgotten in foreign soil. Rhodes avoided the next stop at the Catubig River due to "'Lucaban' and his 'insurrectos.'" On the island of Leyte, Rhodes and his men went ashore to recover a body but could not locate the grave. The troops stationed nearby had previously tried to find the missing soldier's grave but failed. Rhodes commented, "In as much as the 'Padre' had been bitterly opposed to his burial in the Cemetery at the time, they [the soldiers] supposed that the marker, if not the body, had purposely been removed." In some instances, Filipinos refused to cooperate, and burial locations consequently remained hidden to Americans and only known to locals. For example, on the island of Cebu, Rhodes secured a military escort and made shore at Sogod. When the party approached the village, "the native hombres all deserted their shacks and fled to the adjacent hills and ravines." Clearly concerned that the American unit was an occupation force bent on military confrontation, local people fled to the interior. No one remained who could point out the grave. Eventually the corps found the single grave "about a mile back from the shore." Rhodes noted, "No shots were fired and the party returned safely to the ship."[23]

In another instance, the body of Pvt. Albin E. Carter of Company G of the Forty-fourth Volunteers was never recovered. A captured "muchacho" claimed "upon interrogation" that Carter was buried on a mountain near the Ibajay River near Pandan, Panay. But Filipinos dug up the body "and the remains thrown in the Ibajay river to keep the searching party of Americans from finding them." American bodies could serve as sites of protest and anticolonialism for some Filipinos. Indeed, the corps looked for Carter's body but without success.

Rhodes's tour continued until the end of June 1901. The burial corps traveled almost eight thousand miles by land and sea recovering bodies. Rhodes and the rest of the undertakers returned to the United States in July after Rhodes released the Filipino laborers. Despite many hardships he was able to reclaim more than 1,400 bodies; he was unable to identify only 11. But the remains of many other soldiers were left behind because they could not be located. His report to the quartermaster general contained an important reminder: "Relatives, friends, and others, interested in the return home of the remains of deceased officers and enlisted men of the army ... can hardly realize what a tremendous task it is to reach many of the graves of our soldiers and return their remains safely to their homes." Nevertheless, Rhodes greatly improved the recovery practices of the U.S. Army. The burial corps was certainly much more effective at finding and identifying soldiers during the Spanish-Cuban-American and Philippine-American conflicts than during the U.S. Civil War. But Rhodes's criticism of the Army's poor administration never reached the press or the public.

A second tour was needed as more Americans died fighting the insurgency, and the quartermaster general appointed F. S. Croggon to run it. This new round of recovery operations went from April to August 1903. Croggon covered ground missed by Rhodes and recovered bodies from military engagements that occurred after the Rhodes team concluded its activities. Croggon's corps had ten undertakers and forty Filipino laborers; the workers were paid $1.25 per day. Like Rhodes, Croggon had to overcome difficulties. The main problem was locating graves and identifying bodies. Locals sometimes desecrated or robbed the graves, particularly when men were buried in local or "native" cemeteries. On several occasions Croggon found that locals had opened an American gravesite and deposited other bodies in it. "Many of the small native cemeteries kept absolutely no records of the interments made, nor the cause of death of the deceased," Croggon reported. He claimed, "Too much cannot be said in favor of each post having its own cemetery."[24]

The corps handled the bodies of many soldiers who had perished from diseases, such as cholera, malaria, or plague. Although the science of the day accepted germ theory, the military's position was that disease such as cholera and smallpox could be spread from dead to living bodies. Modern scientists understand that cholera is water-borne and does not live on human tissue. Likewise, smallpox and malaria microbes die shortly after the death of the host. Dead bodies do not actually pose much of a threat, but many in the military, including Croggon, believed that the bodies of persons who died from disease should remain untouched for several months and even years before any attempt to disinter them was made. Even then, "diseased" remains should be kept in hermetically sealed caskets, and the caskets should be made hygienic with lye and other chemicals. Croggon recommended the military develop post cemeteries to keep American bodies safe from desecration and to prevent disease. He did not trust local cemetery officials, particularly in areas where disease was rampant, to bury bodies hygienically. He believed they indiscriminately placed bodies, whether "healthy" or "sick," in the same gravesite. Thus Croggon called for the separation in post cemeteries of cholera victims from "adjoining those in which are buried the bodies of those whose death was caused by non-contagious or non-infectious diseases." In circumstances where a post commander could not build a cemetery, bodies should be placed "outside, but close to, the boundary of the native cemetery." This was very different from early in the war, when U.S. soldiers who fell in the fighting in Manila were buried in Paco Cemetery along with remains of cholera victims from the early nineteenth century. Americans had to quarantine the "sick," whether alive or dead.

Creating post cemeteries would also make it easier eventually to recover the remains of the dead. Despite Croggon's hard work, he failed to recover at least sixty-one bodies. Some were very difficult to find, and some corpses simply disappeared. For example, Pvt. Clayton Allard of the Ninth Infantry was never recovered. Although the corps found his grave and identification bottle near DapDap on Samar, the body was missing. The group believed "that the grave was desecrated by wild animals." At Balingiga, Croggon discovered the graves left by Captain Bookmiller and recovered all but three of the bodies. Pvt. John D. Buhrer could not be identified. Although they found remains in his grave, all that was written on the paper in the identification bottle was "Body of an Unknown American Soldier, 9th Inf., found back of the Company sink, Balingiga, Samar, Jan. 7th, 1902." That the body had remained unburied for more than three months was disconcerting. Croggon had no choice but to label the body as unknown, and Buhrer, at least officially, was never recovered. The corps likewise failed to recover Privates Litto Armani and Charles Powers. Croggon could not find their graves, and there was "reason to believe the remains were never recovered."[25]

After Balingiga, newly promoted Gen. Jacob H. Smith had ordered Maj. Littleton Waller of the Marines to "turn Samar into a howling wilderness" and to kill every Filipino over the age of ten. Although Waller largely ignored these unlawful orders, he did attempt to subdue the island. He won some battles, but he could not control the island from the coast. It was necessary to occupy the interior if Waller wanted to suppress Samar insurgents. In January 1902 Waller led his company and several Filipino guides and laborers inland on a march from Lanang to Basey. It was a horrific mistake. The rains had pushed the rivers ever higher, there was no trail, and the men began to run out of food. On top of this, Waller got lost. He decided to split up his force. He would lead the healthy forward to Basey, while the sick and weak would try to make it back to Lanang. Waller placed Capt. David Porter in charge of the second group. After a few days, Waller made it to Basey, immediately resupplied, and led men back into the interior to find the others. But Porter was having problems retracing his steps. His men grew weaker, and the Filipino guides eventually mutinied. This placed the men in a perilous position. Porter split his men up and left Lt. Alexander S. Williams in charge of the weakest men while he looked for a route back to Lanang. Porter made it. He sent a relief party after Williams. When the search party finally found them, most of the Filipinos had either run away or revolted against Williams. Ten marines had wandered away from the group and were left in the interior presumably dead.[26]

Croggon attempted to find these ten men but failed. The burial corps had no location to even begin looking for the men. The superintendent reported, "At every town visited by the Burial Corps in Samar, inquiry was made regarding these cases, but no information was obtained."[27] The recovery of the dead was a remarkable story of dedication and perseverance on the part of U.S. civilians, but it was also a story of bodies misidentified or left behind. Very little information regarding the travails of recovery reached the American public. It was difficult to retrieve sacred bodies from the profane interior of the Philippines, and this made it difficult for Americans to retrieve cultural memories of a confusing war that occurred thousands of miles from home. In a distant colonial war where military officials controlled information from the battlefronts, government officials could use the memory and honor of the war dead to mitigate domestic criticism, as Secretary of War Elihu Root did when campaigning for McKinley's reelection.

The tension caused by a badly run and increasingly bloody war nevertheless was evident on Memorial Day in 1902. Just a few weeks earlier, Major Waller had faced a court-martial trial for his conduct on Samar, and the public began learning about the actions of the U.S. military in turning the island into a "howling wilderness." Although the tribunal acquitted Waller, this trial did significant damage to the public's perception of the war. To counter public criticism, President Theodore Roosevelt opened an investigation into the military leadership in the Philippines. A handful of regular Army officers were court-martialed. To demonstrate further his commitment to the U.S. mission in the Philippines, Roosevelt also used the dead to justify the war. His Memorial Day address to an audience at Arlington National Cemetery marked a first for a sitting U.S. president. Some 30,000 people were present, many of whom were Civil War veterans and their families.[28] The day included a parade by the Grand Army of the Republic, the decoration of graves, and the gathering at the old amphitheater to listen to speeches by government officials. One speaker set the Lincolnian context by reading aloud the Gettysburg Address after which Roosevelt took the podium to cheers "of the immense audience, which stretched outside the limits of the amphitheater."[29]

Roosevelt began by praising the Civil War veterans. "You did the greatest and most necessary task which has ever fallen to the lot of any men on this Western Hemisphere." He praised the men: "You left us a reunited country. You left us the right of brotherhood with the men in gray, who with such courage and such devotion for what they deemed the right, fought against you. But you left us much more even than your achievement, for you left us the memory of how it was achieved." After establishing how the Civil War should be remembered, Roosevelt conceded that conquest of the Philippines was not as grand an accomplishment as what the Civil War veterans had achieved, but the soldiers abroad "are your younger brothers, your sons. They have shown themselves not unworthy of you, and they are entitled to the support of all men who are proud of what you did." Just as Gen. John B. Gordon and President William McKinley had found connections between the Civil War and the Spanish-Cuban-American War, Roosevelt claimed that the Philippine War and the Civil War were linked in purpose and in nobility of white reconciliation. Then Roosevelt responded to the Waller trial, admitting that there were some soldiers who had "so far forgotten themselves as to counsel and commit, in retaliation, acts of cruelty." But these were just a few individuals, he insisted, and not typical of the U.S. military mission in the Philippines. He reminded his audience "that for every guilty act committed by one of our troops a hundred acts of far greater atrocity have been committed by the hostile natives." Roosevelt promised that any U.S. soldier who had committed excesses would be found out and disciplined.[30]

Justifying the war meant that the president had to uphold and praise the actions of the majority of soldiers doing their duty. Historian Paul A. Kramer interprets Roosevelt's speech as evidence of a race war between American "civilization" and Filipino "barbarism." Kramer's emphasis is on the transpacific nature of the conflict.[31] But there was a second aspect of the speech that also deserves mention. Roosevelt justified the war by placing foreign and domestic spaces side by side, which served to describe the American empire inside and outside the nation. Roosevelt reprimanded critics of his administration's policies in the Philippines, who he claimed were too quick to condemn soldiers in the Philippines without admitting that "from time to time, there occur in our country, to the deep and lasting shame of our people, lynchings . . . a cruelty infinitely worse than any that has been committed by our troops in the Philippines." He continued, "The men who fail to condemn these lynchings, and yet clamor about what has been done in the Philippines, are indeed guilty of neglecting the beam in their own eye while taunting their brother about the mote in his." He accused detractors who "afford far less justification for a general condemnation of our army than these lynchings afford for the condemnation of the communities in which they have taken place." In comparing alleged war crimes abroad and lynchings at home, Roosevelt did not condemn the American character. He associated all anti-imperialists with those anti-imperialists who were also outspoken white supremacists, such as Senator Ben "Pitchfork" Tillman of South Carolina. According to Roosevelt, "In every community there are people who commit acts of well-nigh inconceivable horror and baseness."[32]

Linking domestic and foreign violence, Roosevelt revealed a repertoire of U.S. imperial power that many wished to obscure. It was a recognition that some officers in the Philippines were responding to insurrection in the same way some whites attempted to enforce the color line at home. For example, in August 1901 whites in Pierce City, Missouri, lynched three black men after they discovered the body of a young white women murdered on her way home from church. The mob then turned on other African Americans and burned their homes, forcing the victims to scatter into the woods to escape the violence. Mark Twain described the event in his posthumously published essay "The United States of Lyncherdom," sarcastically suggesting that this kind of violence was a lethal combination of "imitation" and "moral cowardice." Twain, too, a committed anti-imperialist, tied foreign and domestic spaces together in his essay, suggesting that the racial violence in small towns all across America that made up the United States of Lyncherdom made attempts to intervene in nonwhite foreign lands an absurdity.[33] Similar to the racial violence in Missouri, Capt. Andrew Rowan ordered the destruction of two villages on Bohol in the Philippines. Rowan acted in defense of one of his corporals, who raped a Filipino woman and was then murdered by her boyfriend. Rowan ordered the destruction of the assassin's village and his girlfriend's village. There was no military investigation into Rowan's actions.[34] The similarities in the ways that some American civilians enforced the color line in Missouri and the ways some American soldiers practiced violence in the Philippines could be seen again and again.

From his podium in Arlington, Roosevelt argued that concentrating only on the bad, without considering the "countless deeds of wisdom and justice and philanthropy," would encourage most people "to condemn the community." In "The United States of Lyncherdom" (1901) Twain made a similar argument in the wake of the Pierce City riot. "Certain of her children have joined the lynchers, and the smirch is upon the rest of us. That handful of her children have given us a character and labeled us with a name, and to the dwellers in the four quarters of the earth we are 'lynchers,' now, and ever shall be." But unlike in Pierce City, Roosevelt insisted that the United States was obeying rules of engagement in the Philippines established during the Civil War. This provided another rhetorical move for Roosevelt to exploit. In the spirit of Lincoln's promise, Roosevelt justified the Pacific war by comparing detractors of the Philippines to the old Confederacy. He noted that the Confederate Congress called General Grant a "butcher" and accused Lincoln of engaging in "contemptuous disregard for the usages of civilized war."

Roosevelt expanded this upside-down interpretation of Lincoln's promise. The great work of "conquering" the Filipinos would bring them peace and stability without the threat of an "'independent' Aguinaldian oligarchy." The Americans could "teach the people of the Philippine Islands not only how to enjoy but how to make good use of their freedom." And in performing this duty to Filipinos, Roosevelt promised not to "forget our duty to our own country":

> The Pacific seaboard is as much to us as the Atlantic.... The shadow of our destiny has already reached to the shores of Asia. The might of our people already looms large against the world-horizon; and it will loom ever larger as the years go by. No statesman has a right to neglect the interests of our people in the Pacific.

This was the global vision that Roosevelt saw unfolding in the Philippines. He justified U.S. expansion on the frontier of the empire because it enhanced or protected U.S. national interests. There could be no nobler cause than this. The speech received raucous applause and "three cheers to our brave President."[35]

Roosevelt believed that soldiers' bodies provided the proof of a benevolent U.S. empire. Dead Americans invoked the public's obligation to remember them and their cause in the Pacific world. But the soldiers' remains that the U.S. Army retrieved often communicated a less than inspiring interpretation of imperialism. In 1900, some of the 1,900 bodies were repatriated home from foreign lands. The vast majority came from the Philippines accompanied by a few from China's Boxer Rebellion. The War Department sent 984 home, buried 487 in the Presidio in San Francisco, and interred 320 in Arlington National Cemetery.[36] Upon arrival, military personnel unloaded the bodies in San Francisco or New York and then shipped them to their kinfolk, who asked for a full military funeral in a local cemetery or a nearby national cemetery. But a major problem arose when state governments refused to allow the military to ship the "diseased" dead across state lines. When the remains of smallpox victims arrived at San Francisco, local authorities refused the bodies because they could not obtain the proper permits from inland state governments whose laws "forbid the transportation of bodies when death was due to this [smallpox] disease." The dead men had been buried in the Philippines for more than a year, their flesh was gone, and all that remained were bones. The military had documented these facts, which eliminated the risk of disease with the authorities in Manila. But state sovereignty interrupted the national commemorative tradition, and thus the military was "compelled to inter in the Presidio National Cemetery at San Francisco 142 of such remains, many of which otherwise would have been sent to their former homes for private burial."[37]

People who were not necessarily anti-imperialist began criticizing the War Department for delays. Deputy Quartermaster W. S. Patton noted these criticisms in his annual report. He stated, "As might be expected, the department has suffered some criticism from relatives and friends of officers and soldiers at delay in shipment of remains, due to failure to fully understand existing conditions." Failure on the part of Americans to understand the reasons behind the delays demonstrated just how much they misunderstood the nature of the counterinsurgency in the Philippines. On top of the difficulty of recovering the bodies, it was necessary to identify, prepare, and transport the remains halfway around the world. This took time and the War Department officials desperately wanted to make sure that they could identify as many men as possible. In the Philippines, Rhodes and Croggon were often hampered by inclement weather, difficult terrain, and far from pacified districts. To mitigate criticism, the War Department established a permanent burial party in the Philippines, complete with an official morgue in Manila, so that "the entire group [of islands] will be visited annually, or oftener when practical," allowing for "the least possible delay after death." This would end the burial parties being organized in the United States and transported to the Philippines and instead allow for military officials stationed in the Philippines to retrieve, identify, and document bodies more efficiently.[38]

Although many of the "healthy dead" were shipped throughout the United States to hometowns where they received honorable funerals, the "sick dead" had to be taken directly to San Francisco or New York. This again showed how unprepared the military was for handling the dead from an unpopular war. Several western states had laws on the books prohibiting the transportation of bodies killed by disease, including malaria and yellow fever. These laws reflected the belief that disease easily could be spread by the dead, even by remains that had been buried for more than a year and only retrieved recently. Nevertheless, the federal military had to honor these state laws, and in this case state sovereignty controlled federal policy of transporting the dead. In the fall of 1903, the transport ship *Sumner* left the Philippines for the United States. It carried much of the returning Fifth Infantry Regiment, which barracked in New York. But the transport also contained 173 dead on board, many of which had succumbed to disease, not conflict, making it impossible for their bodies to be transported from San Francisco overland by rail across state borders to their hometowns in the East.[39] Thus the *Sumner* had to sail through the Indian Ocean through the Suez Canal and the Mediterranean before crossing the Atlantic Ocean to New York. The voyage took more than two months to complete and finally arrived in November, allowing members of the Fifth Infantry to disembark in New York. The military unloaded the bodies on dock 12 on the East River in full view of the public so people could claim their loved ones on the dock and take them home. Those who remained unclaimed were shipped to Arlington to receive burial there. The same exercise of state sovereignty in the West determined the route of the transport ship *Kilpatrick*, which returned 302 dead from Manila, including the bodies from Balingiga. Although some had died in battle, most of the three hundred had died from disease. Most of them, as well as the unclaimed, ended up in Arlington.[40]

Once recovered and identified, the remains of most of the dead were shipped home and received traditional burials with full military honors. The War Department received significant criticism when the process of repatriation went awry. For example, Charles Seigal died in the Philippines in 1900. The War Department shipped his body and buried it in a cemetery on Staten Island. He remained buried there for weeks before his family learned that his body had been returned to the United States. They immediately petitioned for a disinterment but could not pay for the transportation expense to Manhattan, where they lived. A local Jewish charitable organization, not the War Department, helped pay for the removal and shipment of Seigal's body.[41]

Another example that brought embarrassing criticism was the "Many Journeys" of Private Fitzmaurice's remains. The Fitzmaurice family lived in Oklahoma, but requested his remains be shipped to St. Louis, Missouri, for burial. The War Department shipped the corpse to St. Louis, but no one immediately claimed the body. The St. Louis authorities shipped it back to New York, where it was forwarded to Philadelphia for interment. Fitzmaurice's sister wrote the War Department about the body, and military officials sent the remains to her home in Oklahoma. But the family wanted Fitzmaurice buried in St. Louis, so she forwarded the casket via the War Department to St. Louis. When she arrived in St. Louis to claim the body a half-hour late, she learned that local officials had again shipped it to Philadelphia. Eventually military officials delivered Fitzmaurice's remains to St. Louis.[42]

Americans extended Lincoln's promise to the dead from the unwelcome Philippine-American War. The practical and logistical difficulties of retrieval tested the durability of the promise while the nature of the war tested the integrity of American cultural memory. Not everyone agreed with McKinley and Roosevelt that the U.S. pacification and occupation of the Philippines, over the resistance of Filipino nationals and the suffering of many more Filipino civilians, was consistent with the "new birth of freedom" heralded for Americans at Gettysburg forty years earlier. Although the dead could symbolize American righteousness powerfully, the reality was that the War Department was as unprepared for recovering the dead as they were for administering an empire. Neglect, incompetence, desecration became manifest all too often, but government officials obscured the details of recovering the dead. They went on to obscure the realities of imperialism with the rhetoric of nationalism and republicanism. They prevailed and changed the meaning of what Lincoln meant when he committed the state and the citizenry to commemorating the fallen community as well as Americans' sense of their place in the world and their nation's mission.

PART 3

Communication

The complications of America's place in the world grew in the years after the Philippine-American War, which was largely over by 1907 with the first assembly elected in the Philippines. By 1916 U.S. congressmen legislated to relinquish their colonial holdings in the Philippines at some point in the future, although this promise would not be enacted until after the Second World War. Both Republican and Democratic administrations experimented with various strategies to pursue U.S. interests and promote American ascendancy. Theodore Roosevelt continued McKinley's policy in the Philippines while issuing his Roosevelt Corollary to the Monroe Doctrine and implementing "gunboat diplomacy." He helped instigate a civil war in Colombia that ended with the independence of Panama and gave the United States control over the Panama Canal project. It would connect the Atlantic and Pacific Oceans and allow U.S. fleets to move rapidly to destinations where they were needed.[1] Even before the canal was opened, Roosevelt sent the Great White Fleet on a worldwide cruise as a demonstration of naval power. He also sent U.S. forces into Honduras, the Dominican Republic, Cuba, and Nicaragua. President William Howard Taft embraced "dollar diplomacy," but also approved interventions and occupations of Honduras, Panama, Cuba, and Nicaragua. Such moves not only protected American interests but also increased economic and financial integration between the United States and Latin American and Caribbean countries. By the eve of the Great

War, the United States dominated the Western Hemisphere and challenged any unwanted European involvement in the region.

The 1912 election saw Woodrow Wilson, the Virginia-born former president of Princeton University and governor of New Jersey, defeat Roosevelt and Taft. The first Southerner to serve as president since before the Civil War, Wilson brought a new emphasis on self-determination and collective security, dubbed the "New Freedom," to U.S. foreign policy. But the Wilson administration hardly repudiated the quest for U.S. hegemony. Not surprisingly, the president sounded like his predecessors when it came to justifying his shows of force abroad and commemorating the dead from these actions. What was distinctive was the fact that a Southerner now spoke words redolent of Lincoln, revealing to a new generation of Americans embarking on the twentieth century the triumph of reunion and reconciliation in the context of empire.

With each successive presidential administration embracing the politics of empire, government officials had to find ways to pass cultural memory on to a new generation. This was exceedingly difficult because more and more Civil War veterans were dying. French historian Pierre Nora insists that living memories died, or at least turned into sites of memory, when the people with the experience passed away.[2] It was only possible, suggests Nora, to share echoes of memory through monuments of stone, memorabilia, or souvenirs. The actual memories had perished with the dead. Historian Jan Assmann suggests, however, that while memories may not pass from generation to generation through nonritualized, spontaneous, and local communicative memory of people, cultural memory could be passed on from one generation to the next even over millennia. This process, suggests Assmann, is one in which certain memories eventually come to be canonized as part of society's core identity. Canonization here means to take memories and texts that authoritatively define the proper, legal, preeminent, and sacred parameters of civilization into an archival collection that people can consult through the ages. While the textual content of the canon never really changes, texts can be added and subtracted from the canon based on the interpretations of new generations of people. Canonical texts facilitated each new generation to interpret memory even if each generation produced a variation on the long-standing interpretation. This maneuver gained new significance in the age of information where new technologies of communication liberated people from the relatively slow process of print journalism and visual images. Traditions, rituals, and cultural memory could be communicated through aural mediums almost instantaneously and across vast open spaces to reach audiences numbering in the millions. Through cultural memory, politicians could collaborate with citizens in new ways to reinterpret memories of American empire. Abraham Lincoln's Gettysburg Address articulated the generational interpretation of the Protestant Good Death and ancient Athenian democracy, William McKinley's Atlanta speech similarly spoke to the generational variation of Lincoln's promise, and Woodrow Wilson showed again how Americans would transmit cultural memory through the rituals of the martial dead to explain the First World War.

Wilson signaled his acceptance of the Lincolnian tradition within a few months of taking office. In 1913 the State of Pennsylvania hosted one of the largest ever Civil War reunions to commemorate the fiftieth anniversary of the Gettysburg battle. Fifty thousand members of the Grand Army of the Republic and the United Confederate Veterans returned to meet and camp on the battlefield. They ate, talked, and lived together from June 25 to July 4.[3] Wilson arrived on Independence Day. Just as Lincoln had dedicated the country to a "new birth of freedom" fifty years earlier, Wilson renewed the national spirit in his address. Standing nearly in the same spot where Lincoln had spoken, Wilson told the crowd, "I need not tell you what the Battle of Gettysburg meant." Noting that "fifty years have gone by," he said, "I crave the privilege of speaking to you for a few minutes of what those fifty years have meant." In his view, "They have meant peace and union and vigor, and the maturity and might of a great nation. How wholesome and healing the peace has been!" The United States now stood unchallenged: "There is no one within its borders, there is no power among the nations of the earth, to make it afraid."[4]

In spite of the nation's growing strength, it still required from its citizens a willingness to sacrifice and a warlike sense of purpose. He acknowledged the soldiers in the audience by saying that they had "set us a great example of devotion and utter sacrifice," but went on to suggest that their work for reunion was a beginning and not an end. Wilson declared that "the Civil War had shown 'what it costs to make a nation.'" There were still more burdens and challenges, even in peacetime. His call to action against "principalities and powers and wickedness in high places" maintained the martial metaphor admonishing Americans to act like soldiers as they pursued their civic endeavors: "Come, let us be comrades and soldiers yet to serve our fellow-men in quiet counsel, where the blare of trumpets is neither heard nor heeded and where the things are done which make blessed the nations of the world in peace and righteousness and love."[5]

The demands of industrial civilization and globe-straddling empire blurred the old republic's simple distinctions between war and peace or slavery and liberty. Lincoln had dedicated the Gettysburg battlefield to the men who fought and died there, obliging Americans to "never forget what they did here." By contrast, Wilson made the battlefield ubiquitous for Americans. Even if the country's struggles were not always martial in nature, citizens had an obligation to serve their country and mankind. Speaking to the Civil War generation, Wilson attempted to communicate an updated interpretation of Lincoln's promise to a new generation of Americans.

CHAPTER 6

Exiles of American Cultural Memory

> Exile is strangely compelling to think about but terrible to experience. It is the unhealable rift forced between a human being and a native place, between the self and its true home: its essential sadness can never be surmounted. And while it is true that literature and history contain heroic, romantic, glorious, even triumphant episodes in an exile's life, these are no more than efforts to overcome the crippling sorrow of estrangement. The achievements of exile are permanently undermined by the loss of something left behind forever.
> —Edward Said, *Reflections on Exile*

The First World War made exiles of millions of people. Separation from homes, separation from loved ones, and separation from humanity sometimes within one's own homeland defined the tragedy of war. Exile "is produced by human beings for other human beings," claimed philosopher Edward Said. But nations could shelter people from the exiled experience. "Nationalism is an assertion of belonging in and to a place, a people, a heritage. It affirms the home created by a community of language, culture, and customs; and, by so doing, it fends off exile, fights to prevent its ravages."[1] Cultural memory could help provide a home, and proof of the power of cultural memory was its ability to integrate other people into it. But as much as nationalism could shield people from exile, it also had the capacity to banish people. The ability for American cultural memory to integrate people had its obvious limits. African Americans, for example, would barely be incorporated if at all. Government officials and U.S. citizens could use cultural memory to communicate the borders between the integrated and the exiled domestically and at the empire's frontier.[2]

Cultural memory could help ameliorate the tensions of American empire built up over the nineteenth century by helping Americans define who could integrate into cultural memory and who would be exiled from it. As historians Jane Burbank and Frederick Cooper claim, "The United States over the course of the nineteenth century acted with a particular imperial mode—forging a continental empire that sharply distinguished the included from the excluded, giving rise to a polity that defined itself as national." Burbank and Cooper contrast the functioning American empire from the British imperial legacy that explicitly and fundamentally viewed subjects at home as different from those people that the British empire governed in the periphery. While British agents spent time and resources building institutions that marked differences between the metropole and the periphery, agents involved in the American imperial project tended to incorporate their "fixation on territory, property ownership, monogamous family life, and female subordination" as a "firm belief that the American way of life was both superior and based on universalistic values that would be welcomed by all others." They governed colonial subjects with the same expectations of white U.S. citizens while simultaneously failing to acknowledge "the erasure of the sovereignties of the indigenous people of the continent." The reality of the American empire was one in which government officials and citizens collaborated to build a national identity that did not exclude people horizontally across the American empire so much as vertically in relation to those who viewed American values as universal and natural and those who did not. That is to say that people could be incorporated, and likewise exiled, within and beyond the nation's borders depending upon their belief in the universality of the American way of life.[3] American cultural memory helped communicate the boundaries between the integrated and the exiled.

While the reality of imperial power excluded Native Americans, women, and African Americans within the boundaries of the United States, cultural memory had the capacity to integrate, for example, the Jewish citizens of

Wilmington, North Carolina. Arthur Bluethenthal represented one such example during the First World War. He was a volunteer ambulance driver for the American Field Service in Serbia and Albania who then transferred to the French Foreign Legion and flew a bomber for the Lafayette Flying Corps over the western front. He hailed from Wilmington, where he was the son of German Jewish immigrants and attended the reform Temple of Israel. German aircraft pilots shot Bluethenthal down over Maignelay, France, while he was redirecting French artillery fire on June 5, 1918. He was buried in France, but his parents retrieved his body to bury in Wilmington in 1921. Wilmingtonians used well-rehearsed mythologies that remembered the war dead as cavaliers and New Southern gentlemen, developed while implementing Confederate dead into Lincoln's promise during the late nineteenth century. They commemorated Bluethenthal's absent body and honored him again when his body returned home. Wilmington airport officials named a runway after him. The French military awarded him the Croix de Guerre with Star and the Médaille Militaire while alive and the Croix de Guerre with Palm posthumously. He was a highly decorated soldier and a local hero, and memory-makers easily incorporated him into the elite collective memory that honored him for his actions on the western front as a cavalier aviator and New Southern gentleman warrior. Archivist Robert B. House and the North Carolina Historical Commission even included Bluethenthal's heroics in the World War I collection of the North Carolina State Archives to prove the purity of Southern gentlemen who volunteered to fight for the French empire against the German empire. Bluethenthal's commemoration provides an opportunity to examine the remembrances of North Carolinians who volunteered for France on the eastern front well before the United States declared war on Germany. It exposes how these volunteers communicated cultural memory and U.S. borders through letters and print media that shaped the perceptions of citizens about joining the war, about Germany, and about Islam, convincing many to abandon their positions of neutrality. These volunteers had an agenda, and they communicated their experiences of the eastern front using the racialized and gendered memories they learned from home. They were crucial in shaping the way Americans not yet committed to the fight imagined the people and places engulfed by the war. Examining Bluethenthal's experiences as a case study thus illuminates how cultural memory during the war could integrate some while exiling others.[4]

Bluethenthal was a natural hero for Wilmingtonians because his family worked diligently long before the war to integrate themselves into the cultural fabric of the Cape Fear region. Historian Eric L. Goldstein notes that as Jewish people in America integrated more and more into middle-class society, they developed institutions and sought out social boundaries that gave them the flexibility to embrace both Jewish traditions and American culture.[5] The Bluethenthals fit well into this process. Arthur's father, Leopold, immigrated to the United States from Bavaria to work for his uncle Frederick Rheinstein in Wilmington. Rheinstein immigrated, too, and settled in Wilmington among a significant community of German Jewish immigrants who integrated themselves into Southern society even before the Civil War. Many served as soldiers for the Confederacy; Rheinstein served as a purchaser for the Confederate States and was drawn to Wilmington, in part, because it remained one of the few open Atlantic ports that the Union did not control until early 1865. Cape Fear and areas surrounding Wilmington thus became a Confederate hub of trading, blockade running, and ocean access. Rheinstein later settled in Wilmington and drew upon his wartime experience to become the owner and operator of Rheinstein's Dry Goods, a profitable operation that by 1885 yielded Rheinstein half a million dollars per year. He helped start the Reform Jewish Temple of Israel synagogue in Wilmington while cultivating social and business relationships with Jewish and non-Jewish citizens throughout the city. Rheinstein was part of a cadre of successful Jewish business leaders that included Solomon Fishblate, who would serve as mayor of the city, Nathaniel Jacobi, who ran a successful hardware store, and many others who integrated themselves into white Wilmington and Southern culture while supporting Democrat politicians, especially during Reconstruction. Many joined the Masons, the Odd Fellows, and other non-Jewish orders, too. Together they created a significant social and commercial presence in Wilmington.

Leopold eventually inherited his uncle's store, renaming it the Bluethenthal

Company Dry Goods. He met and married his wife, Johanna, in Wilmington and she gave birth to Herbert on September 18, 1890, Arthur on November 1, 1891, Gertrude on November 18, 1892 (she died in 1894), and Elsa on April 2, 1896. Like the Bluethenthals, many Jewish people integrated their experiences into American Southern culture without losing a sense of their Jewish identity.[6] Leopold made enough money to send his younger son, Arthur, to the Irving Institute in Tarrytown, New York, before enrolling him at Phillips Exeter Academy in Exeter, New Hampshire, a boarding school that Abraham Lincoln's son Robert and Ulysses S. Grant Jr. attended. Sending their son to the Academy demonstrated the Bluethenthals' ability and desire to integrate their son with the privileged status of America's elites. Despite this ability to hobnob with America's upper class, young Arthur had to work for his academic accolades. He wrote his German-born parents that while at the Irving Institute, "I found out up here that I don't know the first thing about German grammar.... It was hard for me to keep up with the rest of the fellows." But he worked and improved his German so that he was "get[ting] along as well as the rest of them." He studied algebra and geometry and was assigned to perform the part of Jessica in his English class's performance of *The Merchant of Venice*. He also excelled at football.[7] His successes at Phillips Exeter helped him go on to enroll at Princeton University where he was a five-foot-nine, 186-pound All-American football star. He played center for the team and was inducted into the International Jewish Sports Hall of Fame posthumously in 1997.

As the nineteenth century faded, however, Jewish people encountered more difficulties in integrating themselves. As more Jewish people from parts of Eastern Europe began to arrive in the United States, Jewish identity became multifaceted. The language of Yiddish, the debates between Orthodox and Reform Judaism, and the lack of a singular place of origin, argues Goldstein, confused white Protestant Americans. He argues that Americans tried to understand Jewish Americans through the lens of blackness versus whiteness, which forced Jewish people to embrace the politics of whiteness even if that meant, for example, German Jews who immigrated in the mid-nineteenth century looking unfavorably upon Jewish immigrants from Eastern Europe few decades later. "American Jews became preoccupied," claims Goldstein, "with the need to situate themselves socially as white and to find ways of defining Jewishness that did not interfere with their whiteness."[8] The Bluethenthals were excellent at accomplishing this.

An early expression of the kind of costs that assimilation demanded of some Jewish people may help explain why some Jewish leaders participated in the 1898 Wilmington race riot. Two prominent members of the Temple of Israel, Solomon Fishblate and Nathaniel Jacobi, attended the mass meeting of white citizens at the courthouse the day after the compromised election that the Democrats won. "Many of the city's business leaders were present" as Alfred Moore Waddell read the contents of what has become known as the "Declaration of White Independence," which helped orchestrate the coup d'état against Fusionist politicians. Fishblate and Jacobi proposed amendments to Waddell's declaration that called for the forced resignations of the police chief, the mayor, and the aldermen of the city. They signed the declaration with 445 other men, and at least Fishblate was in the mob of perhaps 1,000 men who burned the *Daily Record*'s office.[9] In the maelstrom that followed, Democrats under the leadership of Waddell overthrew the Wilmington government, forcing Republican and Populist Fusionist politicians to resign under force of arms. Waddell took over the government and implemented white-only policies that saw the coerced (and voluntary) banishment of thousands of blacks and whites, the firing of black workers from their jobs, and Jim Crow laws such as poll taxes and literacy tests keeping many blacks from voting. Jacobi himself seemed to have fired many of his black workers and encouraged other businessmen to do the same. This kind of violence created a great number of exiles within North Carolina.

Not all Jewish people in North Carolina supported this kind of viciousness. Some actively opposed and prevented it. Jewish sheriff Joseph Hahn in New Bern, North Carolina, actively confronted Democratic and Red Shirt intimidation. Hahn and many of his black deputies oversaw an orderly election in New Bern.[10] Certainly many Jewish people in Wilmington were also critical of the violent takeover of their city's political office. Arthur Bluethenthal's seventh birthday came just days before the riot, and no evidence suggests either Arthur or his father participated in or witnessed the riot. In fact, it is entirely conceivable that they could have been critical of the entire affair. Yet somehow historians must explain the hardened racial views that Arthur exhibited regarding African Americans in Wilmington as well as Islamic and Indochinese people he encountered in Serbia and Albania. It is hard to imagine that a young and impressionable boy would have been immune from the racial attitudes exhibited by Jewish and non-Jewish men, many of whom he certainly knew and respected, in the travails of the Wilmington uprising. Fishblate and Jacobi and many in the Jewish community would have likely relished in Arthur's academic and athletic accomplishments as he, perhaps among all other Jewish youth in Wilmington, personified the integration and success of Jewish Americans. It is likely that Arthur at least participated in the communicative memory of the race riot as a small child, even if he and his family did not participate in the violence. These memories and the cost of assimilation certainly influenced the racial views that he would develop during his young formative years and articulate later as an adult. Jewish families in Wilmington worked and worshipped together, socialized even with non-Jews, and grieved together. The Bluethenthals and the Jacobis were friends, if not admirers, of each other over the years. Upon hearing of Arthur's death in combat, Marcus Jacobi—Nathaniel's oldest surviving son, who would have been in his twenties at the time of the race riot—penned a kind letter to Leopold and Johanna Bluethenthal, telling them that Arthur's "sacrifice was a willing one, imbued with duty and patriotism, and he died with a smile and a sense of duty performed." He hoped that the "God of our Fathers" would "console you in your irreparable loss," and he signed the letter as "Sincerely, your friend, Marcus Jacobi."[11]

Arthur's decision to volunteer for France in the fight against Germany seemed to cause a rift between him and his parents. Leopold and Johanna hoped to persuade him not to volunteer. In February 1916 it seems that someone gave Arthur an essay from the Greensboro, North Carolina, publisher Charles Leonard van Noppen titled "Henry Weil." The essay was a tribute to the integrative powers of German Jews in America and seemed to imply that fighting against Germany would compromise the hard work of previous generations. Unlike immigrants from other parts of Europe, the essayist argued that German Jews immigrated to the United States, started businesses, relied on themselves in times of hard luck, pursued education, looked out for the less fortunate, obeyed their parents, and refrained from divorce. If this short essay was supposed to prevent Arthur from fighting the countrymen of his forefathers, it backfired. The essayist noted that Henry Weil—a close friend to the Bluethenthals, Arthur's brother, Herbert, married Weil's youngest daughter, Janet—came from Germany and very quickly joined the Confederate cause as a teenager. "A mere boy, a foreigner, probably without clear understanding of 'what they fought each other for,' the blood of the old Hebrew warriors of Old Testament days so thrilled him that he took his musket and fought well." This suggested Henry Weil's participation in the Civil War was coincidental and even somewhat accidental. Arthur underlined the passage "without clear understanding" and wrote in the margin, "On the contrary he had decided ideas before coming over."[12] In opposition to his parents' wishes for him not to join the French war effort, Arthur seemed to accept just how much German Jews integrated into the fabric of Southern culture and to believe he was completing the full circle of integration by fighting as an American Jew against Germany. Henry Weil's activity in the Civil War only seemed to spur Arthur into joining the American Field Service, even if it meant fighting the countrymen of his parents' birthplace.

His motivation to join the war effort perhaps was a desire to demonstrate, like those before him, the masculine qualities of integrating his Jewishness into the fabric of American society. He may have joined, too, because a love interest spurned him or perhaps he could not live with the boredom that went with working at Bluethenthal's Dry Goods and living under the shadow of his father. He also wrote of duty and fighting for humanity as reasons for volunteering. Probably a combination of these reasons saw Arthur leave Wilmington for France in spring 1916 in a sort of self-imposed exile, shortly after attending his brother Herbert's wedding to Janet Weil.

The United States had not yet entered the war, and Woodrow Wilson would campaign against joining the war in that fall's election. Arthur spent his time driving an ambulance for the AFS as part of Section Three stationed on the eastern front in Monastir, Serbia, near the Albanian border (modern-day Bitola, Macedonia). As fellow driver, Robert Whitney Imbrie described, a cosmopolitan atmosphere dominated the city, "that only war and the Orient could produce: a sprinkling of soldiers, mostly French, although occasionally a Russian or an Italian was noticed; a meditative old Turk, stolid Serbian women, little children—a lively, varied picture" on a street scene that included a "queer little bakery," "odd little shops," and a "hot milk booth" with "English-speaking Montenegrins." Here Bluethenthal and his colleagues exhibited extraordinary heroism as they routinely evaded German and Bulgarian artillery shells to take the wounded from one of the mosques in Monastir (which operated as a collection point to take wounded from the trenches) and transport them out of the city to hospitals safely behind French lines. Death was all around as Imbrie described how "when shells came in there was terror, panic, a wailing and gnashing of teeth, for not even the fatalism of Mohammed could be proof against such sights."[13]

Arthur, however, was tired of his time in Macedonia, and as Section Three prepared to leave the eastern front in the spring of 1917, he contemplated returning home to Wilmington. But he did not want to stay with his parents for very long, he told his sister Elsa. When Congress declared war on Germany in April, Arthur changed his mind about coming home.[14] He decided instead to sign up for the French Foreign Legion to become a pilot. Upset that Arthur had turned down a chance to come home in lieu of signing up to join the Lafayette Flying Corps, his father ceased writing him. On June 12, 1917, Arthur wrote his parents, "Haven't heard a line from you in over a month so I guess you must be pretty sore at me. But still I am sorry."[15] On June 15 Arthur's regret turned confrontational. "Why on earth don't you write?" he asked. "I have not had but one letter in six weeks and that one was waiting for me when I got to France." He lectured, "Even though you are awfully sore at me, I think you ought to drop a line or two." But his anger was short-lived. He reminded his parents he was short on money. He had to pay twenty francs per day for five weeks in Paris while he waited to train for his aviator's license. He had to buy underwear, shirts, and socks as well as a new uniform because his old one "was in tatters." And he had to pay back the "several football bets that I lost last fall." He asked his parents to up his allowance to $100 per month. He claimed the "ordinary food is not fit to eat in any way shape or form." He promised his parents that he "would be much obliged" if they "could send the 100 dollars for the 1st couple of months" as soon as they could.[16] In his July 4, 1917, letter home, Arthur again was quite upset with his parents. "I received your letter June 10th today mama and I can't say that it caused me any very great rejoicing. As usual, you don't understand."

His parents worried about his desire to fly and that it was much more dangerous than serving in the ambulance corps. Contradicting the way many in North Carolina would later commemorate his death, he wrote, "I know you are going to worry about me. I can't help that. I am doing what I consider my duty! I did it in no flush of enthusiasm or burst of patriotism. I had my choice and I took what appealed to me most." Less of patriotism and enthusiasm and more of a choice to avoid home, Arthur signed up as a bomber pilot because he was apparently too heavy to fly a fighter. He told his parents if they did not want to write him, they did not have to, but he would write "every week to say I'm well."[17] By July 11 Arthur had received letters from his parents, and he felt much better about their relationship. Still, in his July 25 letter home, he warned, "The sooner you both realize that Germany simply has to be defeated in order to have any freemen at all on earth, the sooner you will get the point of view that people over here have had for years."[18] He believed his parents had been absent from Europe too long to know what was going on. Lost in the commemorations of the heroic Bluethenthal was the argument with his parents that described what was actually at stake in his volunteering for France. Less a defense of humanity, Arthur and his parents argued over the unacknowledged meaning of Jewish integration in America and whether or not Arthur betrayed his father's generation or enhanced German Jewish integration into American culture by fighting against Germany in a way that even the United States now planned to participate.

While training for his aviator's license, Arthur continued to spend his father's money. In August 1917 he had an oil painting made of himself that cost $100 that he sent to his father, and he paid $80 for surgery to remove an abscess in his ear. He bought the painting "in case something should happen." He promised that he would pay his father back for all the money he used. He was toying with the idea of joining the U.S. Army now that the United States had declared war and claimed that as a lieutenant in the aviation forces, he would get a salary of $3,000 per year, which was "not bad at all." Still, at the moment, he remained a volunteer as the U.S. military prepared to send troops across the Atlantic, and he asked his dad to send money until he could draw his next $100 allowance. By late October 1917 Leopold was still receiving surprise withdrawals from his bank account for $200. Although he had given Arthur $200 six weeks earlier, Leopold was "surprised to put it mildly that you drew again," and he did not know why Arthur "should use so much money." He asked his son "not to abuse my good nature too much" and to come home at least for a visit and "not disappoint us again."[19] In March 1918 Arthur drew his $100 for April because he "needed it a little bit sooner." Additionally, he asked his father to "make arrangements with the United Cigar Stores to send me 100 Egyptian Deities, plain tip, every week" and to "send for two weeks."[20] Such letters betrayed Arthur's dependence on his father's support in order to volunteer, which seemed to contradict the mythology of a self-reliant cavalier.

Upon initially arriving in France in 1916, Bluethenthal had a great time as a young man on a quest almost personifying characters in John Dos Passos's novel *1919*, one of whom declared, "Fellers, this ain't a war.... It's a goddam whorehouse."[21] Once the United States entered the war, military officials would seek to stamp out such mind-sets. Historian Mark Meigs argues that "the army and the American popular press did the best they could to push the French woman into the role of harlot."[22] Yet Bluethenthal arrived in France well before the U.S. propaganda machine was in operation. His full embrace of French culture betrayed his self-imposed exile from Wilmington as a myth; Arthur actually was in near complete control over his identity no matter where he chose to go, and he enjoyed syncing up his Wilmington identity with new exciting experiences in France. His early experiences, indeed, showcased some of the racialized and sexist attitudes that he brought with him to France from Wilmington. He detailed many of his excellent adventures to his childhood friends Davey and Arthur in which Bluethenthal became a kind of Orientalist relating the experiences of the East to his Occidental friends in Wilmington. A letter illustrates just how much Bluethenthal interpreted the cultures of eastern peoples through the gender and racial categories he learned growing up in Wilmington and perhaps practiced at Irving, Phillips Exeter, and Princeton. He seemed to understand, at least on some level, the importance of maintaining his reputation back home. In his long single-spaced six-page letter, he told his friends, "You may show any part to 'Nuts' and the free-from-smut parts to any one at all." It seems that his friends fulfilled his wishes, because someone heavily edited this letter before making it public. The edited version made it into the World War I Collection at the North Carolina State Archives, and Arthur's parents sent copies of the edited letter "which we consider very interesting, and out of which you can use such parts as you deem of interest to your purpose" to the president of Princeton University, who sought to create a memorial volume commemorating all of Princeton's valiant student war dead. The Bluethenthals also sent copies of the edited letter to Phillips Exeter Academy. Thus the biographical memory of Arthur's first months in France made it into cultural memory in a heavily edited version designed to cultivate Arthur's reputation as part of a mythology useful for North Carolinians, Princeton and Phillips Exeter alumni, and Americans across the nation. Some of his erotic Orientalism undermined the Southern gentlemen mythology that commemorators would use to remember him. While his friends edited these sections out, they unapologetically kept his racialized descriptions of the eastern front intact. These Orientalist descriptions of race, at the time, obviously posed no threat to his heroic mythology and demonstrated the kind of racism that people in Wilmington (and much of the nation) accepted uncritically and unapologetically.[23]

Initially stationed in "proximity to the Boches, the excellent wine and all that" of the Côte d'Or, he wrote Davey and Arthur, "Our inn was kept by three very comely wenches called Gaby, René and Lily, and believe me for general speed around the *infield* and all around ability on ground *Balls*, they had—'Tinker to Evers to Chance' crying for help. Needless to say I picked up lots of French here, atmosphere and otherwise." This sexual metaphor for getting around the bases refers to shortstop Joe Tinker, second basemen Johnny Evers, and first basemen Frank Chance, who famously turned double plays for the Chicago Cubs in their World Series appearance in 1906 and their successive championships in 1907 and 1908. This stereotype of French women probably verified the sexual fantasies that Davey and Arthur back in North Carolina held for foreign women and shared with Bluethenthal. They edited this section out of the letter. Unlike respectable women of North Carolina, foreign women in France seemed to be sexual conquests who fulfilled these young men's fantasies. But Bluethenthal's time in the Côte d'Or was short-lived. French military officials soon told him that he would be sent to Paris and then deployed in three days to Salonique (Thessaloniki) in Greece. Upon arriving in Paris, his deployment was delayed for three weeks, so he "started to *live*." The unrevised letter describes him experiencing Parisian life and spending his father's money "at a pace [that] was something awful," relishing in the "swiftest 21 days I ever put-in." He noted that he "didn't go in for the 'King of In-Door Sports but did manage to get away with my share of good wine and better food."[24]

He soon ran out of money but drew "a series of sight drafts" from his father's bank account. He failed to tell his father about the drafts and his incomprehension of foreign exchange rates because, "with very little warning," the French authorized his transfer from Paris to Marseilles via rail. After three days on a freight train, Arthur encountered a city where "the relative proximity between 'Police and Pleasure' were never on a more amicable or mutually profitable basis." Here Bluethenthal and his fellow volunteers daily visited cafés, went sight-seeing, and swam in the Mediterranean. At night, Arthur told his friends, wartime Marseille closed at 11:00 p.m. except for the "Pleasure Palaces" that competed with each other over which establishment had "a better brand of 'Wild Women.'" Arthur exclaimed, "They were—Great!"

Bluethenthal and a dozen of his colleagues accompanied by two Brits got into some trouble when they "blew into Alines' [Pleasure Palace] like a tornado. Twelve bottles of wine were ordered and consumed." Although someone in the group said he paid for the wine, Arthur "was sure he hadn't." A dispute arose between the men and the lady of the house. When the men tried to leave, "the most genial gendarmes I have ever seen" arrived to deal with the dispute. They asked the men to go with them to the Night Court, which they did with "the Madame in the lead and all the other Madames leaning out of their windows" watching the procession. Arthur took it as a comedy and argued sarcastically to the magistrate that as foreigners they were all used to being cheated and this was just the latest example. Arthur wrote, "Lincoln at Gettysburg struck a less noble note. When I finished, the gendarmes were in tears." After his defense, "the Madame stated her case," and the boys, finally done with their fun, agreed to pay for all the wine. The edited letter that made it into the archives slimmed the story down enormously. Although it retained the comedic value of the story, as clearly Arthur's personality was big, editors changed the number of bottles of wine from twelve to ten, eliminated the women from the story, and transformed the owner of the establishment from a woman to a "male proprietor" and the "Pleasure Palace" to a café.[25] This editing made it harder for people in Wilmington to see how Arthur and his friends understood their masculinity in the presence of foreign women in a foreign land. Such censorship made it easier for people back home to acknowledge Bluethenthal as some authentic gentlemen innocently enjoying himself on the town.

From Marseille Bluethenthal boarded the Portuguese ship *Madeira* for Thessaloniki, where the French had established a base of operations from which they were trying to secure Albania from German and Bulgarian penetration and prop up an allied government after the collapse and catastrophic retreat across Albania of the Serbian Army.[26] Unlike his time in France, his encounters in the eastern front demonstrated how Bluethenthal's memories of home kept him distinct from the East and prevented him from integrating into the Slavic culture of the Balkans. Bluethenthal and his American colleagues insisted that the Islamic and Slavic cultural world in which they found themselves was strange and exotic. Much like Edward Said described western artists and novelists who defined the East through their art and travelogues, Bluethenthal and many of his colleagues communicated memories of American power, race, and gender through a process of Orientalism.[27] These memories often looked eerily similar to how people encountered the color line and constructed gender at home in Wilmington. Bluethenthal thus unintentionally exposed how he (and many of his fellow Americans on the eastern front) interlocked cultural memory from home with the way he interpreted the war because he himself was a rivet that tied North Carolinians to the eastern front. Volunteers stationed in the East for the first time came into contact with an array of people and belief systems of the French empire, which "recruited Africans and Indochinese soldiers—coercing and persuading them to be effective fighters in the imperial cause."[28] These interactions with people from the East caused the American volunteers to remember home even as they quickly manifested their Orientalist gaze. When brought face to face with French Indochinese soldiers on board the *Madeira*, American volunteer Robert Imbrie noted that "to occidental eyes they were exactly alike, the same slanting eyes, the same black, wiry hair, the same lack of expression. Each was simply a bifurcated yellow ditto of the others" who spoke in a "high falsetto chant which rang of the East."[29] Harvard graduate and ambulance driver Charles Baird Jr. noted in a letter home that "these Chinese are so small and yellow that you cannot tell them from their khaki packs. They bumped us and jabbered like monkeys. We bumped them and cursed. They continued jabbering. Their talk is a funny, monkeyish twang."[30] These were published accounts meant to describe the situation to a mass audience of Americans. Bluethenthal's Orientalism, in a private letter, seemed to go a bit beyond the general stereotypes of his colleagues. His seemed intimately tied to his experiences growing up in Wilmington. Arthur describes his boarding the *Maderia* as a Portuguese "dirty transport ship" with more than eight hundred "Gambrogians," which unbeknownst to Bluethenthal were French colonial soldiers from Indo-China. "They tried to tell us that a Gambrogian is a sort of Indo-Chinese, but I have not lived all my life in the South for nothing. What they seemed to me to resemble most closely was a cross between a slim respectable Chinese woman and a Pulman [sic] porter."[31]

Bluethenthal's friends may have edited out the "smut parts" of Arthur's letter home, but they kept Arthur's racial views describing French Indochinese people. While it seemed inappropriate to Arthur and his friends to leave his talk of women in the letter perhaps because it would seem to undermine Arthur's status as a Southern gentleman, it seemed unquestionable to all in Arthur's circle—including his parents, who forwarded the letter to Princeton and Phillips Exeter—to edit his racial language. This suggests that neither he nor his friends feared that Arthur's racial views would threaten his heroic standing in Wilmington or at Princeton, and it illustrates how Arthur used memories of home to describe the racial landscape of the eastern front in ways that also helped reinforce domestic memories of race for people in North Carolina. Wilmingtonians could "understand" an Indochinese person because they all understood the racism and sexism embedded in Bluethenthal's references to a Chinese woman and a Pullman porter.

Bluethenthal continued to filter his experiences on the *Madeira* through the memory of racial stereotypes.[32] He and his colleagues were not officers and thus received assignments to sleep in the hold with the colonized passengers. Bluethenthal did not like the arrangement: "It took about three minutes for the hold to resemble in atmosphere and general odor a mixture of a nigger pool room and an opium den. I stayed just long enough to grab my bag and rush on deck, it was so awful I had to laugh." Using such phrases again illustrated to people back home what this encounter was like because they "knew" what the ship's hold smelled like through the racial stereotypes in which many believed unquestionably. The French lieutenant arranged for the Americans to sleep on the deck and in the smoking room when it rained. The American volunteer thought this was very fortunate not because of (in the unedited letter) "the reckless abandon with which a 'Chink' serves lunch, or because of their 'shockin bad habits'—(It was no great trick to catch them doing an 'Admiral Barry,' the one with the other anytime)," but because (returning to the edited letter) "they arranged to develop an epidemic of Spinal Meningitis and very thoughtfully started dying off."[33] In the unedited version, Bluethenthal referred to Rear Adm. Edward Buttevant Barry, who was commander of the U.S. Pacific Fleet for several months before dramatically retiring in 1911 to prevent a scandal in which some of his senior officers accused him of immorality for having sex with a cabin boy. Here we must question Bluethenthal's reliability in relating this story. He said that he was only present in the ship's hold for a few minutes before moving onto the deck permanently, yet he claimed to have witnessed sex between men several times. More probably the case was that he related Orientalist stories to his friends at home, making sure to reinforce the stereotypes that westerners had already developed about the masculinity and sexuality of Asian men.

The meningitis outbreak, nevertheless, began taking its toll. The first victim, a French colonial named Mohammet San Chu, received a formal funeral and burial at sea. Imbrie related that on October 25 three hundred Indo-Chinese soldiers under arms formed a processional at 2:00 p.m. "under a blare of bugles." Eight armed guards escorted the coffin and draped a French Tricolor over it while their comrades presented arms. The commander and the commandant of the ship "clad in full dress and bearing sidearms" took up positions behind the casket. The eight guards came to attention with bayonets while the commander raised his arm. Then a bell rang out and the engines of the ship stopped. The commandant read a service, "his voice sounding very solemn," and when he concluded, the bugles "sounded forth the plaintive, mournful notes of *le repos*." All the officers then stood in salute and "with a swish and click three hundred guns presented arms." "The remains of Mohammet San Chu" then slipped overboard, and "a soldier of the army of France sank to its last cantonment." It was a formal occasion that would not be replicated. Mohammet San Chu received an officer's funeral while the overwhelming scores of Indo-Chinese who would eventually die in transit were unceremoniously buried at sea. Their deaths underscored the reality that "large numbers of colonial subjects—without citizenship rights—died for France."[34] But this realization did not seem to come to the Americans on board. For them this was an annoying consequence of the conditions on the ship. Imbrie noted, "To avoid contact with the 'chinks' was impossible. Sanitation was not existent, filth collected on the decks and, to make matters worse, water, both for bathing and drinking, gave out."[35]

Bluethenthal was less elegant and more irreverent in his description of the worrying number of funerals. "As the epidemic threw itself into *High* ... Brother Gambrog, or Sing Hy, as we called him, had his pedal extremities attached to any non buoyant substance, and calmly eased into the *Drink* by night." As the ship neared the Adriatic Sea, the captain of the ship received a wireless telegraph that German submarines were nearby. The captain appointed Bluethenthal and his fellow Americans to look out for torpedoes and periscopes. "It was during these night watches that we first learned about them dumping the Chinese Chink overboard," wrote Bluethenthal. One morning at 3:00 a.m., they spotted a cruiser in the distance. It turned out to be a British vessel, but before it could be identified, Bluethenthal tried to reach the bridge to warn them. The Portuguese-speaking crew could not understand him as he and his comrades got more agitated about not being able to communicate the potential danger. "Just at the psychological moment," he wrote, "a dead chink having just been eased over board, and becoming detached from his moorings, bobbed up about 30 yards astern. The gunner had everything ready to puncture him" when finally the lookout shone a light and confirmed it was a body and not a periscope. Everything calmed down for the rest of the journey. Upon reaching Thessaloniki, Bluethenthal described a historic city full of Hellenism via the Greeks, Christianity via the Apostle Paul, and Islam via the Ottoman Empire, as "just like any other Oriental city. Women mercifully veiled, Turks, Greeks, Spanish Jews, and in addition to all of these worries, innumerable English nurses, evidently chosen for unusual homeliness of face and form." He continued, "Only the Musselmans and Turks' wives are veiled. The veiled ones deserve one of our President's outbreaks on humanity if the unveiled ones are any criterions."[36]

From Thessaloniki, the volunteer ambulance crew made their way to the Islamic-dominated city of Monastir. The German and Bulgarian militaries had retreated from the city earlier but could still reach beyond the city limits with their artillery pieces fixed in the mountain behind Monastir. The AFS volunteers first set up their operations in Florini beyond the guns' range but decided to move into Monastir to be closer to the mosque collection site and the wounded. Imbrie described Monastir after a bombardment: "It was nothing to . . . see mangled and torn bodies; a man with his head blown off; a little girl dead, her face staring upward, her body pierced by a dozen wounds; a group in grotesque attitudes with, perhaps, an arm or a leg torn off and thrown fifty feet away. These in Monastir were daily sights."[37] Bluethenthal would have seen these scenes, too. In addition to his brave work running among artillery shells to get the wounded out of Monastir, Arthur observed life among Muslim and Slavic people during the horror of war, and his memories of these experiences exposed an Orientalist mentalité. Eager to impress his friends Davey and Arthur, he woefully misinterpreted the cultural practices of people living there. Again verifying the stereotypes constructed of a racialized other in Wilmington, Bluethenthal described Islamic women in town as belonging to a "harem" and that it seemed to be the local "pastime to line the Bitches in heat up in the main square and then watch the fun." He believed that one particular woman "dropped her veil" to "slip me the '*Bed Room Eye*' the other day." But he told his friends that he did not want "to become a *Eunuch*," so he "didn't follow it up." He admitted, however, that he had his eye on "one little *Mangey* one" who performed in the square "so well in fact that I have noted her name and qualifications and have made her my candidate for "The Noble *Pisce* Prize." Again, while in a foreign land, his Orientalist fantasy seemed to get the better of this New Southern "gentleman." None of these descriptions survived the editing process, as his friends deleted these parts from the official letter that would enter the public domain. The encounters he may have had with French women in Côte d'Or and in Marseille help contrast Bluethenthal's Orientalist gaze of Muslim women on the eastern front. French women could be conquered, and Islamic women were forbidden or, in extreme cases, could be reluctantly used. But he did not expect to act as a gentleman with women from foreign places.

He treated women from home quite differently. He answered letters he received in Serbia from three Wilmington girls inviting him to prom. From this response we can triangulate his differing views of women at home and abroad. Although he received individual letters from each woman, he could not respond to them individually because he "was scared to death." He was "by nature very shy," he admitted, and so he wrote the three women collectively in a single letter. "I am as scared as ever. If there is anything more appalling to me than a bursting shell, it is fear of apron strings and what is worse, girls in general! I am utterly lost around them—utterly." And this was made worse, he said, by his time in Serbia where "seeing nothing but Macedonian and Serbian women with faces hidden and feet bare, I find the idea of writing to one girl at a time quelque chose formidable but to a group of real girls, educated and everything. I appeal to your mercies. I am lost!" He was concerned that because he spent all his time with men "that trying to write without being 'risqué' in this country is like—well, I can't do it." He was "terribly cut up" that he could not attend prom, even though he "would like to get loose at a dance again." He told the girls, "Now since our noble country had decided that it has to fight, I feel that I must too." But

Arthur seemed torn, and he regretted missing prom. He believed if he went to prom, "I could fix up that empty feeling," but the war was a "nuisance and can't be helped." Perhaps these three Wilmington girls asked Arthur to the prom—possibly even at the behest of his parents—to get him to come home. His response shows again that Bluethenthal's exile was voluntary and self-imposed, and he could end it if he wanted to do so. What is most striking about the letter is how deferential Arthur was to women at home compared with how he depicted women in Western and Eastern Europe.[38] Even in Serbia, when he responded to women from home, he was compelled to act gentlemanly. He seemed liberated from this obligation when he encountered women abroad.

When his unit moved into Monastir, Bluethenthal told Davey and Arthur that the officers had situated their headquarters in a building between two mosques, and they often had to outrun German artillery shells. "They bombard pretty steadily." With a note of western "Othering" of the East, he reported to his friends that none of the ambulance drivers was hurt because "we know at least enough to duck or dive into a cellar when not driving, while the civilians start running around wild." One attack killed several children of the neighborhood, including a girl of five or seven who "was blown into minute pieces." After the shelling stopped, ambulance drivers and townsfolk emerged to locate the injured. One ambulance driver described the state of his ambulance as "being shot through and through . . . but worst of all the windshield and top were ruined and a horrible piece of the little child wound round and round the steering-wheel."[39] Imbrie described the scene as "appalling." His car's "sides were blown in and the entire machine was plastered with blood and strips of human flesh, the shell which did the damage having torn to shreds a little girl who was standing by at the time." This was a powerfully horrifying scene for Imbrie. "In all the war," he continued, "I have never seen no more horrible sight than that of the child's family gathering the still warm particles of flesh, finding here a hand, there a finger or a foot, the while moaning in anguish, and the rolling on the ground."[40] John Munroe too described his damaged ambulance, but "the worst feature was that a little girl of seven, who used to play around and talk to us while we were oiling and greasing, was literally blown to pieces and fragments of her burned flesh were spattered all over." Munroe described how "half of her head landed on the top of my car and had to be scraped off with *essence*. It was pretty sickening."[41]

In this moment of stunning catastrophe that profoundly affected most who witnessed it, Bluethenthal made a revealing observation to Davey and Arthur that survived their editing process. He said that "the little girl's death was rather ghastly," but that was about all of the emotional commitment he could produce. He described the aftermath: "All the Mothers rush out clucking to their *off-jump* and try by a process of elimination to find the unlucky one." Finally one of the Americans found "two fairly intact legs and a piece of ribbon hanging on his Steering Wheel. By means of these the poor kid was spotted." Bluethenthal continued:

> The grandfather then started picking up the smoking, dripping hunks off the ground, and getting them piled together. Between trips, he tore his hair, and beat his breast in true Biblical style. I took a picture of him with the legs in his hands, not because I am specially fond of it, but it seemed the proper thing to do at the time, which I did nonchalantly. It also shows what an awful point of view you get over here. Fatalists of the worst kind is putting it mildly. (See fig. 12)

In this passage it seems that the horror of the war could not overshadow Bluethenthal's views of the villagers. He had seen a lot of death and injury by then, he had built emotional calluses, but the photograph of such a gruesome moment allowed him to parlay his Orientalist views into imagery that could visualize the East for his western friends in powerful ways.[42] He similarly related the story to his sister, Elsa. He somewhat flippantly wrote, "A little five year old girl standing nearby was blown into what our physicists would call I suppose an excellent example of the 'Atomic Theory.'" But what seemed to trouble him the most was how mothers came running out "calling their children and finally by a process of elimination and employing such syllogisms as All x is not y and such not the poor kid is finally identified." He again mentioned the photo he took and explained, this time to his sister, "Ordinarily it sounds 'perfectly horrid' to think about but you get a simple awful viewpoint here.... You become a fatalist of the worst possible type."[43] When writing to his friends he claimed Muslims were the fatalists, but to his sister he was able to divulge to her that he was, too.

There seemed embedded in Bluethenthal's Orientalist gaze a memory of segregated homeland landscapes jumbled up with the topography of the eastern war front. In the seat where Hellenism was born and spread, Bluethenthal remained disconnected from the geography, the history, and the people of this place. He could gaze at them, but he could not see very well the effects the war had on locals. The war made these people exiles in their own homeland, but instead of exile, Bluethenthal saw only fatalism. People here practiced a different religion and spoke a different language than he did. He did not integrate into Islamic and Slavic culture, and thus he was completely detached and unable to understand the suffering. It seemed that he viewed the Islamic people of Monastir as he would have viewed the color line in Wilmington.

Perhaps he was de-sensitized by all the racial violence that filled his boyhood memories of the 1898 race riot. Perhaps in Serbia he had been too traumatized as a consequence of what he saw. This seems doubtful. On the back of the photograph, he noted that he was ten feet away from the girl when the artillery shell eviscerated her. Some of her blood had splattered onto him as he ducked away. He did not run to where the girl was previously standing, he did not try to console the girl's traumatized family, and he did not help search for her remains, yet he had the presence of mind to take a photograph of the shocking horror unfolding in front of him because "it seemed the proper thing to do." This highlighted his detachment from the place and the people; he was an outside Jewish observer from North Carolina in an Islamic land and not a permanent member of this community. Certainly this detachment reflected his experiences growing up in Wilmington in which his whiteness insulated him from black communities even if he interacted with black men and women who came into his father's store.

His father and his father's uncle worked hard to integrate their Jewish faith with Southern culture in North Carolina, and it is likely that Arthur's views of Serbian Muslims were an extension of him growing up in a society where racial violence regulated the color line. This moment exhibits Bluethenthal's ability to nonchalantly become a documentarian interpreting a narrative of the Islamic "fatalism" and "biblical style" of the East to his friends back home in North Carolina that had no bearing on the actual experiences of the people in Monastir. This moment did not seem traumatic for him. Rather he seemed to believe it was a spectacle that needed to be recorded in the most casual of ways.

By recognizing how Bluethenthal projected the color line of the South onto the geography of Monastir, possibly as a way to integrate his Jewishness in the Protestant world of North Carolina, scholars can de-mystify his photograph to see how the subjects inside it are also gazing back at Bluethenthal's Orientalism without even having to look at his camera.[44] Not only can one see the family tragedy unfolding in the image. As metaphor, the photograph also illuminates some of the contradictions in U.S. cultural memory. This was a war where trauma, not heroes, reigned supreme. The photograph magnifies the contradictions between Bluethenthal's ambivalence about the "Orient" and the public commemoration of him as an "Occidental," a Southern gentleman, a cavalier, and a hero. It was a war with permanent consequences for those whom it exiled. Going beyond the photograph, Bluethenthal's experiences unintentionally remind us of many individuals, communities, and kinships—exiles—affected by the war in the most intimate and violent of ways: a nameless girl, an unknown family, men exploiting and even abusing women, and displaced subjects of the French empire. Exiles had memories, too, and although Bluethenthal refused to acknowledge these exilic memories, he proceeded to document them in letters describing the commemoration of a soldier's death on board the *Madeira* and in photography witnessing the instantaneous and traumatic grief borne out of the memories of a family who lost their innocent little girl. The war's permanent consequences for these exiles all become visible once Bluethenthal's Orientalism becomes de-mystified. Arthur's edited letter only made its way into Robert House's World War I collection in Raleigh, North Carolina, because Bluethenthal could be celebrated in a context where his identity became a mythology of a hybridized cavalier, all-American, Southern gentleman while the texts and images that inverted this symbolism could be obscured through the editing and archival projects.[45]

Heavily edited kinship depictions and North Carolina archival collections stripped Bluethenthal's experiences—and the wisdom that could be gained from them—and replaced him as a caricature of a cavalier aviator and Southern gentleman. His friends helped censor the ungentlemanly aspects of his letter, and his family did their part to promulgate their son's heroic nature. House and the archivists did the rest to strip the storytelling capacity out of Bluethenthal's communications. The fact was that Bluethenthal, as North Carolinians commemorated him, did not really exist. Only his mythology existed in cultural memory. This kind of myth confirmed to German Jews who integrated themselves into American culture, as well as non-Jewish whites in North Carolina, that Southern White Anglo-Saxon Protestantism was authentic, dominant, and even heroic, an assimilationist model for the rest of the nation to emulate. North Carolinians who remembered Bluethenthal thus performed their part in helping define who they could claim as a Southerner and who could be included within the national identity. This fulfilled an imperial project of cultural memory. It communicated a process of integration and exile.

Nation-states, argue Burbank and Cooper, "had the idea—illusion perhaps—that difference could be overcome by the appeal of the national idea and of participation in state institutions, or negatively by exclusion, expulsion, and compulsory assimilation." Frederick Rheinstein and Leopold Bluethenthal, especially when considering the Annales school description of the *longue durée*, had inherited a legacy of Jewish exile-cum-diaspora. But each man also escaped exile by assimilation into the national ideal. A longer family history of making Germany a homeland complemented their more recent history of making Wilmington a homeland. They demonstrated their commitment to their American homeland time and time again without losing their Jewish identity. Arthur was just the latest in a long secession of German Jewish Americans. The work of making homelands, however, came at the expense of others who had to be exiled. The price of assimilation was to adapt and re-present racialized ideas about black Wilmingtonians and sexualized ideas about men and women of France, Asia, and the Balkans. Not all Jewish Americans paid this price, as the example of Jewish leaders in New Bern illustrates. In Wilmington, some non-Jewish and some Jewish

Wilmingtonians allied together in the political, economic, and social milieu of the Cape Fear. Those who escaped exile could define their identities by making observations about the exiled living around them. Thus the assimilated could provide valuable observations through which to observe the exiled once their racialized stereotypes were de-mystified. "Nation-states," again claim Burbank and Cooper, "could never exclude, expel, and assimilate enough to produce uniform populations or erase crosscutting loyalties" either within the borders of the United States or at the edges of the American empire. Bluethenthal's wartime letters not only showcased his attitudes about race, gender, and sex. They underscored his imperialistic behavior, reminding us that this was a war between empires, and American volunteers were more than prepared to participate in this kind of imperialistic behavior as well as to communicate an imperialistic memory to their friends and family at home who easily received this memory without having to interpret it because they readily understood the behavior within their own domestic context. Bluethenthal's experiences, as conflicting and contradictory as they sometimes were, challenged the mythologies of republicanism that state elites were trying to build. His letters communicated his Orientalist experiences of the eastern front—his interactions with Muslim and Slavic people, not to mention with French women and Asian men—to Wilmingtonians who had the ability to verify and validate the social constructions of race and gender that already proliferated the cultural memory of Wilmington's 1898 race riot. Bluethenthal's experiences thus provided evidence—verified by his friends, his family, and his commemorators—communicating that some people could integrate into cultural memory while others were exiled.

CHAPTER 7

Cultural Memory in the Information Age

> If one could be in Israel and think of Egypt, Sinai, and the wandering in the wilderness, then one could be in Babylon and think of Israel.
> —Jan Assmann

In his lament over the "Storyteller's" demise, German Jewish philosopher Walter Benjamin decried that "the securest among our possessions were taken from us: the ability to exchange experiences." In the oral age, storytellers were the gatekeepers of memory. To tell a story, Benjamin argued, one first had to listen to others and then integrate one's own experiences into the memories that tied the community together. Raconteurs authentically archived the stories and communicated them to other members of the community and in the process added and subtracted knowledge, wisdom, and memory based on their own experiences. Their decline began long ago when the printed word supplanted oral tradition. This waning continued into the modern era as "the solitary individual" emerged and became "the birthplace of the novel." Modern writers neither joined nor convened a community of listeners and thus, in solitude, they created narratives bankrupt of truth and wisdom and memory. Novelists were incapable of repeating stories authentically because they never listened. Instead they overly relied on their own knowledge often acquired from texts stored in modern archival collections. The solitude of the novelist meant that novels were powerless to embed memories into their narratives because he or she no longer listened to others. The Great War deepened this crisis, claimed Benjamin, because trench warfare destroyed men's ability to communicate their brutal experiences to people at home while people at the home seemed incapable of making sense of the confusing conflict. "Never has experience," wrote Benjamin, "been contradicted more thoroughly than strategic experience by tactical warfare, economic experience by inflation, bodily experience by mechanical warfare, moral experience by those in power."[1]

The war created an even more significant memory problem for Benjamin. Not even the novelist could oppress communication as effectively as information could. The war, he claimed, ushered in the age of information that "lays claim to prompt verifiability." Information's only "requirement is that it appear 'understandable in itself.'" This medium of communication proliferated through print journalism and challenged tradition and wisdom that "was inclined to borrow from the miraculous" and "possessed an authority which gave it validity, even when it was not subject to verification." Without the aura of authenticity, Benjamin lamented that communication in the information age resulted in making events unmemorable. "The value of information does not survive the moment in which it was new." Experience could no longer be communicated well if information could be transmitted quickly and efficiently to mass audiences. As a consequence, the "*memory* [that] creates the chain of tradition which passes a happening on from generation to generation" was broken by the war. He claimed this powerfully affected the way people communicated their experiences face to face. "Was it not noticeable at the end of the war that men returned from the battlefield grown silent—not richer, but poorer in communicable experience?" Indeed some who experienced shell shock, now described as post-traumatic stress disorder, became mentally and physically incapable of communicating.[2]

Benjamin's lament of the storyteller is an expression of his fear of the information age. At stake in the storyteller's demise was Benjamin's trepidation that industrialized warfare and the mass dissemination of information usurped the role of traditional gatekeepers who communicated wisdom authentically. Benjamin's warning came from Europe, more specifically from

Paris, but his message seemed prophetic in postwar America, too. Hundreds of thousands of casualties and millions of U.S. participants certainly represented a splintering of collective memory. Historian Steven Trout contends that "American memory of the war was fractured and unsettled, more a matter of competing versions of memory—each with its own spokespeople—than a single, culturally pervasive construction of the past."[3] In fact, a whole industry of memory rose up after the Great War. A "memory boom" emerged that saw the proliferation of souvenirs, memorabilia, archival collections, novels, and films that fetishized the war experience of soldiers and indeed helped give the symbols of collective memory seemingly more importance than the actual memories of soldiers. Such resentment between those who experienced trench warfare and those who learned about it produced what historian Jay Winter describes as a "Great War between memory and history" that dominated much of the twentieth century.[4] Winter suggests that soldiers had their memories, too, and they used them to witness against the institutionalized information of the war. The shell-shocked became witnesses of trauma, the bodies of the physically disfigured authenticated the experience of conflict, soldiers' photographs documented a snapshot of experience, witnesses verified events in ways that the information age could never extinguish. These were all innovative moments and were suggestive of how people used technology and developed new ways of remembering and communicating memory. In fact, technology could help communicate soldiers' experiences in unprecedented and unexpected ways to a much larger audience.

The Civil War, not the Great War, was America's deadliest. More than 2 percent of the U.S. population died in this earlier conflict, touching nearly every family directly or indirectly. Communicative memories dominated these postwar years, and very few archival collections sprang up in the war's wake.[5] The Great War impacted Europeans in even more profound ways. France lost more than 4 percent, Britain more than 2 percent, and Germany lost nearly 4 percent of their populations. By contrast American families had lost much less on the battlefields of Europe. Whereas Europeans had lost millions, Americans had lost thousands. Although Americans lost much less, they certainly had significant exposure to the war. The United States drafted 4 million men and sent 2 million across the Atlantic to serve. More than 110,000 died due to battle and disease, and 300,000 were injured.[6] The sheer number of people involved coupled with the ability to disseminate information easily and quickly meant that cultural memory could easily splinter, making it much harder to control. Storytellers and even novelists would never be able to store and communicate so many different experiences of the conflict. Memory-makers would need new storage system technologies to keep up with all the experiences Americans brought back with them. Unlike the Civil War, where state agents relied on dispersed communities across the nation to link up their shared experiences with the cultural memory network often through face-to-face interaction, state governments this time seized the opportunity to document the Great War through state-sanctioned archival collections that fetishized but also ritualized the memories.

Benjamin's fear notwithstanding, his assessment of the information age provides a starting point for historians to examine how Americans communicated cultural memory effectively even when cultural memory was rapidly atomizing in the period after the First World War. This had important implications for Americans who hoped to dilute imperial memories with the mythology of republicanism; in the technological landscape of new media, they would have to communicate memories much more effectively after such a devastating global conflict. American citizens and officials would have to collaborate again to adapt collective memory to the new technologies of the information age. This was particularly true in the South. Indeed, Southern memory-makers had transformed cultural memory during America's wars of empire, but the catastrophe of the First World War gave many Southern Progressives an opportunity to take the Lincolnian tradition and make it their own. Many Southerners hoped to alter profoundly the memory landscape that had dominated cultural memory since the Civil War. Unlike Northern states that had committed to building institutions of government and memory through a bureaucratic system, Southerners resisted such state-building practices. By the late nineteenth and early twentieth centuries, however, states like North Carolina seemed to have recovered from the Civil War and now had thriving tobacco and cotton industries as well as port cities, such as Wilmington, that gave agrarian industries access to global markets. Communities inside this agrarian state, however, remained largely disconnected in infrastructure and in identity.

The historical landscape of the state had been defined by agriculture with disparate spheres of local governance. Communicative memory, which had limited capacity, dominated these local areas. Historian Jan Assmann suggests that communicative memories of ethnic and socioeconomic groups "seldom extend beyond a few thousand" without the "result of enhancements." Postwar Southern Progressives sought to bridge these incongruent agrarian landscapes with libraries, road works, and communication networks emanating out from Raleigh, North Carolina, without threatening the layer of infrastructure that supported racial segregation and the color line. The substructure of cultural memory likewise had designs of a "more complex" urban dominance over rural locations in which "the primary alliance between ethnic, cultural, and political formations" that previously dominated disconnected agrarian parts of the state began to fragment, creating social instability but also creating opportunities to stabilize society along new collaborative frameworks.[7]

Postwar North Carolina officials thus hoped to build a cultural memory that they could synchronize to their political agenda. They hoped to do this by connecting the memories of North Carolinians at home and at war together to demonstrate the state's usefulness during the war and to assert its legitimacy in participating in the U.S. empire. North Carolina officials, many of them Democrats who emerged from the violence of the 1898 election or at least benefited from it, in fact hoped to show that the state should play a leading role in this imperial pursuit—that its model of racial segregation, ethnic purity, and religious morality should be a cornerstone of the U.S. empire just as they claimed it had been during North Carolina's war effort. State officials strategically sought to maneuver North Carolina into a position of national importance to shape the discussion of tobacco and cotton trade but also national security, including the perceived threat of immigration and bolshevism, while also attempting to challenge Northern critics of North Carolina's version of Jim Crow segregation practices.

Southern Progressives adapted cultural memory to the information age by investing in the technology of the archives and building archival collections that would help them uproot and undo the Northern hegemony that had proliferated cultural memory since the end of the Civil War. North Carolina's World War I collection thus provides a unique opportunity to see the unfolding embryonic process of postwar institutionalized memory-making as an interesting case study that illustrates the concealed relationship between shared memories of power at home and abroad during time of war. Although gatekeepers—primarily historians and archivists—could access the archival collection, the archives provided a technology of storage, retrieval, and communication in the information age where the communicative memories of people interacted with the cultural memory that state officials sought to build. The archival collection illustrates how Southerners could adapt cultural memory to new technologies, using them to capture and organize disparate memories, while shedding light on how cultural memory could perform the work of redemption. Politicians, in perhaps the most Progressive Southern state, looked to the archives to ritualize and distribute usable and controllable memories of the war that connected and shaped North Carolina identity in urban and rural communities alike. North Carolinians who donated their individual memories, artifacts, and souvenirs of lost loved ones demonstrated how collaborative this archival project actually was. The war dead thus became crucial archival artifacts that North Carolina elites imbued with myths of cavalier and New South ideologies that came out of the losses of the Civil War and the Industrial Revolution. Now, on the winning side, politicians and documentarians used the archives to achieve a sense of authenticity and verifiability in ritualizing the Lincolnian tradition with a Southern twist that proclaimed Southern legitimacy on national cultural memory.

The main problem archivists had to overcome was figuring out how to transform biographical memories of individuals into cultural memory. They did this by ritualizing the experiences of individuals who hailed from small ethnic and rural communities across North Carolina and transforming those experiences into cultural texts. The archives supplied much of the technology on which experiences were converted into cultural texts and much of the storage and retrieval infrastructure on which the rituals of cultural memory could be communicated. The process of converting experiences into texts and then storing and retrieving them from the archives dramatically reduced the quantity of interpreters and interpretations of collective memory but expanded the number of texts that could be interpreted. This was perhaps the most effective way to undermine the atomization of postwar memory. As Benjamin lamented, new gatekeepers had the power to choose which memories would be authenticated and which would be concealed from the public. They did not rely on the experiences of soldiers to substantiate memories; rather, they relied almost exclusively on the canons of western, American, and, in the case of North Carolina, Southern societies. Thus postwar archivists preserved "authentic" memories in which they did not "begin from scratch" but rather reinterpreted the memories of past generations "linking [them] into a continuous process of communication" over time and space. Communicating memories in postwar North Carolina became a process in which archivists cross-pollinated the memories of the Revolution, the memories of the Lost Cause, the memories of imperialism, and the memories of republicanism to explain the First World War. Polyglots could also communicate continuously across time and space using the texts of Christianity, democratic Athens, and medieval knights to create a cultural memory of the Great War adapted to the realities of the twentieth century. In this way, archivists passed "authentic" cultural memories to the next generation. The World War I collection verifies how state elites and middle-class citizens together relied on archival narratives of western civilization to ritualize war memories that elevated the sacred individual over the profane community. They hoped to demonstrate that the heroic actions of Southern men documented their predetermined memory that saw victory in France as evidence of Southern redemption. Along the way they found that wartime experiences could communicate republicanism anew through the technology of the information age.[8]

North Carolina archivists collected and organized the proliferating artifacts of the Great War as a way to bring order to the chaotic postwar memory boom and to fulfill the Lincolnian tradition. The public would now be obliged to remember the dead through the gateways of the archival record. This was especially effective in this war fought across the vast ocean. Unlike the Civil War battlefields and cemeteries that many Americans could reasonably visit, the battlefields of Europe were too far away and accessible only to the richest Americans. Remembering the Great War took an act of extraterritorial imagination for most Americans in which people needed information so that they could create a "spiritual attachment" to locations they knew nothing about. North Carolinians thus fulfilled their Lincolnian obligations to the dead by developing "an art of memory that is based on the separation of identity from territory." They could be in North Carolina but think of sacred space in France. Thus North Carolinians had to reimagine the memory landscape by overlapping their domestic memories with imagined places far away and never visited. This significantly taxed the rituals of the Lincolnian tradition, and American citizens had to develop new techniques of remembering that juxtaposed their experiences made in the domestic sphere with acquired information they used to learn about the frontier. Their successful separation of territory from memory restructured the cultural memory network, causing Americans not to "forget" the Great War so much as decontextualize their memory of it. The legacy of this network survives. Archives helped store the extraterritorial information and historians helped interpret these memories through the filters of republicanism and nationalism. State officials throughout the country participated in building World War I collections that would document the accomplishments of their citizens and officials in the war effort. State elites in North Carolina were no different. They built the World War I Collection housed in the North Carolina State Archives precisely to fulfill the Lincolnian tradition with a heavy Southern accent. They harnessed the memories of the Great War to serve a Southern, a nationalistic, and an imperialistic agenda.[9]

The archive was a powerful institution allowing the gatekeepers of information to interpret the war for the public. Citizens collaborated with this effort by giving documents and artifacts to the archives. At stake in this collaboration was the postwar history writing that embraced a national history born out of the exercise of imperial power. Historians often use archival collections to construct the history of a nation, but by using the strategies that Ann Stoler describes as the "archival turn," they can also brush against the grain of the archives to find cooperation between history and memory of the war.[10] Although archives became mechanisms designed to support the state, sometimes brutally so, archivists often buried deep within the archives the experiences of people whose eyewitness accounts could potentially undermine or at least critique the bureaucratic legacies of archival power. This especially happened when people contributed artifacts that disrupted or even contradicted the canon of western civilization. One sees a structure rooted in the paternalism and racism of postwar North Carolina. By using the methods of the archival turn, scholars can view the archive itself as a collaboration between history and memory that unearths the concealed topography of empire, at the home front and the war front, that produced a Southern Progressive interpretation of cultural memory. Archivists explicitly built the World War I collection to ritualize cultural memory of the war and conceal the biographical and communicative memories of some North Carolinians. This was an act of colonial power. They ritualized the memories of the heroic dead who served on the western front while ignoring the experiences of North Carolina women who served as nurses and African American soldiers who served North Carolina and the United States. Yet archivists' collection strategies meant that they could not completely sift out the individual and communal experiences that critiqued the colonial power dynamics of the archives and the overdetermined agenda of state officials. Some of the war experiences of women and African Americans also could be inserted into the archives and preserved.

The communication of heroic North Carolinians and the concealment of women and African American experiences was a political and cultural response to a fundamental question in postwar North Carolina: would Southern regions and people be left out of the pursuit of empire like they were during the pursuit of industry after the Civil War? It seemed likely despite the international trade of agrarian commodities that tied the state to the global economy. The separated communities living in rural areas across the state posed an infrastructural access barrier to empire that separated the urban business elites from the rural economic vitality of the state. How could Southern institutions, especially in North Carolina, prevent Northern modernity and materialism from dominating the postwar South again? Part of the answer seemed to lie in integrating the people of the state into a cohesive identity along with integrating them into the state's economy. The memory project of integrating the dispersed people and economies of North Carolina was well under way even before the war began. North Carolina elites had already largely succeeded in building what Catherine W. Bisher describes as a "historical awakening." From 1815 to 1915, she argues, elites were prolific at publishing local histories, writing state history textbooks, dominating architectural styles, and creating monumental depictions "as part of their reclamation of regional and national power" that minimized or eliminated alternative narratives and experiences. "With competing visions of the state's past, present, and future all but silenced in official discourse," she adds, "these leaders shared a powerful sense that both in politics and in the culture at large, matters had been returned to their correct alignment."[11] This alignment represented a cultural tradition based on Southern white Anglo-Saxon Protestantism that defined pure American citizenship through a modified cultural memory stemming from the Lost Cause, the New South, and the color line. This cultural memory seemed under renewed assault after the war when race riots, the fear of bolshevism, anarchist bombings, and state-sanctioned Palmer raids across the nation demonstrated a fundamental and violent critique of American imperial power. Southern Progressive political leaders sought new ways to cover over such naked expressions of imperial power with memories of republicanism that would reinforce their own legitimacy at imposing their urban progressive agenda on the people of a rural state often ambivalent or at odds with their program.

State officials found in the Lincolnian tradition a powerful ritual of commemorating the dead that could aggregate spaces where republicanism and imperialism overlapped. But instead of using the emancipatory traditions of Lincoln's promise, Southern Progressives built a cultural memory based on hybridized older and newer Southern mythologies of the cavalier stemming from the Lost Cause and the Civil War, the New Southern gentleman emerging from the Industrial Revolution, and the xenophobia of pure Americanism. Many Southerners had long been cultivating such memories. Members of the United Confederate Veterans exploited America's wars of empire in the Caribbean and in the Pacific to get the federal government to recognize the Confederate dead. They successfully integrated Confederate graves into the Lincolnian tradition. But the information age emerging out of the devastation of the First World War gave Southern Progressives in North Carolina the opportunity to "prove" Southern identity was redeemable and even desirable for the rest of the nation to emulate during the twentieth century. The World War I collection gave documentarians access to consistent, reliable, instantly verifiable information that artificially enhanced the mythology of cavaliers of the Lost Cause and the gentlemen of the New South, transforming them into factual narratives that demonstrated a Southern embrace of republicanism.[12]

Southern Progressives who built the archives came to dominate North Carolina by emerging from the ashes of the 1898 election, which saw Democrats overthrow the Fusionist ticket in Wilmington and take control of politics throughout most of the state. They were open to adapting their brand of progressivism to a national scale, and many played a key role in Woodrow Wilson's administration, including Josephus Daniels as secretary of the Navy and David Houston as secretary of agriculture. The cultural memories of the cavalier and the gentleman—neither fully deployed nor fully forgotten—provided powerful precedents through which Southern Progressives could remember the Great War and redeem the past debacles of the Civil War and mostly failed industrialism. The objective of the North Carolina Historical Commission, which pushed state legislators to appropriate funds for the creation of the World War I collection, was to fill the gaps in cultural memory that North Carolina's involvement in the war laid bare. White urban elite men who also occupied the highest levels of state bureaucracy in Raleigh during the war made up the commission. Dr. Daniel Harvey Hill Jr. of Raleigh, nominated by Southern Progressive governor Thomas W. Bicket, served. Bicket had also nominated Hill to be head of the North Carolina Council of Defense during the war.[13] The secretary of state and chairman of the North Carolina Historical Commission, Democrat J. Bryan Grimes, provided additional political access to the governor's cabinet. Both Hill and Grimes were sons of Confederate officers from the Civil War. Robert D. W. Connor, who was a founding member of the Historical Society and its current secretary, also served on the Commission. Connor would later become the first archivist of the United States in 1935. These men were politically connected and highly motivated to shape the "historical awakening" of the state's wartime record and their leadership of the war effort.[14]

To oversee the work of collecting records for the archive, the commissioners hired ex-serviceman Robert Burton House.[15] House went to France in August 1917 but came back in April 1918 to serve as a machine gun instructor at Camp Gordon, Georgia. Here he stayed through the duration of the war, marrying his fiancée within one week of returning from France and receiving promotion to lieutenant.[16]

These elites attempted to layer an urban memory over the disconnected rural communities of the state. House was the central organizer of this collection effort. He held a bachelor's degree in history from the University of North Carolina and a master's degree in history from Harvard University. Both of his grandfathers fought for the Confederacy. While in New England, he spent time making friends "with the sons of men who fought against my own people," believing that "I can get on in the world with New Englanders in a better way now that I know more about them."[17] House was a devotee of Woodrow Wilson, but he also recognized the greatness of Abraham Lincoln. After attending one particular lecture on Lincoln during his military training in New York, he wrote that Lincoln was "the greatest example of simple strength on record" primarily because the Republican president had seen "the truth from the very first" and persevered through many challenges. House noted that Wilson, unlike Lincoln, provided "the greatest example of sheer analytical morals on record."[18] House's analysis of Lincoln and Wilson suggested that he was someone steeped in Southern traditions but not burdened by them. And he brought these ideas to his duties as collector of war records for the Historical Commission.

House and the historical commissioners initially based collection efforts on the design of the wartime Council of Defense. Only whites served on these councils interspersed throughout the state to raise money and support the war effort. Now House directed various community volunteers who headed wartime committees in their local areas to collect and organize the records and documents that they produced during the war. He also beseeched them to reinstate their wartime committees to collect documents and memorabilia from the more than 80,000 soldiers returning home. The

Historical Commission thus imposed the very segregated martial structure on their archival collection efforts that was designed to raise money and war materials in support of a war among empires.[19] Mostly white North Carolinians who donated artifacts collaborated with this effort. From very early on, House and the commissioners thus established a structure of collecting documents that guaranteed the archives would exclude whole swaths of populations throughout the state; this skewed the holdings of the archive he was building but showcased the "grain" of the collection. Adding to the inconsistency of their collection efforts, the rural geography of the state meant that House could not impose any universal methods of collection. He had to rely on cooperative partnerships that added additional layers of motivation to the project, such as their partnership with the United Daughters of the Confederacy, who were interested in documenting the wartime experience only of Confederate descendants. Each institution the commissioners worked with brought its own interests and agendas to its methodologies of collection. When commissioners learned that they were capturing too few documents from black communities, for example, House attempted timidly to reach out to black community leaders. They were able to enlist the help of black men in fifty-seven of the state's one hundred counties, but commissioners gave few guidelines to follow, reinforcing a segregated order of collecting these materials that reflected the structure of North Carolina society. The same could be said for materials from women. Although commissioners asked many women to collect archival records in each county, the concentration on soldiers and committee chairmen to organize collection efforts meant archival materials included few female voices. The archival collection of the war thus reflected and replicated the embedded racial and gender hierarchies of counties and was almost entirely white and masculine. This was not accidental but strategic, and it formed a colonial power dynamic of collecting information that North Carolinians used selectively to preserve the polarity of socioeconomic differences established along racial and gender lines that coexisted within the state.[20]

As the lead collector, House accumulated authority from the archives to influence cultural memory. He was charged with promoting the archives as much as collecting and organizing its documents. Thus he produced many speeches, workshops, and outreach opportunities to collaborate with citizens around the state. He used his authority to tell stories about the past but also to speak about the present state and nation. One of House's favorite narratives surrounded North Carolina's beloved son Lt. Kiffin Yates Rockwell, who left home on August 3, 1914, to travel to France where he volunteered for the French Foreign Legion long before the United States entered the war. He fought in the trenches in Champagne during the winter of 1915, where he was wounded in the thigh by machine gun fire in May. After doctors told him that his wound would make it difficult for him to return to the trenches, he transferred to the French Air Force and then helped found the Lafayette Escadrille flying squadron made up of American volunteers. The French military awarded him the Croix de Guerre after he was wounded in the face during a flight over the Verdun battlefield. He had refused to go to the hospital and instead continued to fly missions.

"If I die," Lieutenant Rockwell wrote to his mother, Loula, back home in Asheville, North Carolina, in the autumn of 1916, "I want you to know that I have died as every man ought to die—fighting for what is right. I do not feel that I am fighting for France alone, but for the cause of humanity—the greatest of all causes." Shortly after sending this letter, the twenty-six-year-old Rockwell took flight over Alsace on September 23. An enemy pilot intercepted Rockwell and shot him through the chest; Rockwell died instantly in the cockpit, and his plane crashed behind French lines. His fellow pilots in the Lafayette Escadrille recovered his body and brought it back to the main base where 124 members mourned him and buried his body in Luxeuil-les-Bains.[21] In North Carolina, people commemorated Rockwell with poems, ceremonies, books, monuments, parades, and speeches during and after the war. House used Rockwell numerous times to generate interest in the state's archival mission and to shape the cultural memory of the state's role in the war. Not just an American volunteer fighting and dying for France before the United States entered the First World War, Rockwell had been the first American to shoot down an enemy aircraft, the first American to win the French Médaille Militaire, and only the second American airman to have died in combat. For many in the state, he was the epitome of a North Carolinian soldier.

While Rockwell and other American volunteers described their willingness to sacrifice in terms of democracy, humanity, and civilization, they explicitly sought to pull the United States into this war among empires that would confirm to many that the United States was indeed an imperial power, too.[22] But participating in a war of empires seemingly contradicted American republican virtue, especially in Southern places such as North Carolina where elites negotiated the tricky and sometimes uneasy places close by and in far distant lands where nation and empire overlapped such as where republicanism and Jim Crow or civilization and Orientalism laid side by side. American volunteers involved in the Great War, such as Rockwell, exposed again the anxious conflicting memories of empire and republicanism that had been accumulating since the end of the Civil War.

Americans across the United States, like Rockwell, volunteered for France before the United States declared war. Many of them were highly educated and privileged. Like Rockwell, these volunteers hoped to portray a specific propagandistic message. Many organizers openly admitted that it was also an attempt to bring the neutral United States into the war.

> By personal and published letters, by articles, by books, by lectures, by photograph and cinematograph, they were bringing the war ever nearer to those on the other side of the Atlantic and by the organization of committees in almost every college and university and in nearly every city and town in the United States, they were developing a deeper and more active interest in American participation.[23]

U.S. volunteers of the French Foreign Legion and U.S. administrators, particularly Dr. Edmund Gros, the medical director of the American Field Service (AFS) in Paris, helped form the Lafayette Escadrille in 1916 as a force of propaganda. They conspired to use the media in the United States and in Paris to persuade French officials to authorize the American-only flying corps. The intention of this organization was to lead "their compatriots from the doubt of neutrality to a comprehension of the vital issues at stake—the safety of Liberty, the preservation of Democracy" (as well as the French empire's defeat of the German empire). "The sacrifice of their lives stirred their countrymen beyond all argument of words—theirs was the propaganda by deeds, and they won out."[24] French military officials complied with this propaganda by singling out Americans for French military honors whenever possible. Many American volunteers believed that joining the flying corps "would be more sport, and they also felt that they could thus serve France's cause more directly." Airmen even used two lion cubs, Whiskey and Soda, as mascots to propagandize their wartime efforts. Archivists after the war were able to co-op their carefully articulated propaganda into an expression of North Carolina identity that blended the cause of humanity with the redemption of the South. House, for example, liberally quoted from Rockwell's letter to his mother whenever he made presentations on behalf of his archival mission to demonstrate Rockwell's special heroism as a pure-blooded North Carolinian.

Rockwell's body, however, posed some difficulties for postwar North Carolina historians. In order to synchronize their political agenda with cultural memory they had to reconcile Rockwell's dying for the French empire as an example of North Carolina identity. They would have to do this with Rockwell's body in absentia because his body remained buried in French soil. Rockwell's death and the postwar public commemorations of him had come at a moment when history and memory in North Carolina were in flux. State officials could use Rockwell's death if the symbols of heroism could help people interpret Rockwell's death as a metonym for the state. This cultural memory accounted little for Rockwell's experiences in the trenches or in the air and amounted to a heroic cavalier interpretation of the pilot's death. Commemorating Rockwell suggests that North Carolinians developed an extraterritorial memory of the Great War as a great vindication of Southern identity. One observer memorialized Rockwell through poetry. "Only a country boy, yet / He links hands with Lafayette, / (This gallant Tarheel) . . . Higher than eagles fly, / Higher than eagles die, / No flare or music near him, / In splendid sacrifice, / Alone, he fights and dies. / Not Spartan king nor Roman knight / Ever fought so weird a fight."[25] Here the poet contextualized the fallen aviator's heroism within his Carolina identity and juxtaposed it to Lafayette's Franco-Americanness, an ancient Greek, and an ancient Roman—noble warriors bound together into a cavalier hero for the mechanized ages.[26]

"God's Tarheel" killed and buried in France had a Southern identity that North Carolina elites eagerly sought to authenticate through Rockwell's lineage.[27] House described Rockwell's pedigree as one of a cavalier steeped in the long traditions of military service, Protestantism, and American history. The archivist described the airman's father, James, as a Baptist preacher in Whiteville, North Carolina, who named his son after William Kiffin, a fifteenth-century English missionary, and Matthew Yates, a nineteenth-century foreign missionary from North Carolina. Both of Kiffin Rockwell's grandfathers were Confederate soldiers who survived the Civil War. House noted that Kiffin's ancestors fought and fought well in the War of 1812 for the United States, the Revolution, several colonial wars in the seventeenth and eighteenth centuries in New England, and Queen Anne's War. Many received promotion, merit, and land grants for the role they played in these wars.[28] But House added to Rockwell's cavalier nature an authentication of his gentlemanly status.

According to family genealogy, Deacon William Rockwell ventured to the New World from England in 1630 as part of the Puritan migration to Massachusetts. Going back even earlier, Rockwell's family, according to House, apparently came to England from France when Sir Ralph de Rocheville, a Norman knight, had accompanied Empress Matilda, a grandchild of William the Conqueror, to claim the English throne from her father, Henry I, in the twelfth century. Likewise Rockwell's mother's family history could be traced back to French Huguenots. The connection was clear. Southern values mixed with pure genealogy seemed predestined to create soldiers like Rockwell who would stand and fight when others across the country would not. Connected to such genealogical characters in France, England, and New England gave Rockwell a certain genteel aristocratic cache in North Carolina that traced the arc of the state's history and of the family genealogy to the same location. Rockwell's birth home, his apparent ancestral home, and his burial place thus could be conflated with his constructed identity as an aviator-cavalier to make him a symbol of the history of North Carolina. In their public commemorations around the state, officials thus amalgamated hybridized memories of the cavalier and the gentleman into a pure American machine-age aeronaut who fought for the republican honor of his Carolina homeland and of his ancestral home in France without acknowledging the imperial nature of the war.[29]

Such a projection illuminates the cultural memories of the Lost Cause and the New South in this particular archival project and had important uses for negotiating the spaces of national and imperialistic identity in postwar North Carolina. On Armistice Day 1920, House delivered a speech in Burlington, North Carolina, to celebrate the two-year anniversary of victory. After again describing Rockwell's heroism and genealogy, House tied Rockwell's noble death to the purity of the state.

> Such faith, such loyalty, such moral tenacity characterize North Carolina. . . . North Carolina is the purest blooded of American Commonwealths. There are more people in this state like the original founders of America than can be found elsewhere. Foreign born elements are unknown in North Carolina. Alien enemies do not exist.

Just as Rockwell's genealogy demonstrated the cavalier-aviator's purified gentleman status, House asserted that the people of North Carolina similarly had retained the purest genealogy and the original genes of the original Americans. The proof of these virtues, he claimed, could be found in the attitudes and actions of North Carolinians during the war which were stored in the state's archival collection. Information dominated his speech. He noted that the state easily filled its volunteer draft quotas. He claimed that surveys from draft boards showed that "desertion was practically non-existant [sic] except in the case of a few negroes and ignorant whites." He claimed that General Pershing had noted how "the soldiers of North Carolina were superior in physique and general bodily and mental tone to any soldiers in the South." House noted that more men from the state sacrificed their lives than from any other state in the South and that the Thirtieth Division (made up mostly of North Carolinians) "won more Congressional Medals of Honor for supreme heroism than any other Division." Then he invoked Rockwell as "the first American to volunteer in war, the first to bring down a German plane, and the originator of the phrase 'Lafayette we are here.'" All of these, House insisted, demonstrated that "North Carolina is the most purely American of all the states in the union." The proof was in the archives.[30]

The invocation of Rockwell and other Carolinian achievements highlights the tyranny of information as a tool of ritualizing postwar public commemorations. This cultural memory placed white Southerners in an assertive position of leadership—uprooting the narrative of losing the Civil War—as an example for the rest of the nation to follow. No longer a liability of the Lost Cause or a reflection of failure to industrialize, Rockwell and other North Carolinians demonstrated the purity of Americanism to win the war and a sacred Southern nationalism that could transform the state along political lines and lead the nation by example. All of this could be documented thanks to the World War I collection. This cultural memory was not a remembrance of immigrants, African American contributions, or of the terrible consequences that trench warfare had on the maimed, the traumatized, and the dead. It offered no critique of the color line or of gender inequality. It was an expression of internal domestic repertoire of imperial power that sought to explain the trauma of the war through the lenses of white Anglo-Saxon Protestant individuals and communities. It was an invented cultural memory that evolved out of the cultural memories before it, obscuring and forgetting racial and economic inequality and accentuating the virtues of "one hundred percent Americanism" and North Carolina purity in a context of American empire. It helped integrate the many people and communities spread across North Carolina into a stable cultural memory. The memory of Rockwell thus symbolized an imperial memory of power typical of the World War I collection.

Archivists used the collections they built to shape cultural memory. But this did not go unchallenged. People contested the cultural memory that state officials cultivated by sharing their experiences of the past in ways that resisted ritualization and interpretation. North Carolina nurses who served in Base Camp Hospital No. 65 in France witnessed trauma and death not in mud-filled trenches but in the blood-soaked hospital wards. These experiences proved just as authentic and authoritative as men's and much harder for mythologists to penetrate. Nurses of Hospital No. 65 practiced communicative memory by sharing their experience-based memories surrounding the trauma, heartache, and the success and failures that went along with nursing the wounded from an inhumane war. These memories often functioned as a counter to cultural memory in North Carolina because they could not be regulated. Unlike Rockwell, who documentarians and politicians used to project a cultural memory of purity and pure Americanism to people living in the disconnected communities of North Carolina society, nurses could subtly challenge the purity claims and expose the troubling mythologies of the state's archival collection because they could make their own credible and moral observations of the war. Nurses, historian Mark Meigs claims, were supposed to pose as an alternative "ideal woman," especially when compared with French women who government officials depicted as licentious. Military officials wanted nurses to portray matronly and moral versions of femininity, and so officials often isolated nurses from interacting with enlisted men.[31]

As proper Anglo-Saxon Protestant North Carolinian women, nurses who formed much of Hospital No. 65 could export memories of home to France through what Amy Kaplan describes as nineteenth-century "domesticity," a "mobile and often unstable discourse that can expand or contract the boundaries of home and nation, and that their interdependency relies on racialized conceptions of the foreign." The perceived purity of North Carolinian women accompanied these domestic visions that saw foreign agents as threats to hearth and homeland because they "blurred the boundaries between the domestic and the foreign," especially as they blurred the masculine spaces of the public sphere and the feminine spaces of the private sphere. Kaplan situates her rereading of women's antebellum Civil War novels squarely on elite women, but her analysis also can be used to reread nurse's wartime memoirs of the Great War. While women such as Harriett Beecher Stowe and Sarah Josepha Hale demonstrate how women could imagine ways in which "spatial and gendered *imperial* configurations are linked in complex ways that are dependent upon racialized notions of the foreign," nurses venturing to France who expected to implement these inherited homegrown patterns in a foreign land also had to violate them when they were forced to confront the chaotic conditions of war.[32]

North Carolina nurses who served in France brought their memories of domesticity to Base Camp Hospital No. 65, which was operational from

April 1918 to August 1919 at Kerhoun just outside of Brest, France. The War Department authorized Dr. J. Wesley Long from Greensboro, and Dr. Fred M. Hanes of Winston-Salem to organize the unit. The staff had 29 officers, 97 nurses, and 209 enlisted men. Many of the staff were from the same small towns in North Carolina or had known each other while in college. This military hospital would play an important part in the postwar transitioning of the sick and wounded who would be confined in Hospital No. 65 until they healed and were strong enough to endure the tough transatlantic voyage home. Personnel arriving in France already sick would be taken to Kerhoun to find respite in the hospital until they recovered. North Carolina nurses tried to implement their domestic visions of purity and hygiene within their management of the hospital, but the "Spanish Influenza" outbreak in late 1918 largely scuttled these plans. The unfinished part of the hospital compound was supposed to open fully in October, but almost immediately the North Carolina staff who took over operating the hospital in late September were inundated with sick men contaminated with foreign agents. On top of this, it rained for the first two months after their arrival. Clean water was difficult to acquire and the influenza pandemic was just beginning. Domestic visions that sought to purify foreign elements would have to be implemented later. The first priority for nurses was to stabilize the hospital, already laden with thousands of sick men.[33]

The spontaneous and varied experiences shared in this chaotic environment brought the community of nurses and doctors into a close-knit group. They made lifelong connections and continued to have annual reunions to keep their memories alive long after the war ended. These annual reunions were the very definition of communicative memories, and they exposed some of the inconsistencies inherent in House's elite ritualization of cultural memory. Hospital No. 65 reunions exposed problematic rituals of masculinity, of pure Americanism, of heroizing men, and of the glory of war that went along with cultural memory. They inserted instead memories of the role that women played in France, the trauma of modern warfare and epidemics, and the hard cold reality of death for those whom they could not save. These actions did not fit into the symbol structure and the mythology of cultural memory. In fact, House and the Historical Commission never collected materials from Hospital No. 65 or their reunions because archivists had "no access to official records" about the hospital. Ione Baine and Irene Brewster donated their personal records, which made up the bulk of the file, to the North Carolina archive long after House moved on to the University of North Carolina. In this way, these women explicitly attempted to brush against the grain of the archives, especially at the end of Baine and Brewster's lives when the communicative memory of Hospital No. 65 was being pulled apart by time and death.[34]

Staff members of Hospital No. 65 met every year until 1965. Reunion events usually consisted of meals, memorial services, and business meetings to plan for the next year's reunion. Without rituals or elite interpreters, these events facilitated spontaneous interactions within the group dynamic. Participants usually met in hotels in towns around the state from Blowing Rock to Winston-Salem. Of course, there was lots of time to talk and to share stories. The staff members, but particularly the nurses, were clearly a close-knit group and tried to keep alive the memory of their work in France. Ione Baine recounted their unit cheer, "Rah! Rah! Rah! Sixty-five / Happy, brave and alive / Tar Heel born and Tar Heel bred / But now we are after Kiser's [sic] head. / Carolina! Carolina! U.S.A.!" Baine included a list of all one hundred nurses as "A Word Picture of Each One." Rose Allison was "Witty," Evelyn Armstrong was "Lovely," Irene Brewster was "Lovely Person," Clara Fredere was "Witty Dark," Mabel King was "Loved Fun," and Elizabeth Sears was "So Fine, Wanted a Home."[35] By 1951 the official reunion program began including a "roll call of deceased members." Annual reunions continued until too many had died and the communicative memory perished with them. Baine and Brewster's memories critiqued the separation of masculine public and feminine private spheres and the paternalism that so dominated cultural memory in the state. Women from North Carolina played a crucial role in the war and worked in environments that were nearly as gruesome and traumatizing as the trenches. Neither Baine nor Brewster, nor any of the nurses or doctors, were ever commemorated like Rockwell and Bluethenthal.

Their accounts of Hospital No. 65 reinforced the imperial domesticity of home and nation when confronted with the geography of a foreign place with unfamiliar people and customs. Domesticity could have a particular application to war nurses because "the fear of disease," claims Kaplan, "and of the invalidism that characterizes the American woman also serves as a metaphor for anxiety about foreignness within." As middle-class white North Carolina nurses established their Southern "'habits and system of order'" to "anchor the home [or in this case the hospital at Kerhoun] as a stable center in a fluctuating social world," they tried their best to keep foreign contagions out of men's bodies and out of men's (and their own) souls.[36] Nurses could try to confront "the foreign" within the relative hygienic hospital. Yet they could do little to prevent mass contagion during the chaos of the influenza pandemic. Nursing in this environment brought ample opportunities for women to assert domestic order, but it also forced them to transgress the domestic visions of Southern purity. "When we arrived," claimed Brewster, "50% of the barracks was completed, none of the windows had been fitted with glass but were covered with oiled cloth or burlap." Each ward was built as a barracks and was 150 feet long by 40 feet wide. Each ward could accommodate between 35 and 40 beds. Lights, sewers, and water systems had not been hooked up yet. No stoves were in place to heat the wards. "At night, it was a fantastic picture to go into a ward filled with desperately ill men, dimly lighted by two candles burning on tin pie plates on the floor, one at each end of the ward." Brewster wrote of the kind of difficulties the influenza pandemic caused them and how they attempted to keep contagion from spreading. Lack of heat, light, and water complicated by the massive influx of unanticipated patients posed significant problems. Women and men adapted to the moment transforming the nineteenth-century boundaries of private and public spheres, allowing them to form intimate relationships in these kinds of difficult working conditions. They had to open "Siberia" to accommodate the number of flu victims, which meant opening a mothballed part of the compound. "The nurses, doctors, and stretcher-bearers had to jump ditches, and wade in mud over their ankles in the pouring rain" to move patients from convoy trucks to "Siberia." They tried to accommodate the sick as best they could. "One patient would be placed on the bed, using a blanket for a mattress, and the next patient would be placed on the mattress on the floor. The nurses took temperatures and found the sickest patients for the doctors to visit." While doctors tried to help as many as possible, "hot cocoa was brought from the kitchens and we tried to keep our patients warm and as comfortable as possible." Brewster noted that the staff had to accommodate 2,000 patients within ten days of opening Siberia. They were overrun by foreign contaminants, and they had no vaccines to protect them.[37]

Baine recounted some of the difficulties she faced on her first day. She was assigned to a ward of forty beds occupied by flu victims. She had one assistant who was a tailor by trade. Together they had three plates, three cups, a few blankets, and no sheets at their disposal. They brought water to drink, but the sick patients did not want to take it because the chemicals used to purify the water made it taste terrible. Patients ranged from the unconscious to the delirious to those trying to escape. "I felt ashamed," she wrote, "and tried even harder hour after weary hour and the rains poured outside!"[38] These were difficult circumstances for Brewster, too, who noted how "the constant faithfulness of our unit under these trying conditions was admirable. The cold and the dampness due to the constant rain were a serious source of discomfort, increasing the sickness among the nurses when their services were so greatly needed." Nurses could neither keep the men nor themselves from getting sick. The conditions seemed to bring the community of doctors, nurses, and stretcher-bearers closer together in their shared work of trying (and often failing) to regulate the contagion. "The work," she wrote, "would have been hard if we had had every facility to care for our sick, but good results were obtained with little to work with. The difficulties were overcome by the splendid cooperation among patients, nurses, and doctors." Men and women worked together in their efforts to stabilize conditions that yet remained dire.[39]

Baine noted that in October, 585 patients succumbed to the flu, 66 dying in a single day. Most of the dead were Americans who contracted the flu on board troop ships traveling from the United States to Europe. The hospital had 4,200 beds but was quickly filled to capacity. Baine described the welcome arrival of supplies that helped many men recover as the epidemic rapidly declined in late 1918. "We were able to make the boys comfortable and with efficient treatment countless thousands recovered and returned to their regiments."⁴⁰ Nurses made do with what few supplies were available. They learned to turn wash basins into bathtubs and to eat mess with only a single utensil, usually a knife; they worked while fatigued and in wrinkled uniforms, and developed efficient strategies for sharing water from the street faucet. They were able to institute a sense of domestic order despite their limited means.

North Carolina nurses sought to bring domestic order not only to the chaotic hospital but also to the traumatized lives of the soldiers. They gave the sick hot foot baths and massaged soldiers' callused feet with Vaseline. For Christmas they took gifts of socks and a sweater from the American Red Cross and put their patients' names on them and put them under a homemade tree. They wrote letters for soldiers or gave them advice about what to say to sweethearts and loved ones back home. But there were limits to their ability to stabilize the social lives of the men. Baine remembered, "We were much concerned over one boy that sent his girl a lovely gift and when she thanked him, asked whether it was intended for a Christmas gift or a wedding present as she had just been married." Baine recalled that "he was completely broken up and we found it hard to cheer him."⁴¹

The limits of imposing domestic order in such a traumatic and disheartening place, however, illuminate the difficulty of implementing memories of home in France. Baine noted, "In memory I can still see those boys as they were admitted with horrible suppurating wounds literally dying as infection sapped every ounce of their vitality." They found it difficult, in particular, to deal with shell shock victims because they "would often harm themselves, unless watched closely." They had difficulty preventing the inevitable infection or death. Most of their patients suffered and died ingloriously and were never commemorated like Rockwell or Bluethenthal. Dying under such pathetic circumstances betrayed the heroic mythology of cultural memory. Contrary to commemorations back home, the experiences in the hospital showed how devastating and inhumane the war could be. In an overseas land inflicted with foreign microbes that killed men so easily, Southern nurses often were powerless to implement their domestic memories of North Carolina society. Even after the flu epidemic quelled, nurses had to adapt domestic memories to foreign realities.

Unlike the structure of House's archive (and North Carolina society), for example, these white nurses operated a racially integrated hospital. Baine noted that her black patients were "placed side by side with the white ones" and "were always most obedient and appreciative of our services."[42] Brewster described the "humor" of "Willie Dear," who was one of her black patients suffering from empyema. His drainage tube would continually fall out while he rested in bed. It happened so often that the ward surgeon would habitually ask, "Willie Dear, where is your tube this morning?" Brewster described Willie as an "epicure" because he insisted on eating bread and molasses when the rest of the ward patients could only receive bread and jam.

Nurses also took care of German prisoners of war who were admitted to the hospital to recover. Baine claimed that she and her cohorts "thought we would be very firm and just show them how we felt about their country, but looking at a sick boy one could only see just another lonely, sick boy that might easily be our brother, so we gave them every care and a kind word, and soon they were on their way to recovery." Despite her expectations to treat German men firmly, these "Tarheel" nurses compromised their domestic memories when confronted by all sorts of microbial and cultural foreign elements.[43]

The nurses' control over their world had significant limits. They may have had an ability to blur the lines between public and private as well as domestic and foreign spaces on the ward, but they had very little influence outside the hospital. The military, operating on nineteenth-century views of female purity, took great care to isolate these women from the foreign elements of French society, even when their curiosities brought them into contact with the unfamiliar. Nurses and staff were largely confined to the army base. November brought the armistice and a relief for the hospital. Fewer sick Americans arrived in France, and work for the nurses switched from treating sick arrivals to helping soldiers from the front heal enough to survive the return journey home. To fill some of the downtime, military officers imposed their own types of domestic and military order by organizing regulated dances and social events on the base. Nurses could walk through the countryside unattended and throughout the hospital compound, but they could not leave the base without a pass. They could procure a pass to go into Brest for a day of shopping. Nurses rode into town in ambulances "for tea at the American Nurses Club" but had to be back on base by 9:00 p.m. In a few instances nurses were able to embrace foreign culture when they sought it out. Baine was able to talk her superiors into letting her go to Rome with a ten-day leave pass. She and her friends Mabel King, Rose Allison, Clara Fredere, Elizabeth Sears, and Evelyn Armstrong anticipated a "glorious adventure." They visited Paris for three days and then went by train to Rome where they toured the Forum, the Coliseum, the Appian Way, St. Peter's Basilica, and the Vatican. The women had the trip of a lifetime eating delectable food and seeing historic sites. Baine was saddened to have just missed seeing the pope. The nurses nearly missed their return to France because they did not speak Italian and could not find the train station in Rome. They traveled for a few hours on a tram—lost—until they met American soldiers who gave them directions in English.[44]

Although not wholly exposed to foreign elements, some women at least temporarily suspended their morally pure domestic visions while on tour. These opportunities were rare, though, and most of the time women did not venture beyond the limited boundaries of the hospital or Brest. With the peace treaty finalized, they began sailing home. Brewster returned home in March 1919 and Baine on August 6, 1919. Baine continued working as a nurse, taught Sunday school, performed community volunteer work, and indulged in romanticized domestic memories reinforced by her time abroad: "The splendor of Paris / or the wonder of Rome / never equaled by half / the joy of my home."[45]

While commemorations of Rockwell faded over time, nurses and doctors of Hospital No. 65 built intimate and enduring memories of the war that kept bringing them back together for annual reunions until the very end of their community's existence. They shared their memories of the war that often challenged the paternalistic structure and claims of Southern purity embedded in elite forms of cultural memory. The way House structured his collection methods almost guaranteed that he would never collect the memories of the Hospital No. 65 staff. Their communicative memories entered the archives postscript and suggested that the war had very few if any cavaliers and gentlemen but a great many sick and dying. Hospital nurses completely understood the poor success rate of keeping foreign agents from infecting men's bodies. They also understood, no matter how committed they were to domestic visions of purity, they would never be the same after their time in a strange land. The experiences of nurses at Hospital No. 65 likewise suggest that no matter how much North Carolina elites tried to demonstrate that the cause of victory laid in the magisterial efforts of pure Americanism and pure-blooded white North Carolinian heroes, cultural memory could never be kept purified from the so-called foreign agents of Europe or within the state. Many participants were indeed women who did not fit into the mythology that cultural and political elites of the state championed. Baine and Brewster only sought out the archival collection themselves when they knew all too well that they could no longer keep the communicative memory of their group alive. They had to transform the communicative memory of their group into cultural memory protected by the archives if they wanted their memories of the war to continue beyond their deaths. Baine and Brewster took advantage of the information age to preserve their memories. This group's memory could become a corrective of cultural memory encouraging North Carolinians to reform or abandon the rituals and traditions of an outdated cavalier/gentleman collective memory that confined women to the private sphere and pretended to purify society.

Like communicative memory, biographical memory of individuals could subtly undermine the efforts historical commissioners made at building a collection dripping in xenophobia and white Anglo-Saxonism. Historian Adalaine Holton suggests that archival collections such as that for World War I, failed to exhibit—and even suppressed—the rich tapestry of black literature, history, and identity through which African American/pan-African actors demonstrably and fundamentally contributed to American identity. House's segregated archives were colonial archives that wielded imperial power passively to suppress African American contributions to the war. He concealed the relatively few artifacts of black North Carolina soldiers that he collected deep within the organization of the archives. These memories of Southern black soldiers could destabilize the elite cultural memory that the archives helped to ritualize.

Lt. Thomas J. Bullock, who was born and raised in Henderson, North Carolina, volunteered, much like Kiffin Rockwell, to fight and spent most of his time under the command of the French. Unlike Rockwell, Bullock was black. But Rockwell and Bullock had similar experiences. They both enjoyed college and military school. Bullock enlisted underage to fight in the Spanish-American War and later fought in the Philippines. He then entered the historically black Lincoln University in Pennsylvania. After graduating in 1911, he taught black children and worked for the U.S. Postal Service until he enlisted in the New York Fifteenth Regiment of the National Guard. From here he was selected to go to the first black officers training school in Des Moines, Iowa, where he received his rank as second lieutenant and a commission in the 367th Infantry Regiment making up the Ninety-Second Division of the U.S. Army. In its first action of the war, this black regiment fought well near Frapelle, a small village in Lorraine near the German border, alongside other African American regiments that made up the division. They faced artillery, chemical weapons, and German advances head on without giving up their positions. The brutal fighting would cost Bullock his life; he was killed in action on September 2, 1918. Unlike Rockwell's or Bluethenthal's posthumous superstar status in the state of North Carolina, Bullock was barely mentioned at all even though he surely deserved it.[46]

Back home in North Carolina, Bullock's wife, Cleopatra, attempted to keep her husband's memory alive. Just days after his death she had sent a prepared typewritten brief of her husband's life including his formal photograph in dress uniform to several officials in Washington DC and in North Carolina, as well as to the *Raleigh News and Observer*. When she heard about a roll of honor being established at the State Archives, she made sure to contribute her memories of her husband. Cleopatra utilized the archive to embed the biographical memory of her husband within its structure. This was crucial because few records of black soldiers made it into the archives, as did few voices from women. Unlike Arturo Afonso Schomburg's anticolonial archive, claims historian Adalaine Holton, African Americans tended to collect documents to "counter claims of black inferiority and support their struggle against racist practices."[47] Cleopatra Bullock's aim likewise was not to critique the American empire but to have her husband included in the pantheon of North Carolinian heroes. Her unsolicited submission, nevertheless, helps expose the segregated and masculinized energies on which North Carolina elites built and used the archives. Thomas Bullock was very nearly the same as Rockwell but uncelebrated. When archivists responded to Cleopatra by sending her a questionnaire in October 1918, she included her typed sketch but failed to send a photograph because she only had one left. Later she reluctantly sent in her last copy but asked the state archivists once they were done with it to send it back. Although state archivists eventually completed the Roll of Honor, they failed to return Mrs. Bullock's photograph to her. Even though much of his biography was quite similar to Rockwell's, Thomas Bullock would not be made into a cavalier, a Southern gentleman, or a pure American. Rather than use his biography on speaking tours around the state, those in charge of the archival project buried Bullock's memory and photograph in a file.

This chapter focuses on the collaboration of North Carolinians and state officials to negotiate the places of nation and empire within cultural memory that showcased the political agenda of Progressive Southerners immediately after the war. By comparing memories of white heroes with the reconstruction of memories of the color line and the gender line at home, this chapter suggests that nationalistic and imperialistic memories shared similar cultural memory rituals. State officials and North Carolina citizens attempted to collect and archive the documents and artifacts of the state's soldiers to demonstrate their cultural strength and racial vitality, especially when contrasted with the wartime achievements of Northern soldiers. State officials built an archival collection to deliberately communicate and distribute Southern versions of the cavalier and the New Southern businessman through cultural memory. These memories of war stressed traditional themes of nativism, capitalism, and Protestantism, and added elements of the Lost Cause movement and the New South. But in collecting artifacts, archivists and citizens inadvertently undermined their own efforts because they also opened the archives to communicative and biographical memories gathered in documents and materials from North Carolina nurses and soldiers that challenged the cultural memory of the state and the nation.

While public commemorations and archival collections could help build a cultural memory that obscured the contradictions of imperial and national spaces, they also helped expose the contradictions in places where nationalism and imperialism overlapped. By thinking about the imperial practices of Americans embedded in the cultural memories that they produced, scholars can better understand the legacies of American volunteers in the early days of the war before U.S. involvement. Women were pushed too often from cultural memory, but they retained a strong influence in the realm of communicative memory and, in fact, their forced retreat from cultural memory often meant that women became more influential in communicative memory of the dead. As the nurses of Hospital No. 65 suggest, their presence and participation in communicative memory often posed challenges to cultural memory built on paternalism. Historian Michael Kammen asserts that what is distinctive about American memory and culture is "the American inclination to depoliticize the past in order to minimize memories (and causes) of conflict." Americans forget in order to form a balm around the social bonds of the nation. "That is how we healed the wounds of sectional animosity following the Civil War, and that is how we selectively remember only those aspects of heroes' lives that will render them acceptable to as many people as possible."[48] Rockwell's death and commemoration and Bullock's death and lack of commemoration provide an instructive pattern as to just how undemocratic the American memory that Kammen describes so often operated. Certainly Bullock and the nurses of Hospital No. 65 deserved at least as much recognition and commemoration in North Carolina as Rockwell received. Information age technologies allowed archivists and historians to store, retrieve, interpret, and communicate these memories through archival collections at the time the collection was made and across time as scholars accessed the collection. Historians could use these memories to identify the grain of the archive so that then they would see concealed memories rise to the surface when brushing against the grain of the archives. Nurses from Hospital No. 65 and Cleopatra Bullock's memories of her husband could be shared anew in the twenty-first century but only after someone did the work of exposing them. Americans have not forgotten the First World War; they have decontextualized their memories of it. Remembering the dead from the First World War thus is an intensive active process that requires citizens to understand the geography of the conflict as well as the multifaceted experiences of the men and women who participated. Commemorations, monuments, and architectural structures of cultural memory must be made to engage citizens to pursue the hard work of remembering and not simply to reproduce the memories of the elites.

CHAPTER 8

That Cause Shall Not Be Betrayed

> But I believe that the mind reconstructs its memories under the pressure of society. It is not strange then that society causes the mind to transfigure the past to the point of yearning for it?
> —Maurice Halbwachs

President Woodrow Wilson delivered his Memorial Day speech in 1919, just six months after the November 11 armistice, at the dedication of the Suresnes American Military Cemetery. Just four miles outside Paris's city center, the cemetery overlooked the city; the burial ground became the perfect setting for Wilson to make a final case for Americanism. Wilson was in France attempting to persuade the Paris peace conference to accept his Fourteen Points plan, which Wilson hoped would reshape the world system. The peace conference was not going well for Wilson, and his moral American crusade was losing momentum. By the end of May, British prime minister David Lloyd George and French prime minister Georges Clemenceau had rejected nearly all of Wilson's Fourteen Points on their suspicions that Wilson's policies would not produce an effective transatlantic system of economic and military security. It was a foreign policy disaster for the president; it took incredible energy to keep his fourteenth point—the creation of the League of Nations—on the negotiation table.[1]

Wilson's moment was passing him by. Historian Erez Manela suggests the postwar "Wilsonian Moment" captured the imaginations of hundreds of millions of people around the world who received Wilson's message of self-determination and carved it into their own political agendas. Many were already remembering the war as a new chapter in how the world system would function. African Americans, Vietnamese, Egyptians, Arabs, Chinese, Indians, Africans, and many others on the oppressed side of the global color line ventured to Paris to assert their claims for identity and independence. The Wilsonian Moment nevertheless passed with great disillusionment because Wilson was never able, and had never intended, to fulfill the wishes of those in the periphery. The wake of the Paris peace conference saw disenchantment felt by millions around the world and formed a backdrop to the 1919 revolution in Egypt, the March 1st Movement in Korea, and the May 4th Movement in China, as well as Gandhi's policy of *satyagraha* and the Amritsar massacre, not to mention the ascendance of communism in China and French Indochina. The president dedicated the Suresnes American Military Cemetery in the context of desperately trying to retain public interest in the League of Nations.[2]

In his attempts to make the world "safe for democracy," Wilson committed millions of Americans to what was then the most horrific war in history and sought to limit the liberties of war critics, immigrants, and labor unions at home. Wilson had to demonstrate to the postwar American electorate that the cause was worth the turmoil. He hoped to heal wartime wounds by recommitting Americans to the commemorative traditions surrounding Lincoln's promise. This was a process begun during the American Civil War that sought to define the beginnings of a new republicanism, argues Drew Gilpin Faust, where Americans could look to the dead as symbolic representations of religiosity, republicanism, and modernism.[3] But times and mentalities had changed since the mid-nineteenth century. Jackson Lears suggests that Americans had been reborn from a republic to a nation and had undergone significant transformations of race, empire, and bureaucracy since the years of the Civil War.[4] Consequently, argues Christopher Capozzola, Americans reformulated their relationship to the state replacing nineteenth-century cultures of voluntary obligations with twentieth-century cultures of the law and law enforcement. Americans focused less on their obligations to society and more on society's obligation to fulfill their individual liberties and protect their civil rights.[5] In committing so many young Americans to a war with ambivalent purpose, federal officials seemed ill-equipped to adapt Lincoln's promise to the changing definitions of citizenship, especially as black citizens, union organizers, women, and immigrants began demanding the rights of citizenship. The prospective Lincolnian tradition that Wilson deployed at Suresnes seemed ill-suited for retrieving and communicating retrospective memories from the losses of the Great War.

Despite his initial policy of neutrality, the Wilson administration set about implementing a centralized bureaucracy after Congress declared war in 1917. Wilson's regulation of the domestic economy, claims Adam Tooze, amounted to "a triumphant model of 'democratic capitalism'" that promised abundance and prosperity to Americans at home but probably never really made an impact on the war effort. The "true locus of American power" during the Great War "was founded above all on money not on things." Actual wartime production relied not on U.S. factories but on European "inter-Allied cooperation," which developed in 1915, at a moment of U.S. neutrality when European heads of state felt they could not rely on U.S. financial support. Europeans used this inter-Allied system to disperse European coal, steel, food, and credit to each other through intergovernmental agencies and cooperation even after U.S. financial support steadied. Europeans factories supplied the bulk of the rifles, machine guns, artillery, aircraft, and tanks while the Wilson administration supplied most of the finance and a considerable number of men and women. U.S. officials allowed banks to accumulate huge national debts from belligerent countries, manipulate currencies and inflation, and raise more than $30 billion through the sale of Liberty Bonds. This kind of European financial dependence on American banks created a "new asymmetrical financial geometry" that gave the United States a "position of unprecedented dominance, not over its Caribbean satrapies or the Philippines, but over Britain, France, and Italy, the great powers of Europe." Tooze argues that this provided Wilson with "exactly the kind of unilateral power" that the president wanted in order to leverage his view of a postwar democratic world system. Officials in France, Great Britain, and Italy grew concerned over their lopsided transatlantic financial dependence on the United States but needed financial services to defeat Germany. Europeans would attempt to reconfigure the economic transatlantic world after the war, which meant that they would resist Wilson's Fourteen Points.[6]

While the Wilson administration sent men and credit to Europe, its officials at home instituted a draft to swell the military and handed Gen. John J. Pershing command of the American Expeditionary Force (AEF). Wilson also put journalist and publicist George Creel in charge of the newly formed Committee of Public Information with the explicit job of "selling the war" to the American people. Creel used media in all forms including "four-minute men" who would speak at public functions around the country soliciting support for the war and advocating that Americans buy Liberty Bonds. In an effort to control dissenters—including immigrants and labor leaders—Wilson supported congressional measures in 1917 and 1918 including the Espionage Act, the Alien Act, and the Sedition Act, allowing the government to arrest and prosecute individuals for spying, to deport immigrants, and to jail dissenting voices. Further centralizing the domestic war effort, White House officials worked with Congress to raise income taxes and to levy a tax on war profits. The president also established the National War Labor Board to help prevent strikes by mediating labor disputes and the War Industries Board to coordinate industrial production and eventually "to suspend the antitrust laws for the duration of the war."[7] The United States Railway Administration, meanwhile, nationalized railroads to keep coal trains moving. Despite constant consternation from Republican Party members that some programs did not work as effectively as hoped, the Wilson administration largely succeeded in building the first U.S. military industrial complex.

American families contributed, too, sending their loved ones to the trenches of Europe, and in exchange they demanded from government and military officials a responsible and appropriate handling of the armed forces. But the new trench warfare was extremely effective—and gruesome—at creating unprecedented numbers of casualties and extreme psychological trauma. Austrian psychoanalyst Sigmund Freud published his essay "On Murder, Mourning, and Melancholia" in 1917.[8] Trying to explain the psychological implications of loss, Freud's essay suggested a fine distinction between mourning and melancholia, what today would be called severe depression. This psychological turn toward mourning and grieving made state actors ever more aware that their armies of democracy brought with them a public expectation that soldiers did not die in vain. Thus the public demanded that state agents commemorate the dead in meaningful retrospective ways that allowed them to address their psychological trauma as well as their physical loss by permitting them to bring their memories of the dead with them into the present.

To justify a military buildup that was responsible for the deaths of tens of thousands, the Wilson administration and the War Department needed to adapt the nationalistic commemorative traditions of cultural memory to individuals' psychological demands of memory. This massive undertaking required the hard work of standardizing the imprecise nature of collecting the dead killed in the brutality of trench warfare. Keepers and builders of the commemorative tradition had to recover dead bodies in ways that preserved retrospective functions of memory that used the dead to build individual and group identity, but they also needed to nurture the prospective functions of remembering the dead that accentuated the noble sacrifices that the immortalized fallen community made for the nation. Too many men died too quickly, however, to honor both meanings.

To keep up with the ever-increasing body count, the War Department created a new organization called the Graves Registration Service (GRS) in the summer of 1917. Once U.S. officials committed soldiers to the battlefield, the GRS had the sole responsibility of registering graves. When bodies could be recovered, soldiers usually buried them in makeshift cemeteries near the trenches. Thus the military entrusted GRS men with registering the burial spaces of soldiers who were actually recovered. Those that remained in no man's land or those that were obliterated by artillery shells could neither be recovered nor registered. The GRS registered graves in nearly 2,400 cemeteries resting in seventy-one departments of France; 15,000 soldiers were buried in isolated graves. It was a daunting task that was not completed. Neil Hanson wrote, "Many grave markers had been destroyed in subsequent fighting, or removed by farmers squatting on their ruined land in primitive shelters and desperate to begin ploughing and replanting. As a result, all trace of tens of thousands of graves had been obliterated."[9] After the war, the GRS units would recover as many of the dead as they could and consolidate them into more centralized locations. By early 1920 the number of cemeteries had been reduced to nearly 1,600. GRS leadership refused to separate individual bodies from the community or leave bodies in cemeteries that the War Department did not control. Thus by Memorial Day of 1921, the GRS reduced the 1,600 cemeteries that guarded American dead to 489. By August of that year, the Fine Arts Commission had submitted to President Warren G. Harding for his approval the plans for six permanent cemeteries—four in France, one in Belgium, and one in Great Britain—two more would later be added in France. Harding approved of the proposal, and the GRS began consolidating the remains of the dead into these eight cemeteries.

The creation of the GRS significantly changed the recovery process from previous wars. In the past, commanding generals of the Civil War took control of the burial process and frequently cared little for the recovery and identification of bodies, particularly when this interfered with planning the next battle. In the Philippine and Cuban conflicts, the War Department initially outsourced the jobs of retrieving the dead to private U.S. citizens who oversaw a mix of local and American contractors perform the work of recovering the dead. During the First World War, however, commanders in the field took control of the dead when it came to "emergency acquisitions," but "ordinary acquisitions" now fell under the responsibility of the GRS and would "not be attempted by individual officers or commands." The War Department handed this responsibility not to a civilian contractor but to Col. Charles C. Pierce, who had served as a chaplain in the Plains Indian wars and had headed up the morgue in Manila during the American-Philippine War. Thus he brought with him significant experience of handling the dead on foreign shores. He was responsible for the entire GRS program in Europe. He worked with all the chaplains in the AEF who were "designated by GO [General Order] No. 30, as Sub-inspectors of the GRS."[10] In addition to the chaplains, the chief coordinated the efforts of GRS units, who did the work of identifying the graves and liaison officers who worked with French and

Belgian civil and military officials. Liaison officers coordinated the transfer of American bodies from French and Belgian control to the AEF and vice versa. None of the GRS soldiers were assigned to a specific regiment; rather, their assignments were based on geographic zones. Each group received a sector, and they took their immediate orders from the general in charge of each respective sector. Although GRS men fell under the immediate supervision of the general in charge of their zone, they received their "technical instructions" from the chief of the service. This arrangement basically followed the recommendations outlined by F. S. Croggon in the Philippines and allowed GRS units to work consistently and immediately in accounting for the complexity of shifting troop movements. This system allowed for AEF commanders to enter and leave zones at will without the GRS losing track of the graves and the identification of the dead.

A GRS unit commander supervised work directly and coordinated his efforts with the liaison officer. Each unit received "one light Ford delivery car" and "one light Ford truck." Soldiers in each unit would move through the "zone of advance" to locate and note the graves with informal identification measures, and they would usually return to the back lines to complete the paperwork. After hostilities ended in the sector, working parties would then venture to the region and formally identify each grave. GRS officials built the entire strategy of the system around their desire to keep the bodies of American dead together. The chief instructed GRS units to "prevent by every means the making of isolated interments and the use of any but proscribed places of burial. Every isolated burial endangers the loss of a soldier's body, and such a menace to the comfort of bereaved friends must be prevented at all hazards." The GRS built the community of the fallen in part because innate in their work was a pragmatic efficiency needed to recover so many bodies.[11]

Identifying the graves of Americans had a specific process. When in the field searching for gravesites, GRS men used name pegs, which were "nothing more than V shaped wooden pegs or boards, 1 cm. in thickness, 9 cm. wide at top, and 38 cm. in length." Chaplains were expected to always keep a good supply of name pegs. Attached to the peg was a label in which chaplains and GRS men could write "in BLOCK letters, with hard, black lead pencil," the identification information of each man buried below. "The name pegs are to be securely fixed in the ground at an angle of 45 degrees, with the labeled side underneath to protect the inscription from the weather." GRS workers attached soldiers' duplicate identification tag ("dog tags") to the name peg and took the other one for their records. Although identification bottles could also be used, this was only done if no name pegs were available. The system of identification tags was much more efficient at identifying the remains than the bottles used in the Philippines. Graves were not deemed "fully reported" "until a GRS officer or a responsible NCO [noncommissioned officer] acting under his orders had visited the grave, is reasonably satisfied of its identity and has affixed to the cross, about one foot above the ground, an aluminum strip . . . bearing the letters 'GRS.'" Once a GRS unit fully reported graves and the chief of the service had found an acceptable burial space, GRS men or other military personal removed the bodies from the field to the new cemetery. In all of these new burial spaces, the GRS required a burial officer to supervise the process, and a chaplain had to be present at all burials including those not of the Christian faith. GRS men then had to recheck the battlefields to make sure that they had left no grave behind and no soldier was in an isolated burial spot.[12]

To be sure that the public, including those families that lost someone, derived the appropriate symbolic meaning from the dead, the War Department seized virtually complete control of access to the bodies. This went far beyond simply planning and laying out the new cemeteries; it marked a monopoly on the retrospective and prospective interpretations of the dead. GRS officials, for example, prohibited all photographs of the dead. The GRS ordered its own photographers to document gravesites for two reasons: to "provide relatives of the dead with photographs of graves" and so that officials could reconstruct cemeteries in case they were destroyed "by shell fire or otherwise." Other than GRS photographers, "No photograph of cemeteries or individual graves shall be taken except by written permit approved by the Chief of the GRS." This prohibition included family members and reporters. Negatives of any photograph could only be developed at the Signal Corps laboratory in Paris, and all prints "will be censored and stamped by the Press Officer, Intelligence Section, General Staff, GHQ." Even the cameras used to take images had to be "listed in the office of the Chief." It was a complete takeover of all representations pertaining to the dead and had a chilling effect on communicative memory. Although the principal reason for taking pictures was to send images of the graves to loved ones, photos of gravesites were "issued to relatives of the dead only upon their request" and were subject to "additional censorship." Furthermore, GRS officials forbade soldiers and workers to disclose information to private individuals about the location of their loved ones. The office of the chief of the service maintained the sole archives of information pertaining to the dead, and his office actively censored all information. If a GRS soldier received a personal inquiry about a gravesite, he had to forward it to the chief's office. If the soldier disclosed any information to the private citizen, he was considered to be in a "breach of trust, even though the information is not prohibited by ordinary censorship." That the War Department viewed American war graves as intelligence sites subject to censorship demonstrated just how much military officials felt compelled to control the meaning of the dead.[13] With this level of control, the GRS dressed the dead in all the ornaments of prospective nationalism. From the moment of death to the initial burial, to the body's disinterment and final reburial, military officials wanted to control how citizens honored the unforgettable achievements of the dead.

This kind of GRS-dominated cultural memory, which in so many ways controlled and concealed the dead from communicative memory, provided the backdrop for President Wilson's 1919 Memorial Day address in the Suresnes American Cemetery. The cemetery hosted thousands of U.S. soldiers and foreign dignitaries, including Marshall Foch, who attended the ceremony. After the playing of the "Star Spangled Banner," the "Marseillaise," taps, and a statement read on behalf of the absent Prime Minister Georges Clemenceau, Wilson spoke prospectively of the dead, championing their achievements and sacrifices in the war. He referred to the Great War dead as "a unique breed. Their like has not been seen since the far days of the Crusades." He likened the men who died as fighting "the cause of humanity and of mankind." Wilson's opening move of comparing the men of the AEF to Christian crusaders of the Middle Ages underscored the timelessness of his crusade in which the world war was just the beginning; the peace would complete the crusade. "They are dead; they have done their utmost to show their devotion to a great cause, and they have left us to see to it that that cause shall not be betrayed." These comments inched Wilson toward the real objective of his speech in which he hoped his contested allies, along with his avid supporters, would hold up his League of Nations as the institution that would prevent future wars:

> It is for us, particularly for us who are civilized, to use our proper weapons of counsel and agreement to see to it that there never is such a war again.... So it is our duty to take and maintain the safeguards which will see to it that the mothers of America and the mothers of France and England and Italy and Belgium and all other suffering nations should never be called upon for this sacrifice again.

The president spoke to Europeans and Americans at home about the necessity of the peace treaty to make this a war to end all others. It was a bargain made to European mothers and suffering nations over the dead bodies he commemorated. This was Wilson's best attempt to link the memory of the living to the cultural memory of the dead by amplifying the prospective greatness of the dead's achievements and how they deserved the respect of the living to keep their memories alive forever more. By stressing both functions of remembering the dead, Wilson hoped that the grieving would overwhelmingly convince heads of state and diplomats in France, as well as skeptical congressmen back in the United States, to accept a peace treaty.[14]

Lincoln's long shadow fell over Wilson. Just as Lincoln had helped dedicate Gettysburg, Wilson dedicated a U.S. military cemetery in France. Just as Lincoln had politicized the dead to make the war about "the new birth of freedom" and the abolishment of slavery, so Wilson politicized the sacrifice of the dead to promote his League of Nations. Wilson's most adamant and memorable statement concerned the League: "This can be done. It must be done. And it will be done," perhaps echoed Lincoln's "government of the people, by the people, for the people" in the ears of his listeners. Wilson certainly understood his speech in the context of Lincoln's famous address and even quoted from it. "The League of Nations is the covenant of governments that these men shall not have died in vain." Although not quite as eloquent or brief (Wilson spoke for nearly thirty minutes), Wilson made sure to cast his dedication in the traditions of the Civil War. A Southerner ensconced in the cold memory of what historian Nina Silber describes as the "Romance of Reunion," where white Southerners and white Northerners sought reconciliation at the expense of black civil rights, Wilson suggested the "sons of America [from the Great War] who were privileged to be buried in their mother country will mingle with the dust of the men who fought for the preservation of the Union." The metaphor of the Civil War became the metaphor of the Great War in the president's mind. "As those men gave their lives in order that America might be united, these men have given their lives in order that the world might be united." He continued, "Those men gave their lives in order to secure the freedom of a nation. These men have given theirs in order to secure the freedom of mankind." His next comment focused his political message further: "I look for the time when every man who now puts his counsel against the united service of mankind under the League of Nations will be just as ashamed of it as if he now regretted the union of the States."[15]

New York Times reporter Richard Oulahan found that passages like these illustrated Wilson's direct challenge to senators in Washington DC who opposed the peace terms and the League of Nations.[16] But Wilson did not focus his criticism solely on the American opposition. He claimed that some advisors at the peace conference tried to "insert into the counsel of statesmen the old reckonings of selfishness and bargaining and national advantage" and that "any man who counsels these things advocates the renewal of the sacrifice which these men have made." Instead of private counsel, "the peoples of the world are in the saddle." No longer would courtiers and lobbyists be able to dictate the parameters of the world system; everyone would have a stake in the system through the League. Wilson issued "a challenge that no previous generation ever dared" to undertake. The sacrifice of the men buried beneath Wilson's feet provided the urgency. "We all believe, I hope, that the spirits of these men are not buried with their bodies. Their spirits live." These men, suggested Wilson, underscored the purpose of America's involvement in the war which was "to show mankind the way to liberty." On all of this Wilson urged his listeners to consider "all the great traditions of America to make yourselves soldiers now once for all in this common cause, where we need wear no uniform except the uniform of the heart, clothing ourselves with the principles of right and saying to men everywhere, 'You are our brothers and we invite you into the comradeship of liberty and peace." He concluded with a personal note that he hoped would underscore the legitimacy of his purpose. "I sent these lads over here to die. Shall I—can I—ever speak a word of counsel which is inconsistent with the assurances I gave them when they came over? It is inconceivable."[17]

Wilson proposed a memory of the war dead that suggested Americans would become full-throated interventionists in the world, creating a New World Order that would regulate the world system, including America itself, by eliminating global economic barriers, advocating self-determination for the great nations of Europe, and regulating it all through global institutions such as the League of Nations.[18] As historian Erez Manela suggests, Leninism implemented by the Bolsheviks in the Soviet Union offered the only viable alternative to Wilsonianism.[19] And to this end, Wilson extended Lincoln's promise to Europeans as an expression of Americanism—packaged in commemorative ritual—that could be exported beyond the borders of the United States and to the European continent. But in many ways Wilson's attempt to extend Lincoln's promise to a war-torn Europe fell flat. Wilson had difficulty translating the sacrifice of the fallen community, from the Civil War and the Great War, into real political action. Lincoln had made much of his speech about the idea that the Civil War had been a conflict to emancipate slaves. The irony of this was that at Suresnes the president summoned the cold memory images of reconciliation and reunification—a process at odds with the African American quest for civil rights in the Reconstruction and Progressive eras—and tried to sell the process to Europeans. Had he attempted to warm cultural memory by reinvigorating the emancipatory tradition of Lincoln's promise to commemorate the noble cause of liberty by using the dead to acknowledge the importance of black troops in the war effort, the yoke of colonialism around the world, and the plight of oppressed peoples seeking authentic self-determination, the rhetoric might have better underscored the connection between the League of Nations and the sacrifice of the dead. But the president was not seeking this kind of transformation. Wilson's reliance on a colder memory failed to find any new interpretations from Lincoln's promise. His dedication speech lacked vision and leadership domestically as well as internationally. Just as with his Latin American Pact, Wilson's Fourteen Points disrupted neither the line of colonialism nor the line of Orientalism nor the color line of the world system but rather promised to regulate these lines and manage the world system in a way that benefited the traditional Great Powers with the United States in the lead. It was an address that spoke to Wilson's inability to integrate authentically the communicative memory of the dead with the cultural memory of the war.

Wilson's use of the bully pulpit in an attempt to manipulate cultural memory of the war would not go unanswered. Citizens would respond. He asserted that the war should be remembered through an American lens and that American families made sacrifices to guarantee the memory of America's gift to the world system. But the president offered very little to console the actual families. Some scholars suggest that this was an example of a public official unilaterally manipulating public opinion through cultural memory and using the bureaucracy of the state to shape the way future citizens would come to remember the war. Other scholars contend that efforts like Wilson's had limited effects. They stress the spontaneous memories of soldier groups who, often with the help of grieving families, built their own postwar communicative memories and countermemorials of the dead shunning the self-aggrandizement of public officials pedaling a nationalistic cultural memory.[20] These important interpretations stress the tension, even animosity, that naturally exists between communicative and cultural memory. But these interpretations also often overlook the opposite, if not equally important, tendency for citizens and government officials to collaborate by bringing communicative and cultural memory together over the rituals of the dead. Rather than reading Wilson's Suresnes speech solely as an attempt to influence the memories of millions in the United States and abroad, the president's text becomes the opening statement in a much broader coalition of middle-class citizens, corporate leaders, and government officials negotiating the parameters and meanings of the Lincolnian obligations to honor the dead. Outspoken critics could be seen as collaborating with those in power using communicative memory to critique, readjust, and (re)shape cultural memory around the collective memory project in which Americans tended to layer republican meanings over imperial realities.

There was much at stake for government officials and citizens alike in the immediate postwar milieu. Despite Wilson's negotiations at the Paris peace conference, the Senate and the American people rejected the role of the United States as a global leader, at least as Wilson framed it. The League of Nations required the United States to give up some of its sovereignty, and they believed this price was too much to pay in exchange for collective security even if that meant greater U.S. global hegemony.[21] This not only negated the United States' participation in the League of Nations but also spoiled the prospective interpretation that Wilson had used to commemorate the war dead. The dead were buried in Europe seemingly with no tangible cultural memory to explain the meaning of their sacrifices. Meanwhile the threat of widespread disruption, chaos, and even revolution had already occurred in Russia and was threatening the rest of Europe and the United States. Government officials in Western Europe acted quickly, working together to preserve capitalism through an informal system of cooperation designed to correct their financial dependence on the United States that had come to dominate the transatlantic economic world. They needed this cooperation, in part, to maintain social order within respective national borders and colonial order within respective empires that also saw them jockey for prime position in a postwar colonial world system that promised the spoils of empire. There were significant financial risks, as American bankers had underwritten massive wartime loans to belligerents, and now beneficiaries feared losing their investments, threatening the entire transatlantic world order. Incredible domestic risks existed as well. Wives, parents, and children had given their loved ones over to a government that wanted to build a democratic army and were left to wonder if their husbands, children, and fathers would return home. The end of the war meant returning soldiers, job losses, rapid inflation, a retrenched color line, and the "Red Menace" that dominated the summer of 1919. It also meant mourning the dead on a massive level, and people began questioning U.S. military officials' capacity to retrospectively honor their dead kin.

New commemorative traditions emerged out of American attempts to manage these risks. Americans who expected reverent republican treatment of the dead collaborated with government officials who sought to keep citizens invested in the values of Americanness. Nearly 40 percent of families elected to keep their dead buried in Europe, but 60 percent chose to return their dead to the United States. Those bodies that remained in Europe became the centerpiece of a new tradition that had the effect of producing sentimental European-American connections as they encouraged Americans to participate in a transatlantic pilgrimage that would demonstrate American respect for the dead and American values as a trusted resource in the postwar world. These pilgrimages allowed Americans, both pilgrims and tourists, to retrieve American cultural memory by journeying to Europe and simultaneously demonstrating American republicanism to European observers. This had an effect on extending the Lincolnian tradition to European soil. But few Americans could make this pilgrimage; families who chose to bring home the remains of their loved ones, at government expense, reproduced the ritual of pilgrimage in reverse that came out of the practices of the Spanish-Cuban-American and Philippine-American Wars where Americans desired to sanctify the dead in U.S. soil. War families wanted to bring their dead home so they could more easily keep them in their lives and in their memories. Many families, and many of the electorate too, demanded a responsive, retrospective, and republican retrieval of the nation's dead. At the conclusion of the war, the War Department continued to locate and retrieve the remains of U.S. servicemen through the GRS. With the threat of warfare gone, registration and recovery teams could work much more efficiently.

But the postwar milieu also produced a whole new set of difficulties. It became incredibly difficult for GRS units to retrieve bodies without violating the national sovereignty of other countries. In October 1918, during the dying days of the conflict, William Graves Sharp, the U.S. ambassador to France, negotiated with the French Foreign Office to petition the return of U.S. bodies to U.S. soil. But these negotiations ended with French officials only allowing the GRS units access to French transportation infrastructure for the purpose of embalming and burying U.S. soldiers in France. Returning the bodies to the United States, French officials insisted, would be discussed after the war. France's reconstruction efforts would take precedence, and French authorities needed to use the railways to transport building materials and men. American use of the railways to transport the dead would have to wait through the logistical bottleneck. In addition to French national policy, U.S. retrieval practices had to take into account the various local jurisdictions controlled by local mayors and police officials who held significant power in their dominions. In Lambezellec, near Brest and about ten kilometers from Kerhoun, the Commissaire de Police reported to the French director of general safety at the Ministry of the Interior in late April 1919 that he imposed a work stoppage on African American soldiers who were recovering U.S. dead soldiers that had been buried in mass graves in the city cemetery. Apparently U.S. authorities buried soldiers without coffins for several months beginning in October 1918 because they had no wood. The Commissaire estimated that between 100 and 150 bodies were deposited daily over a few months and assumed they had all been victims of the flu epidemic. French law required that diseased corpses not be exhumed for five years, but GRS men were digging up the bodies just months after their original burial. Many houses bordered the cemetery, and black flies circulated around the "diseased" dead, frightening the townsfolk who feared a public safety disaster in the making. The mayor of Lambezellec heard many grievances from townsfolk complaining about the behavior of their allies, and he too believed the Americans were endangering public health. So he ordered an immediate work stoppage. The director of the General Safety forwarded these concerns to GRS chief Pierce, who embarrassingly issued an apology admitting that his "young zealous officers" had indeed violated French laws. Pierce reminded the French director that the GRS desired to comply with French law in all cases. GRS headquarters sent a telegram to the burial party on May 8, ordering them to cease work. These kinds of legitimate concerns had a deeply consequential effect on living Americans' ability to develop their postwar memory rituals.[22]

The War Department thus felt mounting pressure from U.S. families to return bodies quickly as officials had promised before the war. On top of this, the War Department faced a public relations nightmare in the making that would surely impact collective memories of Americans at home. Col. M. J. Henry in the quartermaster general's office explained, "The temporary coffins in which the bodies have been interred in the National Cemeteries [in Europe] have been made of unseasoned wood as it was impossible at that time to purchase seasoned lumber." The results were that "the coffins have shrunk enormously, leaving cracks and are unsuitable for the purpose of sending remains to the United States." Henry recommended immediate retrieval of all U.S. remains. He advised that the military place experienced officers in charge of the process who would document, in triplicate form, every movement of the remains from the cemeteries in Europe to the United States. Henry wanted the best officers because he believed "the smallest mistake would be greatly exaggerated in the newspapers and in the minds of the people of the United States." In addition, Colonel Henry suggested that bodies be transferred to new coffins and "each coffin should be wrapped" in the "National Colors (storm flags)" presumably to cover over any potential defects in the caskets that might affect the representation of the nation's dead. This marked a clear intent to respect the dead and mitigate any perceived military mishandling of the retrospective form that citizens relied on to keep the dead a part of their collective memory.[23]

By October 1919 the coffins had deteriorated further, and the U.S. government wanted to reclaim the nation's lost sons immediately. But the French government did not want a "general removal of the soldier dead in or out of France." Secretary of War Newton Baker described it as the "determined opposition of the French Government." Baker felt quite a bit of pressure on the domestic front because a year after the war ended, the War Department had not brought back a single body. Baker claimed, "Our Government should do its utmost to keep faith with the relatives of our soldier dead in France, who have been led to believe that, when the war ended, the bodies of such soldiers, if desired by their next of kin, would find their final resting place in their own country." Baker asked Secretary of State Robert Lansing to press French officials into "a modification of that . . . policy as will permit the removal of our dead from France." Secretary Baker urged Lansing to stress to French officials the great distance between the United States and France that made grave visitation "impracticable," and "the comparatively small number of American soldiers" to be recovered should allow French officials to make an exception for U.S. bodies. Baker estimated that only 65,000 Americans would be returned out of an estimated 4.5 million "(including enemy)" dead. Most of the U.S. bodies were buried near battlefields, therefore "transportation of their bodies over any considerable portion of France so as to interfere with traffic to any great extent or create in any marked degree the depression in the morale of the population" could be avoided. Baker pointed out that U.S. soldiers had already been returned from the United Kingdom, Belgium, Russia, Italy, Germany, and Luxembourg. And finally Baker reasoned that the War Department had already sent out inquiries to nearest of kin asking them if they would like their loved ones returned. Failure to return the bodies would "place the War Department in a very embarrassing situation to be compelled to inform such relatives that France now refuses to permit such action." He concluded, "Such information, it is feared, will, moreover, arouse the resentment against France of the relatives of those Americans who gave their lives in defense of France."[24] Such arguments did not seem to sway French officials or change the situation on the ground that France could not spare the rails for transporting the dead.

On top of these failed negotiations, the War Department faced an even larger problem made evident by the return of the dead from Russia. The transportation of bodies from Russia was very important because it formed a test case for the later repatriation of bodies from Western Europe; it failed miserably. The SS *Lake Daraga* was an American freighter built just outside of Detroit in Wyandotte, Michigan, in July 1918. The freighter spent the war hauling coal from Wales to France for the U.S. Army. In October 1919 the *Daraga* made its final voyage for the U.S. Army from Brest, France, to New York and included the cargo of the dead who had fought at Archangel in Russia during the failed invasion of Siberia.[25] Using a coal ship to transport the dead home proved a debacle. Rough seas tormented the entire transatlantic voyage. Seawater spilled over the sides of the freighter, spoiling the coffins and the bodies of the dead. Just as in the Philippine and Cuban conflicts before, dock workers unloaded the decomposing bodies off the ship and directly onto the Hoboken pier for the public to witness. What ensued was a carnival of military officials sorting and unloading bodies, military officials organizing the bodies on the pier, and loved ones claiming the bodies and arranging transportation to take them home. This sort of chaos horribly mortified military officials. Instead of a celebration of nationalism, the saltwater had spoiled the human remains and turned the pier into a stench-ridden wharf of brine and carrion for the public to see and smell. This kind of treatment seemed to violate the Lincolnian obligation for the living to remember the dead and could not be tolerated when the dead from Europe began arriving in large scale. Maj. Charles Elliott sent a report to the commanding general at the Port of Embarkation at Hoboken, New Jersey, in response to the failure. Elliott recommended immediate changes including that cargo ships be outfitted "for transporting bodies in good condition." He proposed that these ships be outfitted "with 'ice boxes' [used] for shipping quantities of beer" and that the refrigeration containers "be used for bodies in a poor state of preservation."[26]

The use of beer coolers as a practical way to transport nationalized remains did not seem, at least to Elliott, to contradict the soberness of the task at hand. In fact, the embarrassment created by the *Daraga* allowed Elliot to reconfigure the entire transportation process into a publicly reverent passage that symbolized the hallowed memory of nationalism and the retrospective memory of the dead. Elliott did so by recommending that the War Department establish a "Disposition of Remains Section" at Hoboken and place Maj. Edwin R. Sharpe in charge. This section dealt only with the bodies—and no other cargo—coming to New Jersey from Europe. Elliott recommended that the military repurpose a warehouse in Weehawken, New Jersey, into a morgue. This warehouse had the advantage of railroad tracks running directly into it, and bodies could be moved from ship to train to warehouse with minimal exposure to the public. Elliott stated it was "absolutely necessary that these remains be handled with the greatest care and accuracy," and therefore he thought it unwise "to use one or more of the Piers for this purpose as there will be too much publicity and proximity to active operations on the piers." He proposed that longshoremen not handle damaged caskets. Rather, "some other force," presumably military personnel under Sharpe's command, should unload them "in a secluded place, away from those in good condition, to avoid the prying eyes of reporters and other morbidly inclined individuals." These sorts of policies could be seen as military officials' attempts to accommodate retrospective memory by withholding the "damaged" and controversial dead from public sight, thereby enabling loved ones to preserve their memories of the dead and bring the dead with them into the present untarnished.[27]

French authorities, meanwhile, slowly relaxed the transportation embargo, and GRS officials began retrieving bodies and shipping them to the United States. Once the dead arrived in Hoboken and passed inspection, workers unloaded the caskets and placed them in the warehouse where they underwent another inspection as workers prepared the bodies and the caskets for their final transportation to their hometowns and public commemoration. Initially individual bodies went straight from New Jersey to their final destination, "with an enlisted attendant accompanying them from Hoboken to destination." But this escort system stopped working once shiploads of bodies began arriving; there were too many bodies to accompany. The quartermaster general changed the process again in 1920 to avoid public criticism. He established several distribution centers in Washington DC, Chicago, Louisville, Atlanta, St. Paul, Omaha, Little Rock, San Antonio, Cheyenne, El Paso, Portland, and San Francisco and required that bodies "be forwarded in group or carload shipments" to one of these centers. The commanding officers in New Jersey telegraphed the respective distribution center depot officer ahead of forwarding the bodies. Once the depot officer made preparations to receive the shipment, the Hoboken center mailed him the identification information of the dead. Once the depot officer received the mailed identification lists, he organized the final leg of the journey from the depot center to the local cemetery and made final arrangements for the funeral. This included obtaining burial permits, transportation permits, baggage checks for the coffin, and receipts for the body. Forty-eight hours after the identification papers left Hoboken through the mail, the Hoboken office shipped the bodies.[28]

Citizens held the military bureaucracy accountable when it failed to fulfill their expectations. "Numerous complaints" filtered into the War Department.

Early complaints focused on the "failure to furnish proper convoy" to the dead. People expected the dead to be escorted and respected. The main problem lay in large urban areas that did not have enough trained military personnel to perform these services consistently. "These complaints," warned the adjutant general, "are hurting the standing, prestige and honor of the Army." To prevent this, the secretary of war changed procedures again and put in place measures to "furnish suitable escort at distribution points, and firing squads at funerals . . . when the relatives of the deceased request it." To secure more labor, the secretary of war authorized general soldiers to fill the role of attendants. The military's staffing resources became strained, especially in 1921, which witnessed the greatest volume of bodies returning from Europe as a consequence of public demand that the military uphold the high standards of retrospective memory.[29]

Despite the best attempts by Elliot and the quartermaster general's office to control the retrieval of the dead, government officials could not eliminate public criticism entirely, especially when republican traditions butted up against national borders in Europe. The United States received permission from the German government to recover the bodies of prisoners of war who died while incarcerated. The GRS retrieved the bodies and sent them by overland vehicles to Leipzig, Germany, and then onto Antwerp, Belgium, where they disembarked for the United States. But the *Washington Post* highlighted the "wasteful inefficiency with which the work has been conducted." The column, published on June 5, 1921, reported, "Twenty-seven men with a touring car and nine trucks have been touring Germany since April recovering the scattered remains of 47 American dead." The author continued, "Five trucks and touring cars were sent all the way to Poland for the single body there" and cited members of the work detail who said, "The work could have been done very simply and expeditiously by the use of trains and streamers [*sic*] instead of transporting the bodies in trucks through an alien country."[30] When questioned, Col. H. F. Rethers, now chief of the service, responded that the land vehicles were the only way to recover the bodies. Rethers cited the Ministerial Decree of July 22, 1920, which forbade the shipment of bodies through Germany. In lieu of this embargo, the GRS proposed to the German government the use of "motor transportation, which would avoid any expense to the German Government, or burden to the railways." German officials granted the proposal, "but with the further precaution that the exhumations were to be carried out with the least publicity possible and that no information regarding the work be disseminated," because German officials did not want to grant "similar authority to other foreign countries." Rethers responded that the newspaper report unfairly criticized the mission, and he insisted that he used only one Cadillac, one white truck, and eight GMC trucks. Contrary to the newspaper report, this kind of work demonstrated an impressive effort to recover American dead from foreign soil and meet the obligations of Lincoln's promise and the expectations of the American citizenry.[31]

U.S. citizens and officials continued to collaborate when shaping retrospective and even cultural memory of the war. Bringing soldiers home at government expense was important to most Americans, especially those who believed that they needed the body close to keep their memories of the dead from fading into the past. The War Department, meanwhile, wanted to capitalize on the symbolic value of the dead. In addition, the death industry in the United States—undertakers, casket builders, cemetery officials—sought profits by pressuring private citizens to encourage the government to bring the dead home. Americans had developed new memory techniques and practiced the now well-formed remembrances through their experiences with capitalism and grief.[32] These corporate expressions of grief and mourning attempted to incorporate the kinship of the individual family into local history and to the larger network of national biography. American citizens, too, had become well versed in using the industry of death to explain loss. Citizens, government officials, and industry leaders thus collaborated to ensure that the rituals of the Lincolnian tradition would cover the war dead from the Great War. This collaboration took place where communicative memory and cultural memory intersected and could be found in the criticisms surrounding the controversy of whether or not the government should return dead soldiers to U.S. soil.

Many found great satisfaction in the newly developed military ritual of reverse pilgrimage in which the military ritualized the transportation of the dead body back home. H. F. Richards, for example, reburied his son, Sgt. Joseph Clifford Richards, on November 11, 1920, in Williamsport, Pennsylvania. Richards and his wife participated in the early Bring Home the Soldier Dead movement. They received their son's body at Williamsport on November 8, and Richards praised government efforts in a letter to Col. Charles Pierce: "The casket was entirely satisfactory and my wife and I are greatly pleased because of the manner in which it was delivered. The flag that draped the casket is being preserved by us as a sacred souvenir." The Richards family kept the casket closed during their entire time in Williamsport and relied "solely on the identification made by the representatives of the war department." The undertaker inadvertently broke the handles of Sergeant Richards's coffin when removing it from the exterior packaging. This, claimed Richards, was the only problem in the entire ceremony. Mr. and Mrs. Richards found comfort in their memories of their son within the cultural memory that the War Department was attempting to build. Mr. Richards continued, "The knowledge that the body of our son now lies in the homeland is a great solace to the lad's mother and myself. I have great hope that his mother now soon will regain her normal health. It has been a long and anxious two years for both of us, as the boy died Nov. 15, 1918."[33]

But not everyone felt the way the Richards family did. Diverse opinions from numerous people argued that the war dead should remain in France. This too marked a collaborative, albeit contentious, effort between the citizenry and the government to commemorate the dead, and again this collaborative effort took place in interconnected locations where people traversed the spontaneous living memories of families and the coinciding ritualized institutionalized cultural memory of the nation-state. One citizen argued for the economic importance of the dead remaining buried in Europe. "After the war there will be an increased number of business relations between the United States and France and England and each citizen who visits these countries would have an opportunity of paying the respect due to the dead soldiers."[34] William Whitman of Chicago, meanwhile, believed that returning the bodies somehow violated the honor of their sacrifice. Whitman claimed, "The soul of man is not bound up in the putrid flesh nor scattered bones."[35] Dr. H. A. Hewlingo of San Bernardino, California, likewise did not favor the plan. He asked the secretary of war, "If you have humane feelings would it not be well to manifest it by prohibiting the shipment of the dead bodies of soldiers? Having these dead bodies brought home for burial can be of *no* possible *good*; and the excitement which it entails is conducive of much sorrow and also bitterness." Dr. Hewlingo argued that the dead posed health problems to the living and should be cremated. He argued, "The Battle-fronts are liable to be Pest Fields in the no distant future. The soil is already contaminated—Pure drinking water *will be* an impossibility—And it is thro this source diseases are communicated."[36]

The *New York Times* published a letter cabled from novelist Owen Wister detailing what he described as the "desecration that would shock mothers" in the U.S. cemeteries in France. The author of the 1902 novel *The Virginian* and close friend of Theodore Roosevelt—one of Wilson's most vocal critics—Wister believed the dead should remain buried in Europe and claimed the cemeteries were a disgrace due to the massive removal of bodies. En route to visiting the grave of Theodore Roosevelt's son, Quentin, who crashed his plane in rural France and whose father insisted that his body remain buried near the site of his death, Wister claimed that the nearby U.S. military cemetery had numerous craters and that bodies, only recognizable as "things without shape," were regularly pulled out of the ground as the cemetery officials readied them for shipping. According to Wister, retrieval of the dead did not enhance the process of cultural memory; rather, it demolished it. He claimed that the necessity of burying the dead quickly meant that cemetery officials put bodies in the ground without coffins and often buried them only in blankets or baskets. When gravediggers disinterred bodies, they "often place the basket on top of a stove to melt the mud off and find something to send to America." Wister's accusations continued as he suggested that most of the dead were not embalmed but only "sprinkled with disinfectant and shipped to Hoboken." Wister claimed that many of the bodies, once they reached Hoboken, lay unclaimed, and so military and municipal officials buried them in potters fields in local cemeteries. The problem was that the death industry in America was adept at "exploiting mothers' grief to put money in certain pockets." The end result was that soldiers were taken "from the soil their sacrifice made sacred." The massive disinterment spoiled the once beautiful national cemeteries. He claimed that the Romagne American Military Cemetery was a beautiful site. "Its grass was green, its crosses white. Peace and beauty filled it." But after 40 percent of the dead were dug up and shipped to America, Romagne looked like "an old mouth, half teeth, half gums." Wister asked, "Can nothing stop this hideous mockery of the living and the dead?"[37]

Beneath Wister's letter, the *Times* published a letter from Wilson's ambassador to Italy, Thomas Nelson Page of Virginia. The ambassador had just returned from a visit to France where he too had visited several cemeteries including Romagne. Page believed that the dead should remain buried in France, but he also challenged Wister's suggestion that the U.S. military cemeteries were dilapidated and the buried uncared for. Page claimed, "No more impressive tribute to American valor and American love of freedom can be imagined than these cemeteries." At Romagne, Page viewed the white grave markers and noted the American flag flying above; he wrote, "One felt personal pride in every gallant spirit whose mortal dust reposes there." When he found out that the War Department would return many of the bodies to the United States, Page responded, "It seemed desecration to dig them up." A graduate of Washington and Lee University, Page looked to the quintessential Southern gentleman for guidance on the subject of removal. "When General Lee was asked to lend his name to a plan to remove the Confederate dead from Gettysburg he replied that he had always felt that the fittest resting place for a soldier was the field of honor on which he had nobly laid down his life." The ambassador insisted that the dead should not be brought home but rather remain in France.[38]

Such accusations echoed the sentiments of Wilsonianism stressing that the presence of the dead powerfully symbolized Americanism in Europe. By implication, however, arguments such as Wister's seemed to insinuate negligence on behalf of the GRS units in their responsibilities of returning the dead. It prompted a response from the GRS chief, Col. H. F. Rethers, who wrote to the newspaper to correct the "flagrant falsehood and insult" that came from Wister's letter. Here government officials again responded to citizen critics. Rethers claimed, "This solemn duty is performed silently and without ostentation, with every precaution taken by means of orders and instructions and direct supervision by commissioned officers of the army to insure careful and reverent handling of the dead." He cited a Massachusetts State Memorial Commission report that investigated the cemeteries in 1920 with the permission of the War Department. The commissioners claimed that "every effort has been made to do the business part accurately, decently, and with all respect and after that to bestow the honors due to the heroic dead." Rethers pointed to cemetery records showing that Wister had visited the cemetery at Seringes-et-Nesles before disinterment began. When he returned a few weeks later, disinterment had begun, but he was not allowed to see the operations because "the work is screened from the public." The chief of the service pointed out that GRS supervisory embalmers had to be graduates of embalming schools. None, claimed Rethers, came from the dregs of society.[39] The GRS office in Hoboken also issued a statement denouncing Wister's letter and solicited support from the American Legion, which was founded in 1919 by soldiers returning from Europe. The American Legion national commander, Col. F. W. Galbraith Jr., did not believe Wister's accusations but claimed that Legionnaires would never allow soldiers to be buried in potters fields should the U.S. Army fail in its responsibilities. Capt. R. E. Shannon, who headed the Hoboken office for the GRS, asserted that out of 14,852 bodies so far coming through his jurisdiction, only two had been unclaimed, and they were shipped to Arlington National Cemetery to receive burial with full military honors. Shannon quoted the report submitted by Maj. William F. Deegan, who was vice commander of the New York American Legion, that stated his investigation had found no cases of neglect and only one case of oversight.[40]

Others invested in returning bodies to the United States also criticized Wister. A. B. Pouch was president of the Bring Home the Soldier Dead League, a group that actively lobbied Congress to return the dead at government expense. Pouch denounced Wister's "cowardly propaganda" and attested that in his own visits to the cemeteries, "work that is being carried out by the Government is all that any one could reasonably expect." Nevertheless, Pouch and others like him remained "more convinced and more determined than ever not to have a single bone left in France." Rev. Paul D. Moody, who served as assistant senior chaplain of the AEF during the war, however, agreed with Wister. He shared the observations of one of his fellow chaplains who did not serve at the front but had visited it a couple of times. The chaplain recounted that on one occasion he saw six hundred gravediggers making graves; so many died that sometimes a few weeks passed before individual corpses were buried. A former captain in the AEF, Theron J. Damon, wanted his fallen comrades to remain buried in France. It was too "ghoulish," he suggested, for bodies to be brought back to America to "tear off the healing scab of time and reopen some of the deepest wounds which humanity knows." Mary Gates of New York complained that her friend, who had lost her son in the war, had to inform the government on four occasions that she did not want her son moved from his gravesite in a Catholic cemetery in a rural French village. When notified that they moved her son to a larger cemetery and again to another cemetery, she became quite distressed. Gates blamed this on the people intent on bringing the dead home. "It is about time someone did something toward finding out who is back of the movement of bringing home our dead," wrote the indignant Gates.[41]

Although critical and even acrimonious, the public discourse demonstrated how citizens and government officials collaborated over the meaning of the dead. The U.S. government allowed family members to bring their loved ones home at government expense or to keep them buried in France. The bureaucratic process proved flexible enough to make corrections in the face of criticism, but officials also defended its operations when they believed the public unfairly attacked the retrieval rituals. Despite some rancor within the debate, the federal government worked out multiple interpretations of Lincoln's promise in order to make the tradition applicable to the realities of the First World War. Most of these variations added new rituals without inhibiting tradition. Military officials, for example, used the U.S. flag to cover over damaged caskets, and the grieving saw this as an opportunity to collect a souvenir that represented their family's sacrifice for the nation. Families could keep the Civil War tradition alive by keeping their dead soldier buried near the spot where he died. For many this signaled a profound ability to remember the war dead extraterritorially. But it also expanded the values of Americanism across the Atlantic and beyond America's borders. Historian

Mark Meigs notes that U.S. war cemeteries in France marked "an outpost of American culture that American tourists can visit abroad and an American stage upon which American dignitaries can act in a foreign place."[42] These cemeteries, particularly in Memorial Day celebrations, would continually reaffirm Franco-American relationships. Americans who wanted to bring their loved ones home could do so, too. They could also criticize the government bureaucracy that made plenty of mistakes in maintaining care for the dead. But it seems that an accumulation of these mistakes never seriously amounted to a betrayal of Lincoln's promise even as people asserted multifarious interpretations of the dead. Indeed, the controversies over burial locations, bureaucratic recordkeeping, and the sacred handling of the dead demonstrated how citizens and government agents collaborated to reinforce cultural memory when it easily could have been deconstructed in the aftermath of the First World War.

American cultural memory remained a cold expression of American empire. Wilson demonstrated this at Suresnes when he provided a pastless interpretation of the Lincolnian tradition to Europeans. Wilson simply could not bend the memory of reunionism to his globalist agenda. It was hard for Europeans to contextualize the American dead of the Great War continuing a tradition started during the U.S. Civil War. Europeans interpreted the war through a different past and had different memories of empire and colonialism. Americans also found this articulation of memory hard to use when they interpreted the Great War. American participation in the war seemed much vaguer and more open-ended for many in the United States. Atomization of memory could not be so easily contained through rituals that relied on the Civil War dead, a war that for many Americans had a singular purpose of reunion even as most citizens forgot the war as an emancipatory cause. It seems that Wilson's call for a League of Nations at Suresnes found the limit of Americans' and Europeans' abilities and willingness to imagine the extraterritoriality of the war. Wilson's Fourteen Points plan and the League of Nations, nevertheless, served as a reminder of just how asymmetrical the Atlantic world economy had become during the war. U.S. banks had more financial leverage over European states than ever before. British and French governments at the Paris peace conference in

1919 understood that Wilson's demands would likely throttle their ability to govern their respective colonies around the world and would likely facilitate a trade network that benefited the producers in the United States even at the cost of sovereignty claims from British and French governments. Prime Minister David Lloyd George and President Raymond Poincaré accepted financial dependence on U.S. banks during the war, and successive British and French governments would seek to remedy the lopsided nature of this economic relationship before the total economic collapse of the 1930s. The memory that Wilson invoked at Suresnes simply was not warm enough to convince heads of state and their subjects and citizens they governed that America would govern the world system any more democratically than before. Americans too became suspicious of European entanglements that collective security seemed to obligate them to uphold. Wilson soon suffered a stroke and was unfit to carry out his political objectives. Americans would turn to another president with a different vision of the postwar world and use new technologies to craft a more sustainable cold memory of the Great War.

CHAPTER 9

Listening to Empire

The monument of death will outlast the memory of the dead. The pyramids do not tell us the tale that was confided to them; the living fact commemorates itself. Why look in the dark for light? Strictly speaking, the historical societies have not recovered one fact from oblivion, but are themselves, instead of the fact, [that] which is lost. The researcher is more memorable than the researched.
—Henry David Thoreau, *A Week on the Concord and Merrimack Rivers*

President Warren G. Harding gave the eulogy at the dedication ceremony to the Tomb of the Unknown Soldier in Arlington National Cemetery on November 11, 1921, the day before the Washington Naval Conference began and nearly two and a half years after President Woodrow Wilson's Memorial Day address in Suresnes, France. Harding's speech was particularly remarkable because American Telephone & Telegraph's (AT&T) newly developed electric public address system passed its first major test transmitting the president's words through amplifiers to an audience of more than 100,000 people at the cemetery and over telephone lines to 50,000 New Yorkers in Madison Square Garden and 22,000 people at the Auditorium in San Francisco. This was a coast-to-coast mnemonic and aural event.[1] The electric transmission gave Harding the ability to project his voice in real time directly to a much wider audience than any president before him and without the journalistic filters of newspaper and magazine editors. Similar to the way

Abraham Lincoln, without the aid of a microphone, had spoken of the fallen soldiers at Gettysburg as sacrifices for liberty, Harding declared the Unknown Soldier a symbol of liberty that stood in for all the other American bodies that remained buried in Europe, lost at sea, or never recovered.[2] While only a handful of people actually heard Lincoln's speech (or Wilson's speech at Suresnes), most people, even those in attendance, had to wait to read it in the papers. Tens of thousands heard Harding's speech as he spoke the words.[3]

Harding and his secretary of state, Charles Hughes, sought to cultivate an international "community of ideals, interests, and purposes" at the next day's Washington Naval Conference (also known as the Arms Limitation Conference) in response to the rise of the Soviet Union and other threats to the American ideal of a world made safe for democracy. "Compared to the solemnity of Versailles, the Washington Conference was a truly spectacular exercise in public diplomacy," claims historian Adam Tooze. It was the first conference of its kind and posed a model for other conferences that would take place throughout the interwar period. The conference, which began on November 12, 1921, and ended in February 1922, was one of the Harding administration's first official attempts to cultivate a community of interests. Harding used the dedication ceremony at Arlington as his opening move "to launch the conference amidst a refreshingly straightforward celebration of wartime solidarity." This "community of interests" did not amount to a Wilsonian League of Nations that restricted the sovereignty of Great Powers or the self-determination that held the hopes of nation-states not yet formed. It framed a smaller group of Great Powers that worked together against common threats, particularly communism. It was a relationship based on shared interests. The talks initially were a great success for Harding's administration. Delegates created a multinational nonbinding agreement in which the United States, Britain, France, Italy, and Japan committed to limiting their naval armaments in the Pacific World, thus preventing an arms race like the rivalry between Britain and Germany before World War I. This agreement set the ground rules for transpacific collective security and for America's "Open Door Policy" regarding China. It set the American, British, and Japanese fleet ratio at 5:5:3, which allowed the United States to keep pace with the British naval presence in the Pacific while simultaneously reducing armaments. British officials agreed to the treaty because it offered the "trilateral agreement" that allowed the British to avoid "the choice between Japan and the United States" in competition for the Pacific Rim. "Never before had an empire of Britain's stature so explicitly and consciously conceded superiority in such a crucial dimension of global power," claims Tooze. But it also circumvented the League of Nations and revived prewar-style diplomacy, in which great powers acted in concert to impose limits on their shared adversaries and to control the destiny of smaller nations.[4]

Harding's and Wilson's speeches commemorated the dead of the Great War within the context of the U.S. imperial power. Many Americans, however, could not quite make the Wilsonian commitment to the world and sought instead to remember the war as a conflict that would allow the United States to finally control its own destiny without the burdens of collective security and international entanglements. They elected Harding in 1920, and he too hoped to use cultural memory to help make America's case to the world for economic and political postwar global leadership. Despite raising and implementing tariffs, refusing to sign the Peace of Paris, and rebuffing the League of Nations, Republicans ultimately agreed with Wilson that the United States should significantly influence the world system. The Republican dislike of Wilson's League of Nations, as one historian describes, was that they desired to "avoid the policy of collective security on the grounds that it might easily weaken the United States, both defensively and offensively, by tying it to various features of the status quo that were sure to disappear—and others that ought to be altered by America itself."[5] Thus the Harding administration rejected the League of Nations in favor of expanding the "informal empire." Harding and his advisors sought something much closer to the prewar "dollar diplomacy" of Republican president William Howard Taft, in which the softer power of U.S. business and democracy became the overarching strategy for asserting U.S. postwar influence on the global system. This was especially clear in Harding's hosting Pacific naval powers at the Washington Naval Conference, which began with Harding's eulogizing the Unknown Soldier. By examining the role of the dead, scholars can examine the shifting political meaning of cultural memory within the technological revolutions emanating from the Great War.

But this chapter also illustrates the role played by U.S. citizens explicit in their collaborations with private corporations and government intermediation to keep the Lincolnian tradition functional and purposeful. As Americans turned from the Progressivism of Wilsonianism to the more laissez-faire Republican policies that helped open the age of the Roaring Twenties, Americans developed new innovative memory technologies and techniques that showcased a cool cultural memory of the war and that relied on the rhetoric and metaphors of republicanism to cover over the difficult realities that came out of U.S. imperialist power. This amounted to an incredibly difficult maneuver in the wake of the First World War. Historians such as George Mosse suggest that the cult of the fallen soldier became a centerpiece of various government officials' attempts to control the meanings and memories of the Great War. They often failed to accommodate the spontaneous communicative memories of people who were intimately tied to the dead. "A tendency has thus grown in the Western world," suggests German historian Reinhart Koselleck, "to represent death in foreign or civil war only as a question and no longer as an answer, only as demanding meaning and no longer as establishing meaning." He surmises that "what remains is the identity of the dead with themselves; the capability of memorializing the dead eludes the formal language of political sensibility."[6]

If officials failed to incorporate readily the communicative memories of loved ones into cultural memory, many citizens chose to abandon them altogether in favor of grieving through their communicative memories. Jay Winter's *Sites of Memory, Sites of Mourning* details the efforts of many Europeans to cultivate a culture of grief and memory on their own terms. Thus a conflict of memory immediately followed the First World War, pitting the official rituals and interpreters of cultural memory attempting to cover over the abuses and disillusions of the conflict against the spontaneous living memories of citizens who demanded their fathers, sons, and husbands be remembered even if that meant criticizing state actors for their leadership during the war. The tension between official and citizen remembrances of the war often were contentious and real. Historian Jan Assmann suggests, however, that the memory of the dead could have a more conterminous effect. Because remembering the dead occupied a space between the local spontaneous communicative memory and official ritualized cultural memory, it had the potential to bring cultural and communicative memories together in the same place. What Lincoln accomplished in his Gettysburg Address and Harding reproduced at Arlington was to convene the memories of the dead through a process of reciprocity between the living and the dead, in which the living could measure their fulfillment of Lincoln's promise in direct correlation to the "amount of respect that [they] show[ed] for [their] own forebears." This reciprocity could be contentious and even scandalous at times, but it could also provide opportunities for the grieving and the bureaucrats to collaborate. "Whether the monument is a war memorial with thousands of names or the anonymous Tomb of the Unknown Warrior," suggests Assmann, "the motif of group identification is unmistakable."[7]

Harding, however, found an effective prospective metaphor to reconvene the Lincolnian tradition and communicate it through the technology of sound and the enduring sacrifice of a single unknown man obliging individuals to recognize that "our part is to atone for the losses of heroic dead by making a better Republic for the living."[8] Harding infused republican traditions onto the Tomb of the Unknown Soldier to help join fracturing cultural memories together again by covering over the new imperialistic nature of cultural memory that thrived on the politics of reunification and the politics of difference (along racial, gendered, and religious lines), both domestically and internationally. The Harding administration knotted American identity to cultural memory in innovative ways that no one since Lincoln had accomplished. Harding, however, benefited from the technological advances of corporate capitalism and from the bureaucratic reforms of Progressive politicians that were in their infancy during Lincoln's presidency. Harding's key innovation was using new technologies of telephony to add sounds to the already established visual communication of democratic war dead. Sounds of the dead, stemming from the Lincolnian metaphor of "mystic chords of memory" from the sixteenth president's first inaugural address took on a new meaning by attaching individual citizens together into an aurally networked cultural memory. After the Civil War, Northern and Southern men had fought together in the American West, Cuba, the Philippines, and France. New political virtuosos could now add notes of imperial expansion to the chords of memory metaphor, accentuating the unforgettable legacy of the dead, while listeners could continue to hear the themes of republican and national unity arpeggiate over the body of a single unknown American through the new aural medium of telephony. This was a reciprocal synchronization of retrospective and prospective memories. Aural retrieval and communication of cultural memory produced a collaborative network between sights, sounds, and peoples' memories that now could transcend geography like never before. This memory network incorporated an expansive geography connecting an American killed in France, transported across the Atlantic, and buried in Arlington within a transcontinental landscape from New York to San Francisco. Great distances could be traversed and geographies could be brought closer not by Lincoln's moral quip that relied on the "better angels of our nature" but by telephone wires, radio waves, and print journalism. Middle-class Americans participated in these social and technological networks that helped bridge the geographies of the Atlantic and the Pacific. People retrieved and communicated memories differently in this age of mass communication. In front of the microphone behind the newly constructed Arlington Amphitheater, Harding, AT&T, and the audiences in Washington DC, New York, and San Francisco fashioned a live transcontinental studio performance that played upon overlapping geographies of empire, death, and sound and played between communicative and cultural memory.[9]

On the surface the memory project seemed finished. Civil War reunification had been built around white Anglo-Saxon Protestantism, capitalism, nativism, and segregation. Wars with Native Americans in the West, with Spain and in Cuba and the Philippines, a war with Cubans and Filipinos themselves, invasions of Mexico, interventions, occupations, and colonial takeovers of nations in the Caribbean, South America, and the Pacific "reunified" the American political landscape in ways that required Americans to locate the United States in relation to the Atlantic and the Pacific worlds while considering how the American empire fundamentally attempted to bridge their "exotic" nonwhite inhabitants.[10] The calamity of the Great War and the confusion surrounding U.S. participation, however, threatened to undo the cultural memory landscape that middle-class Americans earlier had constructed. The postwar chaos of 1919 revealed many of the deep-seated prejudices that the war effort on the home front had covered over; the turmoil exposed just how disunited Americans actually were. The return of black men from a segregated battlefront somehow threatened white masculinity, and racial violence intensified. The Red Summer of 1919 bled into 1920 as violence and bloodshed showcased the color line inside the United States, the Palmer Raids against union leaders, immigrants, and suspected Bolsheviks, the anarchist bombings directed at politicians and Wall Street, and massacres in places like Centralia, Washington, that pitted lumber barons and war veterans against workers and fellow veterans who had joined the Industrial Workers of the World. American interests abroad also seemed to be unraveling. Congress rejected the Peace of Paris and the League of Nations, which brought more uncertainty to the United States' role in the world. The United States had very limited capacity to intervene in the Ruhr crisis in Europe, for example. They also had little voice with European and Asian empires that were reorganizing the Pacific world and its peoples in the wake of the Paris peace conference.

One way to help bottle up this sort of disunity was to produce postwar symbols that condensed unity and massaged nationalistic feelings. The commemorative tradition initiated by Lincoln and amended by McKinley after the Cuban conflict and Roosevelt during the war with the Philippines could easily incorporate the tropes of nativism, Protestantism, and capitalism into new prospective traditions that stressed the achievements of the war dead. But the United States had become increasingly multicultural, and the rituals of cultural memory poorly addressed the need of a cosmopolitan citizenry to retrospectively remember the dead. Different groups played an ever-increasing role on the home front and on the battlefield, and they demanded that government officials respect the dead when they retrieved bodies from Europe. Officials often responded imperfectly, and sometimes callously, to the concerns of the citizenry, but they also adapted their methods to public criticism, and this kind of collaboration continued to shape how Americans remembered the war and the dead. What the collective memory needed was a symbol that suggested Americanness was open to all groups to claim symbolic—even if not real—access. Commemorative traditions based on Lincoln's rhetoric of liberty and government for the people had to appear to have the stuff of diversity by the end of the Great War, even if it retained its Protestant, capitalist, and nativist underpinnings. The Tomb of the Unknown Soldier became the epitome of this effort. The success of commemorating an unknown soldier was that the ceremony subtly inverted the communal aspects of Lincoln's promise. As an individual soldier, the Unknown violated Lincoln's original principle that the community of the fallen, not individual soldiers, would be remembered. But as a metaphor, the unknown warrior changed the topography of memory. Diverse groups could look at the Unknown and see a reflection of themselves as part of a national community.

The creation of the Tomb of the Unknown Soldier was negotiated by the military, the federal government, and the middle-class citizenry. The original idea came from Brig. Gen. William Durward Connor, who had learned of the French plans to dedicate a monument to an unknown French soldier. Connor suggested that the United States likewise commemorate an unknown, but U.S. Army chief of staff Peyton C. March did not like the idea. March believed that the GRS might eventually identify most, if not all, of the American dead and did not want to commemorate someone whose identity would later be found out. But the incredible public response to the British and French Unknowns who were reburied on November 11, 1920, convinced American politicians that they could recuperate similar retrospective sentiments from the public. New York congressman Hamilton Fish Jr. reintroduced the idea to the War Department and eventually won concessions from military leaders. Congress authorized the return of a single unknown soldier in the spring of 1921; President Wilson signed the legislation in the last month of his presidency.[11]

But America had no central location like London or Paris to commemorate such a symbol. British authorities buried the remains of the Unknown Warrior in Westminster Abbey, where he rested among monarchs, poets, and scientists of renown in the heart of London. French officials likewise buried the Poilu Inconnu in the heart of the French Empire. The Place de l'Étoile was the intersection of Paris's twelve major roads and the center of the Axe historique, which connected the Louvre Palace through Paris to La Defense (a monument dedicated to the French defenders of Paris in the Franco-Prussian War) on the outskirts of the city. Napoleon Bonaparte commissioned the magnificent Arc de Triomphe at the center of the Place de l'Étoile as a victory arch dedicated to the soldiers of the Napoleonic Wars. These locations reified the British and French imperial histories to a specific place on which the subjects of Britain and the citizens of France honored their unidentifiable soldiers from the Great War.

The United States had no such location. The French and British commemorated their unknowns as spectacles of empire while Americans had cast the war as a conquest that made the world safe for democracy. The new traditions may have been popular in London and Paris, but they violated the traditions of the American collective memory. As an editorialist from *Life* magazine wrote, "A ceremony of this kind is an imitation and seems rather too likely to be a cheap one."[12] About this time GRS officials had come out in opposition to the congressional legislation that would produce the Unknown Soldier. The GRS had slowly reduced the number of unknown dead through the use of dental records, which had to be sent to the War Department to be compared with dental charts taken at the time of enlistment. Although theirs was a pragmatic rather than an ideological opposition, GRS officials claimed, "The time is not yet ripe for the selection of the unknown hero to be honored."[13]

Added to this controversy, there was little consensus on where the unknown warrior should be buried. Although Arlington National Cemetery accepted the dead from the Philippine and Cuban conflicts and soldiers of the Civil War who died near Arlington and Alexandria, Virginia, it had not yet completely become reified as the Valhalla of the American empire. Americans had decentralized commemorative space through its national cemetery system and dispersed it throughout the nation. By 1920 Arlington served as just one of ninety cemeteries that the War Department oversaw from San Francisco to Santa Fe, New Mexico, to Elmira, New York, to Marietta, Georgia. Military officials shipped bodies home where they buried the remains in a local cemetery or in a nearby national cemetery. The War Department largely, although not exclusively, used Arlington for victims of disease, the unclaimed, and those whose families explicitly requested that they bury their loved ones there. There were other suggestions. Philadelphians wanted the soldier buried in Independence Hall or at least in Independence Square.[14] Some New Yorkers planned to bring to the city a second unknown soldier, but Secretary of War Newton Baker did not support this proposal.[15] Many disagreed with sentiments that accentuated such local importance over nationalism. Bringing back an unknown American soldier, argued the editors of the *New York Times*, "should not be associated with any State nor with any particular army organization. As in England and France, it is the nation that should do honor to the unidentified soldier, and his tomb should be a shrine for the Americans of all the States and all the lands under the flag." The editors argued that the body should be placed in Arlington, "where the bravest lie, men of the South as well as men of the North, who fought for the Stars and Stripes."[16]

Arlington was a controversial choice for some. There already existed a tomb for unknown Civil War soldiers. Dedicated in September 1866, the very first tomb for the unknowns marked a burial of more than two thousand unidentified Union dead. It served as the central location for Decoration Day ceremonies in the early years after the war and became one of the most important locations in the cemetery. But by the twentieth century the cemetery had also become the location for a Confederate section first authorized in 1900 after McKinley's Atlanta speech the previous year. Confederates from surrounding areas around Washington DC had been disinterred and reburied in the national cemetery. In 1914 Jewish American, Confederate soldier, and sculptor Moses Ezekiel completed a monument to the Confederate dead funded by the Confederate Memorial Association. President Woodrow Wilson received the monument as a welcomed example of reunification. For some the placing of the Unknown from the Great War just yards away from the Confederate monument in Arlington was too controversial. Soldiers from the North and South had fought shoulder to shoulder in the war with Spain, but the Unknown brought back from France, some feared, might arouse feelings of sectionalism, not nationalism. Was the Unknown a Northerner or a Southerner? Editors of the *New York Times* even reversed their positions and began calling for the burial space to be the U.S. Capitol instead of Arlington. "The revival of memories that affect national unity and concord should be guarded against."[17] They argued that not everyone who visited Washington visited Arlington, but "all America finds its way to the Capitol." The rotunda's paintings and its traditions had been "a shrine of the American people," and the structure created "an irresistible impulse of interest and patriotism." The location in the Capitol rotunda "would have a more solemnizing and reverential effect than if the sepulture were in the cemetery at Arlington across the Potomac."[18]

After considerable debate in which the public played an important role, military officials decided to place the Unknown's body in the U.S. Capitol, where it would lie in state before being buried at Arlington. On Armistice Day 1921, the Unknown's funeral procession full of mourners began at the U.S. Capitol and moved through Washington to Arlington. The *New York Times* reported that "Washington had witnessed many notable ceremonies, but never one like this." The funerals of Lincoln, Garfield, and McKinley were impressive, but the tears shed for the Unknown were "carried away by the emotion of the symbolism of patriotism which this unknown American embodied." The casket was "taken from that central spot in the Capitol's rotunda where before this only the bodies of Presidents had lain in state, and where it had been designed to place the body of George Washington." The procession lasted three hours, and participants walked seven miles from the Capitol onto Pennsylvania Avenue and passing by the White House before making the trek across the Potomac River to Arlington. Following the caisson along the route were President Harding and other dignitaries who would convene the Arms Limitation Conference the next day, including Field Marshal Foch and Premiere Aristide Briand of France, General Diaz of Italy, Arthur J. Balfour, former prime minister of Great Britain who was now serving as lord president of the council in Prime Minister Lloyd George's government, and Prince Tokugawa of Japan.

Crowds witnessing the spectacle cheered when the gold star mothers walked by and cheered louder when Woodrow Wilson and his wife passed. Wilson's poor health, the remnants of a stroke suffered during his presidency in 1919, prohibited him from reaching Arlington, but he made it as far as the White House "and received an ovation all along the route." The *New*

York Times reporter noted the sobriety of the crowd. "But when they saw this stricken man who had been Commander-in-Chief of the forces with which the Unknown Warrior fought they broke into cheers."[19] This was a significant recognition of the former president. A defeated body, defeated in politics, and some argued defeated by Lloyd George and Clemenceau in Paris, Wilson's inclusion perhaps foreshadowed just how unifying the symbolism of the Unknown could be.

At Arlington, President Harding delivered the eulogy. Harding was not able to eliminate criticisms of efforts to retrieve the dead, but he was able to take advantage of innovative cultural memory techniques. He did so by hearkening back to the Lincolnian tradition, this time finding inspiration in Lincoln's metaphor of sound and memory from his first inaugural address. Before Gettysburg, when he first took the oath of office, Lincoln initially relied on an aural and mnemonic metaphor that he described as the "mystic chords of memory" that existed between Northerners and Southerners. This was a calculated but natural metaphor especially because at this time sounds could not be mechanically reproduced. Americans in the early republic period had cultivated a political culture of music and singing that stressed themes of political harmony.[20] Lincoln drew from this preexisting aural literacy to remind disillusioned Southerners threatening secession of the "mystic chords of memory, stretching from every battlefield and patriot grave to every living heart and hearthstone all over this broad land." The mystic chords that connected the dead to the living constituted more than just a metaphor; they also convened a republican social network of grief and memory. The patriot dead, Lincoln surmised, helped form cultural memory networked through a harmonious chord progression connecting the war dead's sacrifice to the living's cultural memory. Many Northerners and Southerners had family connections, experiential connections, or political connections to the patriot dead. These dead thus represented a real social network to which living people inserted themselves. Lincoln hoped most would remember the sacrifices of the dead and thus still hear the chords and the harmony that "will yet swell the chorus of this union, when again touched, as surely they will be, by the better angels of our nature." This republican memory network relied heavily on already obsolete notions of Jeffersonian civic virtue, individualism, agrarianism, and decentralized local government, and it was drowned out by the cacophony of Southern secession.[21]

Harding reapportioned the mysticism of Lincoln's aural metaphor at the Unknown's dedication. "If we give rein to fancy," asserted Harding, "a score of sympathetic chords are touched for in this body there once glowed the soul of an American, with the aspirations and ambitions of a citizen who cherished life and its opportunities." Harding's refurbishing the aural metaphor in the postwar period of the early twentieth century had the capacity to help Americans recontextualize a republican memory useful enough to mystify the boundaries between individual grief and collective memory, the profane and the divine, as well as the boundaries between American nation and empire. "Through metaphor," historian Mark M. Smith suggests, "sounds broke free of their physical space, slipping into the social and cultural realm." Once this slippage happened, claims Smith, "non-visual senses frequently play[ed] very powerful roles in not only stimulating memories of the past but in activating and shaping them."[22] Thus Harding's dedication speech spoke to and incorporated several different audiences and had multiple layers of meaning, but he intended to aggregate atomized memories into a single harmonized national memory. The president thus sought to reassure and remind Americans of their sacrifice during war and the need to stay committed to the Republican plan for security and economic recovery.

Activating nineteenth-century social networks of grief and memory proved difficult. These networks originally lacked structures powerful enough and people skilled enough at communicating them effectively. At stake was the efficacy of Benedict Anderson's observation that "the nation's biography snatches against the going mortality rate, exemplary suicides, poignant martyrdoms, assassinations, executions, wars, and holocausts," but "to serve the narrative purpose, these violent deaths must be remembered/forgotten as 'our own.'"[23] While Europeans could reach across the centuries to find notable and violent deaths, the American Valhalla was too small and overwhelmingly made up of white elites committed to capitalism, nativism, and Protestantism to represent a truly multicultural republican narrative. The dead of the Civil War, along with congressional support of national cemeteries, enlarged the pool of notable dead from which Americans could draw to establish national identity.[24] But this was a visual, not an aural, representation of republicanism. Row upon row of uniform tombstones adjacent to actual battlefields accentuated the visual representation of many people who sacrificed their lives for the nation and were now commemorated in utilitarian landscapes benefiting a national memory. Neither Lincoln nor Congress made this cultural memory alone. Government officials collaborated with the patriot graves and the living kinfolk and countrymen who helped activate it. Users attached a visual landscape and an architectural style that added breadth and depth to the hagiography of this republican imagined community. After the Great War, designers of the Tomb of the Unknown attempted to connect a single body to the national cultural memory as the "last step in this democratization of death."[25] It became particularly effective because it projected a grief ritual of a private body onto the scale of the American social body.[26] Conflating individual tragedy with collective nostalgia for the dead thus helped build a useful cultural memory that reframed grief within a social and even national context and thereby diluted the political language of liberty that Lincoln voiced at Gettysburg.[27]

The making of a middle-class industry to manage death occurred simultaneously with the attempt to manage sound. Early Americans believed, according to Sarah Keyes, that the new western geographies of American expansion needed new sounds. Survivors of the Overland Trail in the early nineteenth century, for example, sought to "make the graves of the overlanders and the surrounding land part of the American domain" by replacing the "howling of wolves with the proper, civilized sounds of tolling bells," which "symbolized American mastery over nature."[28] Inventors, meanwhile, pioneered machines that could control sound. Corporations built and marketed these technologies, and middle-class Americans gained the technical skills to listen through these new machines.[29] Just as with the death industry, the sound industry fashioned a network of consumers and producers via an industry of telephones, gramophones, and emerging technologies of radio. Similar to the railroad industry's subjugation of western spaces, AT&T subdued the sounds of the West with considerable investment leveraged by banks and the federal government's willingness to let AT&T operate as a monopoly. The corporation thus produced an electronic soundscape, and Harding used the dedication ceremony to help signal the completion of these imagined possibilities emanating from an imperial past of conquering the West. Harding thus did not simply speak into a microphone; he performed his commemoration ceremony through an aural medium to an audience already experienced in using visual, sound, and grief networks. This was a studio-produced performance despite its open-air delivery, and it fulfilled audience expectations as an entirely scripted event. The national cemetery provided the perfect studio for sound and memory (re)production, becoming a constructed visual representation of national sacrifice while AT&T engineered it into a landscape to control the production of electronic sound.

The sights and sounds of the national cemetery seemed to provide a strong imperial legacy in which the unknown body would be placed. One newspaper reporter described the terrain entombing "dead from the Mexican and Spanish Wars, as well as from France, and men drowned in the battleship *Maine*." It was an open-air studio where one could even hear the acoustics of the past through the "echoes of the spirit of the Pilgrims [that] reach us and do not seem weakened by the elapsed time." The reporter also promised the location of the ceremony would allow Americans to again "hear the winged words of Lincoln in his Gettysburg Address" that the living would continue "the unfinished work" that the dead "thus far so nobly advanced."[30] Arlington thus became an ideal location where cultural memory could utilize sound and geography to layer a harmonic memory of reunified national biography of republicanism over the discord of the Great War.

Harding's commemoration signaled a moment when Americans from many walks of life interacted with the dead through innovative and acquired technical skills of remembering they had developed from the sound and death industries.[31] All facets of studio production were in place at the commemoration of the Unknown: sound technicians seeking fidelity; a network of trained consumers across the country who had developed modern mourning practices and technical listening skills from years of practicing with gramophones and telephony; a vocal performance of articulation, authority, and authenticity; and an interaction between people and machines that produced new sounds of empire across thousands of miles of space.[32] Memories could now cross greater distances faster and access larger networks of people in more meaningful ways.

Prior to the twentieth century, sound had always been magical and mystical. Scientists, inventors, and philosophers had largely demystified sound by the end of the Great War, and this had consequences for the mystical chords of memory metaphor.[33] The human ear is able to sense and to select vibrations in the air and send this information through neurons to the brain. The brain receives these messages from the neural pathways and filters them through previous experiences and memories before interpreting and storing them internally.[34] But the mind can also interpret these neurological memories through a cultural network to help it process the meaning of the selected vibrations detected by the ear.[35] Sound metaphors can help people select certain sound waves and filter out others, interpret them internally, and connect their memories to the realm of collective memory where social interactions help the living and the dead vouch for each other.[36] Telephony increased the number of potential network connections and increased the speed through which individuals could connect their individual memories to cultural memory.[37]

The technological manipulation of sound developed by AT&T engineers allowed more people than ever before to listen to (and share) the sounds of nation and empire. Emily Thompson suggests that electronic sound manipulation had the ability to mystically transport "20,000 San Franciscans [to] Arlington" and connect distant and even isolated people at a time when the "nature of sound and the culture of listening were undergoing a "reformulation of the relationship between sound and space."[38] One reporter claimed, "It was one of the most remarkably impressive scenes ever known in San Francisco" where "every sound of the Arlington ceremony affected the great crowd within hearing of the waves of the Pacific Ocean."[39] The ability to transform space with sound, Thompson writes, meant that "sound was gradually dissociated from space until the relationship ceased to exist" requiring "new criterion by which to evaluate [sounds]." People had to learn new ways of listening within the context of reevaluating the changing memory landscape of nation, space, and empire. East and West

Coast people could now be connected to the nation in aural ways that were based on similar communication strategies but much more immediate than print journalism. While the electronic technology of telephony demystified the nature of sound waves, it also helped produce magical imaginings of the relationship between space, nation, and empire. New mysticism of space went hand in hand with the updated chords of memory metaphor. Harding and his listeners thus were at the cusp of a new age of memory-making in the United States where they had to reimagine and restructure the topography of cultural memory.

Commemorating the body of an American unknown showcased amalgamating middle-class networks where citizens could consume kinship, identity, a cultural memory, a republican national identity, and a highly motivated agenda without acknowledging an imperial identity. Here laid the key obfuscation surrounding the cult of the Unknown Soldier: the body had no kinship. Harding himself noted that in "return[ing] this poor clay to its mother soil" was recognition that "some mother gave him in her love and tenderness, and, with him, her most cherished hopes." The brilliance of using an unknown soldier was that the body's anonymity ensured that it could not be linked absolutely to any specific family or group. It represented a powerful retrospective manipulation of time, space, and genealogy. Without kinship there was no individual identity, and thus no kinship could assert any evidence of remembrance. All that anyone knew of the unknown was that he was an American soldier and that he was dead. No one could know his surname or his experiences. And yet people could retrospectively remember his body through the axis of family hearthstone even if some were excluded from national politics. The unknown monument nearly matched the family grief ritual, contour for contour, but simulated social connections through cultural memory and not kinship relations. As individuals conjured up memories of respective loved ones in Madison Square Garden, one reporter wrote, "Thousands, including many of the gold star mothers . . . were in tears, as the president in touching words told how many American families, whose sons were buried where they fell, might hope that the unknown soldier was their boy."[40] This kinship simulation provided a usable historical collaboration for the public to keep the memory of the dead alive retrospectively and for government and military elites to mystically and directly tie individual memory to cultural memory. The audio network transmitted sights and sounds of cultural memory expeditiously and efficaciously over telephone wires around the country with limited feedback.

Much of the ceremony played on the nativist, Protestant, and capitalist traditions of American culture. The ceremony borrowed its ethos from the Good Death tradition of the nineteenth century in which an unknown body received a secularized commemoration that honored his acceptance to the national pantheon. Steven Trout and other historians have illustrated the Protestant underpinnings of the dedication ceremony. Organizers draped the official monument and the ceremony with Protestant hymns, speeches, and ornamentation. Most Americans believed that the Unknown represented a cultural memory of the unchanging middle-class aspirations of white Americans.[41] But this cultural memory was not absolute, and many people could interpret the monument differently especially in the face-to-face interactions that defined communicative memories of different groups. As G. Kurt Piehler contends, "Few white Americans envisioned the Unknown Soldier as being black, but a delegation of African-American leaders disagreed and went to the Capitol to lay flowers by his casket."[42] Even during the ceremony, visible cracks in the hegemonic interpretation of the Unknown emerged that could be seen and heard. Harding noted that the dead man before him "may have been a native or an adopted son; that matters little because they glorified the same loyalty, they sacrificed alike."[43] Multiple groups with competing yet complementary historical remembrances could bend the monument to correspond to their own respective experiences of the past, especially when they shared memories with each other without the decorum and protocols of cultural memory. The Tomb of the Unknown was such an ambivalent monument that members of several real and fictive kinships could connect their experiences to it, and they did especially during the interwar years.

Northerners could believe the Unknown came from the North while Southerners could claim he had a Southern birth. The tomb thus projected a narrative of completed reunification, and it helped resolve any lingering fissures, symbolic or real, between the North and the South. But this also allowed disparate groups to experience at least a symbolic presence in the imagined community defined by multiple segregations. Trout illustrates how the interwar years brought a plethora of protests from "dozens of poets, fiction writers, editorialists, and clerics [who] appropriated this national symbol and turned it against its official makers."[44] Maybe the Unknown was native born and white, but perhaps he was an immigrant or, as poet James Weldon Johnson's *Saint Peter Relates an Incident of the Resurrection Day* suggested, the Resurrection would show that the soldier was black.[45] Perhaps he harbored Bolshevik or anticapitalist beliefs if we are to take John Dos Passos's irreverent description of "An American Body" seriously.[46] Certainly many with socialist leanings did. Possibly he was Native American, as the presence of Chief Plenty Coups at the dedication ceremony might imply, or perhaps he was Catholic or Jewish. A single "American Soldier Known but to God" implied a divination of the Unknown's body and his memories that allowed immigrants, black Americans, and white Americans to infer that the Unknown might be one of them. Interpreters such as Johnson and Dos Passos registered their protests a decade later and within cultural memory during the interwar years, but their criticisms did not suddenly appear years after the dedication ceremony. Instead of inventing these criticisms of official cultural memory, these interwar poets, writers, and editors should be seen as co-opting communicative memories for their own cultural projects of literature and critique. These storytellers could transcend the boundaries of social memories and give voice to memories of the war that cultural memory could not detect. Rather than invention, authors based their critiques on communicative memories that had always been present within collective memories of marginalized groups but could not be detected very well because they flourished within the spontaneous personal oral interactions of group members that left no paper trail. These undocumented memories coalesced throughout the country even as government officials were planning the dedication ceremony. Poets and authors registered unofficial or vernacular critical interpretations of the tomb within their literature, which, in turn, formed the evidence of a cultural critique that historians could then detect. The dedication ceremony and its accompanying pageantry can only provide evidence of cultural memory; it cannot help scholars detect the countermemories that lived within the communicative interactions of local people operating orally within their groups. Harding's speech, meanwhile, infused the monument and the body with the politics of reconciliation and extended the retrospective gesture of citizenship to many people without offering any real political power to minority populations. It was the furthest that people operating in a paradigm of Jim Crow America would go toward acknowledging a symbolic citizenship to disenfranchised people. The absence of kinship helped symbolize at least a shadow of cosmopolitan republicanism even if it obscured the imperialistic realities of the nation. Mystical chords tied the unknown individual to a national cultural memory and reflected back to the individual transcendent and muddled symbolic impressions of family, nation, and democracy; the monument worked as an ambivalent cultural symbol to help diverse and often excluded people see and hear the retrospective and prospective memories of the dead that symbolized the living national community at least for a moment. The Unknown thus was neither a son of Pennsylvania nor of Georgia nor of California, nor was he the son of his own father and mother; he was a son of America.[47]

On Armistice Day 1921, several cultural memory network users imagined prospective connections between the dead Unknown and the reconfigured spaces of American empire that would be showcased beginning the next day at the Arms Limitation Conference. Sound and visual networks communicated these unforgettable achievements of the dead efficiently. Chaplain John T. Axton delivered an invocation at the beginning of the Unknown's funeral, praying into the microphone for all to remember the dead. He asked God to "accord exceptional judgment, foresight, and tactfulness" to delegate leaders attending the next day's disarmament conference who sought to "end that discord, which provokes war" so that there "may be world tranquility."[48] Using the audio network to communicate across the continent, Axton asserted a prayerful memory of America's role in the war that assigned a divine and even sacredness to the unknown body and to the disarmament conference, suggesting a mystical relationship between sacrifice, peace, and empire. At least one editor of the *New York Times* praised Harding's speech, claiming that the world was "'a world awakened,' of 'a wider freedom.' This objective, vaguely seen, led us into the Great War. It should lead us on into the Great Peace."⁴⁹ Again this exhibited a tacit memory of America's ability to influence the world beyond its borders because of its contributions to the war. Most of the churches in New York performed special services simultaneous with the dedication ceremony in Washington DC. Although churchgoers did not hear the commemoration over the phone line, they too were able to access the cultural memory that tied the Unknown to the peace conference. All the Episcopal churches put on a "service in memory of those who gave their lives for their country in the World War and in supplication for God's blessing upon the Conference on the Limitation of Armament." At St. Patrick's, Msgr. Michael J. Lavelle explicitly tied Armistice Day to the peace conference but told his parishioners that "unless the peoples and their governments loved and imitated Christ, all treaties were but 'scraps of paper.'" At St. John the Divine Cathedral, "one of the greatest crowds in its history gathered," and Bishop William T. Manning spoke to children and their parents, stating that "Armistice Day, 1921, might ever be remembered as the beginning of a new era of brotherhood and peace." After a two-minute silence, Manning "concluded with a prayer for the Washington conference." Rabbi Joseph Corcos of the Spanish and Portuguese Synagogue along Seventieth Street bordering the west edge of Central Park lamented that the world is "still suffering from its unhealed wounds, though war has robbed it of material wealth and the flower of its manhood, yet they still construct more warships and invent more deadly instruments for a further carnage." Corcos believed the Arms Limitation Conference would help the world "march, no matter how slowly, in the direction of peace and tranquility. He claimed President Harding would be a "great prince of peace, a veritable messiah through whose instrumentality God's kingdom of peace will have been established in the world." Here the commemoration of the Unknown held significant symbolism of divination and of an empire of peace.⁵⁰

Although he never directly tied the two events together in his speech, the president claimed, "I can sense the prayers of our people, of all peoples, that this Armistice Day shall mark the beginning of a new and lasting era of peace on earth, good-will among men." Here the dedication ceremony can be viewed beyond its nationalistic metaphor and can be interpreted as an attempt to establish a cultural memory governing the "community of interests" that Harding and the Republicans were attempting to cultivate in the Pacific. Foreign representatives from every participating nation in the next day's Arms Limitation Conference attended the ceremony.[51] Of course Britain, France, Italy, and several other countries had also used the remains of unknown soldiers to commemorate their respective nations and empires. But Harding went beyond this and sought to link these burgeoning national memories to reflect a democratic world order. He argued in his eulogy that the Unknown typified an Americanism that could lead the world out of depression and toward peace. Unlike the officials of Britain and France, who took extra steps to ensure that their Unknowns were authentic representatives of Englishness and Frenchness, Harding celebrated the American Unknown as a metaphor for the cosmopolitanism of the American people. Harding spoke to what he believed was a uniquely American consensus formed out of the willingness of diverse Americans not only to defend the liberty of the United States but also to extend that liberty to a recovering Europe and a Pacific world in turmoil:

> The loftiest tribute we can bestow today . . . is the commitment of this Republic to an advancement never made before. If American achievement is a cherished pride at home, if our unselfishness among nations is all we wish it to be, and ours is a helpful example in the world, then let us give of our influence and strength, yea, of our aspiration and convictions, to put mankind on a little higher plane, exulting and exalting, with war's distressing and depressing tragedies barred from the stage of righteous civilization.[52]

The intersection for Harding's view of nationalism and the expansion of America's postwar informal empire was located at the "heroically earned tribute" to the Unknown Soldier. The cosmopolitanism and the sacrifice symbolized by the Unknown, at least for the president, was evidence of America's ability to lead the new world order.

In Washington some saw an implicit connection between the dedication ceremony and the limitation talks. "A charming atmosphere is prevailing," claimed one observer. "It is an atmosphere of good-will. Nobody has anything to ask for himself and everybody is ready to make the happiness of humanity."⁵³ Meanwhile the Japanese delegation's official statement, issued the same day as the dedication ceremony, agreed: "All the nations of the world, with their war wounds still sore, are clamoring for peace. And, though some of these wounds are of the flesh, there are equally deep economic wounds." Prime Minister Briand similarly declared, "France wishes to arrive at an accord that will create an atmosphere of peace, in which the nations may work in complete security." Senator Schanzer of Italy reflected on the conference just an hour or two after the ceremony: "Now, the supreme condition in order that the equilibrium of the world may be re-established and in order that the countries more severely struck by the war may rise and reconstruct their economy is peace. That is why all our efforts must be directed toward creating political guarantees for the lasting maintenance of peace." Perhaps the British empire delegation's official statement made the strongest connection between the unknown and the conference:

> The stately and impressive symbolism of America's mourning for her sons and daughters dead in the cause of liberty had deeply moved the hearts of their British comrades in the Great War. It is a worthy prelude to the labors of the conference which begins tomorrow, and to this end the British Empire delegations, representing all parts of the empire, look to aid in the task of extricating the world from the unhappy conditions into which war has plunged it, and to make the peace, secured at so great a cost, a heritage of mankind.

A reporter noted, "Upon every hand were heard expressions of satisfaction that in paying his tribute to America's soldier dead the Chief Executive grasped his opportunity to renew the pledge of the United States to take its full share of leadership in the attainment of a better order."⁵⁴

The next day the president officially opened the conference by welcoming the delegates to the Washington conference. He reminded them, "Here in the United States we are but freshly turned from the burial of an unknown American soldier, when a nation sorrowed while paying him tribute." Americans across the country, he claimed, "were summarizing the inexcusable cause, the incalculable cost, the unspeakable sacrifices, and the unutterable sorrows, and there was the ever-impelling question: how can humanity justify or God forgive?" The dedication of the Tomb of the Unknown Soldier was a showcase of the chords of memory metaphor that bound biological memories of Americans together through a cultural memory that Harding could use to represent America's unique selling point of a mission in the Pacific that would prevent war and allow for trade and industry to revive the world economy. From this perspective, the Tomb of the Unknown ceremony and the social network built around mystic sounds of remembrance is evidence of an adept diplomatic use of cultural memory to impress upon foreign delegates a chorus sounding that the United States could lead the world.[55]

Throughout the ceremony the fidelity of sound, although not pure, was very good as song and words were transmitted with only a few moments of distortion. Sounds from the amplifiers in both cities spilled out of the respective venues and onto the surrounding streets where an estimated crowd stood outside the Auditorium that matched the numbers inside hoping Harding's voice could help them make sense of the tragic war and perhaps even heal their grief. "In the open air," claimed one observer, "the President's voice seemed to come from the chest of a giant."[56] Roland Barthes describes this kind of sound as the "grain of the voice," in which he refers to the sounds that vocal cords make moments before those sounds form words.[57] Although Harding's performance was powerful, the meaning of his voice was illusory. Mladen Dolar suggests that although the grain of the voice can produce sound waves and can be detected by its accent, its timbre, and its intonation, it is "recalcitrant to meaning" because the voice has no linguistics. This suggests that the microphone voice that Harding performed and that came "from the chest of a giant" to comfort the grief-stricken and heal the wounds of society was in fact an illusion made possible by electrical current moving sound waves across telephone lines.[58]

Similar to the way Lincoln spoke on behalf of the dead at Gettysburg, Harding spoke for the dead man and depicted him as an anonymous hero for the American empire who "fired his shot for liberation of the captive conscience of the world." The materiality of the Unknown Soldier thus was also for the world according to Harding. It stood in not just for Americans but for the millions who died in the war. It was the living's responsibility "to testify undying gratitude and reverence for that thought of a wider freedom."[59] Harding's vocal performance accentuated democracy and the progress of modernity as a universal pursuit shared by millions of soldiers collectively. The president concluded:

> Standing today on hallowed ground, conscious that all America has halted to share in the tribute of heart and mind and soul to this fellow-American, and knowing that the world is noting this expression of the republic's mindfulness, it is fitting to say that his sacrifice, and that of the millions dead, shall not be in vain. There must be, there shall be, the commanding voice of a conscious civilization against armed warfare.

An American voice, he implied, spoke clearly on behalf of civilization. The world could yet be made safe for peace as well as democracy.

But this metaphorical "voice of conscious civilization" too was illusory on the domestic and international fronts. After finishing his eulogy, the president stepped away from the microphone and sat down. American and foreign dignitaries decorated the tomb with numerous medals of respective national honor. Finally, Chief Plenty Coups, a Crow Indian representing all Indians in the United States, placed his headdress and war stick on the tomb. Chief Plenty Coups stated, "I feel it an honor to the red man that he takes part in this great event because it shows that the thousands of Indians who fought in the Great War are appreciated by the white man." He added, "I hope that the Great Spirit will grant that these noble warriors have not given up their lives in vain and that there will be peace to all men hereafter." Chief Plenty Coups called for peace "to all men" including those marginalized within the borders of the United States. His words, perhaps unintentionally, pointed to the sacrifice of the subjugated and to the illusory sounds of the chords of memory metaphor.[60]

Harding's voice, meanwhile, aided the illusion that America could deliver peace and prosperity to the Pacific world.[61] The president understood the monument as a site of memory that guaranteed that America would be a global leader and a voice of peace. Harding articulated a "memory of power extended over space" that envisioned the United States as bridging the

Atlantic and Pacific worlds.[62] The kind of bridge Republicans in the United States hoped to build did not reject outright the kind of globalism entrenched in the postwar world system so much as they wanted much greater federal control over it, and they sought this by limiting immigrants, lowering taxes, creating tariffs, and negotiating treaties such as the Naval Limitation Pact, none of which offered much economic prosperity or political liberty to people living in the periphery. But these politicians, led by Harding, could not fully roll back the interventionism of the Progressive years even if they refused to participate in the League of Nations. The memories of the war along with the technology and business interests that dominated the postwar world system demanded that the United States play a global role. Memories of the dead accompanied the technologies of a rapidly globalizing capitalist age in which Americans (re)imagined citizenship within an accumulation of imperial power that now bridged the wide-open spaces of the Atlantic and Pacific worlds. The Tomb of the Unknown became a symbol of the contradictory and ambivalent intentions of Americans who wanted to use imperial power to intervene in the world system while also seeking to remain free from the entrapments and entanglements of European colonialism. From this perspective, American cultural memory, as interpreted by Wilson and Harding, could offer few republican memories to people who lived in Asia, the Pacific, and on reservations within the United States. It was not a cultural memory that commemorated the experiences of people seeking self-determination; it was re-presenting the peace and prosperity that the United States was now offering the Pacific and Atlantic worlds and their inhabitants. This network did not contain memories of self-determination or a new world order; rather, they echoed American nationalism and America's expansion westward in a world system that would soon see the United States become the core of that system.[63]

Epilogue

Reclaiming Lincoln's Promise?

> The journey into the unknown or the transgression of a border represents a prime example and model for the process of forgetting. The child forgets his parents, the envoy, his message, the prince, his noble birth, the soul, its heavenly origin, because there is nothing in the new world to bear or support memory.
> —Jan Assmann

The cold cultural memory that brought U.S. citizens, government agents, and corporate capitalism together after the First World War had significant staying power. By insulating the present from the past and restricting social change, cultural memory helped undergird Jim Crow segregation and the military-industrial complex that organized and protected the United States. Effective collaboration between middle-class citizens, officials, and corporations continued for the next sixty years, incorporating the imperialistic memories of the Second World War and much of the Cold War into the republican mythology of the nation. But American cultural memory was also threatened by the inconsistencies of a nation that acted imperialistically while claiming to be republican. This threat did not pose a technological undermining to the cultural memory that Americans built in the twentieth century; rather, it was a moral weakness embedded in cultural memory. The republican memory that Americans folded into national and then imperialistic memories was never completely forgotten, but the context changed dramatically over time. Imperialism became the dominant context through which Americans made cultural memory. Americans' envelopment of republican memory within the imperial context created profound fissures within the cultural memory that could not be hidden forever. The tension was too profound and needed only a moment to cut it. That moment came in Santiago de Cuba during the Cuban Revolution of the 1950s and 1960s. Since the USS *Maine* had been resunk in international waters, there were very few symbols of U.S. involvement in Cuba. U.S. and Cuban governments had collaborated to build a few monuments in Havana, but nature was reclaiming the actual battlefields of El Caney, Daiquiri, and San Juan Hill. Some Americans involved in the invasion of Cuba and the Spanish surrender of Santiago grew quite concerned when they visited Cuba in the late 1950s as tourists. Now as old men retracing their steps, they found few memorials that described their actions as young men.

One of these Americans was retired Maj. Gen. Ralph E. Truman, a cousin of former president Harry S. Truman. General Truman toured Cuba in 1955 and 1956, and to his dismay, he found the Santiago battlefield to be "our FORGOTTEN BATTLE FIELD."[1] He came home and enlisted his cousin's help in persuading U.S.-backed Cuban president and dictator Fulgencio Batista to turn the Santiago battlefield into a Gettysburg-style national park.[2] Harry Truman wrote to Gen. Carl Spatz, head of the American Battle Monuments Commission (ABMC), petitioning Spatz to seek legislative approval from Congress for the ABMC to take over care of the battlefield and the Santiago Surrender Tree, where Spanish forces had signed the surrender terms.[3] President Warren G. Harding had asked Congress to create the ABMC in 1923 to extend the Lincolnian tradition to military dead buried in foreign nations. This institution used similar sorts of memory techniques that Americans deployed at the Tomb of the Unknown. Gen. John J. Pershing oversaw the ABMC, which took control of the American military cemeteries abroad as well as building and maintaining monuments and memorials of the First World War. Later the ABMC planned and managed the cemeteries and monuments of the Second World War. Sites in Cuba did not fall under the ABMC's jurisdiction, as there were no cemeteries from the Spanish-Cuban-American war. Instead, the ambassador to Cuba and the U.S. secretary of state, with money from the U.S. Army, controlled the Santiago Surrender Tree memorial. No one looked after the battlefield.

General Truman collaborated with members of the Missouri Chapter of the Spanish-American Veterans, Congress, leaders of the ABMC, and the Cuban government. He enlisted the help of Congressman and Spanish War veteran Barrett O'Hara, who made official visits to Cuba in 1955 and supported Truman's plan. Truman hoped to jointly fund the restoration program as a "reaffirmation of the mutual friendship of the Cuban and American people." American organizers were particularly sensitive to enlisting the Cuban government because they feared the Cuban veterans organizations in the Oriente Province, where the Santiago battlefield and Surrender Tree are, could "nullify some of the goodwill" of the American-led commemorative program. Cuban veterans of the Oriente, according to Truman's report, were mainly "of Negro ancestry and it is for this reason that this [U.S.] Consulate recommends procuring the full endorsement of the Cuban government." Such comments in the confidential foreign service report anticipated possible protest from Cuban veterans because the whole commemorative venture threatened to accentuate U.S. actions during the war while obscuring Cubans' participation in their own struggle to become independent from Spain. As an illustration of this tension, one of the War Department's judge advocates general ruled in 1909 that "the monuments, markers, and other objects established on the battlefield in the vicinity of Santiago are the property of the United States and were acquired in the operation of appropriate acts of appropriation." According to the Pentagon, the United States owned the battlefield and the Surrender Tree. Cuban governments over the years tacitly, but never formally, accepted the American claim of sovereignty. It was feared that Cuban veterans could undermine the U.S. effort if the Cuban government failed to play a significant role in building the site of memory. In fact, the consulate in Santiago recommended that military officials seek a public proclamation from Cuban authorities of "acknowledged sovereignty" over the sites and suggested that during the rededication ceremony, the ABMC rename the site the "Cuban-American Friendship Tree" to mitigate "objections [that] have been voiced locally over the present title 'Surrender Tree Site.'" Congress eventually passed legislation to cede control of the Santiago Surrender Tree to the ABMC. Turning the Santiago battlefield into a national park would take Congress longer to consider, but Truman and his chapter of the Spanish War Veterans believed it was promising.[4]

Congressional willingness to work jointly with the Batista dictatorship may have ameliorated some of the Cuban veterans groups in Oriente Province, but it failed to recognize a more significant form of protest growing in the Sierra Maestra. Fidel Castro's fledgling group of revolutionaries landed in the Oriente Province in December 1956. Batista's forces seemingly defeated them, but this forced the insurgents into the mountains, where they mounted a memory war over their own radio channel as well as print media when the *New York Times* interviewed Castro. The revolutionaries likened themselves to charismatic and powerful Cuban leaders of the 1895 revolution such as Antonio Maceo. Castro himself channeled the imagery of José Martí and of Jesus Christ. Their campaign appealed to a growing number of people in the Oriente Province who joined his movement in the mountains. Others who did not join were still influenced by the revolutionaries' ability to connect their movement to memory of Cuban history before U.S. involvement.

Like Castro's revolutionaries, Americans during the 1950s had a stake in the Oriente Province and the Surrender Tree in particular. The Surrender Tree, claimed one, "is perhaps the most important tree in American history because of the role it played in making the United States a world power and a consequent rise to pre-eminence in world affairs." The U.S. consulate in Santiago thus recommended that "there is a pressing need to maintain it in a neat and presentable state and in a manner which will reflect on the prestige of the United States."[5] Truman, meanwhile, continued to meet with Cuban military and civilian authorities as "official guests" of the Cuban government to study the site of the battlefield and make provisions to restore it "as an added tourist attraction" for the growing number of Americans visiting sites of the war.[6] Gen. M. Diaz Tamayo of the Cuban Army along with members of the Cuban Tourist Commission met Truman at the airport for his visit in 1958. Truman and his wife toured the battlefields, met with the U.S. ambassador, and even received an invitation to meet with President Batista. The Cuban president had sought to strengthen U.S. tourism in Cuba.[7] Truman met with Batista, who "speaks perfect English," for an hour. According to Truman, Batista agreed that "the suggestion about the restoration of certain portions of the battlefield was excellent." The dictator believed "it would not only be of historic value to his country and the United States, but other historic spots in and around Santiago, dating back to the 15th Century," wrote Truman. Batista called on his aides to begin the process and described to Truman how Cuba was planning to celebrate the centennial of President Theodore Roosevelt's birthday and that perhaps under cover of the Roosevelt centennial Truman could create a memorial tablet celebrating the anniversary of "Cuba getting her freedom from Spain and the 60th anniversary of the Hispano-Americano war." Batista suggested that if this marker could be placed at Gen. William Shafter's headquarters, then "it could mark the beginning of the program for the restoration of the battlefield." Truman left the meetings with Batista excited, believing "this time [we] really accomplished what we had been attempting to do on two previous visits." Congress approved the ABMC takeover of the monument and battlefield for July 1, 1958. Truman and the Spanish War Veterans could now work with the ABMC and the Cuban dictator to restore the fields of battle surrounding Santiago, but the U.S. arms embargo against Cuba that began shortly after Truman returned to the United States complicated the plan.[8]

The ABMC first set to work in preserving the Surrender Tree. It had deteriorated over the years, and it needed new concrete curbing, updated parking areas, driveways, and walkways. The site needed an updated fence and floodlights "at each corner of the site which now habitually serves after dark as a trysting place for hot blooded Cubans." The recommendations from the embassy in Havana noted that "while neither the Embassy nor the Consulate necessarily wish to discourage nocturnal activities of this sort, it is not believed the 'Surrender Tree Site,' appropriate though the name may be, should be used for these purposes." The embassy also suggested that the ABMC tear down the caretaker's shack that housed the caretaker, Julio de Lay, a Cuban national, his wife, and four children and replace it with a stone-mason home complete with electricity and running water. Because the site "marks the scene of the birth of a new nation," the house should be "maintained in keeping with the dignity of the United States and the Republic of Cuba."[9] The State Department reminded ABMC officials in November 1958 that "the assistance given by the United States to the Cubans in achieving their independence is an important and traditional factor in the relations between the two countries and appropriate reminders of our efforts on behalf of Cuba are useful in maintaining close ties between Cubans and Americans."[10]

As the ABMC began preparations to inspect the site, Fidel Castro engaged in guerilla war tactics against Batista's forces. The Cuban military could not defeat the guerillas, and Batista resigned and fled the country on December 31, 1958. Castro marched into Santiago on January 2, 1959, while his comrades Camilo Cienfuegos and Ernesto "Che" Guevara marched into Havana. Together they instituted a provisional government under President Manuel Urrutia Lleó. Castro and his armed revolutionaries would keep close control over the new president's policies. In January 1960 the ABMC received a request from the Cuban government to return five eighteenth-century cannon from the Surrender Tree site to Santiago's Moro Castle. Dr. Francisco Pratt Puig of the University of Oriente, who directed the Cuban Public Works Department, argued that these cannon had nothing to do with the 1898 conflict and should be handed over to the Moro Castle restoration project where they would be remounted in their historically correct locations. The American consulate officer agreed and recommended that the ABMC return the cannon.[11] Cuban public works officials also made known their plans to enlarge the Santiago Zoological Garden, which bordered the battle monument. Architect Nerma del Maza was placed in charge of the project. The U.S. official reported that while some of her choices were different in style from the monument, they were in good taste. He reported that the Cuban government was "doing a considerable amount of work locally in beautifying old monuments and other tourist attractions." He stated that "San Juan Hill is maintained in excellent condition," and he believed that the battle monument would benefit from the changes as a whole.[12]

By April 1960, however, something ominous occurred. Just one month after the explosion of the *La Coubre* in Havana Harbor—a French ship carrying Belgian weapons whose explosion while in port Castro blamed on the Eisenhower administration—the ABMC became alarmed over a report from the U.S. embassy in Havana in which the consulate in Santiago reported that on April 21, a member of the Cuban police ordered the caretaker of the Surrender Tree site to replace the U.S. flag with a Cuban flag and "to fly it in place of honor."[13] The consulate, however, continued to fly the U.S. flag and to maintain control of the site. In October 1960, the U.S. government extended the arms embargo against the Cuban government to include exports as tensions rose between the outgoing Eisenhower administration and Castro's ever closer embrace of communism. ABMC officials were not pleased with recent events, and Gen. Thomas North suggested that the ABMC dismiss the caretaker and abandon the site altogether, "since the Cuban authorities were encroaching on the site, and had previously engaged in harassing tactics as regards flying the flag." Others on the committee believed that the Cuban government would use the withdrawal as propaganda against the United States, and Spanish War Veterans groups in the United States would be upset with the decision. The ABMC committee agreed to continue with the project, but they instructed the consulate officer "not to indicate approval of the proposed changes at the Surrender Tree site, nor to authorize the removal of the Moro Castle cannon."[14]

In January 1961, President Eisenhower authorized the closure of the U.S. embassy in Havana, removing diplomats from Cuba as Castro nationalized American-owned industries. The ABMC nevertheless hoped to continue to oversee the Surrender Tree site. Officials moved forward with improvement plans and increased the caretaker's annual salary from $840 to $1,200, allowing him and his family to find accommodation while they hoped to begin constructing the new caretaker's home. The ABMC would liaison with the State Department to work through the Swiss embassy still operating in Havana.[15] By February, however, shortly after John F. Kennedy formally entered the White House, U.S. embassy officials received a report from their counterparts in the Swiss embassy in Havana. Julio de Lay, caretaker of the Surrender Tree site, abruptly quit his job as caretaker for a position with the Cuban Ministry of Public Works, which offered a higher salary. De Lay now oversaw the tree, the adjacent Santiago Zoological Gardens, and the San Juan Hill battle site for the Cuban government while continuing to live in the caretaker's shack. He employed his nephew to look after the

Surrender Tree site when he was pulled away by his new responsibilities. The report also noted that the fence separating the Surrender Tree site from the zoo had been taken down.[16] This signaled to the ABMC that the Cuban government was effectively encroaching on the site. On 17 April, the Bay of Pigs invasion took place. This force of Cuban exiles trained by the Central Intelligence Agency (CIA) invaded Cuba. They hoped to connect with anti-Castro Cubans and to overthrow Castro, who by now had deposed Manuel Urrutia Lleó and appointed himself prime minister as well as president of the National Tourist Agency. He also appointed Che Guevara to important positions. The ABMC received another report from the Swiss embassy officer who toured the Surrender Tree site on behalf of the ABMC. He reported that the Castro regime now hoped to combine the Surrender Tree site, the zoo, the agricultural experimental farm, and the San Juan Hill battlefield into one massive park. In fact, the Cuban government closed fences and entrances to the tree site, thus forcing sightseers to funnel themselves through the zoo first before seeing the Surrender Tree.[17]

While the ABMC officials retained control over the site, they did not sustain their monopoly over the interpretation of the site or the surrounding battlefield. After the United States extended the embargo to include imports and then visitation, few Americans since the Cuban Revolution have seen the Surrender Tree site in person. Yet the ABMC still claims legal responsibility for the site. Absent a U.S. embassy in Cuba, the ABMC completely depended on third parties, such as the Swiss embassy, to channel money to the caretaker. American officials also had to rely on the honorable intentions of Cuban nationals to maintain the site through the decades. The tenuous control that the ABMC maintained was evident as the tree's health declined over the years and finally died. The Cuban government replaced the tree in 1998.[18] Cuban authorities thus subtly undermined the ABMC to take away their paid caretaker without them knowing, closed off the entrance of the site from non-zoo patrons, and prevented the ABMC from turning the battlefield into a national park. Today the battlefield is dominated by sprawling suburbs. Although the Cuban government acknowledges and even maintains the few American sites that remain, they have superimposed revolutionary sites throughout the country that far outnumber the monuments dedicated to U.S. involvement in the Spanish-Cuban-American war. Sites include where Fidel Castro's *Granma* made land, where the revolutionaries held out in the Sierra Maestra, and sites in Santiago, such as the Antonio Maceo equestrian statue at the center of Revolutionary Square. The Castro regime understood well the vulnerability of American presence in Cuba. If U.S. diplomats were correct that reminding Cubans of U.S. efforts in Cuban independence was crucial to maintaining good relations between Cubans and Americans, then the Castro government successfully outmaneuvered General Truman, ABMC officials, and U.S. embassy personnel who built their commemorative efforts in Cuba on the crumbling dictatorship of Fulgencio Batista. Such a strategy demonstrated a failure of U.S. cultural memory, and it also exposed just how undemocratic U.S. cultural memory could be. Cuban communists exposed cracks in the U.S. cultural memory project that Americans had covered over previously. As the Cuban-American political and economic relationship continued to worsen, U.S. cultural power lost the ability to remind Cuban citizens of the myth of U.S. republicanism, which allowed the Cuban government to expose the imperial nature of U.S. cultural memory. Cuban communist interpretations offered a new interpretation of the Spanish-American War, one that was much warmer than U.S. interpretations. These revolutionary memories invoked the past to bring about change and transformation and suggested that U.S. democracy that facilitated the interests of corporations and dictators was not all that different from Spanish colonial governance. Cuban revolutionaries stubbornly confronted U.S. cold cultural memory with a much warmer alternative of the Spanish-Cuban-American War in the early days of the revolution. It took U.S. cultural memory-makers, both government agents and citizen tourists, completely by surprise.

The cultural memory that Americans built was exceedingly powerful in convincing people that the United States was a republic and not an empire. This was true even as government officials wielded imperial power in some of the most brutal and corrupt ways in conflicts across the Pacific, the Atlantic, and at home. But U.S. cultural memory came under attack in the second half of the twentieth century not only by people such as Fidel Castro but also by U.S. citizens closer to home. The deaths of people such as Emmitt Till and Viola Liuzzo and the life of Malcolm X, forced many Americans to separate their memories of republicanism from the repertoire of domestic imperial power. The United States' wars in Asia also forced imperial memories to the surface especially as tens of thousands of casualties from the Korean conflict and the tens of thousands of Americans suffering from PTSD and Agent Orange contamination challenged, along with the dead, the republicanism that politicians used to justify these conflicts. Politicians and military leaders throughout the twentieth century would use the Tomb of the Unknown Soldier to cover over the imperialistic wounds that their political agendas created, including adding more bodies to the tomb such as unknowns from the Second World War, the Korean War, and the Vietnam War. Ronald Reagan's administration attempted to cover over the failure in the Vietnam War by actively searching for an unknown. Congress authorized the expansion of the Tomb for a Vietnam soldier in 1973, but none could be found. Only four sets of remains were unknown from the entire Vietnam conflict, and three would later be identified. In the election year of 1984, the Reagan administration put an incredible amount of pressure on military officials to produce an unknown especially so they could counteract Mia Lin's critically acclaimed and popular Vietnam War Memorial Wall, which some conservatives believed was too critical of the United States. Hoping to mimic fellow Republican Warren G. Harding's interpretation of the Lincolnian tradition, Reagan eulogized the Vietnam Unknown on Memorial Day 1984 in Arlington National Cemetery.[19]

Kinship, however, posed a potential threat to the "authenticity" and linearity that undergirded the Tomb of the Unknowns as a monument. As Michael Naas suggests, DNA science makes identification of the dead almost universal, as evidenced in the American Unknown from the Vietnam War whose plane was shot down in 1972 and who was later identified as 1st Lt. Michael Blassie.[20] The U.S. military discovered Blassie's remains within a few weeks of his plane being shot down. They collected only six bones as well as material effects from his plane including an identification card and a photo of his family, but they never told the Blassie family. Because of the limited amount of physical remains recovered, military officials discounted the material objects found with the bones and mistakenly reclassified Blassie's remains as unknown. The Reagan administration selected these remains—as Blassie's were the only "unknown" to select—and ordered the military to destroy all the artifacts and evidence that could tie Blassie's identity to the remains. In addition to the shocking and inappropriate nature of this act, the Reagan administration essentially undermined the Lincolnian tradition because Blassie should have been incorporated into the community of the fallen rather than have his identity erased. But the Reagan administration found it more politically powerful to isolate him from his family and his comrades by obscuring his identity. Although Harding could accomplish this maneuver in 1921, it would be more difficult for Reagan to do so. Reagan did benefit from the politics of the interment in 1984, but by the 1990s some involved in the POW/MIA movements began hard investigations and produced enough paper evidence to suggest that Michael Blassie could be identified. These researchers informed the Blassie family, who were stunned because they had never been told Blassie's remains had been recovered, let alone quickly identified.[21] After much controversy and reluctance from government officials, the Blassie family successfully petitioned the military to disinter and identify the remains of what DNA evidence would later identify as Blassie's. DNA identification restored Blassie's kinship, and the Blassie family reinstituted their family rituals of mourning within the Lincolnian tradition as they reburied him in a national cemetery near their home in St. Louis.[22] The Blassie family unintentionally exposed the collaboration between the middle class and elites and the government by disrupting the harmonious metaphor that mystified family ritual and national identity. Identifying Blassie helped undermine the Tomb of the Unknowns as prosthesis of kinship because it demystified the cultural memory that obscured the traditional family mourning ritual. DNA science thus helped expose cultural memory as an invented tradition and revealed the simulacra of filial tradition that it was built upon.

As technology developed in the digital revolution, America's naked wars of imperialism in Iraq and Afghanistan during the early twenty-first century would be exposed for its blatant contradictions of the Lincolnian tradition. While the Blassie family perhaps unintentionally challenged the foundations of American cultural memory, the Tillman family intended to expose the way cultural memory covered over imperialism with the mythology of republicanism. Pat Tillman left the National Football League (NFL) and a multi-million-dollar contract in 2002 to enlist in the U.S. Army. A potent metonym of republicanism, Tillman fought in Iraq and then Afghanistan, where he died under mysterious circumstances. Here Tillman can be inserted into a comradeship of citizen soldiers that also includes the Unknown Soldier. But while the Unknown Soldier helped obscure the repertoire of American imperial power, Tillman's notoriety helped illuminate it. In an attempt to incorporate Tillman into cultural memory, the U.S. Army posthumously promoted Tillman and awarded him the Silver Star and the Purple Heart. Although he was originally reported to have been killed by enemy combatants, accusations of an alleged military cover-up brought forth official investigations that showed that friendly fire at relatively close range actually killed him. This kind of commemoration was not what Lincoln promised at Gettysburg. In fact, it seemed a betrayal of Lincoln's promise.

This became a more powerful threat when people close to Tillman suggested the U.S. government was attempting to silence the corporal's growing criticism of U.S. involvement in Iraq before his death. Tillman was not an unknown soldier; he was a known soldier. He had a family, and they used their communicative memory of Tillman to shield him from the cultural memory in which military and political elites tried to shroud the Iraq and Afghanistan conflicts. This made it difficult for elites, the military, or even George W. Bush to speak on Tillman's behalf, despite the president's attempts to emulate Harding and Lincoln. Tillman's family could speak out, too, and they did so, using new digital technology and the power of social media networks to reach millions of people exponentially. They suggested that the "military and the government created a heroic tale about how their son died to foster a patriotic response across the country."[23] The imperialistic chords of memory that Harding played so effectively at the beginning of the American century could no longer be performed once technology of the digital age demystified cultural memory. Government agents, corporate entities such as the NFL, and citizens who sought to manipulate Tillman's death for political and cultural purposes only exposed how obsolete cultural memory had become and how complicit corporations and government officials were in failing to live up to the Lincolnian tradition.[24]

Further erosion of the Lincolnian tradition as the war against terror continues to rage threatens the power of cultural memory to cover over the wounds of imperialism. Sgt. La David Johnson's death just outside the village of Tongo Tongo in Niger on October 4, 2017, illustrates how Lincoln's promise remains unfulfilled. Johnson, who was black, and three white soldiers, Sgt. Bryan C. Black, Sgt. Jeremiah W. Johnson, and Sgt. Dustin M. Wright, fell under ambush from fighters loyal to the Islamic State. While Black, Johnson, and Wright died not far from the vehicle they had been riding in, La David Johnson became separated from the others and was killed by gun fire. Several hours later American military personnel arrived in helicopters operated by civilian contractors. They retrieved the bodies of Black, Wright, and Jeremiah Johnson, but they could not find La David Johnson. The contractors and military recovery team eventually left the site, and Johnson's body remained on the field of battle. Two days later, nearly a mile away from the ambush site, children from the village herding cattle stumbled upon his remains. Village eyewitness accounts claim they found his hands bound with rope and a gaping hole in his head; they suggested he had been captured and executed by militants connected to the Islamic State. However, military officials later decided that he had died "in a hail of bullets, hit as many as 18 times as he took cover in thick brush."[25] Shockingly, five weeks after his death and a month after his burial, FBI and military investigators discovered more bone fragments that they had overlooked during their initial retrieval of his body. At the behest of the military, Johnson's funeral was closed-casketed. Myeshia Johnson, his pregnant wife, voiced her frustration with the military. "Every time I asked to see my husband, they wouldn't let me," she said in a nationally televised interview. "They told me that he's in a severe wrap—like I won't be able to see him. I need to see him so I will know that that is my husband," she exclaimed. Seemingly losing faith in the credibility of the military's retrieval process, she questioned why the military would not let her see his remains. "They won't show me a finger, a hand, I know my husband's body from head to toe, and they won't let me see anything. I don't know what's in that box. It could be empty for all I know."[26]

President Donald Trump further inflamed the controversy when he called Mrs. Johnson. His call, she claimed, was poor. She recalled that the president, who had received deferments from military service during the Vietnam War, did not even know her husband's name during the conference call, and his statement that "he [Sergeant Johnson] knew what he signed up for" seemed irreverent if not disrespectful. While Trump denied that this conversation went the way Mrs. Johnson described it, Congresswoman Frederica Wilson, a Democrat from Miami and family friend, was listening and verified Mrs. Johnson's account. This set off a firestorm of controversy across the nation in which Trump's White House chief of staff and a retired general, John F. Kelly, held a press conference on October 19, 2017, that defended Trump's handling of the call by attempting to defame Congresswoman Wilson. "There's no perfect way to make that phone call," Kelly said. Kelly himself had lost a son in the Afghanistan conflict in 2010. But he claimed that Wilson's comments were inappropriate and that they, not the president's phone call, represented a level of disrespect that seemed to dominate the American landscape too much. "When I was a kid growing up, a lot of things were sacred in our country," Kelly noted. He described how "women were sacred, looked upon with great honor. That's obviously not the case anymore as we see from recent cases." He lamented how "life—the dignity of life—is sacred. That's gone." He then said, "Religion, that seems to be gone as well." And then Kelly added, "Gold Star families . . . I just thought—the selfless devotion that brings a man or woman to die on the battlefield, I just thought that might be sacred."[27]

Kelly then segued into what amounted to an anti–Gettysburg Address in his defense of the president. His main complaint was that citizens no longer respected what members of the military did or how they made sacrifices for civilians. Kelly devoted a large portion of his presentation to outlining the military retrieval process of bringing dead soldiers home. "Most Americans don't know what happens when we lose one of [our] soldiers, sailors, airmen, Marines, our Coast Guardsmen in combat. So let me tell you what happens." He then sketched out a process that the military had developed over several wars and updated over the twentieth century. He described the retrieval of the body from the field of battle and transfer to Dover Air Force Base wrapped in a shroud and packed in ice. He then described how a casualty officer escorts the body to the killed soldier's home. While this is happening, another casualty officer informs the family and stays with them through the grieving process and the funeral. And then, speaking of the fallen soldiers, Kelly made a stunning accusation. "Most of you, as Americans, don't know them. Many of you don't know anyone who knows any one of them." After his speech, Kelly took three questions from the media, and then he left the stage. But before exiting, he reminded the citizenry, "We don't look down upon those of you who haven't served. In fact, in a way we're a little bit sorry because you'll never have experienced the wonderful joy you get in your heart when you do the kinds of things our servicemen and women do—not for any other reason than they love this country. So just think of that."[28]

Kelly's anti–Gettysburg Address posed a direct threat to the Lincolnian tradition. It overtly described a breaking point between military service and civilian life and went on to claim that civilians could not understand the sacrifices that soldiers made because citizens held very little sacred in modern society, including the idea of sacrifice. Responding critically to General Kelly's comments, Phil Klay, an Iraq war veteran and winner of the National Book Award for his collections of essays, *Redeployment*, responded, "Veterans feel very keenly that America is disengaged from these wars," but added, "The problem is not going to be fixed with the idea only people who are personally involved have the right to ask questions. It's the exact opposite." Philip Carter, a veteran and director of the military, veterans, and society program at the Center for a New American Security in Washington DC, said of Kelly's speech, "It was odd. The military does not have a monopoly on loss and hardship."

These kinds of criticisms echoed the long tradition of obligation that the military and the citizenry held toward each other. But Kelly's speech highlighted a divide between civilian sacrifice and military sacrifice. At Gettysburg, Lincoln, the first Republican president, promised the military dead that civilians would remember them for their sacrifice. Chief of Staff John

Kelly, working for another Republican president more than 150 years later, suggested that this sacred promise was no longer in effect. Soldiers volunteered, he said, despite the fact that civilians reneged on their obligations to remember their sacrifices even as the Trump administration failed to uphold the government's end of the promise to Sgt. La David Johnson's family.[29]

This kind of finger-pointing, however, obscured a larger issue that was at stake in cultural memory. Why were these four soldiers in Niger anyway? Pentagon officials claimed they were on a routine reconnaissance mission, but Senator Lindsey Graham of South Carolina said, "I didn't know there was 1,000 troops in Niger," and declared that the war against the Islamic State was "an endless war without boundaries, no limitation on time or geography." He added, "We don't know exactly where we're at in the world militarily and what we're doing." This was a shocking statement from a man who serves on the Senate Armed Services Committee. Johnson's death thus exposed an American presence in a part of the world to which much of the citizenry and even members of Congress were oblivious. The president mangled the attempts to cover over this imperialistic presence when he failed to explain Sergeant Johnson's death to a widow who demanded answers. And this failure to use the Lincolnian tradition effectively ended with the president's chief of staff blaming Americans for defaulting on Lincoln's promise.[30]

Social media of the digital age and DNA science were new technologies that weakened American cultural memory because they allowed families who lost loved ones in conflicts from Vietnam to Afghanistan to Niger to accomplish what the Castro regime accomplished in Cuba. They all could challenge the moral contradictions on which Americans constructed cultural memory. By bringing the past into the present, they warmed cultural memory and exposed the cold imperialistic rituals that were incongruent with the republican Lincolnian tradition. Proof of this outmoded cultural memory can be seen coming from President Trump's gross mishandling of Lincoln's promise and General Kelly's anti–Gettysburg Address. The successive failures to take care of survivors of war from Korea, Vietnam, and more recently Iraq and Afghanistan only cause more people to doubt the government's willingness to fulfill Lincoln's promise when soldiers die. Technology and also moral contradictions within cultural memory have exposed the imperialistic nature of collective memory of the war dead. What is needed is a new cultural memory with new rituals, one that interacts warmly with American citizens in ways that encourage them to think critically about the past and keep the past persistently in the present. Only then can a republic confront the imperialism of the nation and truly fulfill Lincoln's promise.

APPENDIX A

Stops in D. H. Rhodes's Tour of the Philippines, October 1900–July 1901

HAWAII

Oahu Cemetery, Honolulu	October 9	33*
Catholic Cemetery, Honolulu	October 10	3

GUAM

Catholic Cemetery, Agana	October 23	4
Agana	October 23	2
Soumaye	October 23	1

PHILIPPINES

Malate, Manila	November 14–24	280
Paco Cemetery, Manilla	November 23–24	89
Small Pox Hospital, Manilla	November 2	24
Corregidor Island	December 3	14
Canocoa, Luzon	December 6	31*
San Roque, Luzon	December 8	2
Balanga, Luzon	December 11	12
Santa Cruz, Luzon	December 14	18*
Siniloan, Luzon	December 18	10
Calamba, Luzon	December 20	1

Los Banos, Luzon	December 20	3
Majayjay, Luzon	December 20	2
Magdalena, Luzon	December 20	1
Indang, Luzon	December 28	9
Niac, Luzon	December 29	3
"Camp Dewey" Manilla	January 2	1
Bacoor, Luzon	January 2	3
San Mateo, Luzon	January 5	3
Dagupan, Luzon	January 11	41*
Catholic Cemetery Dagupan	January 12	27
Sual, Luzon	January 13	1
Alaminos, Luzon	January 13	2
Pozorrubio, Luzon	January 13	1
Binalonan, Luzon	January 14	7
San Manuel, Luzon	January 14	1
San Nicolas, Luzon	January 15	4
Bayabang, Luzon	January 19	6
Alcala, Luzon	January 19	1
Camiling, Tarlac	January 19	1
Rosales, Luzon	January 21	1
Tayug, Luzon	January 22	12
Humingan, Luzon	January 23	3
San Quintin, Luzon	January 23	2
San Jose, Luzon	January 24	12
Mangaterem, Luzon	January 27	2
Panique, Luzon	January 27	1
Guyapo, Luzon	January 27	1
Matalang, Luzon	January 27	1
Tarlac, Luzon	January 28	2
Angeles, Luzon	January 29	4

Florida Blanca, Luzon	January 30	1
Mexico, Luzon	January 30	2
San Luis, Luzon	February 2	2
Gandaba, Luzon	February 2	2
Arayat, Luzon	February 3	1
Cabiao, Luzon	February 4	3
San Isidro, Luzon	February 5, 6, 10	38*
Cabanatuan, Luzon	February 7–8	29
Bongahong, Luzon	February 8	4*
Aliaga, Luzon	February 9	2
Maasin, Luzon	February 14	1
San Miguel, Luzon	February 14	7
San Ildefonso, Luzon	February 15	1
Malolos, Luzon	February 16	1
Carranglan, Luzon	January 26	3
Solana, Luzon	January 30	8*
Bagabag, Luzon	January 31	2
Bayombong, Luzon	January 31	5*
Santa Maria, Luzon	February 13	1
Angat, Luzon	February 14	1
Norzagaray, Luzon	February 14	1
Santa Tomas, Luzon	February 23	4*
Tanauan, Luzon	February 23	5
Lipa, Luzon	February 24	14
San Pablo, Luzon	February 24	14
Paranaqe, Luzon	March 24	1
Balayan, Luzon	March 28	1
Lemery, Luzon	March 28	5
Batangas, Luzon	March 29	5*
San Jose, Luzon	March 29	10

Loboo, Batangas, Luzon	March 30	1
San Juan de Boc Boc, Luzon	March 31	1
Tayabas, Luzon	April 3	13
Lucban, Luzon	April 3	2
Stiaon, Luzon	April 3	4
Sariaya, Luzon	April 3–4	9*
Candelaria, Luzon	April 4	1
Lucena, Luzon	April 5	19
Laguimanoc, Luzon	April 6	2
Guinayangan, Luzon	April 7	1
Pasacao, Luzon	April 7	4
Donsol, Luzon	April 8	1
Sorsogon, Luzon	April 8	7
Gubat, Luzon	April 9	1
Ligao, Luzon	April 10	4
Legaspi, Luzon	April 10	24
Camilig, Luzon	April 11	1
Albay, Luzon	April 11	2
Virac, Luzon	April 12	2
Tabaco, Luzon	April 12	6
San Jose de Lagonoy, Luzon	April 13	9
Nueva Caceres, Luzon	April 17	32
Baao, Luzon	April 17	2
Bato, Luzon	April 17	1
Iriga, Luzon	April 18	1
Buhi, Luzon	April 18	3
Nabua, Luzon	April 18	1*
Libmann, Luzon	April 18	2
Daet, Luzon	April 20	2
Antimonan, Luzon	April 21	3

Mauban, Luzon	April 22	5
Baler, Luzon	April 23	8
Aparri, Luzon	April 25	16*
Boac, Marinduque	May 7	5
Santa Cruz, Marinduque	May 8	4
Torrijos, Marinduque	May 8	5
Romblon, Romblon	May 9	1
Masbate, Masbate	May 10	2*
Laguan, Samar	May 11	1
Borongan, Samar	May 12	2
Abuyog, Leyte	May 13	1
Dulag, Leyte	May 13	3
Tacloban, Leyte	May 14	5
Palo, Leyte	May 14	3
Dagami, Leyte	May 14	1
Jaro, Leyte	May 14	2
Alang, Leyte	May 15	2
Tanauan, Leyte	May 15	1
Barugo, Leyte	May 16	5*
Carigara, Leyte	May 17	2
Catbalogan, Samar	May 17	12*
Calbayog, Samar	May 18	7*
Bogo, Cebu	May 19	1
Palompon, Leyte	May 19	1
Ormoc, Leyte	May 20	1*
Maasin, Leyte	May 20	1
Hilongas, Leyte	May 21	2
Danao, Cebu	May 22	1
Sogod, Cebu	May 22	1
Cebu, Cebu	May 23	22*

Naga, Cebu	May 25	1
Carcar, Cebu	May 25	1
Sibonga, Cebu	May 25	1
Tagbilaren, Bohol	May 26	2
Jagna, Bohol	May 26	6
Cagayan, Mindanao	May 27	18
Iligan, Mindanao	May 28	10
Misamis, Mindanao	May 28	12
Jimenez, Mindanao	May 29	2
Oroquieta, Mindanao	May 29	1
Jolo, Sulu	May 31	2
Siasi, Sulu	May 31	1
Davao, Mindanao	June 2	7
Parang, Sulu	June 3	5
Cotabato, Mindanao	June 4	10
Malabang, Mindanao	June 5	2
Zamboanga, Mindanao	June 6	5
Cebu	June 7	3
Dumanjug, Cebu	June 7	4
Mualbual, Cebu	June 8	2
Alegria, Cebu	June 8	1
Balamban, Cebu	June 9	7
Escalante, Negros	June 9	2
Manapla, Negros	June 10	1
Sara, Panay	June 11	5
Banate, Panay	June 12	2
Iloilo, Panay	June 13–14	82*
Calinog, Panay	June 14	5
Barotoc Nuevo, Panay	June 14	2
Dumangas, Panay	June 15	4

Bacolod, Negros	June 17	21
Silay, Negros	June 17	1
La Carlota, Negros	June 17	1
Binalbagan, Negros	June 18	3
San Jose de Buena Vista	June 19	12
Bugason, Panay	June 19	6
Colasi, Panay	June 20	4
Pandan, Panay	June 20	1
Ibajay, Panay	June 20	1
Calivo, Panay	June 21	5
Capiz, Panay	June 23	19
Panitan, Panay	June 23	2
adao, Panay	June 23	6
Dumarao, Panay	June 24	4
Mambusao, Panay	June 24	3
Carigara, Leyte	May 17	2
Catbalogan, Samar	May 17	12*
Calbayog, Samar	May 18	7*
Bogo, Cebu	May 19	1
Palompon, Leyte	May 19	1
Ormoc, Leyte	May 20	1*
Maasin, Leyte	May 20	1
Hilongas, Leyte	May 21	2
Danao, Cebu	May 22	1
Sogod, Cebu	May 22	1
Cebu, Cebu	May 23	22*
Naga, Cebu	May 25	1
Carcar, Cebu	May 25	1
Sibonga, Cebu	May 25	1
Tagbilaren, Bohol	May 26	2

Jagna, Bohol	May 26	6
Cagayan, Mindanao	May 27	18
Iligan, Mindanao	May 28	10
Misamis, Mindanao	May 28	12
Jimenez, Mindanao	May 29	2
Oroquieta, Mindanao	May 29	1
Jolo, Sulu	May 31	2
Siasi, Sulu	May 31	1
Davao, Mindanao	June 2	7
Parang, Sulu	June 3	5
Cotabato, Mindanao	June 4	10
Malabang, Mindanao	June 5	2

Total Number of Locations: 177

Total Number of Days: 228

Total Number of Graves: 1,423

*Denotes one or more bodies not disinterred due to status of recent death, smallpox victim, cholera victim, ex-soldier, desertion, native, or no body found in grave.

Note: I have kept the U.S. spellings of cities and islands of the Philippines to accentuate the colonial forms of knowledge that Americans produced and used when they retrieved the dead from a foreign land.

APPENDIX B

Stops in F. S. Croggon's Tour of the Philippines, November 1902–August 1903

Abra de Ilog, Mindoro	November 14	1
Palauan, Mindoro	November 15	4
Mangarin, Mindoro	November 16	1
Pinamalayan, Mindoro	November 17	2
Pola, Mindoro	November 17	2
Calapan, Mindoro	November 17	3*
Gasan, Marinduque	November 18	4
Boac, Marinduque	November 19	1
Santa Cruz, Marinduque	November 20	5
Romblon, Romblon	November 21	1
Masbate, Masbat	November 22	3*
Calbayog, Samar	November 23	18
Mauo, Samar	November 29	2
Weyler, Samar	November 29	1
Blanca Aurora, Samar	December 1	2
Taviron, Samar	December 3	2
Dumaloong, Samar	December 3	12
Dap Dap Hills, Samar	December 4	0*
Tarangnan, Samar	December 5	11

Catbalogan, Samar	December 7	6*
Santa Rita, Samar	December 7	2
Villa Real, Samar	December 8	3
Calbiga, Samar	December 8	1
Carigara, Leyte	December 10	7*
Barugo, Leyte	December 11	1
Bogo, Cebu	December 12	1
Ormoc, Leyte	December 12	1
Bay Bay, Leyte	December 13	7*
Matalom, Leyte	December 13	1
Cebu, Cebu	December 15	12*
Danao, Cebu	December 19	1
Ubay, Bohol	December 19	1
Loboc, Bohol	December 20	1
Tagbilaren, Bohol	December 21	1
Oslob, Cebu	December 21	1
Dumanjug, Cebu	December 22	1
Balamban, Cebu	December 22	1
Argao, Cebu	December 23	1
Tubigon, Bohol	December 23	1
Naga, Cebu	December 24	1
Maasin, Leyte	December 26	3
Malitbog, Leyte	December 27	1
Dulag, Leyte	December 28	2
Barauen, Leyte	December 29	1
Tanauan, Leyte	December 30	2*
Tacloban, Leyte	December 31	17
Basey, Samar	January 3, 1903	9
Balangiga, Samar	January 13	35*
Quinapundan, Samar	January 14	3

Guinan, Samar	January 16	2
Borongan, Samar	January 17	9*
Dolores, Samar	January 18	2
Oras, Samar	January 18	1
Laguan, Samar	January 19	9*
Catarman, Samar	January 20	4*
Bobon, Samar	January 21	10
Catubig, Samar	January 22	1
Cagayan, Mindanao	January 28	6
Iligan, Mindanao	January 30	4*
Misamis, Mindanao	February 2	1
Jimenez, Mindanao	February 3	2
Oroquita, Mindanao	February 3	7*
Langaran, Mindanao	February 4	3
Zamboanga, Mindanao	February 5	6*
Isabela, Basilan	February 6	3
Malabang, Mindanao	February 10	36*
Camp Vicars, Mindanao	February 12	12*
Mataling Falls	February 13	1
Tucuran, Mindanao	February 14	2
Parang, Mindandao	February 15	4
Makar, Mindanao	February 17	2
Davao, Mindanao	February 18	1
Mati, Mindanao	February 19	3
Jolo, Jolo Island	February 22	4
Calivo, Panay	March 7	2
Capiz, Panay	March 9	6
Dumarao, Panay	March 9	1
Dao, Panay	March 9	1
Sara, Panay	March 11	2

Iloilo, Panay	March 13	24*
Binalbagen, Negros	March 16	2
San Jose de Buena Vista	March 17	1
Cuyo, Cuyo Island	March 18	1
Puerta Princesa, Paragua	March 19	2
Culion, Island of Culioa	March 20	1
Coron, Busuanga	March 21	1
Dasmarinas, Luzon	April 4	2
Silang, Luzon	April 4	2
Santa Cruz, Luzon	April 4	2
San Francisco de Malabon	April 4	2
Baliuag, Luzon	April 23	2
Sorsogon, Luzon	June 4	4
Bacon, Luzon	June 5	3
Neuva Caceres, Luzon	June 8	25
Pili, Luzon	June 8	1
Bulan, Luzon	June 9	1
Matnog, Luzon	June 9	3
Gubat, Luzon	June 9	2
Nabua, Luzon	June 9	2
Iriga, Luzon	June 9	10
Donsol, Luzon	June 10	2
Libmanan, Luzon	June 12	9
Legaspi, Luzon	June 16	3
Albay, Luzon	June 16	7
Camalig, Luzon	June 17	2
Guinabaton, Luzon	June 17	9
Ligao, Luzon	June 19	4
Antimonan, Luzon	June 19	3
Mauban, Luzon	June 19–20	2*

Polangui, Luzon	June 20	1
Binangonan, Luzon	June 20	3
Paracale, Luzon	June 22	1
Dael, Luzon	June 22	7
Indan, Luzon	June 22	2
Tobaco, Luzon	June 23	2
Virac, Luzon	June 24	1
Pandan, Luzon	June 25	1
San Jose de Lagonoy	June 26	2
Pasacao, Luson	July 3	3
Guinayangan, Luzon	July 4	1
Ragay, Luzon	July 4	3
Pitago, Luzon	July 4	1*
Laguimanoc, Luzon	July 5–6	2
Lucena, Luzon	July 7	11*
Lucban, Luzon	July 9	2
Candalaria, Luzon	July 9	1
Sariaya, Luzon	July 8	4
Canacao, Luzon	July 16	27*
Naga, Luzon	July 20	4*
Los Banos, Luzon	July 22	2
Calamba, Luzon	July 22	2
San Pablo, Luzon	July 22	9
Dagupan, Luzon	July 25	4
San Manuel, Luzon	July 27	2
Binalonan, Luzon	July 27	1
Lingayen, Luzon	July 27	1
Calasio, Luzon	July 29	1*
Gerona, Luzon	July 30	1
Tiason, Luzon	August 2	2

San Juan de Boc Boc	August 2	1
Taal, Luon	August 3	6*
Bamban, Luzon	August 3	1
Batangas, Luzon	August 4	6*
Lobo, Luzon	August 4	5*
Balayan, Luzon	August 5	3*
San Isidro, Luzon	August 5	3
Mt. Niaga	undated	2
Nasugbu, Luzon	August 19	7

Total Number of Locations: 148

Total Number of Days: 260

Total Number of Graves: 619

*Denotes one or more bodies not disinterred due to status of recent death, smallpox victim, cholera victim, ex-soldier, desertion, native, or no body found in grave.

Note: I have kept the U.S. spellings of cities and islands of the Philippines to accentuate the colonial forms of knowledge that Americans produced and used when they retrieved the dead from a foreign land.

NOTES

INTRODUCTION

1. Carpenter, "Letter on the Battle of Gettysburg."
2. "Laurence Kent a Suicide," *New York Times*, July 12, 1921.
3. Tocqueville, *Democracy in America*, 68–72.
4. See LeFeber, *The Cambridge History of American Foreign Relations*, vol. 2; Hunt, *The American Ascendancy*. See also Lears, *No Place of Grace*. While some anti-Moderns, as historian Jackson Lears has described them, were successful in resisting the stresses of modern society, solitary individualism seemed to be unchecked and accelerating faster after the war had ended.
5. Assmann, *Cultural Memory*, 51–53.
6. Jacobs, *Incidents in the Life of a Slave Girl*, 27, 46.
7. Halbwachs, *On Collective Memory*. Halbwachs felt that collective memory was a social dynamic of human interaction.
8. Kandel, *In Search of Memory*, especially 281–85, 300–306. See also Craver, "The Making of a Memory Mechanism." Long-Term Potentiation (LTP) is a synaptic plasticity that probably stimulates memories and learning. According to this theory, experiencing trauma may make LTP semipermanent or at least function much longer than normal.
9. Assmann, *Cultural Memory*, 21–44.
10. Assmann, *Cultural Memory*, 62–63. In the illiterate medieval world of Europe, this was largely accomplished through rituals, festivals, relics, icons, and oral communication. But the mass production of books together with the increase in literacy in the modern age produced an exponential increase in opportunities for people to share their memories. The rise of new writing, listening, and visualizing technologies (since the sixteenth century but particularly in the nineteenth century)

threatened to overload the communicative process and erode the sacredness of collective memories.
11. Blair, *Cities of the Dead*, 12.
12. Finley, *History of the Wyandot Mission*, 51–52. See also Widder, "The Convergence of Native Religion," 170–71. Widder suggests that Native Americans allowed very few whites to view these traditions and rituals.
13. Adelman and Aron, "From Borderlands to Borders," 814–41.
14. Thoreau, *A Week on the Concord and Merrimack Rivers*, 296.
15. French, "The Cemetery as Cultural Institution."
16. See Schuyler, *The New Urban Landscape*; Rauch, *Intramural Interments in Populous Cities* (1866). Rauch connected health to public parks and inner-city burial.
17. Sloane, *The Last Great Necessity*, 70, 80.
18. Farrell, *Inventing the American Way of Death*, 7–8; Sloane, *The Last Great Necessity*, 94.
19. Wiebe, *The Search for Order*.
20. For a discussion of the Good Death and its history, see Houlbrooke, *Death, Religion, and the Family in England*; Jalland, *Death in the Victorian Family*; Faust, *This Republic of Suffering*, 6–17.
21. Shantz, *Awaiting the Heavenly Country*, 2, 19, 179.
22. Ariès, *The Hour of Our Death*.
23. Hobsbawm and Ranger, *The Invention of Tradition*.
24. Nora, *Realms of Memory*.
25. Assmann describes the historical analysis of memory as "mnemohistory." Mnemohistory here is concerned less with how the past actually happened and more with how the past was remembered. See Tamm, "History as Cultural Memory"; Rosenfeld, "A Looming Crash or a Soft Landing?"
26. Assmann, *Cultural Memory*, 45–46.
27. Hahn, *A Nation without Borders*, 143.
28. Renan, "What Is a Nation?"
29. Lears, *Rebirth of a Nation*, 2–5; Mosse, *Fallen Soldiers*.
30. Warren, "The Living and the Dead," 163–67.
31. Assmann, *Cultural Memory*, 263, 269, 262.
32. Bodnar, *Remaking America*.
33. Shantz, *Awaiting the Heavenly Country*, 92.
34. Wills, *Lincoln at Gettysburg*, 146–47, 37–38; Foner, *Who Owns History*, 172. Wills places the Gettysburg Address in the tradition of ancient Greek funeral oratory and the elite intellectual politics of the antebellum period without considering popular and working-class voices who expressed similar intellectual ideas. Selzer, "Historicizing Lincoln." Selzer reminds, "Indeed, Lincoln's address might be best understood as wedding these two [elite and popular] great traditions—one of them, as we have

seen, with a long history of *popular* veneration for the Declaration as America's original 'founding' text." Wills describes this as a sleight of hand designed to trick Americans into reorienting the Declaration as the core edifice of the American political system and decentering the Constitution.

35. Hahn, *A Nation without Borders,* 265, 8, 239.
36. Koselleck, "War Memorials," 368.
37. Assmann, *Cultural Memory,* 41.
38. Carrie Chamberlin to James Moore, NARA92L, Office of the Quartermaster General, Letters Received Relating to Cemeteries, 1873–78, box 1.
39. Igler, *The Great Ocean.*
40. Hahn, *A Nation without Borders,* 359.
41. Hahn, *A Nation without Borders,* 398–400.
42. Burbank and Cooper, *Empires in World History.*
43. Homans, *Symbolic Loss,* 29.

PART 1

1. Downey, *The Play of Destiny,* 5–8.
2. See the Stephen W. Downey Papers at the Rocky Mountain Online Archive, http://rmoa.unm.edu/docviewer.php?docId=wyu-ah10555.xml, accessed March 31, 2016.
3. Downey, *The Play of Destiny,* 4.
4. See Winter, *Remembering War,* 20–26.
5. Donald, *Origins of the Modern Mind,* 325–33.

1. WHERE THE GRAPES OF WRATH ARE STORED

1. See Mosse, *Fallen Soldiers.*
2. Hahn, *A Nation without Borders,* 275.
3. Hahn, *A Nation without Borders,* 313–15, 375, 366–67. For a succinct history of the Freedmen's Bureau, see DuBois, "Of the Dawn of Freedom."
4. Blair, *Cities of the Dead,* 5, 13, 50.
5. Hahn, *A Nation without Borders,* 375.
6. Faust, *This Republic of Suffering.*
7. United States Census, 1860. Henry Cole, Marietta, Georgia. In prison letters to his wife, Georgia Cole tells his wife that Bill and Mollie should plant peas, mend fences, and not ride the horses. After Union troops took Marietta in 1864, Cole's wife states in a letter to her husband, "I tell you that our once good and faithful Mollie has left us." She continues, "Mollie has *never* been the same good servant since the Yankees came. She got to be very insulting and neglectful of me. I always treated her as kindly as possible. My friends say that I *spoiled* her." Mrs. Henry Cole to Henry Cole, November 22, 1864, MHM, Henry Cole Box.

8. Commissioners of Claims, *Henry G. Cole vs. The United States*, Case No. 13312, February 12, 1873, MHM, Henry Cole Box. Cole had learned that Gen. James Longstreet was leaving Richmond, Virginia, to reinforce Gen. Braxton Bragg's troops at Chickamauga. Cole claimed he had spent $500 to send the information to Thomas. Cole stated to the commissioners, "The General always gave me a great deal of credit for that act and said that what was saved at Chickamauga was saved by that means."
9. Dix Fletcher to General Butler, September 28, 1864, MHM, Henry Cole Papers.
10. Stephens, *Recollections*. After the war, Cole, finally freed, likewise tried to use his Northern connections to get the captured Confederate leader freed from his Boston prison cell.
11. Henry Cole to Mary Cole, May 14, 1864, MHM, Henry Cole Papers.
12. Henry Cole to Mary Cole, May 21, 1864, MHM, Henry Cole Papers.
13. Dix Fletcher to General Butler, September 28, 1864, MHM, Henry Cole Box.
14. Henry Cole, "Parole of Honor," January 24, 1865, MHM, Henry Cole Papers.
15. Stephens, *Recollections*, 418. The gold came from Mrs. Judge Erskine of Georgia while the cash came from Cole.
16. Fletcher, *The Journal of a Landlady*, 173.
17. C. M. Meigs to Edwin M. Stanton, September 7, 1866, NARA92C, box 43, folder Marietta GA. Edmund Whitman documented these ten graves in his journal. NARA92E, v. 2, Entry Marietta.
18. Meigs to Stanton, September 7, 1866.
19. S. Montgomery to Julia Montgomery, September 23, 1863, MHM, Henry Cole Papers.
20. For a brief history of Marietta Confederate Cemetery, see Ratledge, "The Confederate Cemetery." Ratledge includes a succinct overview of the cemetery and those involved in its construction, pp. 1–5, and a history of the railroad collision, 6–15.
21. Memorial Committee of Marietta, Georgia to His Excellency Andrew Johnson, NARA92C, box 43, folder Marietta GA.
22. Report, Brevet Major W. A. Wainwright to Ma. Gen. J. Donaldson, August 22, 1866, NARA92C, box 43, folder Marietta GA.
23. Wainwright to Donaldson, August 22, 1866.
24. Report, C. W. Folsom to D. H. Rucker, July 25, 1867, NARA92C, box 43, folder Marietta GA.
25. Report, "Confidential" addendum, Folsom to Rucker, July 25, 1867, NARA92C, box 43, folder Marietta GA.
26. For a discussion of the politics of pilgrimage and tourism of World War I cemeteries in a British context, see Lloyd, *Battlefield Tourism*.
27. Report, "Confidential" addendum.
28. Report, "Confidential" addendum.
29. Ratledge, "The Confederate Cemetery," 2–3, 30.

30. Ratledge, "The Confederate Cemetery," 27.
31. Memorandum, October 22, 1867, NARA92C, box 3, folder Andersonville.
32. "History of Cole Manor," MHM, Henry Cole Papers.
33. "Decoration of Soldiers Graves," *Harper's Weekly*, June 20, 1868, 388.
34. "Fort Myers, Virginia (Arlington)," NARA92CC, box 49, folder Arlington Estate; "Arlington Estate," NARA92CC, box 49, folder Arlington Estate.
35. Adjutant General Thomas to Col. J. Taylor, January 3, 1862, NARA92CC, box 49, folder Arlington Estate.
36. Elias M. Greene to Chief of the Quartermaster, Washington DC, May 5, 1863, NARA92CC, box 49, folder Arlington Estate.
37. See Nora, *Realms of Memory*.
38. Freedman's Village to Redfield Proctor; A. H. Holmes to Redfield Proctor, September 27, 1890; John W. Daniel to Redfield Proctor, NARA92CC, box 49, folder Arlington Estate; U.S. War Department, *Annual Report of the Secretary of War*, 311.
39. Richard Batchelder to A. H. Holmes, October 27, 1890, NARA92CC, box 49, folder Arlington Estate; Report Richard Batchelder, December 20, 1890, NARA92CC, box 49, folder Arlington Reservation.
40. Chas Bird to Depot Quartermaster, New York City, July 13, 1900, NARA92C, box Arlington VA, folder, Arlington.
41. Todorova, "The Mausoleum of Georgi Dimitrov."
42. Nikolai Voukov, "The Destruction of Georgi Dimitrov's Mausoleum in Sofia: The 'Incoincidence' between Memory and Its Referents," in *Places of Memory*, ed. Augustin Ioan, special issue of *Octogon* (Bucharest, 2003), quoted in Todovora, "The Mausoleum of Georgi Dimitrov," 411.

2. THE NATION, A MONUMENT OF EMPIRE

1. "Sitka National Cemetery," U.S. Department of Veteran Affairs, http://www.cem.va.gov/cems/nchp/sitka.asp, accessed July 9, 2008.
2. Hahn, *A Nation without Borders*, 242, 243, 398–99.
3. Igler, *The Great Ocean*; Jones, "Running into Whales," 349–77; Cushman, *Guano and the Opening of the Pacific World*; Melillo, "The First Green Revolution," 1028–60.
4. Blair, *Cities of the Dead*, 50, 5–6.
5. Assmann, *Cultural Memory*, 53. Of course, many historians from DuBois, *Black Reconstruction in America* to Foner, *Reconstruction*.
6. See Blair, *Cities of the Dead*. By 1871 freedmen attempts to create memories around celebrations of Emancipation Day, Surrender Day, and, in Richmond, Virginia, Evacuation Day had largely ceased. Women had come to dominate Decoration Day ceremonies throughout the South.

7. Girardeau, "Confederate Memorial Day," 7–8, HL; Hahn, *A Nation without Borders*, 426, 430.
8. Zerubavel, *Time Maps*, 40.
9. Girardeau, "Confederate Memorial Day," 7–8.
10. Girardeau, "Confederate Memorial Day," 8, 9, 20, 17–18.
11. Girardeau, "Confederate Memorial Day," 22.
12. Jacobson, *Barbarian Virtues*.
13. LaFeber, *Cambridge History of American Foreign Relations*, 2:14–18.
14. The U.S. Department of Veteran Affairs claims that General Davis built the cemetery.
15. Jessup, "Connecting Alaska," 388–89; John H. Keatley to General Holabird, October 6, 1888, NARA92R, box 67, folder Sitka AK; Jackson, *A Statement of Facts*.
16. Keatley to Holabird, October 6, 1888.
17. Keatley to Lt. Col. N. H. Batchelder, March 17, 1889, NARA92R, box 67, folder Sitka AK.
18. Report, Lt. Col. M. I. Ludington to Quartermaster General, December 20, 1889, NARA92R, box 67, folder Sitka AK.
19. Hahn, *A Nation without Borders*, 245–47, 315.
20. Pratt, "'A Curious Compound of the Hero and the Dandy,'" 37–55.
21. Hahn, *A Nation without Borders*, 413, 414–17.
22. "Funeral of General Custer," *Harper's Weekly*, October 27, 1877.
23. Lindeman, *Pretty Shield*, 128–41.
24. Welch, *Killing Custer*.
25. Blair, *Cities of the Dead*, 4.
26. Fish, "American Union," 5, 6, 9, 12, 13.
27. Stiles, *Address at the Dedication of the Monument to the Confederate Dead*, 2–3.

3. REMEMBERING DOMESTIC FOREIGN SPACES
1. Assmann, *Cultural Memory*, 53.
2. Blight, "For Something beyond the Battlefield," 1156–78.
3. Nelson, *Federal Writers' Project*.
4. Renan, "What Is a Nation?"
5. Pérez, "Incurring a Debt of Gratitude"; Pérez, "The Meaning of the Maine."
6. Dunlap, *Address . . . in the Confederate Cemetery*, 8, 6.
7. Dunlap, *Address . . . in the Confederate Cemetery*, 12, 13–14.
8. Lears, *Rebirth of a Nation*.
9. "The Confederate Reunion," *New York Times*, July 21, 1898.
10. See Kinzer, *The True Flag*. Kinzer recovers the debate over American empire after the war with Spain to show the intensity, dynamism, and acrimony of advocates on both sides of the debate.

11. *Chicago Times-Herald,* as quoted in *An Address by Booker T. Washington . . . at the Thanksgiving Peace Jubilee Exercises,* 1.
12. *An Address by Booker T. Washington,* 7.
13. Blair, *Cities of the Dead,* 179.
14. Washington, *Story of My Life and Work,* 284.
15. Wilmington Race Riot Commission, "Final Report," May 31, 2006.
16. Blair, *Cities of the Dead,* 179.
17. Washington, *Story of My Life and Work,* 284, 289.
18. *Speeches and Address of William McKinley,* 158–59.
19. *Speeches and Address of William McKinley,* 369–70.
20. "Atlanta's Peace Jubilee Is Ended." *New York Times,* December 16, 1898.
21. "Atlanta's Peace Jubilee Is Ended."
22. "Atlanta's Peace Jubilee Is Ended."
23. "Atlanta's Peace Jubilee Is Ended."
24. "Atlanta's Peace Jubilee Is Ended."
25. Washington, *Story of My Life and Work,* 293, 294, 295.
26. Blair, *Cities of the Dead,* 179–86.
27. *Report on the Re-Burial,* 20; Poole, *On Hallowed Ground,* 116–17.
28. Janney, *Burying the Dead but Not the Past.*
29. *Report on the Re-Burial,* 13, 35, 28, 25, 26. For a detailed examination between UCV leaders and various women's groups who protested and supported Confederate reburials in Arlington, see Blair, *Cities of the Dead,* "Arlington Sectional Cemetery."

PART 2

1. Wilmington Race Riot Commission, "Final Report," May 31, 2006, 126; Prather, "The Red Shirt Movement."
2. The North Carolina legislature formed the Wilmington Race Riot Commission in 2000. No state officials had ever investigated the riot. Legislators charged commissioners with establishing a historical record and making recommendations. Commissioners found the white leaders of the riot had committed a coup d'état that severely transformed the city socially, politically, and economically. Commissioners recommended that the state offer economic, educational, and commemorative reparations including financial compensation to the victims' heirs and provide incentives for business development and investment for minority homeownership in Wilmington. The state failed to implement most of the committee's recommendations. Wilmington Race Riot Commission, "Final Report," May 31, 2006, chaps. 1–3.
3. Wilmington Race Riot Commission, "Final Report," 122–55.
4. Kirk, *A Statement of Facts,* 10; Wilmington Race Riot Commission, "Final Report," 141, 150, 173–74.

5. John Bass, "Fighting in the Philippines—The Revolt," *Harper's Weekly*, April 8, 1899, 358.
6. Bass, "Fighting," 348.
7. Assmann, *Cultural Memory*, 24, 25, 44.
8. Burbank and Cooper, *Empires in World History*, 8, 458.
9. For a discussion of the color line, see DuBois, *The Souls of Black Folk*, chap. 1. For a discussion of Orientalism, see Said, *Orientalism*.

4. RETRIEVE THE *MAINE*!

1. Pérez, "Incurring a Debt of Gratitude," 359.
2. Assmann, *Cultural Memory*, 130, 2.
3. Kandel, *In Search of Memory*, 281.
4. Assmann, *Cultural Memory*, 72.
5. Assmann, *Cultural Memory*, 6.
6. Pérez, "The Meaning of the Maine," 299, 319, 317, 300.
7. Klein, "Spaniards," 313, 366.
8. Klein, "Spaniards," 312.
9. Leonard M. Cox, "Plan for Raising USS *Maine*," NARA77G, USS *Maine*, box 1266, folder 1.
10. William M. Black to the Chief of Engineers, August 20, 1910, NARA77G, USS *Maine*, box 1266, folder 1; John Jackson to Secretary of State, September 24, 1910, NARA77G, USS *Maine*, box 1266, folder 3.
11. William Bixby to Secretary of War, October 10, 1910, NARA77G, USS *Maine*, box 1266, folder 3.
12. Joseph Jacoby to Secretary of War, November 1, 1910, NARA77G, USS *Maine*, box 1266, folder 2.
13. Second Indorsement, William Black to Chief of Engineers, November 15, 1910, NARA77G, USS *Maine*, box 1266, folder 2.
14. Report, Mason Patrick to William Black, January 26, 1911, NARA77G, USS *Maine*, box 1266, folder 5.
15. William Bixby to Secretary of War, February 27, 1911, NARA77G, USS *Maine*, box 1266, folder 5. One million dollars in 1911 currency would approximately equate to $26,455,072 in 2019 currency based on an average inflation rate of 3.08 percent per year.
16. Garrison, *Final Report*, 12. The record for an eight-hour shift was 28 piles.
17. William Ellis to Secretary of War, June 5, 1911, NARA77G, USS *Maine*, box 1267, folder 7.
18. Appendix KKK, NARA77G, USS *Maine*, box 1267B, 20.
19. John Arbuckle to Henry Stimson, September 13, 1911, NARA77G, USS *Maine*, box 1267, folder 12.

20. "Raise, Not Sink, the *Maine*," *American Marine Engineer*, September 1910, NARA77G, USS *Maine*, box 1266, folder 2.
21. War Department to Editor of the *American Marine Engineer*, September 26, 1910, NARA77G, USS *Maine*, box 1266, folder 2.
22. "The Mystery of the Maine," *Morning Star*, June 27, 1911, NARA77G, USS *Maine*, box 1267, folder 11.
23. "Remember the Maine!" *Inter-Ocean*, July 1911, NARA77G, USS *Maine*, box 1267, folder 11.
24. "Remember the Maine!" *Inter-Ocean*.
25. John Harvey to Henry Stimson, July 8, 1911, NARA77G, USS *Maine*, box 1267, folder 11.
26. Garrison, *Final Report*, 21.
27. Addendum KKK, NARA77G, USS *Maine*, box 1267B, 20.
28. William Black to William Bixby, May 16, 1912, NARA77G, USS *Maine*, box 1267A, folder 19; Addendum KKK, NARA77G, USS *Maine*, box 1267B, 20.
29. Telegram, Beaupré to Secretary of State, April 2, 1912, NARA77G, USS *Maine*, box 1267A, folder 19.
30. Isaac Auchenbach to Secretary of War, August 11, 1911, NARA77G, USS *Maine*, box 1267, folder 9.
31. Cablegram, Mason Patrick to William Bixby, August 17, 1911, NARA77G, USS *Maine*, box 1267, folder 9.; Chief Clerk to the Secretary of War to Secretary of War, September 5, 1911, NARA77G, USS *Maine*, box 1267, folder 9.
32. W. H. Ludwig to Benjamin Focht, June 24, 1911, NARA77G, USS *Maine*, box 1267, folder 11.
33. Eberhard Faber to William Bixby, October 12, 1911, NARA77G, *Maine*, box 1267, folder 11.
34. Assistant Secretary of War to City of Moline, Illinois, March 25, 1912, NARA77G, USS *Maine*, box 1267A, folder 18.
35. First Indorsement, June 20, 1912, NARA77G, USS *Maine*, box 1267A, folder 20.
36. Emilio Heredia to F. A. Pope, November 20, 1912, NARA77G, USS *Maine*, box 1267B, folder 22.
37. Mayor of Pompton Lakes to Henry Stimson, December 11, 1912, NARA77G, USS *Maine*, box 1267B, folder 22.
38. H. Barnhart to Henry Stimson, May 19, 1914, NARA77G, USS *Maine*, box 1267B, folder 22.
39. William Bixby to Congressman E. L. Taylor, February 12, 1912, NARA77G, USS *Maine*, box 1267A, folder 15.
40. Report, William Black to William Bixby, May 15, 1911, NARA77G, USS *Maine*, box 1267, folder 7.

41. George H. Maines to William Taft, September 11, 1911; NARA77G, USS *Maine*, box 1267, folder 11; Acting Secretary of War to George Maines, October 3, 1911, NARA77G, USS *Maine*, box 1267, folder 12.
42. A Patriot to the editor, October 24, 1911, NARA77G, USS *Maine*, box 1267, folder 12.
43. Joseph Jacoby to Secretary of the Navy, December 29, 1910, NARA77G, 1894–1923, USS *Maine*, box 1266, folder 4.
44. William Black to William Bixby, January 24, 1911, NARA77G, USS *Maine*, box 1266, folder 5. For a discussion of vernacular and official memory, see Bodnar, *Remaking America*.
45. Seventh Indorsement, William Bixby to Secretary of War, January 25, 1911, NARA77G, USS *Maine*, box 1266, folder 4.
46. Secretary of War to Joseph Jacoby, January 26, 1911, NARA77G, USS *Maine*, box 1266, folder 5.
47. William Maybury to William Taft, June 14, 1911, NARA77G, 1894–1923, USS *Maine*, box 1267, folder 11.
48. Klein, "Spaniards," 342.
49. Henry Ide to Secretary of State, August 24, 1911, NARA77G, USS *Maine*, box 1267, folder 9.
50. "Remember the *Maine*," *El Hogar Espanol*, August 1911, NARA77G, USS *Maine*, box 1267, folder 8.
51. "Cuba Desires a 'Maine Island,'" *Lewistown Evening Journal* [Maine], September 1, 1911, NA, RG 77, Records of the Office of the Chief of Engineers, General Correspondence, 1894–1923, USS *Maine*, box 1267, folder 8.
52. Isidoro Ojeda to Henry Stimson, September 12, 1911, NARA77G, box 1267, folder 8.
53. Second Indorsement, William Bixby to William Black, October 25, 1911, NARA77G, USS *Maine*, box 1267, folder 8.
54. Harry Gradel to Henry Stimson, NARA77G, USS *Maine*, box 1267A, folder 16.
55. James Wolferdern to William Bixby, June 29, 1911, NARA77G, USS *Maine*, box 1267, folder 11.
56. Helen Temple to Bixby, NARA77G, USS *Maine*, box 1267, folder 11.
57. Comet Film Company to Bixby, February 13, 1912, NARA77G, USS *Maine*, box 1267, folder 15.
58. E. Johnston to Edwin Ray, 6 March 1912, NARA77G, USS *Maine*, box 1267, folder 17.
59. Charles Funck to William Taft, February 20, 1912, NARA77G, USS *Maine*, box 1267A, folder 16.
60. Beekman Winthrop to Henry Stimson, February 24, 1912, NARA77G, USS *Maine*, box 1267A, folder 15.
61. William Taft to Secretary of the Navy, December 16, 1911, NARA77G, USS *Maine*, box 1267A, folder 15.

62. Klein, "Spaniards," 345.
63. Zanetti and Knight, *Sugar and Railroads*; José Miguel Gómez to William H. Taft, translated, December 6, 1910, NARA77G, USS *Maine*, box 1266, folder 3.
64. Beekman Winthrop to Secretary of State, February 29, 1912, NARA77G, USS *Maine*, box 1267A, folder 17; Acting Secretary of State to the American Legation at Habana, March 2, 1912, NARA77G, USS *Maine*, box 1267A, folder 17; American Minister to Cuba to the Secretary of State, February 26, 1912, NARA77G, USS *Maine*, box 1267A, folder 16.
65. Klein, "Spaniards," 346.
66. E. N. Johnson to Alfred King, March 4, 1912, NARA77G, USS *Maine*, box 1267A, folder 15; Memorandum for the Secretary of the Navy, February 15, 1912, NARA77G, USS *Maine*, box 1267A, folder 15; William Black to H. B. Ferguson, February 24, 1912, NARA77G, USS *Maine*, box 1267A, folder 16.
67. Garrison, *Final Report*, 34–35. Note that 620 fathoms equate to 3,720 feet or 0.7 miles. E. N. Johnson to Alfred King, March 4, 1912; Memorandum for the Secretary of the Navy, February 15, 1912, NARA77G, USS *Maine*, box 1267A, folder 15; William Black to H. B. Ferguson, February 24, 1912, NARA77G, USS *Maine*, box 1267A, folder 16; William Black to H. B. Ferguson, March 7, 1912, NARA77G, USS *Maine*, box 1267A, folder 18.
68. Memo for Bureaus and Officers of the Navy Department, February 20, 1912, NARA77G, USS *Maine*, box 1267A, folder 15; Program of USS *Maine* Memorial and Funeral Ceremonies, March 25, 1912, NARA77G, USS *Maine*, box 1267A, folder 18; Telegram, American Minister to Cuba to the Secretary of State, February 26, 1912, NARA77G, USS *Maine*, box 1267A, folder 16.

5. MEMORIES OF A FOREIGN LAND

1. Miller, *"Benevolent Assimilation"*; Kramer, *Blood of Government*; Kramer, "Violence in the U.S. Empire."
2. LaFeber, *Cambridge History of American Foreign Relations*, 170–200; Hahn, *A Nation without Borders*, 487.
3. Hahn, *A Nation without Borders*, 490.
4. Van Dyke, *American Birthright and the Philippine Pottage*, 4, v, 11; Kinzer, *The True Flag*.
5. Schurz, *For the Republic of Washington and Lincoln*, 1, 20.
6. Agoncillo, *To the American People*, 64. This sort of argument foreshadowed Ho Chi Minh's famous reading of the Declaration of Independence in 1945 after the Japanese left Vietnam in the wake of the Japanese defeat in the Second World War. It also foreshadowed how the United States would approve the reestablishment of French colonial rule in Vietnam before financially supporting the French regime much to the dismay of many Vietnamese people.

7. Chadwick, *Present Distress*, 15, 16, 20–21. For a detailed description of Sam Hose's death, see Wells, *Lynch Law in Georgia*; *Atlanta Journal*, April 24, 1899.
8. Chadwick, *Present Distress*, 21, 22, 26.
9. Taft, *Duty of Americans in the Philippines*, 1, 17.
10. Root, "Speech," Canton OH, October 24, 1900, 9, 11, 19, 31, 14, HL.
11. Miller, *Benevolent Assimilation*, 148; LaFeber, *Cambridge History of American Foreign Relations*, 159.
12. Kramer, *Blood of Government*.
13. Miller, *Benevolent Assimilation*, 207–8.
14. Miller, *Benevolent Assimilation*, 200–206. See also Ileto, "The Philippine-American War."
15. Miller, *Benevolent Assimilation*, 204.
16. *Annual Reports of the War Department for the Fiscal Year Ended June 30, 1902*, 607–8.
17. John F. Bass, "Our New Possessions—The Philippines," *Harper's Weekly*, February 4, 1899.
18. Kramer, *Blood of Government*, 76–79; Aguilar, "Tracing Origins."
19. Report, D. H. Rhodes to Quartermaster General of the Army, September 30, 1901, 3, NARA92D, box 1.
20. F. S. Croggon to Chief Quartermaster Division of the Philippines, April 1, 1903, NARA92D, box 1.
21. Croggon to Chief Quartermaster.
22. Report, D. H. Rhodes to Quartermaster General, September 30, 1901.
23. Report, D. H. Rhodes to Quartermaster General, September 30, 1901.
24. Report, F. S. Croggon to Chief Quartermaster, Division of the Philippines, August 31, 1903, 3–4, NARA92D, box 1.
25. Report, F. S. Croggon to Chief Quartermaster, August 31, 1903, 3–4.
26. Miller, *Benevolent Assimilation*, 220–25.
27. Report, F. S. Croggon to Chief Quartermaster, August 31, 1903, 13–15.
28. Kramer, *Blood of Government*, 155–57.
29. "President Strikes at Army Critics," *New York Times*, May 30, 1902.
30. "President Strikes at Army Critics."
31. Kramer, *Blood of Government*, 155–57.
32. "President Strikes at Army Critics."
33. Twain, "The United States of Lyncherdom."
34. Miller, *Benevolent Assimilation*, 206.
35. "President Strikes at Army Critics."
36. Annual Report, Deputy Quartermaster-General M. I. Ludington, 302–3.
37. Annual Report, Deputy Quartermaster-General W. S. Patton, 362–63.
38. Annual Report, Deputy Quartermaster-General W. S. Patton, 364, 362.
39. "Brings 173 Soldier Dead," *New York Times*, November 22, 1903.

40. "Brings 302 Dead Soldiers," *New York Times*, September 13, 1903.
41. "A Soldier's Reburial," *New York Times*, July 29, 1901.
42. "Dead Body's Many Journeys," *New York Times*, November 29, 1903.

PART 3

1. For an overview of U.S. interventions in Latin America and elsewhere, see Kinzer, *Overthrow*.
2. Nora, *Realms of Memory*, vol. 1.
3. "Voices of Battle: The Great Reunion of 1913," *National Park Service*, http://www.nps.gov/archive/gett/getttour/sidebar/reunion13.htm, accessed December 20, 2010.
4. Wilson, "Address at Gettysburg," 370–72.
5. Wilson, "Address at Gettysburg," 371–72.

6. EXILES OF AMERICAN CULTURAL MEMORY

1. Said, *Reflections on Exile and Other Essays*, 174, 6.
2. Assmann, *Cultural Memory*, 133.
3. Burbank and Cooper, *Empires in World History*, 321, 4, 271.
4. Hill, *History of the American Field Service in France*, "Part II: In the Orient, Section V-Monastir." For an obituary of Arthur Bluethenthal published in France shortly after his death, see Hall and Nordhoff, *The Lafayette Flying Corps*, 1:134–35, https://archive.org/stream/TheLafayetteFlyingCorpsvolume1/The_lafayette_flying_corps1#page/n11/mode/2up, accessed September 21, 2015.
5. Goldstein, *The Price of Whiteness*, 11–31.
6. Hieke, "Jews at the Cape Fear Coast."
7. Arthur Bluethenthal to Leopold and Johanna Bluethenthal, October 1906, ABC, folder 14; Arthur Bluethenthal to Elsa, October 5, 1906, ABC, folder 14.
8. Goldstein, *The Price of Whiteness*, 35–50, quote on p. 50.
9. Wilmington Race Riot Final Report, 111–14; Cecelski, *Democracy Betrayed*.
10. Rogoff, "A Tale of Two Cities."
11. Marcus Jacobi to Leopold and Johanna Bluethenthal, June 19, 1918, ABC, folder 1.
12. "Henry Weil," ABC, folder 14.
13. Andrew, *History of the American Field Service in France*, 364.
14. Bluethenthal to Sis, undated, ABC, folder 11.
15. Bluethenthal to Mama and Papa, June 12, 1917, ABC, folder 10.
16. Bluethenthal to Mama and Papa, June 15, 1917, ABC, folder 10.
17. Bluethenthal to Mama and Papa, July 4, 1917, ABC, folder 10.
18. Bluethenthal to Mama and Papa, July 11, 1917, ABC, folder 10; Bluethenthal to Mama and Papa, July 25, 1917, ABC, folder 10.

19. Bluethenthal to Leopold Bluethenthal, August 11, 1917, ABC, folder 10; Leopold Bluethenthal to Arthur Bluethenthal, October 27, 1917, ABC, folder 12.
20. Bluethenthal to Leopold and Johanna Leopold, March 28, 1918, ABC, folder 11.
21. Dos Passos, *1919*, 74.
22. Meigs, *Optimism at Armageddon*, 125.
23. Leopold Bluethenthal to V. L. Collins, January 28, 1919, ABC, folder 3. This edited version made it online at the State Archives of North Carolina and is currently at http://digital.ncdcr.gov/cdm/ref/collection/p15012coll10/id/1488, accessed May 15, 2017.
24. Bluethenthal to Davey and Arthur, January 27, 1917, ABC, folder 12.
25. Arthur Bluethenthal to Davey and Arthur, ABC; Arthur Bluethenthal to Davey and Arthur, January 27, 1917, SANC, Private Collections, Arthur Bluethenthal Papers, box 1.
26. Bluethenthal to Davey and Arthur, ABC. The *Madeira* was formally a German ship sailing under a Portuguese flag. Imbrie, *Behind the Wheel*, 137.
27. Said, *Orientalism*.
28. Burbank and Cooper, *Empires in World History*, 371.
29. Imbrie, *Behind the Wheel*, 138, 141.
30. Baird, "Part II: In the Orient, Section I–En Route to the Orient," 1:341–43.
31. Bluethenthal to Davey and Arthur, ABC.
32. I have retained Bluethenthal's offensive language in his quoted texts to illustrate the ways he connected the racism from home to interpret exiled men when abroad. His language survived the edited version of his letter, which suggests just how uncontroversial the words were to his audiences.
33. Bluethenthal to Davey and Arthur, ABC.
34. Burbank and Cooper, *Empires in World History*, 376.
35. Imbrie, *Behind the Wheel*, 141–42.
36. Bluethenthal to Davey and Arthur, ABC. See also Imbrie, *Behind the Wheel*, 138.
37. Andrew, *History of the American Field Service in France*, 364.
38. Arthur Bluethenthal to Dear Girls, April 22, 1917, New Hanover County Public Library, ABC, folder 11.
39. Hill, *History of the American Field Service in France*, "Part II: In the Orient, Section I-En Route to the Orient."
40. Imbrie, *Behind the Wheel*, 192.
41. Andrew, *History of the American Field Service in France*, 370–71.
42. Bluethenthal to Davey and Arthur, ABC.
43. Bluethenthal to Sis, ABC.
44. Winter, *Remembering War*, 102.
45. Bluethenthal's family donated his papers to the Cape Fear Museum and archives in Wilmington NC. No acquisition record exists, but it appears that an archivist from the North Carolina State Archives secured a copy of Bluethenthal's letter to Arthur and

Davey. The World War I collection does not have the original letter, only a copy. It seems that this was the only document that the Historical Commission obtained from the Bluethenthal Papers. The Cape Fear Museum meanwhile never understood the context of Bluethenthal's photo. They never cross-referenced the photo of the grandfather weeping over the remains of his dead granddaughter with the letter and thus described the event as happening "somewhere in France, likely Moraslin." Without connecting the letter to the photograph, Bluethenthal's Orientalism would remain obscured.

7. CULTURAL MEMORY IN THE INFORMATION AGE

1. Benjamin, "Storyteller," 99, 100, 101–2.
2. Benjamin, "Storyteller," 101.
3. Trout, *On the Battlefield of Memory*, 2.
4. Winter, *Remembering War*.
5. See Faust, *This Republic of Suffering*. Some notable exceptions might include the Official Records of the Civil War.
6. For these statistics see Huebner, "Interchange," 498. Huebner is quoting Clodfelter, *Warfare and Armed Conflicts*. The 300,000 wounded includes physical and mental casualties of war.
7. Assmann, *Cultural Memory*, 124–25.
8. Assmann, *Cultural Memory*, 87–110, 196, 257, 338–44.
9. Assmann, *Cultural Memory*, 192. North Carolina archivists built an artificial collection. A "natural" collection conforms to a structure of order imposed by the donors and is handed over in totality, whereas an artificial collection is a highly selective and highly motivated collection in which archivists impose their own order on the records. Thus the "impressions" of an artificial collection reflect the archivists' own values and interpretations much more than a "natural" collection. See also Derrida, *Archive Fever*.
10. Stoler, "Colonial Archives and the Arts of Governance," 87–109. I have already attempted to brush along the grain of the World War I Collection elsewhere. See Bontrager, "The Means of Instilling That Spirit of Americanism." See also Arondekar, "Without a Trace." In this study, the author suggests that colonial overseers suppressed reports of homosexual activity—preventing them from archival storage—because homosexual practices threatened the colonial order in India.
11. Bisher, "Landmarks of Power," 149.
12. Singal, *The War Within*, 12–15, 18. SANC.
13. President Woodrow Wilson created the Council of Defense to help promote the war and raise money and materials. North Carolina officials, like their counterparts in other states, had organized citizens' domestic war efforts around the state's counties based on this federal model. It oversaw fuel rationing, organized Four Minute Man,

solicited war bonds, and helped with enlistments among many other aspects of the home front.

14. Secretary of State J. Bryan Grimes to Chairman of the Council of Defense Dr. D. H. Hill, June 26, 1918, SANC, box North Carolina Council of Defense, folder Memorials; North Carolina Historical Commission, "Do Your Part," SANC box County War Records, folder Warren County, 5.
15. House would later go on to serve as the first chancellor of the consolidated campuses of the University of North Carolina at Chapel Hill.
16. Robert B. House, "Letters and Diary of First Lieutenant Robert Burton House," SANC, Private Collections, House Papers, box 8; Robert B. House to C. R. Cabbott, February 12, 1921, SANC, Private Collections, House Papers, box 6.
17. Robert House to Sue Eldridge House, May 12, 1917, SANC Private Collections, House Papers, box 8.
18. Robert B. House, unbound scrapbook, entry xxxix, SANC Private Collections, House Papers, box 8.
19. Lears, *Rebirth of the Nation*. This was part of what historian Jackson Lears has described as the "martial ideal," a "destructive regeneration" used by Progressives to push through their remaking of the American and North Carolinian systems.
20. Burbank and Cooper, *Empires in World History*, 452, 456.
21. House, "Kiffin Yates Rockwell," speech, SANC, Kiffin Rockwell Papers, Biographical Sketches and Information, 4.
22. Burbank and Cooper, *Empires in World History*, 371.
23. Andrew, *History of the American Field Service in France*, 8.
24. Thenault, *Lafayette Escadrille*, xiv, 13. Thenault discusses the Americans' explicit strategy for forming the flying unit as a propaganda tool for the American public.
25. Speech, George Tayloe [sic] Winston, "Kiffin Yates Rockwell"; poem by T. Maryon of the *Charlotte Observer*, 1–2.
26. This was not an unusual tendency. Germans, Britons, and French memory-makers were seeking to build similar misleading mythologies about their respective "heroes of the First World War." See Morrow, "Knights of the Sky."
27. House, "Kiffin Yates Rockwell," 2–4, SANC.
28. "Some Military Ancestry of Kiffin Yates Rockwell," SANC, Kiffin Rockwell Papers, Biographical Sketches and Information.
29. House, "Kiffin Yates Rockwell," 2–3, SANC. Handwritten section on back of speech.
30. House, speech at Burlington NC, November 11, 1920, SANC, Private Collections, House Papers, box 6.
31. Meigs, "'Mad'moiselle from Armentieres, Parlez-vous?' Sexual Attitudes of Americans in World War I," in *Optimism at Armageddon*.

32. Kaplan, "Manifest Domesticity," 23–50, quote on 26; 581–606, quote on 583. This earlier version demonstrates Kaplan's thinking at a more theoretical level.
33. Ione Branch Baine, "History of Base Hospital #65," SANC, Private Collections, Ione Branch Baine Papers, folder Typescript Histories of Base Hospital No. 65, 1–19.
34. Baine, "History of Base Hospital #65," 1.
35. See list of Reunion Announcements, Scrapbook Word List of Each One; Baine, "History of Base Hospital #65," 4.
36. Kaplan, "Manifest Domesticity," 591.
37. Irene Brewster, "The Nurses' Side of It," SANC, Private Collections, Ione Branch Baine Papers, folder Typescript Histories of Base Hospital No. 65, 14–15.
38. Baine, "History of Base Hospital #65," 9–10.
39. Brewster, "The Nurses' Side of It," 14–15.
40. Baine, "History of Base Hospital #65," 10, 16.
41. Baine, "History of Base Hospital #65," 13, 16.
42. Baine, "History of Base Hospital #65," 12.
43. Baine, "History of Base Hospital #65," 14.
44. Baine, "History of Base Hospital #65," 16–19.
45. Baine, "History of Base Hospital #65," 1–3, 19.
46. Cleopatra Bullock, "Thomas Bullock," SANC, Individual Service Records, Negroes and the War, Thomas Bullock folder.
47. Holton, "Decolonizing History," 230.
48. Kamman, *Mystic Chords of Memory*, 701.

8. THAT CAUSE SHALL NOT BE BETRAYED

1. "Suresnes American Cemetery and Memorial," American Battle Monuments Commission, http://www.abmc.gov/cemeteries/cemeteries/su_pict.pdf, accessed October 26, 2009.
2. Manela, *The Wilsonian Moment*.
3. Faust, *This Republic of Suffering*.
4. Lears, *Rebirth of a Nation*.
5. Capozzola, *Uncle Sam Wants You*, 18–19.
6. Tooze, *The Deluge*, 200, 201, 204–5, 215, 211.
7. Clements, *The Presidency of Woodrow Wilson*, 89, 143–55.
8. Freud, *On Murder, Mourning, and Melancholia*.
9. Hanson, *Unknown Soldiers*, 254.
10. Report, "Proposed Technical Instructions," September 30, 1918, NARA92C, box 3, folder General 1919–1922.
11. Report, "Proposed Technical Instructions," September 30, 1918.
12. Report, "Proposed Technical Instructions," September 30, 1918.

13. Report, "Proposed Technical Instructions," September 30, 1918.
14. Wilson's speech taken from "Soldiers Hear President," *New York Times*, May 31, 1919.
15. "Soldiers Hear President."
16. Richard Oulahan, "Americans Applauded Wilson's Criticisms," *New York Times*, June 2, 1919.
17. "Soldiers Hear President"; Oulahan, "Americans Applauded Wilson's Criticisms."
18. Hunt, *The American Ascendancy*, 56–62.
19. Manela, *The Wilsonian Moment*. For a shorter introduction, see Manela's essay "Imagining Woodrow Wilson in Asia," 1327–28.
20. See Winter, *Remembering War*.
21. For an in-depth discussion of this, see Knock, *To End All Wars*, and Clements, *The Presidency of Woodrow Wilson*.
22. Report, Commissaire de Police de Lambezellec to le Directeur de la Sureté Général, April 26, 1919, MAÉA, Etats-Unis B 170A; Chief of the Graves Registration Service to Chief de la Mission Militaire Francaise des SOS, May 8, 1919, MAÉA, Etats-Unis B 170 A; Telegram, Knight to QM Brest, May 8, 1919, MAÉA, Etats-Unis B 170 A.
23. Col. M. J. Henry to Chief Quartermaster of France, memorandum, August 19, 1919, NARA92C, box 3, folder General 1919–1922.
24. Secretary of War to Secretary of State, October 20, 1919, NARA92C, box 3, folder General 1919–1922.
25. "USS *Lake Daraga* (ID #4428)," Online Library of Navy Ships, Naval Historical Center, http://www.ibiblio.org/hyperwar/OnlineLibrary/photos/sh-usn/usnsh-l/id4428.htm, accessed October 23, 2009. Also see Budreau, *Bodies of War*, 64–67.
26. Report, Charles Elliott to Port Utilities Officer Hoboken, November 19, 1919, NARA92C, box 3, folder General 1919–1922.
27. Report, Charles Elliott, November 19, 1919.
28. Memorandum, Quartermaster General to Depot Officer, San Francisco CA, June 16, 1920, NARA92C, box 3, folder General 1919–1922.
29. Memorandum, Adjutant General to All Corps Area Commanders, August 8, 1921, NARA92C, box 3, folder General 1919–1922.
30. "To Bring Bodies from Germany," *Washington Post*, June 5, 1921, NARA92C, box 19, folder Germany.
31. H. F. Rethers to Quartermaster General, June 27, 1921, NARA92C, box 19, folder Germany.
32. Ariès, *The Hour of Our Death*. Also see Sappol, *A Traffic of Dead Bodies*; Richardson, *Death, Dissection, and the Destitute*.
33. H. F. Richards to C. C. Pierce, November 27, 1920, NARA92C, box 3, folder General 1919–1922.

34. Memorandum for the Adjutant General, August 9, 1918, NARA92C, box 3, folder General 1919–1922.
35. William Whitman to Secretary of War, September 11, 1918, NAR92C, box 3, folder General 1919–1922.
36. Dr. H. A. Hewlingo to Secretary of War, October 8, 1918, NARA92C, box 3, folder General 1919–1922.
37. Owen Wister, "Plead for Our Dead in France," *New York Times*, April 15, 1921.
38. Thomas Nelson Page to *New York Times*, April 15, 1921.
39. H. F. Rethers to *New York Times*, June 8, 1921.
40. "Only Two Unclaimed," *New York Times*, April 16, 1921.
41. "Writers Disagree on Soldier Dead," *New York Times*, April 17, 1921.
42. Meigs, *Optimism at Armageddon*, 186.

9. LISTENING TO EMPIRE

1. For a discussion on the history of sound, see Bailey, "Breaking the Sound Barrier." For an example of sound and history, see Bijsterveld, "The Diabolical Symphony of the Mechanical Age"; Van der Kloot, "Lawrence Bragg's Role in the Development of Sound-Ranging in World War I," 273–84.
2. Wills, *Lincoln at Gettysburg*; Schwartz, "Collective Memory"; Verdery, *The Political Lives of Dead Bodies*.
3. Diner, *A Very Different Age*.
4. Williams, *Tragedy of American Diplomacy*, 125; Tooze, *The Deluge*, 397, 396, 401.
5. Williams, *Tragedy of American Diplomacy*, 108. See also Manela, "Imagining Woodrow Wilson in Asia," 1337, 1340, 1348; Lentin, "The Treaty That Never Was"; Keylor, "The Rise and the Demise of the Franco-American Guarantee Pact," 96–105.
6. Koselleck, "War Memorials," 369.
7. Assmann, *Cultural Memory*, 45–47.
8. President Harding's address at the Burial of an Unknown American Soldier, *New York Times*, November 12, 1921.
9. Savage, *Standing Soldiers, Kneeling Slaves*; Blight, *Race and Reunion*; Silber, *The Romance of Reunion*; Bodnar, *Remaking America*; Thelen, "Memory and American History"; Piehler, *Remembering War the American Way*; Blackhawk, *Violence over the Land*.
10. Murphy, *Hemispheric Imaginings*. Also see Grazia, *Irresistible Empire*.
11. Hanson, *Unknown Soldiers*, 331–33.
12. "The Unknown Soldier," *Life*, March 17, 1921, 385.
13. "Asks Unknown Hero Delay," *New York Times*, February 17, 1921.
14. "The Unknown Soldier," *Life*.
15. Hanson, *Unknown Soldiers*, 333.

16. "The Unknown Soldier," *New York Times*, December 9, 1920.
17. Hanson, *Unknown Soldiers*, 333.
18. "The Unknown Soldier's Tomb," *New York Times*, February 3, 1921.
19. Program, "Ceremonies at Memorial Amphitheater," November 11, 1921, NARA 319, box 001, folder WWI Unknown Soldiers; "Solemn Journey of the Dead," *New York Times*, November 12, 1921.
20. Wood, "'Join with Heart and Soul and Voice,'" 1083–1116.
21. Abraham Lincoln, First Inaugural Address, March 4, 1861, http://www.bartleby.com/124/pres31.html, accessed May 5, 2015.
22. Smith, "Producing Sense, Consuming Sense, Making Sense," 852. Focusing on print capitalism, Benedict Anderson suggests that cultural memory exploits the visual sense over the aural for its ontological and democratic underpinnings and the United States was no different. Yet sound historians such as Mark M. Smith and Jonathan Sterne and others have insisted that an "aural past" also existed and that the visual hegemony over the past has relied too much on the gaze, the image, and the act of visualization. See Sterne, *Audible Past*.
23. Anderson, *Imagined Communities*, 206.
24. Sloane, *The Last Great Necessity*, 114.
25. Koselleck, "War Memorials," 368.
26. See Poovey, *Making a Social Body*.
27. Koselleck, "War Memorials," 369.
28. Keyes, "'Like a Roaring Lion,'" 35, 42.
29. Sternes, *Audible Past*, 137–78. This was individualized through the use of headphones.
30. "Finds Pilgrim's Echo in Honors to Dead," *New York Times*, November 12, 1921.
31. Stanyek and Piekut, "Deadness," 307–8. Their definition of this "intermundane" agency describes a process not a thing—something one uses to collaborate, not something one possesses or accumulates.
32. Sterne, *Audible Past*, 208–11.
33. Schmidt, *Hearing Things*.
34. Kandel, *In Search of Memory*, 281–85, 300–306. Also see Craver, "The Making of a Memory Mechanism."
35. Brower, "Memory and the Perception of Rhythm," 19–35.
36. Sterne, *Audible Past*, 61–62. Also see Donald, *Origins of the Modern Mind*, 325–33.
37. Sterne, *Audible Past*, 171–75. Before corporations had completely realized the power of radio, they experimented with telephone lines to transmit sounds through amplifiers to a mass audience. Within a few years radio would be the preferred media of mass communication. For example, after Harding's death, President Calvin Coolidge outfitted the White House with a radio transmitter in 1924 and he gave several broadcasts.

38. Berland, "Contradicting Media," 41–42; Schafer, "The Soundscape"; Thompson, "Sound, Modernity and History," 117–18.
39. "Cities Observe the Day from East to West," *New York Times*, November 12, 1921;
40. "Host in Madison Sq. Honors the Dead," *New York Times*, November 12, 1921. The Wilson administration originally gave mothers of soldiers a "gold star" if their son had died in service to the country.
41. Trout, *On the Battlefield of Memory*, 131.
42. Piehler, "The War Dead and the Gold Star," 175.
43. "President Harding's Address at the Burial of an Unknown American Soldier," *New York Times*, November 12, 1921.
44. Trout, *On the Battlefield of Memory*, 131.
45. Johnson, *Saint Peter Relates an Incident of the Resurrection Day*.
46. Dos Passos, *1919*, 466.
47. Edelman, *The Symbolic Uses of Politics*, 6. Murray Edelman described condensation symbols as symbols that "condense into one symbolic event, sign, or act patriotic pride, anxieties, remembrances of past glories or humiliations, promises of future greatness." The Unknown Soldier was one such condensation symbol.
48. "Solemn Journey of the Dead," *New York Times*, November 21, 1921.
49. "Why We Went to War," *New York Times*, November 21, 1921.
50. "City Pays Silent Tribute," *New York Times*, November 21, 1921.
51. "Solemn Journey of the Dead," *New York Times*, November 12, 1921; "Seven Nations Laud Work of Red Cross," *New York Times*, November 14, 1921.
52. "President Harding's Address," *New York Times*, November 12, 1921.
53. "Advises Delegates to Watch Senate," *New York Times*, November 9, 1921.
54. "Leaders Hail Conference," *New York Times*, November 12, 1921.
55. If the world system operated on the notion that security of the high seas was the most important aspect of empire building, the United States was able to further its imperial interests at the Washington conference while checking its competition. Goldstein and Maurer, *The Washington Conference*; Kissinger, *Diplomacy*, 373; "Why We Went to War," *New York Times*, November 21, 1921; Warren G. Harding, "Address of the President of the United States at the Concluding Session of the Conference on Limitation of Armament," February 6, 1922, NARA319, box 001, folder, WWI Unknown Soldiers.
56. "President Harding's Address," *New York Times*, November 12, 1921; "Host in Madison Sq. Honors the Dead," *New York Times*, November 12, 1921.
57. Barthes, "The Grain of the Voice," 505, 509.
58. Dolar, "The Linguistics of Voice," 540–41, 551–52.
59. "President Harding's Address," *New York Times*, November 12, 1921.
60. "President Harding's Address," *New York Times*.

61. Subaltern studies should be acknowledged here, especially the work of Spivak, "Can the Subaltern Speak?" and Bhabha, *Location of Culture*.
62. Burbank and Cooper, *Empires in World History*, 8.
63. This had significant implications for the rest of the twentieth century. Historian K. S. Inglis has shown the cult of the unknown spinning out from London to Paris to Baghdad. Tombs of unknowns constituted a phenomenon that transcended time and war and allowed elites to craft respective national identities in the world. Inglis, "Entombing Unknown Soldiers."

EPILOGUE

1. Ralph E. Truman to Leslie L. Biffle, May 31, 1957, NARA117, box 42, Records Concerning Other Cemeteries and Memorials.
2. "Battle of Santiago 60 Years Ago," *St. Louis Globe Democrat*, section F, p. 4, in NARA117, box 42, Records Concerning Other Cemeteries and Memorials.
3. Harry S. Truman to Gen. Carl Spatz, June 3, 1957, NARA117, box 42, Records Concerning Other Cemeteries and Memorials.
4. Foreign Service Despatch, American Consulate Santiago to Cuba to the Department of State, Washington DC, "Spanish American War Veterans Renew Their Interest in Battle Monuments in Santiago de Cuba Area," August 15, 1957, NARA117, box 42, Records Concerning Other Cemeteries and Memorials.
5. Foreign Service Despatch, "Spanish American War Veterans Renew Their Interest in Battle Monuments in Santiago de Cuba Area," August 15, 1957.
6. Foreign Service Despatch, American Consulate Santiago to Cuba to the Department of State, Washington DC, "Major General (Ret.) Ralph Truman Promotes Restoration of Santiago de Cuba Battlefields," February 19, 1958, NARA117, box 42, Records Concerning Other Cemeteries and Memorials.
7. Foreign Service Despatch, American Consulate Santiago to Cuba to the Department of State, Washington DC, "Visit of Major General (Ret.) Ralph Truman to Cuba," April 7, 1958, NARA117, box 42, Records Concerning Other Cemeteries and Memorials.
8. Ralph E. Truman to Leslie L. Biffle, March 7, 1958, NARA117, box 42, Records Concerning Other Cemeteries and Memorials.
9. Operations Memorandum, American Embassy in Havana to Department of State, October 22, 1958, NARA117, box 42, Records Concerning Other Cemeteries and Memorials.
10. William Wieland to Col. William A. Walker, memo, November 4, 1958, NARA117, box 42, Records Concerning Other Cemeteries and Memorials.

11. Foreign Service Despatch, American Consulate in Santiago to Department of State, October 12, 1960, NARA117, box 42, Records Concerning Other Cemeteries and Memorials.
12. Foreign Service Despatch, American Consulate in Santiago to Department of State, September 23, 1960, NARA117, box 42, Records Concerning Other Cemeteries and Memorials.
13. Telegram, American Embassy in Havana to Department of State, April 25, 1960, NARA117, box 42, Records Concerning Other Cemeteries and Memorials.
14. Memo for General North, American Battle Monuments Commission, December 8, 1960, NARA117, box 42, Records Concerning Other Cemeteries and Memorials.
15. William A. Walker to Robert A. Hurwitch, memo, January 9, 1961, NARA117, box 42, Records Concerning Other Cemeteries and Memorials.
16. Foreign Service Despatch, Swiss Embassy to U.S. Department of State, February 28, 1961, NARA117, box 42, Records Concerning Other Cemeteries and Memorials.
17. Foreign Service Despatch, Swiss Embassy to U.S. Department of State, April 28, 1961, NARA117, box 42, Records Concerning Other Cemeteries and Memorials; Memo, Department of State to Charles B. Shaw, May 18, 1961, NARA117, box 42, Records Concerning Other Cemeteries and Memorials; Foreign Service Dispatch, Swiss Embassy to U.S. Department of State, August 15, 1961, NARA117, box 42, Records Concerning Other Cemeteries and Memorials
18. Santiago Surrender Tree Memorial, American Battle Monuments Commission, https://www.abmc.gov/cemeteries-memorials/americas/santiago-surrender-tree-memorial, accessed May 30, 2017.
19. Bill Thomas, "Last Soldier Buried in Tomb of the Unknowns Wasn't Unknown," *Washington Post Magazine*, November 8, 2012, https://www.washingtonpost.com/lifestyle/magazine/last-soldier-buried-in-tomb-of-the-unknowns-wasnt-unknown/2012/11/06/5da3e7d6-0bdd-11e2-a310-2363842b7057_story.html, accessed May 28, 2017.
20. Nass, "History's Remains."
21. Thomas, "Last Soldier Buried."
22. The Blassies took their son's remains back to their home in St. Louis, Missouri, and reinterred them in nearby Jefferson Barracks National Cemetery.
23. Josh White, "Tillman's Parents Are Critical of Army," *Washington Post*, May 23, 2005, http://www.washingtonpost.com/wp-dyn/content/article/2005/05/22/AR2005052200865.html, accessed April 7, 2015.
24. Krakauer, *Where Men Win Glory*.
25. NBC News, https://www.nbcnews.com/news/military/army-sgt-la-david-t-johnson-fought-end-after-ambush-n830681, December 18, 2017.

26. Sudarsan Raghavan, "U.S. Soldier in Niger Ambush Was Bound and Apparently Executed ,Villagers Say," *Washington Post*, November 10, 2017, https://www.washingtonpost.com/world/africa/us-soldier-in-niger-ambush-was-bound-and-apparently-executed-villagers-say/2017/11/10/3aebba3e-c442–11e7–9922-4151f5ca6168_story.html?utm_term=.05ae48b5926f, accessed April 2, 2017; Alex Horton, "More Remains Belonging to Sgt. La David Johnson Found in Niger, Military Says," *Washington Post*, November 21, 2017, https://www.washingtonpost.com/news/checkpoint/wp/2017/11/21/more-remains-belonging-to-sgt-la-david-johnson-found-in-niger-military-says/?utm_term=.e96331ed11bd, accessed April 2, 2017.
27. *New York Times*, "Full Transcript and Video: Kelly Defends Trump's Handling of Soldier's Death and Call to Widow," October 19, 2017, https://www.nytimes.com/2017/10/19/us/politics/statement-kelly-gold-star.html?action=click&contentCollection=Politics&module=RelatedCoverage&region=Marginalia&pgtype=article, accessed April 2, 2018; Alex Horton, "For Some Veterans, John Kelly's Remarks Add to a Worrying Military-Civilian Divide," *Washington Post*, October 21, 2017.
28. *New York Times*, "Full Transcript and Video."
29. Alex Horton, "For Some Veterans."
30. Rukmini Callimachi, Helene Cooper, Erick Schmitt, Alan Binder, and Thomas Gibbons-Neff, "'An Endless War': Why 4 U.S. Soldiers Died in a Remote African Desert," *New York Times*, https://www.nytimes.com/interactive/2018/02/17/world/africa/niger-ambush-american-soldiers.html?smid=fb-share, accessed April 3, 2018.

BIBLIOGRAPHY

MANUSCRIPTS AND ARCHIVES

ABC. Arthur Bluethenthal Collection, New Hanover County Public Library, Wilmington NC.

Archives, Politique et Economique, Paris.

HL Huntington Library, San Marino CA.

MAÉA. Ministere des Affaires Étrangères.

MHM. Henry Cole Papers. Marietta History Museum, Marietta GA.

NARA. National Archives and Records Administration.

    77G. Record Group 77, General Correspondence, 1894–1923.

    92C. Record Group 92, General Correspondence, Cemetery file, 1865–1914.

    92CC. Record Group 92, Consolidated Correspondence file, 1794–1915.

    92D. Record Group 92, Reports of D. H. Rhodes and F. S. Croggon, in charge of burial corps associated with interments and disinterment in the Philippine Islands, 1900–1903.

    92E. Record Group 92, Edmund Whitman Journal.

    92L. Record Group 92, Letters Received Relating to Cemeteries.

    92R. Record Group 92, Records Relating to Functions Cemeterial, 1828–1929, General Correspondence, Cemetery file.

    117. Record Group 117, Records of the American Battle Monuments Commission.

    319. Record Group 319, Records of the Office of the Chief of Military History, Records of the Historical Services Division, Publications, Unpublished Manuscripts, and Supporting Records, 1943–1977, "The Last Salute, Studies of State Official and Special Military Funerals."

SANC. State Archives of North Carolina, World War I Collection, Raleigh.

Stephen W. Downey Papers at the Rocky Mountain Online Archive. http://rmoa.unm.edu/docviewer.php?docId=wyu-ah10555.xml.

American Battle Monuments Commission. "Suresnes American Cemetery and Memorial." http://www.abmc.gov/cemeteries/cemeteries/su_pict.pdf, accessed October 26, 2009.

American State Papers, 1789–1838. Indian Affairs, vol. 1. "The Wyandots, Communicated to the House of Representatives, February 28, 1812. www.loc.gov, accessed June 1, 2008.

Carpenter, Alfred P. "Letter on the Battle of Gettysburg." In *A Civil War Journal: Company K, 1st Minnesota Volunteer Infantry Regiment at Gettysburg, July 1–4, 1863*. http://www2.smumn.edu/deptpages/~history/civil_war/, accessed June 18, 2007.

Fish, Daniel. "The American Union: The Fittest Monument to Its Dead Defenders." Address given on Memorial Day 1888, Nashville TN. Huntington Library, San Marino CA.

Hill, Lovering. *History of the American Field Service in France*. "Part II: In the Orient, Section V-Monastir." http://net.lib.byu.edu/estu/wwi/memoir/afshist/afs1j.htm#orient, accessed September 21, 2015.

Lincoln, Abraham. *First Inaugural Address*, March 4, 1861. http://www.bartleby.com/124/pres31.html, accessed May 5, 2015.

Nelson, Henry. *Federal Writers' Project: Slave Narrative Project, Vol. 2, Arkansas, Part 5, McClendon-Prayer*. 1936. Manuscript/Mixed Material. Retrieved from the Library of Congress, image 206-7. https://www.loc.gov/item/mesn025/, accessed February 8, 2017.

The Martyred President Collection at Emory University, Atlanta. http://lincoln.digitalscholarship.emory.edu/.

Root, Elihu. "Speech." Canton OH, October 24, 1900. Huntington Library, San Marino CA.

Schurz, Carl. *For the Republic of Washington and Lincoln*. An address delivered at a conference convened by the American Anti-Imperialistic League in Philadelphia on February 22, 1900. Pamphlet. Huntington Library, San Marino CA.

Thenault, George. *The Story of the Lafayette Escadrille*. Translated by Walter Duranty. Boston: Small, Maynard, 1921. https://archive.org/stream/storylafayette00thengoog#page/n6/mode/2up, accessed September 21, 2015.

U.S. Department of Veterans Affairs.
"Sitka National Cemetery." http://www.cem.va.gov/CEMs/nchp/sitka.asp, accessed July 9, 2008.
"Johnson's Island." http://www.cem.va.gov/CEM/cems/lots/confed_stockade.asp, accessed December 22, 2008.

PUBLISHED WORKS

Adelman, Jeremy, and Stephen Aron. "From Borderlands to Borders: Empires, Nation-States, and the Peoples in between in North American History," *American Historical Review* 104 (1999): 814–41.

Agoncillo, Felipe. *To the American People*. Paris: Imprimerie Chaix, 1900.
Aguilar, Filomeno V., Jr. "Tracing Origins: 'Ilustrado' Nationalism and the Racial Science of Migration Waves." *Journal of Asian Studies* 64 (August 2005): 605–37.
Anderson, Benedict. *Imagined Communities: Reflections on the Origin and Spread of Nationalism*. New York: Verso Books, 1998.
Andrew, A. Piatt, ed. *History of the American Field Service in France, "Friends of France," 1914–1917*. Vol. 1. Boston: Houghton Mifflin, 1920.
"Annual Report, Deputy Quartermaster-General M. I. Ludington." *Annual Reports of the War Department Fiscal Year 1900*. Washington DC: Government Printing Office, 1900.
"Annual Report, Deputy Quartermaster-General W. S. Patton." *Annual Reports of the War Department Fiscal Year 1900*. Washington DC: Government Printing Office, 1901.
Ariès, Philippe. *The Hour of Our Death*. Translated by Helen Weaver. New York: Knopf, 1981.
Arondekar, Anjali. "Without a Trace: Sexuality and the Colonial Archive." *Journal of the History of Sexuality* 14 (January–April 2005): 10–27.
Assmann, Jan. *Cultural Memory and Early Civilization: Writing, Remembrance, and Political Imagination*. Translated by David Henry Wilson. New York: Cambridge University Press, 2011.
Bailey, Peter. "Breaking the Sound Barrier: A Historian Listens to Noise." *Body & Society* 2, no. 2 (1996): 49–66.
Baird, Charles, Jr. "Part II: In the Orient, Section I—En Route to the Orient." In *History of the American Field Service in France, "Friends of France," 1914–1917*. Boston: Houghton Mifflin, 1920.
Barthes, Roland. "The Grain of the Voice." In *The Sound Studies Reader*, edited by Jonathan Sterne. New York: Routledge, 2012.
Bass, John F. "Our New Possessions—The Philippines." *Harper's Weekly*, February 4, 1899, 119.
Bederman, Gail. *Manliness and Civilization: A Cultural History of Gender and Race in the United States, 1880–1917*. Chicago: University of Chicago Press, 1996.
Benjamin, Walter. "The Storyteller." In *The Collective Memory Reader*, edited by Jeffrey K. Olick, Vered Vinitzky-Seroussi, and Daniel Levy. New York: Oxford University Press, 2011.
Berland, Jody. "Contradicting Media: Toward a Political Phenomenology of Listing." In *The Sound Studies Reader*, edited by Jonathan Sterne. New York: Routledge, 2012.
Bhabha, Homi K. *The Location of Culture*. 2nd ed. London: Routledge, 2004.
Bijsterveld, Karin. "The Diabolical Symphony of the Mechanical Age: Technology and Symbolism of Sound in European and North American Noise Abatement Campaigns, 1900–40." *Social Studies of Science* 31, no. 1 (February 2001): 37–70.
Bisher, Catherine W. "Landmarks of Power: Building a Southern Past in Raleigh and Wilmington, North Carolina, 1885–1915." In *Where These Memories Grow: History,*

Memory, and Southern Identity, edited by W. Fitzhugh Brundage. Chapel Hill: North Carolina University Press, 2000.

Blackhawk, Ned. *Violence over the Land: Indians and Empires in the Early American West.* Cambridge: Harvard University Press, 2008.

Blair, William A. *Cities of the Dead: Contesting the Memory of the Civil War in the South, 1865–1914.* Chapel Hill: University of North Carolina Press, 2004.

Blight, David W. "For Something beyond the Battlefield: Frederick Douglass and the Struggle for the Memory of the Civil War." *Journal of American History* 75, no. 4 (1989): 1156–78.

———. *Race and Reunion: The Civil War in American Memory.* Cambridge: Belknap Press of Harvard University Press, 2002.

Bodnar, John. *Remaking America: Public Memory, Commemoration, and Patriotism in the Twentieth Century.* Princeton: Princeton University Press, 1993.

Bontrager, Shannon. "'The Means of Instilling That Spirit of Americanism': North Carolina, Cultural Memory, and the First World War." In *North Carolina and the Great War*, edited by Shepherd McKinley. Knoxville: University of Tennessee Press, 2018.

The Boston Common, or Rural Walks in Cities. By a Friend of Improvement. Boston, 1838.

Brower, Candace. "Memory and the Perception of Rhythm." *Music Theory Spectrum* 15 (Spring 1993): 19–35.

Budreau, Lisa M. *Bodies of War: World War I and the Politics of Commemoration, 1919–1933.* New York: New York University Press, 2010.

Burbank, Jane, and Frederick Cooper. *Empires in World History: Power and the Politics of Difference.* Princeton: Princeton University Press, 2011.

Capozzola, Christopher. *Uncle Sam Wants You: World War I and the Making of the Modern American Citizen.* New York: Oxford University Press, 2008.

Cecelski, David S. *Democracy Betrayed: The Wilmington Race Riot of 1898 and Its Legacy.* Chapel Hill: University of North Carolina Press, 1998.

Chadwick, John White. *The Present Distress: A Sermon upon Our Oriental War.* New York: William Green, 1899.

Clements, Kendrick A. *The Presidency of Woodrow Wilson.* Lawrence: University of Kansas Press, 1992.

Clodfelter, Michael. *Warfare and Armed Conflicts: A Statistical Reference to Casualty and Other Figures, 1500–2000.* New York: McFarland, 2008

Cloyd, Benjamin G. *Haunted by Atrocity: Civil War Prisons in American Memory.* Baton Rouge: Louisiana State University, 2010.

Coetzee, Marilyn Shevin, and Franz Coetzee, eds. *Authority, Identity, and the Social History of the Great War.* Providence RI: Berghahn Books, 1995.

Craughwhell, Thomas J. *Stealing Lincoln's Body.* Cambridge MA: Belknap Press, 2007.

Craver, Carl F. "The Making of a Memory Mechanism." *Journal of the History of Biology* 36 (Spring 2003), 153–95.

Cushman, Gregory T. *Guano and the Opening of the Pacific World: A Global Ecological History*. Cambridge: Cambridge University Press, 2013.

Derrida, Jacques. *Archive Fever: A Freudian Impression*. Translated by Eric Prenowitz. Chicago: University of Chicago Press, 1998.

Diner, Steven J. *A Very Different Age: Americans of the Progressive Era*. New York: Hill and Wang, 1998.

Dolar, Mladen. "The Linguistics of Voice." In *The Sound Studies Reader*, edited by Jonathan Sterne. New York: Routledge, 2012.

Donald, Merlin. *Origins of the Modern Mind*. In *The Collective Memory Reader*, edited by Jeffrey K. Olick, Vered Vinitzky-Seroussi, and Daniel Levy. New York: Oxford University Press, 2011.

Dos Passos, John. *1919*. New York: Harcourt, Brace, 1932.

Downey, Stephen W. *The Play of Destiny*. New Creek WV, 1867.

DuBois, W. E. B. *Black Reconstruction in America, 1860–1880*. New York: Free Press, 1992.

———. "Of the Dawn of Freedom." *The Souls of Black Folk*. New York: Library of America, 1987.

Dunlap, Myron E. *Address Delivered by Major Myron E. Dunlap in the Confederate Cemetery at Appomattox, Va., on Memorial Day, May 30, 1898*. Lancaster PA, 1900.

Edelman, Murray. *The Symbolic Uses of Politics*. Urbana: University of Illinois Press, 1964.

Farrell, James. *Inventing the American Way of Death, 1830–1920*. Philadelphia: Temple University Press, 1980.

Faust, Drew Gilpin. *This Republic of Suffering: Death and the American Civil War*. New York: Alfred A. Knopf, 2008.

Finley, James B. *History of the Wyandot Mission at Upper Sandusky, Ohio*. Cincinnati OH: Wright and Swormstedt, 1840.

Fletcher, Louisa Warren. *The Journal of a Landlady*. Edited by Henry E. Huggins, Connie M. Cox, and Jean Cole Anderson. Chapel Hill NC: Professional Press, 1995.

Foner, Eric. *Reconstruction: America's Unfinished Revolution, 1863–1877*. New York: Harper and Row, 1988.

———. *Who Owns History? Rethinking the Past in a Changing World*. New York: Hill and Wang, 2003.

Foucault, Michel. *History of Sexuality, Vol. 1: An Introduction*. New York: Vintage, 1990.

French, Stanley. "The Cemetery as Cultural Institution: The Establishment of Mount Auburn and the "Rural Cemetery" Movement." *American Quarterly* 26 (March 1974): 37–59.

Freud, Sigmund. *On Murder, Mourning, and Melancholia*. Translated by Michael Hulse. New York: Penguin Modern Classics, 2005.

Fritzche, Peter. "The Archive." *History and Memory* 17 (Winter 2005): 13–44.

Garrison, Lindley M. *Final Report on Removing Wreck of Battleship "Maine" from Harbor of Habana, Cuba*. Secretary of War Report to the U.S. House of Representatives. Washington DC: Government Printing Office, 1914.

Gillis, John R. Ed. *Commemorations: The Politics of National Identity*. Princeton: Princeton University Press, 1994.

Girardeau, John L. "Confederate Memorial Day: Re-internment of the Carolina Dead from Gettysburg." Charleston SC: William G. Myzock, 1871. Huntington Library, San Marino CA.

Goldstein, Eric L. *The Price of Whiteness: Jews, Race, and American Identity*. Princeton: Princeton University Press, 2006.

Goldstein, Erik, and John Maurer, eds. *The Washington Conference, 1921–1922: Naval Rivalry, East Asian Stability, and the Road to Pearl Harbor*. London: Routledge, 1994.

Grazia, Victoria de. *Irresistible Empire: America's Advance through Twentieth-Century Europe*. New York: Belknap Press, 2005.

Hahn, Steven. *A Nation without Borders: The United States and Its World in an Age of Civil Wars, 1830–1910*. New York: Penguin Books, 2017.

Halbwachs, Maurice. *On Collective Memory*. Edited and translated by Lewis A. Coser. Chicago: University of Chicago Press, 1992.

Hall, James Norman, and Charles Bernard Nordhoff, eds. *The Lafayette Flying Corps*. Vol. 1. Boston: Houghton Mifflin, 1920.

Hanson, Neil. *Unknown Soldiers: The Story of the Missing of the First World War*. New York: Vintage, 2005.

Harrell, Carolyn L. *When the Bells Tolled for Lincoln: Southern Reaction to the Assassination*. Macon GA: Mercer University Press, 1997.

Hart, John Mason. *Empire and Revolution: The Americans in Mexico since the Civil War*. Berkeley: University of California Press, 2002.

Hellwig, David J. "The Afro-American Press and Woodrow Wilson's Mexican Policy, 1913–1917." *Phylon* 48 (Winter 1987): 261–70.

Hieke, Anton. "Jews at the Cape Fear Coast: A Portrait of Jewish Wilmington, 1860–1880." *Southern Jewish History* 13 (2010): 1–43.

Hobsbawm, Eric, and Terence Ranger. *The Invention of Tradition*. New York: Cambridge University Press, 2003.

Hoganson, Kristen L. *Fighting for American Manhood: How Gender and Politics Provoked the Spanish-American and Philippine-American Wars*. New Haven CT: Yale University Press, 1998.

Holton, Adalaine. "Decolonizing History: Arthur Schomburg's Afrodiasporic Archive. *Journal of African American History* 92 (Spring 2007): 218–38.

Homans, Peter. *Symbolic Loss: The Ambiguity of Mourning and Memory at Century's End.* Charlottesville: University of Virginia Press, 2000.

Houlbrooke, Ralph, ed. *Death, Religion, and the Family in England, 1480–1750.* Oxford: Clarendon Press, 1989.

Huebner, Andrew. "Interchange: World War I." *Journal of American History* 102 (September 2015): 463–99.

Hunt, Michael. *The American Ascendancy: How the United States Gained and Wielded Global Dominance.* Chapel Hill: University of North Carolina Press, 2007.

Igler, David. *The Great Ocean: Pacific Worlds from Captain Cook to the Gold Rush.* New York: Oxford University Press, 2013.

Ileto, Reynaldo C. "The Philippine-American War: Friendship and Forgetting." In *Vestiges of War: The Philippine-American War and the Aftermath of an Imperial Dream, 1899–1999,* edited by Angel Velasco Shaw and Luis H. Francia. New York: New York University Press, 2002.

Imbrie, Robert Whitney. *Behind the Wheel of an Ambulance.* New York: Robert M. McBride, 1918.

Inglis, K. S. "Entombing Unknown Soldiers: From London and Paris to Baghdad." *History and Memory* 2 (Fall/Winter 1993): 7–31.

Jackson, Sheldon. *A Statement of Facts Concerning the Difficulties at Sitka, Alaska, in 1885.* Washington DC: Thomas McGill, 1886.

Jacobs, Harriet. *Incidence in the Life of a Slave Girl.* New York: Bedford Books, 2009.

Jacobson, Matthew Frye. *Barbarian Virtues: The United States Encounters Foreign Peoples at Home and Abroad, 1876–1917.* New York: Hill and Wang, 2000.

Jalland, Patricia. *Death in the Victorian Family.* New York: Oxford University Press, 1996.

Janney, Caroline E. *Burying the Dead but Not the Past.* Chapel Hill: University of North Carolina Press, 2008.

Jessup, David Eric. "Connecting Alaska: The Washington-Alaska Military Cable and Telegraph System." *Journal of the Gilded Age and Progressive Era* 6 (October 2007): 385–408.

Johnson, James Weldon. *Saint Peter Relates an Incident of the Resurrection Day.* New York: Viking Press, 1931.

Jones, Ryan Tucker. "Running into Whales: North Pacific History from Below the Waves." *American Historical Review* 118 (April 2013): 349–77.

Kamman, Michael. *Mystic Chords of Memory: The Transformation of Tradition in American Culture.* New York: Vintage, 1993.

Kandel, Eric R. *In Search of Memory: The Emergence of a New Science of Mind.* New York: W. W. Norton, 2006.

Kaplan, Amy. *The Anarchy of Empire in the Making of U.S. Culture.* Cambridge: Harvard University Press, 2002.

———. "Manifest Domesticity." *American Literature* 70 (September 1998): 581–606.

Kasson, John F. *Houdini, Tarzan, and the Perfect Man: The White Male Body and the Challenge of Modernity*. New York: Hill and Wang, 2001.

Keefer, Bradley. *Conflicting Memories: The Chickamauga Battlefield and the Spanish American War, 1863–1933*. Kent OH: Kent State University Press, 2013.

Keyes, Sarah. "'Like a Roaring Lion': The Overland Trail as a Sonic Conquest." *Journal of American History* 96 (June 2009): 19–43.

Keylor, William R. "The Rise and the Demise of the Franco-American Guarantee Pact, 1919–1921." In *The Legacy of the Great War: Peacemaking 1919*, edited by William R. Keylor. Boston: Houghton Mifflin, 1998.

Kinzer, Stephen. *Overthrow: America's Century of Regime Change from Hawaii to Iraq*. New York: Henry Holt, 2006.

———. *The True Flag: Theodore Roosevelt, Mark Twain, and the Birth of the American Empire*. New York: Henry Holt, 2017.

Kirk, J. Allen. *A Statement of Facts Concerning the Bloody Riot in Wilmington, North Carolina, of Interest to Every Citizen of the United States*. Chapel Hill: University of North Carolina Documenting the American South, 2002. http://docsouth.unc.edu/nc/kirk/kirk.html, accessed March 26, 2017.

Kissinger, Henry. *Diplomacy*. New York: Simon and Schuster, 1995.

Klein, John Marshall. "Spaniards and the Politics of Memory in Cuba, 1898–1934." PhD diss., University of Texas at Austin, 2002.

Knock, Thomas J. *To End All Wars: Woodrow Wilson and the Quest for a New World Order*. Princeton: Princeton University Press, 1992.

Koselleck, Reinhardt. "War Memorials Identity Formations of the Survivors." In *The Collective Memory Reader*, edited by Jeffrey K. Olick, Vered Vinitzky-Seroussi, and Daniel Levy. New York: Oxford University Press, 2011.

Krakauer, Jon. *Where Men Win Glory: The Odyssey of Pat Tillman*. New York: Anchor Books, 2010.

Kramer, Paul A. *The Blood of Government: Race, Empire, the United States, and the Philippines*. Chapel Hill: University of North Carolina Press, 2006.

———. "Violence in the U.S. Empire: The Philippine-American War as Race War." *Asia-Pacific Journal: Japan Focus*. http://www.japanfocus.org/-Paul_A_-Kramer/1745, accessed October 16, 2009.

LaFeber, Walter. *The Cambridge History of American Foreign Relations*. Vol. 2: *The American Search for Opportunity, 1865–1913*. Cambridge: Cambridge University Press, 1995.

Lears, T. J. Jackson. *No Place of Grace: Antimodernism and the Transformation of American Culture, 1880–1920*. Chicago: University of Chicago Press, 1994.

———. *Rebirth of a Nation: The Remaking of Modern America, 1877–1920*. New York: Harper, 2009.

Leiker, James N. *Racial Borders: Black Soldiers along the Rio Grande*. College Station: Texas A&M University Press, 2002.

Lentin, Antony. "The Treaty That Never Was: Lloyd George and the Abortive Anglo-French Alliance of 1919." In *The Legacy of the Great War: Peacemaking 1919*, edited by William R. Keylor. Boston: Houghton Mifflin, 1998.

Levy, George. *To Die in Chicago: Confederate Prisoners at Camp Douglass, 1862–65*. New York: Pelican, 1999.

Lindeman, Frank. *Pretty Shield: Medicine Woman of the Crows*. 2nd ed. Lincoln NE: Bison Books, 2003.

Lloyd, David W. *Battlefield Tourism: Pilgrimage and the Commemoration of the Great War in Britain, Australia, and Canada, 1919–1939*. Oxford: Berg Press, 1998.

Loudon, John Claudius. "Hints Respecting the Manner of Laying Out the Grounds of the Public Squares in London, to the Utmost Picturesque Advantage." *Literary Journal* 2 (December 1804). Reprinted in *Furor Hortensis: Essays on the History of the English Landscape Garden in Memory of H. F. Clark*, edited by Peter Willis. Edinburgh: Elysium Press, 1974.

Manela, Erez. "Imagining Woodrow Wilson in Asia: Dreams of East-West Harmony and the Revolt against Empire in 1919." *American Historical Review* 111 (December 2006): 1327–28.

———. *The Wilsonian Moment: Self-Determination and the International Origins of Anticolonial Nationalism*. New York: Oxford University Press, 2007.

Matsuda, Matt K. *The Memory of the Modern*. New York: Oxford University Press, 1996.

McClintock, Ann. *Imperial Leather: Race, Gender, and Sexuality in the Colonial Contest*. London: Routledge, 1995.

McCook, Henry C. *The Martial Graves of Our Fallen Heroes in Santiago de Cuba*. Philadelphia: George W. Jacobs, 1899.

McNeil, John R. *Mosquito Empires: Ecology and War in the Greater Caribbean, 1620–1914*. New York: Cambridge University Press, 2010.

Meigs, Mark. *Optimism at Armageddon: Voices of American Participants in the First World War*. New York: New York University Press, 1997.

Melillo, Edward. "The First Green Revolution: Debt Peonage and the Making of Nitrogen Fertilizer Trade." *American Historical Review* 117 (October 2012): 1028–60.

Miller, Stuart Creighton. *"Benevolent Assimilation": The American Conquest of the Philippines, 1899–1903*. New Haven CT: Yale University Press, 1984.

Morrow, John H., Jr. "Knights of the Sky: The Rise of Military Aviation." In *Authority, Identity, and the Social History of the Great War*, edited by Frans Coetzee and Marilyn Shevin-Coetzee, 305–23. Providence RI: Berghahn Books, 1995.

Mosse, George L. *Fallen Soldiers: Reshaping the Memory of the World Wars*. New York: Oxford University Press, 1991.

Murphy, Gretchen. *Hemispheric Imaginings: The Monroe Doctrine and Narratives of U.S. Empire*. Durham NC: Duke University Press, 2005.

Nass, Michael. "History's Remains: Of Memory, Mourning, and the Event." *Research in Phenomenology* 33 (2003): 75–96.

Nora, Pierre, ed. *Realms of Memory: Rethinking the French Past*. 3 vols. Ithaca NY: Columbia University Press, 1996.

Nudelman, Franny. *John Brown's Body: Slavery, Violence, and the Culture of War*. Chapel Hill: University of North Carolina Press, 2003.

Oates, Stephen B. *A Woman of Valor: Clara Barton and the Civil War*. New York: Free Press, 1994.

Pérez, Louis A. *Cuba under the Platt Amendment, 1902–1934*. Pittsburgh: University of Pittsburgh Press, 1986.

——— . "Incurring a Debt of Gratitude: 1898 and the Moral Sources of United States Hegemony in Cuba," *American Historical Review* 104 (April 1999): 356–98.

——— . "The Meaning of the Maine: Causation and the Historiography of the Spanish American War." *Pacific Historical Review* 58 (3): 293–322.

Piehler, G. Kurt. *Remembering War the American Way*. Washington DC: Smithsonian, 2004.

——— . "The War Dead and the Gold Star: American Commemoration of the First World War." In *Commemorations: The Politics of National Identity*, edited by John R. Gillis. Princeton NJ: Princeton University Press, 1994.

Poole, Robert M. *On Hallowed Ground: The Story of Arlington National Cemetery*. New York: Walker, 2009.

Poovey, Mary. *Making a Social Body: British Cultural Formation, 1830–1864*. Chicago: University of Chicago Press, 1995.

Prather, H. Leon. "The Red Shirt Movement in North Carolina, 1898–1900." *Journal of Negro History* 62, no. 2 (1977): 174–84.

Pratt, Adam. "'A Curious Compound of the Hero and the Dandy': George Armstrong Custer, the Cavalier Image, and White Masculinity in the Postwar South." In *Black and White Masculinity in the American South, 1800–2000*, edited by Lydia Plath and Sergio Lussana. Newcastle, UK: Cambridge Scholars, 2009.

Putney, Clifford. *Muscular Christianity: Manhood and Sports in Protestant America, 1880–1920*. Cambridge: Harvard University Press, 2003.

Ratledge, Curt. "The Confederate Cemetery at Marietta Powder Springs Road Marietta, Georgia." City of Marietta, Georgia, 1995.

Rauch, John H. *Intramural Interments in Populous Cities, and Their Influence upon Health and Epidemics*. Chicago: Tribune, 1866.

——— . *Public Parks: Their Effects upon the Moral, Physical, and Sanitary Condition of the Inhabitants of Large Cities: With Special Reference to the City of Chicago*. Chicago: S. C. Griggs, 1869.

Renan, Ernest. "What Is a Nation?" In *Becoming National: A Reader*, edited by Geoff Eley and Ronald Grigor Suny, 41–55. New York: Oxford University Press, 1996.

Report on the Re-Burial of the Confederate Dead in Arlington Cemetery. Washington DC: Judd and Detweiler, Printers, 1901.

Richardson, Ruth. *Death, Dissection, and the Destitute*. Chicago: University of Chicago Press, 2000.

Rogoff, Leonard. "A Tale of Two Cities: Race, Riots, and Religion in New Bern and Wilmington, North Carolina, 1898." *Southern Jewish History* 14 (2011): 37–75.

Rorabaugh, W. J. *Alcoholic Republic: An American Tradition*. New York: Oxford University Press, 1981.

Rosenfeld, Gavriel D. "A Looming Crash or a Soft Landing? Forecasting the Future of the Memory 'Industry.'" *Journal of Modern History* 81 (March 2009): 122–58.

Rotundo, E. Anthony. *American Manhood: Transformations in Masculinity from the Revolution to the Modern Era*. New York: Basic Books, 1994.

Said, Edward. *Orientalism*. New York: Vintage Books, 1979.

———. *Reflections on Exile and Other Essays*. Cambridge: Harvard University Press, 2002.

Sanders, Charles W., Jr. *While in the Hands of the Enemy: Military Prisons of the Civil War*. Baton Rouge: Louisiana State University Press, 2005.

Sappol, Michael. *A Traffic of Dead Bodies: Anatomy and Embodied Social Identity in Nineteenth-Century America*. Princeton: Princeton University Press, 2002.

Savage, Kirk. *Standing Soldiers, Kneeling Slaves: Race, War, and Monument in Nineteenth-Century America*. Princeton: Princeton University Press, 1997.

Schafer, R. Murray. "The Soundscape." In *The Sound Studies Reader*, edited by Jonathan Sterne, 95–103. New York: Routledge, 2012.

Schmidt, Leigh Eric. *Hearing Things: Religion, Illusion, and the American Enlightenment*. Cambridge: Harvard University Press, 2002.

Schuyler, David. *The New Urban Landscape: The Redefinition of City Form in Nineteenth-Century America*. Baltimore: John Hopkins University Press, 1986.

Schwartz, Barry. "Collective Memory: How Abraham Lincoln Became a Symbol of Racial Equality." *Sociological Quarterly* 38 (1998): 469–96.

Scott, Rebecca J. "Race, Labor, and Citizenship in Cuba: A View from the Sugar District of Cienfuegos, 1886–1909." *Hispanic American Historical Review* 78 (November 1998): 687–728.

Selected Addresses and Public Papers of Woodrow Wilson. Edited by Albert Bushnell Hart. New York: Modern Library, 1918.

Selzer, Linda. "Historicizing Lincoln: Garry Wills and the Canonization of the 'Gettysburg Address." *Rhetoric Review* 16 (Autumn 1997): 128.

Shantz, Mark S. *Awaiting the Heavenly Country: The Civil War and America's Culture of Death*. Ithaca NY: Cornell University Press, 2008.

Silber, Nina. *The Romance of Reunion: Northerners in the South, 1865–1900*. Chapel Hill: University of North Carolina Press, 1997.

Silbey, David J. *A War of Frontier and Empire: The Philippine-American War, 1899–1902*. New York: Hill and Wang, 2008.

Singal, Daniel Joseph. *The War Within: From Victorian to Modernist Thought in the South, 1919–1945*. Chapel Hill: University of North Carolina Press, 1982.

Sloane, David. *The Last Great Necessity: Cemeteries in American History*. Baltimore: Johns Hopkins University Press, 1995.

Smith, Mark M. "The Political Economy of Sugar Production and the Environment of Eastern Cuba, 1898–1923." *Environmental History Review* 19 (Winter 1995): 31–48.

———. "Producing Sense, Consuming Sense, Making Sense: Perils and Prospects for Sensory History." *Journal of Social History* 40 (Summer 2007): 841–58.

Speeches and Address of William McKinley. New York: Doubleday, 1900.

Spivak, Gayatri Chakravorty. "Can the Subaltern Speak?" In *Marxism and the Interpretation of Culture*, edited by Cary Nelson and Lawrence Grossburg. Urbana: University of Illinois Press, 1988.

Stanyek, Jason, and Benjamin Piekut. "Deadness: Technologies of the Intermundane." In *The Sound Studies Reader*, edited by Jonathan Sterne. New York: Routledge, 2012.

Stephens, Alexander. *Recollections of Alexander H. Stephens*. Edited by Myrta Lockett Avary. Baton Rouge: Louisiana State University Press, 1998.

Sterne, Jonathan. *The Audible Past: Cultural Origins of Sound Reproduction*. Durham NC: Duke University Press, 2003.

Stiles, Robert. *Address at the Dedication of the Monument to the Confederate Dead*. Richmond VA: Taylor and Taylor Printers, 1893.

Stoler, Ann. "Colonial Archives and the Arts of Governance." *Archival Science* 2 (2002): 87–109.

———. *Race and the Education of Desire: Foucault's History of Sexuality and the Colonial Order of Things*. Durham NC: Duke University Press, 1995.

———. "Tense and Tender Ties: The Politics of Comparison in North American History and (Post) Colonial Studies." *Journal of American History* 88, no. 3 (December 2001): 829–65.

Taft, William Howard. *The Duty of Americans in the Philippines*. Washington DC: Government Printing Office, 1903.

Tamm, Marek. "History as Cultural Memory: Mnemohistory and the Construction of the Estonian Nation." *Journal of Baltic Studies* 39 (December 2008): 499–516.

Thelen, David. "Memory and American History." *Journal of American History* 75 (March 1989): 1117–29.

Thompson, Emily. "Sound, Modernity, and History." In *The Sound Studies Reader*, edited by Jonathan Sterne. New York: Routledge, 2012.

Thoreau, Henry David. *A Week on the Concord and Merrimack Rivers*. 1849. New York: Book of the Month Club, 1996.
Tocqueville, Alexis de. *Democracy in America*. In *The Collective Memory Reader*, edited by Jeffrey K. Olick, Vered Vinitzky-Seroussi, and Daniel Levy. New York: Oxford University Press, 2011.
Todorova, Maria. "The Mausoleum of Georgi Dimitrov as lieu de mémoire." *Journal of Modern History* 78 (June 2006): 377–411.
Tooze, Adam. *The Deluge: The Great War, America, and the Remaking of the Global Order, 1916–1931*. New York: Penguin, 2015.
Trostel, Scott D. *The Lincoln Funeral Train: The Final Journey and National Funeral for Abraham Lincoln*. Fletcher OH: Cam-Tech, 2002.
Trout, Steven. *On the Battlefield of Memory: The First World War and American Remembrance, 1919–1941*. Tuscaloosa: University of Alabama Press, 2010.
Twain, Mark. "To the Person Sitting in Darkness." In *Vestiges of War: The Philippine-American War and the Aftermath of an Imperial Dream, 1899–1999*, edited by Angel Velasco Shaw and Luis H. Francia, 62–68. New York: New York University Press, 2002.
———. "The United States of Lyncherdom," *Ozarks Afro-American History Museum Online*, https://oaahm.omeka.net/items/show/8, accessed March 23, 2017.
U.S. War Department. *Annual Report of the Secretary of War*. Washington DC: Government Printing Office, 1888.
———. *Annual Reports of the War Department for the Fiscal Year Ended June 30, 1902*. Washington DC: Government Printing Office, 1902.
Van der Kloot, William. "Lawrence Bragg's Role in the Development of Sound-Ranging in World War I." *Notes and Records of the Royal Society of London* 59, no. 3 (September 2005): 273–84.
Van Dyke, Henry. *The American Birthright and the Philippine Pottage*. New York: Charles Scribner's Sons, 1898.
Verdery, Katherine. *The Political Lives of Dead Bodies*. Ithaca NY: Cornell University Press, 2000.
Warren, W. Lloyd. "The Living and the Dead: A Study of the Symbolic Life of Americans." In *The Collective Memory Reader*, edited by Jeffrey K. Olick, Vered Vinitzky-Seroussi, and Daniel Levy. New York: Oxford University Press, 2011.
Washington, Booker T. *An Address by Booker T. Washington . . . at the Thanksgiving Peace Jubilee Exercises*. Chicago: October 16, 1898.
———. *The Story of My Life and Work*. Cincinnati: W. H. Ferguson, 1900.
Welch, James. *Killing Custer: The Battle of Little Bighorn and the Fate of the Plains Indians*. New York: Penguin, 1995.
Wells, Ida B. *Lynch Law in Georgia*. Chicago: Circulated by Chicago Colored Citizens, 1899.

Widder, Keith. "The Convergence of Native Religion, Roman Catholicism, and Evangelical Protestantism at Mackinaw Mission, 1823–1837." *Journal of Presbyterian History* 77 (Fall 1999): 167–80.
Wiebe, Robert. *The Search for Order, 1877–1920*. New York: Hill and Wang, 1966.
Williams, William Appleman. *The Tragedy of American Diplomacy*. New York: W. W. Norton, 1972.
Wills, Garry. *Lincoln at Gettysburg: The Words That Remade America*. New York: Simon and Schuster, 1993.
Wilmington Race Riot Commission. "Final Report," May 31, 2006, Office of Archives and History North Carolina Department of Cultural Resources. http://www.history.ncdcr.gov/1898-wrrc/report/report.htm, accessed March 26, 2017.
Wilson, Woodrow. "Address at Gettysburg." In *Woodrow Wilson: Essential Writings and Speeches of the Scholar-President*, edited by Mario R. Di Nuzio, 370–72. New York: New York University Press, 2006.
Winter, Jay. *Remembering War: The Great War between Memory and History in the Twentieth Century*. New Haven CT: Yale University Press, 2006.
———. *Sites of Memory, Sites of Mourning: The Great War in European Cultural History*. New York: Cambridge University Press, 1998.
Wood, Kirsten E. "'Join with Heart and Soul and Voice': Music, Harmony, and Politics in the Early American Republic." *American Historical Review* 119 (October 2014): 1083–1116.
Zanetti, Oscar, and Franklin Knight. *Sugar and Railroads: A Cuban History, 1837–1959*. Chapel Hill: University of North Carolina Press, 1998.
Zerubavel, Eviator. *Time Maps: Collective Memory and the Social Shape of the Past*. Chicago: University of Chicago Press, 2004.

INDEX

Illustrations are indicated by F with a numeral

Abanador, Valeriano, 159
ABMC. *See* American Battle Monuments Commission (ABMC)
Adams, Samuel, 154
AEF (American Expeditionary Force), 248
Afghanistan War, 311–12
African Americans: enfranchisement of, 39; Freedman's Village and, 55–58, 59, 102; memory and, 37–38, 106; military service of, 91, 92; recovery and burial of, 55, 260; segregation and, 58, 64, 70, 90, 238, 240; violence against, 39, 69, 113–14, 174–75
African Methodist Episcopal Church, 39
Agoncillo, Felipe, 153–54
Aguinaldo, Emilio, 115, 151–52, 154, 156, 163
Alaska, 24, 64, 70–71, 72, 74
Aleutian Islands, 24
Alien Act, 248
Allard, Clayton, 171
Allison, Rose, 234, 239
All Saints Day, F1, 161–62
alternative memory networks, 106

American Battle Monuments Commission (ABMC), 302, 304, 305–6, 307, 308
American Expeditionary Force (AEF), 248
American Foreign Policy and Its Thinkers (Anderson), 24
Americanism, immigration and, 70
American Marine Engineer (magazine), 130
American Telephone & Telegraph. *See* AT&T (American Telephone & Telegraph)
amnesia, 3, 5, 7, 13, 33; collective, 87
Anderson, Benedict, 287, 352n22
Anderson, Perry, 24
Anti-Imperialist Leagues, 153
anti-imperialists, 152, 154, 156
Arapaho Indians, 74, 75
Arbuckle, John, 128–29
Arbuckle Company, 125
Arlington National Cemetery: Confederates and, 101–2, 103, 104; controversy of, 136–37, 138, 283–85; overview of, 52–60; symbolism of, 289. *See also* Tomb of the Unknown Soldier

Armani, Litto, 171
Arms Limitation Conference, 276, 294
Armstrong, Evelyn, 234, 239
Army Corp of Engineers, 123, 125, 130, 144
Articles of Confederation, 5
Asia, casualties within, 310
assimilation, 192, 210–11
Assmann, Jan: quote of, 4–5, 7, 8, 116, 120, 121–22, 213, 217, 279, 301, 334n25; viewpoint of, 7, 13–14, 15, 16, 19–20, 184, 278–79
Atlanta GA, 42, 43, 89
Atlanta Peace Jubilee, 92, 97, 99–100
AT&T (American Telephone & Telegraph), 275, 288–89
Auchenbach, Isaac, 134
aural past, 352n22
Axton, John T., 294

Baine, Ione, 234, 236, 237, 239, 240
Baird, Charles, Jr., 201
Baker, Newton, 261–62, 284
Balingiga, Philippines, 159, 160
Barry, Edward Buttevant, 202
Barthes, Roland, 298
Barton, Clara, 37
Bass, John, 115, 116, 161–62
Batchelder, N. H., 73
Batchelder, Richard Napoleon, 58
Batista, Fulgencio, 302, 305, 306
Battle of Gettysburg, 1–2, 19–20, 22, 38, 62, 65–66, 76, 97–98, 141, 159, 185–86, 269, 276
Battle of Kennesaw Mountain, 46, 50
Bay of Pigs invasion, 308
Beaupré, Arthur M., 143
benevolent assimilation, 152, 160, 163
Benjamin, Walter, 213, 214–15
Berry, James, 105

Bicket, Thomas W., 223
biographical memories, 218–19, 240
biological memories, 14
Bisher, Catherine W., 222
Bixby, William H., 126, 129, 130, 138, 140
Black, Bryan C., 313
Black, William M., 127, 133, 137–38, 144
Black Hills SD, 75
Blair, William A., 9, 40, 65, 81, 101
Blassie, Michael, 310–11
Blight, David, 85
Bluethenthal, Arthur: background of, 189, 190–91, 195–96, 197, 198–200; beliefs of, 192–93, 201–2, 204–5, 208–9; commemoration of, 210; Orientalism of, 197–98, 200, 204–5, 208; photo of, F9, F10, F11, F12; quote of, 194, 195–96, 198, 203–4, 207–8; service of, 193–94, 195–97, 204, 206; writings of, 346–47n45
Bluethenthal, Johanna, 193
Bluethenthal, Leopold, 190–91, 193, 210
Bodnar, Jon, 137
Bookmiller, Edwin, 159–60, 171
Bosley, William, 46
Boxer Rebellion, 176
brain, 6, 34, 120–21, 290
Brewster, Irene, 234, 235, 236, 239, 240
Briand, Pierre Henri, 297
Bring Home the Soldier Dead movement, 267, 270
Bryan, William Jennings, 94, 152, 156
Buhrer, John D., 171
Bullock, Cleopatra, 241–42
Bullock, Rufus, 89
Bullock, Thomas J., F18, 241–42, 243
Burbank, Jane, 25, 117, 188, 210, 211
Burying the Dead but Not the Past (Janney), 102

Bush, George W., 312
Butler, Benjamin Franklin, 44

Caloocan, Philippines, 115–16
Campbell, J. B., 72
canonization, 184–85
capitalism, 11, 70
Capozzola, Christopher, 26, 246
Caribbean, 150
Carnegie, Andrew, 63
Carpenter, Alfred P., 1–2
Carter, Albin E., 169
Carter, Philip, 315
Castro, Fidel, 304, 306, 308, 309
Cavite, Philippines, 165–66
cemeteries: building of, 10; events at, 10, 65; France, F20, F23, F25; politics and, 11, 40, 65; post, 170–71; reduction of, 250. *See also specific cemeteries*
Central America, U.S. forces within, 183
Centralia WA, 281
Chadwick, John White, 154, 155
Chafee, Adna, 158–59
Chamberlin, Isaac and Carrie, 21–22
Chance, Frank, 198
chaplains, work of, F19, 145, 251–52
Charleston SC, 65–66
Chase, Salmon P., 63
Cheyenne Indians, 74, 75, 79
Chicago Peace Jubilee, 91
Chidwick, John P., 145
China, 71, 150, 151, 176, 276
cholera, 170–71
chords of memory, 279–80, 286–87, 290, 298, 312
Christianity, 8, 11–12, 70
Cienfuegos, Camilo, 306
Cities of the Dead, 65
citizenship, 15–16, 25, 26, 39, 120

Civil Rights Act, 90
civil rights movement, 106
Civil War: casualties of, 52, 88, 163, 164, 215, 283, 284, 287–88; comparisons to, 95–96, 98, 153, 173, 186, 255–56; grief rituals of, 12, 246, 271, 272; legacy of, 68, 173; memory and, 14, 17–18, 32, 53, 63, 65, 66, 80, 81, 82, 83, 85, 87, 106–7, 117, 185, 218, 231, 243; migration and, 23; reunification, 280
Cleland, George W., 47
Clemenceau, Georges, 245
cofferdam, F5, F6, F7, 125, 127, 128–29, 130, 132
Cole, Henry Greene, 42, 43, 44–50, 52, 336n8, 336n10
Cole, Georgia Caroline (Fletcher), 335n7
Colfax LA, 69
collective memory, 3, 6, 13–14, 16, 333n7
colonialism, 9–10
Colombia, 183
Columbia, Department of, 72
Comanche Indians, 75
Comet Film Co., 141
Committee of Public Information, 248
communication, 184–85, 213–14
communicative memory, 7–8, 13, 14, 217, 231–32, 243
Confederate Memorial Association, 284
Confederate Memorial Day, 65–66, 69
Confederates: Arlington National Cemetery and, 101–2, 103, 104; customs of, 65; exclusion of, 62, 63; Hollywood Cemetery and, 103; memory and, 37–38, 69–70, 96, 101–2; reburial of, 65–66; women's memorial associations and, 102–3
Connor, Robert D. W., 223
Connor, William Durward, 282

contrapresent functions, 8
Coolidge, Calvin, 352n37
cooling memory, 4, 79, 81, 82, 107
Cooper, Frederick, 25, 117, 188, 210, 211
Corcos, Joseph, 295
core memory, 120–21
Council of Defense, 224, 347–48n13
Crazy Horse, 74, 75
Creel, George, 248
Croggon, F. S., 163, 164, 170–72, 251
Cuba: conditions within, 309; conflict within, 94, 97, 119–20, 123, 302, 304; Cuban-American Treaty and, 123; elections within, 123, 124; expansion in, 151; Havana Harbor, F4, F5, F6, F7, F8, 123, 132, 306–7; leadership of, 123, 124; memorial sites within, 308; Partido Independiente de Color and, 124; recovery of dead from, 121–22; Santiago Surrender Tree, F28, 302, 303–4, 305–8; United States and, 123–25, 133, 139, 146–47, 183; USS *Maine* casualties and, 143–44; veterans of, 303
Cuban-American Friendship Tree, F28, 302, 303–4, 305–8
cult of the fallen, 16, 38
cultural memory: archivists and, 231; aural retrieval of, 280, 352n22; biographical memory and, 218–19; citizenship and, 120; Civil War and, 87; communication of, 280; cult of the fallen and, 16; domestic politics and, 17; empire and, 82; grief and, 26; historiography of, 15; history of, 15; information age and, 217–18; integration and, 188–89; Lost Cause movement and, 68; modern, 17; moral contradictions and, 316–17;

nationalism and, 187–88; network of, 40; Northerners and, 63, 69; Philippines and, 117; practice of, 13–15; reconciliation and, 100; retrieval system of, 20, 118, 120–21; segregation and, 301; slavery and, 21; Southerners and, 65–66, 222–23; storage of, 4; storage systems and, 65; technology and, 316–17; time maps and, 67; United States and, 5; USS *Maine* and, 123, 133–34, 135–36, 146; visual sense and, 352n22; Wilmington NC and, 116–17; women and, 21
Custer, Elizabeth "Libbie," 76–77, 80, 88
Custer, George Armstrong, 74, 75–80
Custis, G. W. P., 53

Daily Record (newspaper), 111, 112
Damon, Theron J., 271
Daniel, John W., 57
Daniels, Josephus, 223
Davis, Jefferson, 33, 35
Davis, Jefferson Columbus, 71
dead: identification of, F19, F20, F21, F22, 163–65, 166–67, 169, 171, 251–52, 283; processing of, 177; recovery of, 170, 249–51, 259, 268, 270–71; transporting, 167, 176, 177, 178, 261, 262–63, 264, 265–66
death industry, 12, 266, 288
Declaration of Independence, 149
Declaration of White Independence, 192
Decoration Day, 53, 65, 337n6
Deegan, William F., 270
democratic capitalism, 247
Department of the Northwest, 74
Dewey, George, 115
diseased bodies, 58–59, 170–71, 176–77, 178, 260

distended society, 3, 11
DNA science, 316
Dolar, Mladen, 298
dollar diplomacy, 150, 183, 277
domesticity, 234–35
Dominican Republic, 183
Donald, Merlin, 34
Douglass, Frederick, 86, 105, 106
Downey, Stephen Wheeler, 31–33, 34–35, 38
Du Bois, W. E. B., 106
Dunbar, Paul Laurence, 106
Dunlap, Myron E., 88

Eckstrom, J. S., 165
Edelman, Murray, 353n47
education, role of, 100
Eisenhower, Dwight D., 306–7
El Cano (ship), 167, 168
Elliott, Charles, 263–64
Elliott, William, 104
Ellis, William, 128
emancipation: geopolitics and, 59; memory of, 19, 56–57, 69, 86, 87, 103, 105–6, 277; national cemeteries and, 62; new era of, 14
Emancipation Proclamation, 54
Emerson, Ralph Waldo, 8
empire, 25, 64–65, 81–82, 83, 87–88, 117, 154
Empires in World History (Burbank and Cooper), 117
Enforcement Act of 1871, 90
Espionage Act, 248
Europe, 9, 247, 258, 259, 269, 272, 273. See also specific countries
Evers, Johnny, 198
exile, 187, 209
external memory storage, 34
Ezekiel, Moses, 102, 284

Faber, Eberhard, 135
fatalism, 207–8
Faust, Drew Gilpin, 246
Fenton, Rebecca L., 112
Field, Cyrus, 71
Finley, James B., 9
Fish, Daniel, 81, 82
Fish, Hamilton, Jr., 282
Fishblate, Solomon, 190, 192
Fletcher, Dix, 44
Fletcher, Louisa, 44–45
Fletcher family, 42
Focht, Benjamin K., 135
Folsom, C. W., 48–50
Foraker, Joseph, 104
Foraker Bill, 104
Forsyth, John, 78
Fort Laramie, 75
Fort Myers, 53
Fort Whipple, 53
Fourteen Points plan, 245, 257, 272
Fourteenth Amendment, 39, 50
Fourth Artillery, 71
Fourth of July, 14
France: American military cemetery in, F20, F23; casualties of, 203, 215; commemoration and, 203; economy of, 247–48; Graves Registration Services and, 259–60, 261–62; Poilu Inconnu in, 282–83, 296; reconstruction of, 260; women of, 198–99
Fredere, Clara, 234, 239
Freedman's Village, 55–58, 59, 102
freedmen, 55, 337n6
Freedmen's Bureau, 39, 55
Freemont, Commandant Captain, 165, 166
Freud, Sigmund, 248–49
Full Dinner Pail, 151
Funck, Julius, 141–42

funeral industry, 12, 266, 288
Fusionists, 112

Galbraith, F. W., Jr., 270
GAR. *See* Grand Army of the Republic (GAR)
Gates, Mary, 271
Geertz, Clifford, 1
gender, reunion movement and, 87–88
George, David Lloyd, 245, 273
Georgia, 50, 90, 154–55
Georgia Memorial Association, 50
Germany, 215, 265–66
Gettysburg, 19–20, 38
Gettysburg Address, 17–18, 20, 38
Gilded Age, 70
Girardeau, John Lafayette, 66, 67, 68–69, 81, 90, 99–100, 103
Glover, Jane Porter, 50
Goldstein, Eric L., 190, 191–92
Gómez, José Miguel, 124, 126, 133, 143, 144
Good Death, 11–12, 18, 37, 96
Gordon, John B., 89, 90, 101–2, 104, 173
Gould, Jay, 63, 77
Gradel, Harry, 140
Grady, Henry, 89
Graham, Lindsey, 316
Grand Army of the Republic (GAR), 32, 40, 87
Grant, Ulysses S., 175
Graves Registration Service (GRS): challenges of, 259–60; chaplains of, F19; criticism of, 270; establishment of, 249; tintypes of, F20, F21; viewpoint of, 283; work of, 2, 250–53, 264, 265–66; workplace of, F22, F23
Great Britain, 188, 215, 247–48, 276–77, 282, 296, 297
Great Railroad Strike, 70, 77–78

Great War, 3, 187, 215, 217–20, 277, 278
Great White Fleet, 150, 183
Green, Mary Jan, 50
Greene, Elias M., 54–55
grief: cultural memory and, 13, 15, 26, 33, 278, 291; death industry and, 268; rituals of, 3, 12, 266; social networks of, 41, 287, 288, 289
Grimes, J. Bryan, 223
Gros, Edmund, 227–28
group memory, 121
Guam, 151
Guevara, Ernest "Che," 306, 308
gunboat diplomacy, 150, 183

Hahn, Joseph, 192
Hahn, Steven, 18–19, 23, 39, 40, 66–67
Halbwachs, Maurice, 6, 245
Hale, Sarah Josepha, 232
Hanes, Fred M., 233
Hanna, Mark, 151
Hanson, Neil, 249–50
Harding, Warren G.: cemetery plans and, 250; election of, 277; leadership of, 277, 302; photo of, F26; speech of, 275–76, 279, 286–87, 289, 291, 292, 295–96, 297–300
Harper, William R., 91
Harvey, John, 132
Havana Harbor, F4, F5, F6, F7, F8, 123, 132, 306–7
Hawaii, 151
Hawley, Joseph, 101–2
Henry, M. J., 261
Herbert, Hilary A., 103–4
Hewlingo, H. A., 267–68
Hill, Daniel Harvey, Jr., 223
historiography, 15
Hogar Espanol, El (magazine), 139

Hollywood Cemetery, 103
Holmes, A. H., 57
Holton, Adaliane, 240, 241
Homestead Act, 23
Honduras, 183
Hose, Sam, 154–55
Hospital No. 65, F15, F16, F17, 231–39
House, Robert Burton, 189, 209, 224–26, 229, 230
Houston, David, 223
Howell, Clark, 98
Hughes, Charles, 276
Hurbache, France, F23
hypolepsis, 14, 16, 17–18

Ide, Henry Clay, 139
Imbrie, Robert Whitney, 194–95, 201, 204, 206
immigrants, immigration, 24, 66, 70, 146, 190–91, 193–94, 217, 231, 247, 248, 281, 293, 300
imperialism: concerns of, 80, 81; effects of, 302, 309–10; experimentation with, 146; foreign *versus* domestic, 101; geopolitics and, 59; justification of, 119; power of, 117; vision of, 83; war of, 159
imperialists, beliefs of, 155–56
imperial memory, 154, 211, 301–2
imperial power, 117
indigenous people, 4, 64, 75
Industrial Revolution, 3
industry, access to, 64
information age, 217–18
Inglis, K. S., 354n63
Inter-Ocean (newspaper), 131
Iraq War, 311–12
isolation, 3
Italy, 247–48

Jackson, Andrew, 8, 9
Jacobi, Marcus, 193
Jacobi, Nathaniel, 190, 192
Jacobs, David, 114
Jacobs, Harriet, 5–6, 7
Jacoby, Joseph, 126–27, 137
Janney, Caroline, 102
Japan, 276–77, 297
Jefferson, Thomas, 8
Jenkins, Friend W., 141
Jewish people, 190–92
Jim Crow laws, 87, 106, 114–15, 154
Johnson, Andrew, 45, 46–48
Johnson, James Weldon, 293
Johnson, Jeremiah W., 313
Johnson, La David, 313
Johnson, Myeshia, 313–14
Jones, Harry, 93

Kammen, Michael, 243
Kandel, Eric R., 120
Kaplan, Amy, 232, 235
Katipunan Society, 163
Keatley, John H., 72, 73
Kelly, John F., 314–15
Kennedy, John F., 307
Kennesaw Mountain, 50
Kent, Laurence, 2
Kerhoun, France, F17
Keyes, Sarah, 288
Kilpatrick (transport ship), 178
King, Mabel, 234, 239
Kinney, Samuel H., 61–62, 71–72
kinship simulation, 291–92, 310, 311
Kiowa Indians, 75
Kirk, J. Allen, 114
Klay, Phil, 315
Klein, John Marshall, 123, 139, 143
Koselleck, Reinhart, 278

Kramer, Paul A., 149, 158, 174
Ku Klux Klan (KKK), 39, 89

Lackawanna Steel Co., 125
La Coubre (ship), 306–7
Ladies' Aid Society, 46
Ladies' Memorial Association, 65–66, 103
Ladies' Southern Relief Society, 103
Lafayette Escadrille, 227–28
LaFeber, Walter, 71
La Liga Filipina, 163
Lansing, Robert, 261–62
Lavelle, Michael J., 295
Lay, Julio de, 305–6, 307–8
League of Nations, 245, 258, 272, 277, 281
Lears, Jackson, 16, 89, 246
Lee, George Washington Custis, 53, 54, 57
Lee, Robert E., 53
Lee, Stephen D., 104
Life (magazine), 283
Lin, Mia, 310
Lincoln, Abraham: administration, vision of, 63–64; assassination of, 33, 35; Emancipation Proclamation, 19; first inaugural address of, 13; Gettysburg Address and, 17–19; Good Death and, 18, 37; The Play of Destiny (play) and, 31–33; quote of, 13
Lincoln's promise: Confederate dead and, 189; contradictions to, 222, 247, 272, 312, 313, 316–17; international interpretation of, 175, 179, 256; limitations of, 70, 74, 80; overview of, 19–20; traditions of, 25, 38, 83, 246, 266; variations of, 37, 54, 55, 65, 69, 75, 94–95, 101, 117, 121, 185–86, 257, 271
literacy, memory and, 333n10
Little Bighorn, 76, 80
Little Round Top, 1

Liuzzo, Viola, 310
Lleó, Manuel Urrutia, 306, 308
Long, John Davis, 99
Long, J. Wesley, 233
Long-Term Potentiation (LTP), 333n8
Lost Cause movement, 34, 63, 65, 68, 102–3
Ludwig, William, 135
lynching, 154–55, 174–75

MacArthur, Arthur, 158
Maceo, Antonio, 304
Maderia (transport ship), 201, 202
Madison Square Garden, 291
Magnolia Cemetery, 65–66
Magoon, Charles Edward, 124
Maines, George, 136
Malcolm X, 310
Manela, Erez, 245–46, 256
Manila, Philippines, F1, 116, 158, 160–62
Manley, Alexander, 111, 112
Manning, William T., 295
March, Peyton C., 282
Marietta GA, 42, 43–44, 45–46
Marietta Confederate Cemetery, 50, 51
Marietta National Cemetery, 41–43, 44–50, 52
Martí, José, 304
Martinsburg WV, 77
materialism, 3
Maybury, William, 138–39
Maza, Nerma del, 306
McKinley, William: Atlanta Peace Jubilee and, 92; background of, 94; benevolent assimilation and, 152; Booker T. Washington and, 92, 93–94; Chicago Peace Jubilee and, 91; compromise of, 94–95, 101–2; election of, 151, 152, 157–58; influence of, 173; leadership

of, 93, 94, 104–5, 122, 149, 156, 157–58, 183; promise of, 96; quote of, 85, 94, 95, 97, 98, 100; speech of, 95, 96, 97; time map of, 97–98, 99; Tuskegee Institute and, 100–101
McMahon, Theodore, 129
Meigs, Mark, 197, 232, 272
Meigs, Montgomery, 53
Memorial Burying Ground, 45–46
Memorial Committee, 47
Memorial Day, 14, 65
memory: alternative networks of, 106; atomization of, 272; biographical, 218–19, 240; biological, 14; boom, 105; canonical obligations of, 25; chords of, 279–80, 286–87, 290, 298, 312; collective, 3, 6, 13–14, 16; communication and, 184–85; communicative, 7–8, 13, 14, 215, 217, 231–32, 243; conflict of, 278; construction of, 6; cooling, 4, 79, 81, 82, 107; core, 120–21; countercultural, 69; equidistant, 16; group, 121; heating, 8, 67; hypolepsis and, 14, 17–18; imperial, 154, 211, 301–2; industry of, 32, 37; landscape, 116; literacy and, 333n10; living, 184; materialism and, 3; militarist regeneration of, 32; modernity and, 3; moralistic, 8; mythologizing and, 34; network of, 33; official, 137; power and, 117; prospective, 15; regulation of, 14; religious, 8; republican, 13, 301–2; retrieval process of, 120–21; retrospective, 15; shared experiences and, 7, 56; site of, 56, 184; slavery and, 6–7; social experience and, 6; spatialization and, 116; stimulation of, 65; storage of, 19–20, 34; storytellers and, 213; techniques of, 14, 19–20; technology and, 300, 316–17; time map and, 67, 69, 97–98, 99–100; vernacular, 137; war and, 214. *See also* cultural memory
meningitis, 202–3
mental maps, 67
Merritt, Darwin, 134
Merritt, Wesley, 158
migration, 23, 63
Military Reconstruction Act, 39
Miller, Stuart Creighton, 149
Miller, William, 45
mining industry, 75
Minnesota, 74
mnemohistory, 334n25
mnemotechnologies, 14
modernity, 3
Monastir, Serbia, F12, 204
monopolies, actions of, 77
Monroe Doctrine, 150, 183
Montgomery, S., 46
Moody, Paul D., 270–71
Moore, James, 55
Moranville, France, F25
Morgan, J. Pierpont, 63
Morning Star (newspaper), 112
Morrill Act, 39
Mosse, George, 16, 38, 278
Moyer, Ann, 46
Munroe, John, 206–7
Murphy, Gretchen, 24

Naas, Michael, 310
name pegs, 251–52
national cemeteries, 37, 38, 40–41, 59–60, 62. *See also specific cemeteries*
nationalism, 187–88
National War Labor Board, 248
nation-state, 117

Native Americans, 9–10, 23, 74–75, 79, 83
nature, empire and, 25
Naval Cemetery, 165–66
Naval Limitation Pact, 300
Nelson, Henry, 86
neurons, 6, 34, 120
New Freedom, 184
New Southerners, 82, 87, 103
New York Times (newspaper), 284–85, 286, 294–95
Nicaragua, 183
Niger, 313, 316
1919 (Passos), 197
Nora, Pierre, 56, 61, 184
North, Thomas, 307
North Carolina: archives, 217–18, 220–21, 240; communicative memory and, 217; Fusionists within, 112; industry in, 216–17; nurses in, F15, F16, 231–33; officers from, F21; politics of, 217, 223–24; Wilmington Race Riot Commission, 339n2; Wilmington race riots, 92–93; World War I collection in, 218–20, 224–26, 231, 242–44, 347n9
North Carolina Historical Commission, 223, 224–25
Northerners, 64–65, 69, 85–86, 94
nurses, F15, F16, 231–33, 234–37, 238–40

Oates, William C., 104–5
Office of Commissioner for Marking Graves of Confederate Dead, 104
official memory, 137
O'Hara, Barrett, 303
Ojeda, Isidoro, 139–40
"On Murder, Mourning, and Melancholia" (Freud), 248–49
Open Door Policy, 276
oral tradition, 213

Order Number 100, 158–59
Organic Act, 72
Orientalism, 161–62, 197–98, 200, 201, 204–5, 208, 346–47n45
Oriente Province, 304
O'Rourke Construction Co., 125
Otis, Elwell Stephen, 158
Oulahan, Richard, 255
Overland Trail, 288

Paco Cemetery, F1, 160–62
Page, Thomas Nelson, 269
Palma, Tomás Estrada, 123–24
Palmer Raids, 281
Panama, 183
Panama Canal, 150, 183
Paris Commune, 66, 68
Partido Independiente de Color, 124
Passos, John Dos, 197, 293
Patrick, Mason M., 127, 128
Patton, W. S., 177
Peace of Paris, 281
Peck, George, 99
Pender, Phoebe, 50
Pérez, Louis A., Jr., 119, 122–23
Pershing, John J., 230, 248, 302
Philippine-American War, 179
Philippines: anticolonial space within, 163; Balingiga, 159, 160; casualties within, F1, F2, F3, 115–16, 157, 158, 159–62, 163, 165, 169, 172; conflict within, 94, 97, 158–59, 161, 171–72, 175; cultural memory and, 117; expansion in, 151; financial investments within, 155–56; government within, 116; Naval Cemetery in, 165–66; U.S. colonies within, 124, 149, 151, 183; white rule within, 115
photography, grave site identification and, 252–53

Pickett, George Edward, 1
Piedmont Park, 89
Piehler, G. Kurt, 292
Pierce, Charles C., 250–51, 260
Pierce City MO, 174–75
Platt Amendment, 123
The Play of Destiny (play), 31–33
Plenty Coups (Chief), 299
Poilu Inconnu monument, 282–83
Poincaré, Raymond, 273
polyglots, 219
Pope, John, 74
Porter, David, 172
post cemeteries, 170–71
Pouch, A. B., 270
Powers, Charles, 171
Pratt, Adam, 76–77
Presidio National Cemetery, 176–77
Pretty Shield, 79
Princeton University, F9, 198
printed word, oral tradition and, 213
prisoner exchange, 44
Proctor, Redfield, 57, 58
property tax codes, 53
prospective memory, 19
Puerto Rico, 151
Puig, Francisco Pratt, 306

Race and Reunion (Blight), 85
race riots, 92–93, 192
racial violence, 69, 281
racism, reunification and, 85, 87–88
raconteurs, 213
Radical Republicans, 38–39
radio, 352n37
railroad industry, 63, 75–76
Ratledge, Curt, 50–51
Ray, Edwin, 141
Reagan, Ronald, 310–11

reciprocity, 279
Reconstruction, 34, 63, 65, 67, 68–69
Redeployment (Klay), 315
Red Shirts, 39, 111, 112–13
Red Summer, 281
Reflections on Exile (Said), 187
"Remember the *Maine*," 122, 123, 140–42, 146
Renan, Ernest, 16, 86–87
republicanism, 2–3, 13, 310
republican memory, 13, 301–2
republic of suffering, 41
reservations, Native American, 64, 75
Rethers, H. F., 265, 269–70
retrospective memory, 19
reunification, 85–86, 105
reunion movement, 87–88
Rheinstein, Frederick, 190, 210
Rhodes, David H., 163, 164–69
Richards, H. F., 266–67
Richards, Joseph Clifford, 266–67
Richmond VA, 103
Rizal, José, 161, 163
Rockwell, William, 229–30
Rockwell, James, 229
Rockwell, Kiffin Yates, F14, 226, 228–29, 243
Romagne American Military Cemetery, 269
The Romance of Reunion (Silber), 85
Roosevelt, Theodore, 104, 124, 150, 158, 173–74, 175–76, 183
Roosevelt Corollary, 150, 183
Root, Elihu, 156–57
Rough Riders, 111, 112–13
Rowan, Andrew, 175
Russia, 71, 150, 258, 262

Said, Edward, 161–62, 187
Saint Peter Relates an Incident of the Resurrection Day (Johnson), 293
Samar, 159

San Chu, Mohammet, 203
Santiago battlefield, 302–3
Santiago Surrender Tree, F28, 302, 303–4, 305–8
Santiago Zoological Garden, 306
Schanzer, Carlo, 297
Schofield, John, 78
Schurz, Carl, 149, 153
Scott, Winfield, 9
Sears, Elizabeth, 234, 239
Sedition Act, 248
segregation, 58, 64, 70, 90, 170–71, 238, 240, 301
Seigal, Charles, 178
Seward, William, 23–24, 64, 71
Seward's Folly, 71
Shantz, Mark S., 12, 18
Sharp, William Graves, 259–60
Sharpe, Edwin R., 263
Sherman, William Tecumseh, 42, 75
Sierra Maestra, 304
Silber, Nina, 85, 255
Sino-U.S. treaty, 71
Sioux Indians, 74–75, 79
site of memory, 56, 184
Sites of Memory, Sites of Mourning (Winter), 278
Sitka AK, 61, 71–72
Sitka National Cemetery, 61, 72–74
Sitting Bull, 74, 75, 79
slavery, 5–7, 15–16, 19, 21, 54, 154
sleeping with the dead, 1–2
Sloane, David, 10
Smith, Charles Emory, 99
Smith, Jacob H., 171
Smith, Mark M., 287, 352n22
social experience, 6
socialism, 66
social media, effects of, 316

solitary individualism, 333n4
sound, use of, 288–90, 294, 298
South Dakota, 75
Southerners: beliefs of, 68, 89; cultural memory and, 65–66, 222–23; empire pursuit and, 221–22; George Armstrong Custer and, 77; Lost Cause movement and, 63; military service of, 94; New Southerners, 82, 87, 103; Northerners and, 64–65; protection for, 89–90; Reconstruction and, 63, 68–69; reunification and, 85–86; vision of, 68
Spain, 94, 139, 151
Spanish-American War, F8, 88
Spanish-Cuban-American War, 3
Spanish Influenza, 233, 235, 236
Spatz, Carl, 302
SS *Lake Daraga*, 262–63
Stanton, Edwin, 48, 52, 54
Stephens, Alexander Hamilton, 43, 44
Sterne, Jonathan, 352n22
Stiles, Robert, 82, 83
Stimson, Henry L., 129, 140
storage systems, cultural memory and, 65
storytellers, purpose of, 213
Stowe, Harriett Beecher, 232
structural amnesia, 7
suicide, 2, 61–62
Sumner (transport ship), 178
Suresnes American Military Cemetery, 245, 246, 253–54
synaptic connections, 6

Taft, William Howard: dollar diplomacy, 150, 183, 277; leadership of, 105, 145, 150, 155–56, 158, 183; quote of, 143, 152
Tamayo, M. Diaz, 304
Taylor, Walker, 113
Taylor, Zachary, 9

telephony, 290–91
Temple, Helen, 141
theater, influence of, 33–34
Theater of the Universe, 31, 32
Thomas, George H., 42
Thompson, Emily, 290
Thoreau, Henry David, 10, 275
Till, Emmitt, 310
Tillman, Ben "Pitchfork," 174
Tillman, Pat, 312–13
time map, 67, 69, 81, 97–98, 99–100
Tinker, Joe, 198
tintypes, F19, F20, F21
Tlingit people, 71–72
Tocqueville, Alexis de, 2, 3, 13
Todorova, Maria, 59
tomb of the unknowns, 53–54
Tomb of the Unknown Soldier: commemoration production of, 289–90, 294–96, 298; creation of, 282, 283–84; dedication of, F26, F27; international quotes about, 296–97; prosthesis of kinship of, 311; symbolism of, 276, 282, 287–88, 292–93, 294, 298–99, 300, 310
Tooze, Adam, 247, 276, 277
To the American People (Agoncillo), 154
transatlantic pilgrimage, 259
transcontinental railroad, 23, 63–64, 75–76
Treaty of Paris, 94
Trout, Steven, 215, 292, 293
Truman, Harry, 302, 305
Truman, Ralph E., 302, 303
Trump, Donald, 314
Tuskegee Institute, 100–101
Twain, Mark, 119, 175
Twentieth Kansas Regiment, 115, 116

Union League, 39
United Confederate Veterans (UCV), 32, 87, 101–2, 103, 106, 222–23
United Daughters of the Confederacy, 102
United Spanish War Veterans, 137
United States: Capitol, Unknown body and, 285; economy of, 77, 151, 247, 258; elections within, 92–93, 111–13, 114, 151, 152, 157–58, 184, 277; expansion and, 3, 4, 22–25, 64, 79–80, 81–82; global competition and, 150; global empire of, 88, 121–22; immigration and, 70; military, F23, F24, 51–52, 70, 75, 105, 152, 215, 276–77; republicanism of, 2–3; reunification and, 105, 280; western vision for, 63–64
Unknown Soldier, 285–86, 291, 292–94, 296, 312, 353n47. *See also* Tomb of the Unknown Soldier
Unknown Warrior monument, 282
U.S. Claims Commission, 42
U.S. Railway Administration, 248
USS *Birmingham*, 144, 145
USS *Maine*: casualties of, 122–23, 127, 129–30, 131, 132, 134, 143–44, 145, 147; commemoration of, F8; cultural memory and, 123, 133–34, 135–36, 146; destruction of, 122–23, 130–31, 132, 141; memorial for, 137–38, 141–42, 144, 145; photo of, F4, F5, F6; recovery of, F5, F6, 124–32; relics of, 134–36; resinking of, 132–33, 144–45; symbolism of, 122, 140
USS *North Carolina*, 144, 145

van Dyke, Henry, 152–53
van Noppen, Charles Leonard, 193–94
vernacular memory, 137
Vietnam War, 310–11, 343n6
Vietnam War Memorial Wall, 310

Index · 383

Voukav, Nikolai, 59–60

Waddell, Alfred Moore, 111–12, 113, 114, 192
Wainwright, W. A., 47–48
Waller, Littleton, 171–73
War Department: Arlington National Cemetery and, 283–84; criticism of, 177, 179, 260–61, 262, 264–65; Freedman's Village and, 57–58, 59; influence of, 106; Marietta National Cemetery and, 47–48; Philippines and, 164; quote of, 130, 177; role of, 56, 58, 252; Sitka National Cemetery and, 73; traditions of, 4; USS *Maine* and, 125–26, 129–30, 134, 137, 142; work of, 176
War Industries Board, 248
Washington, Booker T., 91–92, 93–94, 100, 105, 106
Washington, George, 9
Washington Naval Conference, 276, 294
Washington Post (newspaper), 265
Wayne, Anthony, 9
A Week on the Concord and Merrimack Rivers (Thoreau), 275
Weil, Henry, 194
Wells, Ida B., 86, 105, 106
Western Union Telegraph Co., 71
West Point, 76–77
Wheeler, Joseph, 99
White Declaration of Independence, 111
White Government Union (WGU), 111
White Leagues, 39
white supremacy, 34
Whitman, William, 267
Wiebe, Robert, 11
Wilkes, Tom, 154–55
Williams, Charles J., 50

Williams, Alexander S., 172
Wills, Garry, 18
Wilmington Light Infantry (WLI), 111, 113, 114
Wilmington NC, 92–93, 113, 114–15, 116–17, 192
Wilmington Race Riot Commission, 339n2
Wilson, Frederica, 314
Wilson, Woodrow: Abraham Lincoln and, 254–55; administration of, 223, 247; challenges of, 256–57; congressional measures and, 248; democratic capitalism and, 247; election of, 184; Fourteen Points plan by, 245, 257, 272; leadership of, 150, 246, 248, 347n13, 353n40; speech of, 185–86, 245–46, 253–58, 272; Tomb of the Unknown Soldier and, 282; Unknown funeral procession and, 285–86
Wilsonian Moment, 245–46
Winter, Jay, 215, 278
Winthrop, Beekman, 142–43
Wisconsin, 74
Wister, Owen, 268–69
WLI. *See* Wilmington Light Infantry (WLI)
Wolferdern, James, 140
women's memorial associations, 102–3
World War I, 3, 187, 215, 217–20, 277, 278
World War I Collection, 220–21, 224–26, 231, 242–44
Wright, Daniel, 113
Wright, Dustin M., 313
Wright, Silas P., 114

Zerubavel, Eviatar, 67

STUDIES IN WAR, SOCIETY, AND THE MILITARY

*Military Migration and State Formation:
The British Military Community in
Seventeenth-Century Sweden*
Mary Elizabeth Ailes

*Managing Sex in the U.S. Military:
Gender, Identity, and Behavior*
Edited by Beth Bailey, Alesha E. Doan,
Shannon Portillo, and Kara Dixon Vuic

The State at War in South Asia
Pradeep P. Barua

*Marianne Is Watching: Intelligence,
Counterintelligence, and the Origins
of the French Surveillance State*
Deborah Bauer

*Death at the Edges of Empire: Fallen
Soldiers, Cultural Memory, and the Making
of an American Nation, 1863–1921*
Shannon Bontrager

An American Soldier in World War I
George Browne
Edited by David L. Snead

*Beneficial Bombing: The Progressive
Foundations of American
Air Power, 1917–1945*
Mark Clodfelter

*Fu-go: The Curious History of Japan's
Balloon Bomb Attack on America*
Ross Coen

*Imagining the Unimaginable: World
War, Modern Art, and the Politics of
Public Culture in Russia, 1914–1917*
Aaron J. Cohen

*The Rise of the National Guard: The
Evolution of the American Militia, 1865–1920*
Jerry Cooper

*The Thirty Years' War and German
Memory in the Nineteenth Century*
Kevin Cramer

*Political Indoctrination in the U.S. Army
from World War II to the Vietnam War*
Christopher S. DeRosa

*In the Service of the Emperor: Essays
on the Imperial Japanese Army*
Edward J. Drea

*American Journalists in the Great War:
Rewriting the Rules of Reporting*
Chris Dubbs

*America's U-Boats: Terror
Trophies of World War I*
Chris Dubbs

*The Age of the Ship of the Line: The
British and French Navies, 1650–1815*
Jonathan R. Dull

*American Naval History, 1607–1865:
Overcoming the Colonial Legacy*
Jonathan R. Dull

*Soldiers of the Nation: Military Service
and Modern Puerto Rico, 1868–1952*
Harry Franqui-Rivera

*You Can't Fight Tanks with Bayonets:
Psychological Warfare against the
Japanese Army in the Southwest Pacific*
Allison B. Gilmore

*A Strange and Formidable Weapon: British
Responses to World War I Poison Gas*
Marion Girard

Civilians in the Path of War
Edited by Mark Grimsley
and Clifford J. Rogers

A Scientific Way of War: Antebellum Military Science, West Point, and the Origins of American Military Thought
Ian C. Hope

Picture This: World War I Posters and Visual Culture
Edited and with an introduction by Pearl James

Indian Soldiers in World War I: Race and Representation in an Imperial War
Andrew T. Jarboe

Death Zones and Darling Spies: Seven Years of Vietnam War Reporting
Beverly Deepe Keever

For Home and Country: World War I Propaganda on the Home Front
Celia Malone Kingsbury

I Die with My Country: Perspectives on the Paraguayan War, 1864–1870
Edited by Hendrik Kraay and Thomas L. Whigham

North American Indians in the Great War
Susan Applegate Krouse
Photographs and original documentation by Joseph K. Dixon

Remembering World War I in America
Kimberly J. Lamay Licursi

Citizens More than Soldiers: The Kentucky Militia and Society in the Early Republic
Harry S. Laver

Soldiers as Citizens: Former Wehrmacht Officers in the Federal Republic of Germany, 1945–1955
Jay Lockenour

Deterrence through Strength: British Naval Power and Foreign Policy under Pax Britannica
Rebecca Berens Matzke

Army and Empire: British Soldiers on the American Frontier, 1758–1775
Michael N. McConnell

Of Duty Well and Faithfully Done: A History of the Regular Army in the Civil War
Clayton R. Newell and Charles R. Shrader
With a foreword by Edward M. Coffman

The Militarization of Culture in the Dominican Republic, from the Captains General to General Trujillo
Valentina Peguero

A Religious History of the American GI in World War II
G. Kurt Piehler

Arabs at War: Military Effectiveness, 1948–1991
Kenneth M. Pollack

The Politics of Air Power: From Confrontation to Cooperation in Army Aviation Civil-Military Relations
Rondall R. Rice

Andean Tragedy: Fighting the War of the Pacific, 1879–1884
William F. Sater

The Grand Illusion: The Prussianization of the Chilean Army
William F. Sater and Holger H. Herwig

Sex Crimes under the Wehrmacht
David Raub Snyder

In the School of War
Roger J. Spiller
Foreword by John W. Shy

On the Trail of the Yellow Tiger: War, Trauma, and Social Dislocation in Southwest China during the Ming-Qing Transition
Kenneth M. Swope

The Paraguayan War, Volume 1: Causes and Early Conduct
Thomas L. Whigham

Policing Sex and Marriage in the American Military: The Court-Martial and the Construction of Gender and Sexual Deviance, 1950–2000
Kellie Wilson-Buford

The Challenge of Change: Military Institutions and New Realities, 1918–1941
Edited by Harold R. Winton and David R. Mets

To order or obtain more information on these or other University of Nebraska Press titles, visit nebraskapress.unl.edu.

www.ingramcontent.com/pod-product-compliance
Lightning Source LLC
Chambersburg PA
CBHW021140240426
43661CB00075B/1594